# ETHNICITY, NATIONALISM, AND THE PAKHTUNS

# ETHNICITY, NATIONALISM, AND THE PAKHTUNS

## The Independence Movement in India's North-West Frontier Province

Stephen Alan Rittenberg

**Carolina Academic Press**
Durham, North Carolina

For my parents
Beatrice and Sydney Rittenberg

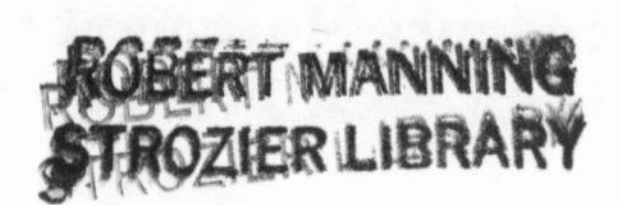




Library of Congress Catalog Card Number: 84–70181
International Standard Book Number: 0–89089–277–6

CAROLINA ACADEMIC PRESS
P.O. Box 51879
Durham, North Carolina 27717

Printed in the United States of America

# CONTENTS

## LIST OF TABLES



## LIST OF MAPS

## LIST OF ABBREVIATIONS USED IN FOOTNOTES

| | |
|---|---|
| AICC | All-India Congress Committee Papers. Nehru Museum. |
| BP | F.L. Brayne Papers. India Office Library. |
| Best Memorandum | L/P&J/7/17, 1931. Part I. No. 1423. Memorandum 703-S, 9/13/30. W.H.D. Best, Deputy Commissioner of Kohat. |
| CD | Sir George Cunningham's Diary. India Office Library. |
| CLAD | *Indian Legislative Assembly Debates.* |
| CP | Sir George Cunningham Papers. India Office Library. (Volume number follows abbreviation.) |
| FR | Fortnightly Administration Reports of the NWFP. Government of India Archives. (I)—Report for the first half of the month. (II)—Report for the second half of the month. |
| Gidney Memorandum | L/P&J/7/17, 1931. Part I. No. 1423. Memorandum 187-S.T., 10/4/30. C.H. Gidney, Deputy Commissioner of Bannu. |
| GoI | Government of India Archives. Home (Political) Department. |
| GP | Sir Hamilton Grant Papers. India Office Library. (Volume number follows abbreviation.) |
| GR | Governor's Report. L/P&J/5. India Office Library. (Volume number follows abbreviation.) |
| HM | All-India Hindu Mahasabha Papers. Nehru Museum. |
| HP | Lord Halifax Papers. India Office Library. (Volume number follows abbreviation.) |
| ID | Intelligence Bureau Diaries. The 1929–30 diaries are in L/P&S/10/1300; the 1931–32 diaries in L/P&S/12. Collection 23. File 16. India Office Library. |
| Isemonger Report | GoI File 11/111, 1930. F.C. Isemonger. "The Frontier Provincial Youth League (Subah Sarhad Zalmo Jirga)." |
| LAD | *North-West Frontier Province Legislative Assembly Debates.* |
| LCD | *North-West Frontier Province Legislative Council Debates.* |

| | |
|---|---|
| LCP | Lord Chelmsford Papers. India Office Library. (Volume number follows abbreviation.) |
| MIL/14 | L/MIL/14. India Office Library. (Volume number follows abbreviation.) |
| ML | All-India Muslim League Papers. Karachi University. |
| MP | A.N. Mitchell Papers. |
| NWFP | North-West Frontier Province Archives. Files of the Peshawar Deputy Commissioner's Office. Part II. |
| NWFP. Swabi Column | NWFP. Bundle 70. S.No. 2095. File 47. "Swabi Column, June 1930." |
| Patel Report | *Report (With Evidence) of the Peshawar Enquiry Committee* (Allahabad: Allahabad Law Journal Press, 1930). |
| PJ6 | L/P&J/6. India Office Library. (File number follows abbreviation.) |
| PJ7 | L/P&J/7. India Office Library. (File number follows abbreviation.) |
| PJ8 | L/P&J/8. India Office Library. (File number follows abbreviation.) |
| PJ9 | L/P&J(c)/9. India Office Library. (File number follows abbreviation.) |
| PO | L/PO. India Office Library. (File number follows abbreviation.) |
| PP | Great Britain. Parliamentary Papers. Accounts and Papers. |
| PR | Provincial Reports. L/P&J/5. India Office Library. (File number follows abbreviation) |
| PS12/23 | L/P&S/12. Collection 23. India Office Library. |
| Register *Ruadad* | Muslim League Subcommittee *Khavatin*. (Part of the collection of Aziz Javed.) |
| RKP | Sir George Roos-Keppel Papers. India Office Library. (Volume number follows abbreviation.) |
| RP | Lord Reading Papers. India Office Library. (Volume number follows abbreviation.) |
| Sulaiman-Panckridge Report | GoI File 393/30-Pol. S.M. Sulaiman and H.R. Panckridge. *Report of the Peshawar Disturbance Enquiry Committee.* |
| VC | Viceroy's Correspondence. L/P&J/5. India Office Library. (File number follows abbreviation.) |

# ACKNOWLEDGMENTS

This book is based on my doctoral dissertation which was submitted to Columbia University in 1977. However, my interest in the North-West Frontier dates back much further to my earliest years as a graduate student. From the beginning, I received assistance and encouragement from many people in many places. It is with pleasure that I acknowledge their contributions and help.

Funding came from four sources. A fellowship from the School of International Affairs of Columbia University allowed me to conduct preliminary research in India and Great Britain in 1970-71. My field work in Pakistan in 1973-74 was sponsored by the Foreign Area Fellowship Program. I completed the research in 1978 on a postdoctoral fellowship from the SSRC-ACLS Joint Committee on South Asia. Finally, a grant from the Council of Social Science Research at Columbia gave me the opportunity to refine the ideas in my dissertation and to rewrite it in its present form. While these organizations provided the financial means which made this book possible, they are not responsible for its contents or conclusions.

I am indebted for their help to the librarians and staffs of the Indian Office Library and British Museum in Great Britain, the Indian National Archives and Nehru Museum in India, and the NWFP Provincial Archives and Karachi University in Pakistan.

Wherever I went in the North-West Frontier Province, I invariably encountered the hospitality and generosity for which its people are justly famous. My deepest thanks go to everyone there who made my field work a success and an enriching personal experience. In particular, Dr. Munavvar Khan and his colleagues in the History Department of the University of Peshawar spent hours listening to my ideas and offering advice. Dr. Riaz Ahmad assisted me in establishing a home in Peshawar and in starting my field work. Mian Ziauddin was always available to help me find my way through the Pakistan bureaucracy. Aziz Javed made available to me the documents he had collected on the nationalist movement and assisted me in tracking down others. Inamullah Jan translated materials in Pashtu for me. Three close friends—Shaukat Ali Khan, Azmat Hayat Khan, and Iftiharuddin—also helped me with my research. I owe a special thanks to Shaukat who devoted countless hours to my work and who taught me more about the Pakhtuns than I suspect he ever imagined. I am also grateful to his father, Khanji, who opened his home to me on many occasions.

In India, I profited from the encouragement, good sense, and excellent memory of the late Gopal Das Khera. I had the good fortune to meet him at the very start of my research, and I continued to draw upon his assistance throughout the course of the following decade.

At Columbia University, Ainslie Embree introduced me to the nationalist history of the Frontier, guided me through the dissertation, and subsequently encouraged me to turn it into a book. Howard Wriggins, Leonard Gordon, and Dennis Dalton read the dissertation and made suggestions on how it could be improved, while Philip Oldenburg and Charles Lindholm commented on portions of the revised manuscript. My thanks go to Arlene Jacobs for typing the manuscript and to Agha Imran Hamid for proofreading it. Finally, I am grateful for the help and patience of Keith Sipe and his staff at Carolina Academic Press.

# ETHNICITY, NATIONALISM, AND THE PAKHTUNS

# 1

# INTRODUCTION

Scholarly studies of the Muslims' role in the Indian independence movement have tended to concentrate on their problems as a religious minority. In light of the eventual partition of the subcontinent, communalism amply warrants the attention it has received,[1] but only so long as it does not obscure the existence of other, often conflicting issues, ambitions, and identities which also influenced the Muslims' political development. Religious polarization was not the natural state of affairs in Indian politics. Communalism represented only one theme in the Muslims' nationalist experience, and it was not necessarily the dominant one until the last years before independence. Like other Indians, Muslims were divided by region, class, caste, and a host of other differences, all of which helped to shape their responses to the broader questions of Islamic separatism and Indian nationalism. Thus, Muslim solidarity cannot be assumed. The process by which a distinctive identity, forged around the symbol of Islam, became the overriding determinant of Muslim political behavior requires explicit examination.

No part of India so dramatically underscores the existence of the divisions within the Muslim community, and the problems created by ignoring them, than the North-West Frontier Province (NWFP). Although the NWFP contained a higher percentage of Muslims than any other province except Baluchistan, its inhabitants consistently stood apart from what has been taken to be the communal mainstream of Muslim politics. The Frontier remained a Congress bastion for seventeen years, long after most other Indian Muslims had come to regard that party as the archenemy of their community. It did not abandon the Congress for the Pakistan movement until the final months before partition. Even then, in the midst of the feverish atmosphere generated by the promise of independence and the worst Muslim-Hindu rioting in India's history, an influential segment of the province remained unpersuaded by the arguments of the Muslim League.

In view of the resistance of its people to the League's ideology, the Frontier Province constitutes a useful regional case study in how and to what ex-

1. By definition, "communalism" refers to a sense of community solidarity regardless of whether it is based on ethnic, religious, or other sentiments. In this work, it will be used exclusively to refer to India's Hindu-Muslim problem.

tent a separate nationalist identity was built up among India's Muslims. Its nationalist history also deserves attention in its own right, for the province acquired a political significance out of proportion to its small size. In addition to being the only province in which the Congress seriously competed for Muslims' loyalties, the NWFP was located along the most strategically important and unstable border of the Indian empire. Together, these factors strengthened the Congress' bargaining position vis-a-vis the British. They also turned the North-West Frontier Province into a major obstacle in the way of a resolution of the Muslim-Hindu conflict and the transfer of power to Indian hands.

As long as politics in the Frontier are judged exclusively by communal criteria, the preferences of its inhabitants make little sense. To date, in fact, the tendency has been to regard the province as little more than a dramatic anomaly in the larger Muslim-Hindu conflict or, as an advisor to the last Viceroy is reputed to have remarked in exasperation, as a "bastard situation."[2] The difficulty in assessing the Frontier's nationalist history does not rest in the eccentricities of its inhabitants. The problem lies in scholars' predilection toward the view that Muslim political choices were dictated primarily by religious affiliation.

The key to the Frontier's politics was ethnicity, not religion, and the crucial group was the Pakhtuns,[3] not the Indian Muslim community. An indigenous Pakhtun movement, the Khudai Khidmatgars,[4] undercut the Muslim League's appeal to communal nationalism by espousing an ideology of ethnic regionalism within the framework of the Indian National Congress' all-India secular nationalism. Why this should have been the case and how the province was ultimately converted to the cause of Pakistan form the central concerns of this study. While it covers the entire pre-independence lifetime of the NWFP, it concentrates particularly upon two pivotal periods of ferment in the province's history, 1929-32 and 1945-47. The first period saw the emergence of the Khudai Khidmatgars as the authoritative spokesmen of Pakhtun interests and their alliance with the Indian National Congress. The second witnessed a steady rise in the influence of the Muslim League until it overcame the Pakhtuns' ethnic loyalties and wrested control of the province from the Congress.

Ethnicity has spawned a vast body of literature whose theoretical concerns and controversies go beyond the scope of this study. An imprecise con-

---

2. D. G. Tendulkar, *Abdul Ghaffar Khan* (Bombay: Popular Prakashan, 1967), p. 427.

3. Most scholarly works on the North-West Frontier follow the Indian practice of referring to the group as "Pathans." "Pathan" is a corruption of the name by which the people call themselves. This study will follow local usage. It will, moreover, conform to the northern dialect of Pashtu and use "Pakhtun" rather than "Pashtun," the southern pronunciation.

4. Technically, the Khudai Khidmatgars were a volunteer body, subordinate first to the Afghan Jirga, an indigenous Frontier party, and later to the Frontier Congress. Due to their popularity, however, their name has commonly been applied to the entire Frontier movement, a practice which will be followed in this study.

cept, ethnicity has been defined and used in widely varying ways. Here, it will be taken to mean a form of group identity, the sense of belonging to a unique community on the basis of common cultural traditions, social institutions, historical experiences, and sometimes real or imagined blood ties.[5] The exact characteristics will vary from one ethnic group to another. In all cases, however, certain shared attributes unite group members and mark them off in their own minds, if not in others', as different from the people living around them.

Ethnicity, then, is determined by a complex of distinctive characteristics. No one feature acts as the exclusive basis for an ethnic group's identity, although one or more are usually treated as the primary indicators of group membership. The attributes on which ethnicity can hinge are as diverse as human behavior. They can include anything from language, religion, and ancestry to eating habits, style of dress, and aesthetic tastes. Whatever the traits, they reinforce one another to build up a composite definition of who belongs to the community and who does not. A mere laundry list of differences, however, is insufficient to set off a body of people as a separate group. As George DeVos has observed: "As a subjective sense of belonging, ethnicity is determined by what a person feels about himself, not by how he is observed to behave."[6] What counts, in other words, is not the sum of the objective differences between groups but those which people invest with symbolic meaning and thereby turn into indices of ethnicity. Moreover, as Fredrik Barth has written, members of an ethnic community consciously or unconsciously differentiate among their common attributes in terms of importance to their collective personality.[7] Some attributes, which are deemed critical in distinguishing them from other people, are singled out as symbolizing the essence of their separateness. Others, which are viewed as more peripheral in importance, are assigned a subordinate role in their group definition. Still others may be ignored or may actually have their existence denied.

Leaders of the All-India Muslim League emphasized the centrality of religion in defining India's Muslims as a community and dismissed those factors which internally differentiated Muslims as insignificant, or meaningless, in the face of the overriding unity created by their common faith. This constituted a reversal of the manner in which Pakhtuns normally viewed

---

5. I have relied for my understanding of ethnicity and its political implications primarily on Paul Brass, "Ethnicity and Nationality Formation," *Ethnicity*, Vol. 3, no. 3, 9/76, pp. 225-40; and *Language, Religion and Politics in North India* (New York: Cambridge University Press, 1974). Also see Frederik Barth, ed., *Ethnic Groups and Boundaries* (Boston: Little, Brown and Company, 1969); and George DeVos & Lola Romanucci-Ross, eds., *Ethnic Identity and Change* (Palo Alto: Mayfield Publishing Company, 1975).

6. George DeVos, "Ethnic Pluralism: Conflict and Accommodation," in DeVos and Romanucci-Ross, *op. cit.*, p. 17.

7. Frederik Barth, "Introduction," in Barth, *op. cit.*, p. 14.

themselves. While Islam formed an integral component of the Pakhtuns' collective self-definition, it was not the critical element. They attached primary significance to a combination of more restrictive criteria, the most important of which was the belief in a common descent.[8] This was reinforced by their system of values (called *Pakhtunwali*), tribal institutions, language, history, mythology, aesthetic traditions, and identification with a specific territory. The identity these characteristics fostered distinguished Pakhtuns from other Indian Muslims almost as much as from Hindus.

Politics among the Pakhtuns revolved predominantly around their ethnic concerns before 1947. The overwhelming Islamic composition of their own country, and of the territory surrounding it, insulated them from the communal fears of other Indian Muslims until 1946-47. Hence, they had no intrinsic bias toward an alliance with their Indian co-religionists. As their history shows, Pakhtuns were ready to join any party that helped them achieve their own distinctive objectives and allowed them autonomy within the all-India context. The Indian National Congress met these criteria to the satisfaction of the Pakhtun nationalists, whereas the Muslim League did not. Other Muslims may have viewed the Congress as a threat to their religious and cultural integrity, but so far as the Khudai Khidmatgars were concerned, it gave them valuable political support on terms that did not compromise their ethnic identity. They saw much less scope for the expression of Pakhtun regionalism within the Muslim League, for its ideology demanded that they abandon their separate ethnic ambitions in the interest of communal unity.

The Pakhtuns' ethnic exclusiveness created divisions within NWFP politics as well as giving them a character which ran counter to the general trend in India. The province's boundaries ignored the pattern of ethnic settlement in the region. Its outer districts—Hazara and Dera Ismail Khan—and its towns were inhabited primarily by a non-Pakhtun Muslim population of heterogeneous origins.[9] Numerically too few and too divided to challenge the Pakhtuns' dominance of provincial public life, non-Pakhtuns still played an important role in the NWFP's nationalist history. Their presence contributed an additional element of ethnic tension to Frontier politics which fed into the larger conflict between the forces favoring Pakhtun regionalism and Muslim separatism.

Due to their unequivocal commitment to Pakhtun interests, the Khudai Khidmatgars and Congress never attracted a sizeable following in the province's non-Pakhtun zones. The Frontier Muslim League, on the other hand, elicited an immediate response in those areas precisely because it was not identified with the NWFP's dominant community. Non-Pakhtuns, espe-

8. See Chapter 2 for a discussion of Pakhtun identity. For a further discussion, see Frederik Barth, "Pathan Identity and Its Maintenance," in Barth, *op. cit.*, pp. 117-34.

9. See *Census of India, 1931*, Vol. 15, Part I, pp. 187 and 201. For a further discussion, see Chapter 2.

cially in Hazara District and Peshawar city, provided the party with its first major sources of support in the province. In the long run, however, this compounded the League's problems, for the key to provincial power lay in the Pakhtun countryside, and the League's non-Pakhtun support tended to reinforce its image as being unsympathetic to Pakhtun needs and ambitions.

While the concept of ethnicity helps explain in ideological terms why the Muslim League encountered such difficulty in convincing Pakhtuns to support Pakistan, it does not provide a complete answer to why they consciously chose Hindus as their political partners rather than Muslims. There was nothing inherent in the League's ideology which prevented it from coupling its call for Muslim solidarity with an appeal to Pakhtun interests. Superficially, in fact, that combination would appear more probable than the accommodation which did occur between Pakhtun regionalism and secular Indian nationalism, since Pakhtuns had a sense of identification with Islam which surpassed any loyalty to a territorially defined Indian nation until well into the twentieth century. To understand why the League could not harness Pakhtun ethnic sentiments to its own cause and why the Khudai Khidmatgars allied themselves so closely to the Congress, one must look at the manner in which political ideologies interacted with the patterns of elite competition and class conflict in Pakhtun society.

Pakhtuns possessed a vigorous polity which gave underlying structure to the province's nationalist experience. Beginning as early as the 15th century, they had organized a society in which they owned the land while non-Pakhtuns, with a few exceptions, were relegated to a position of economic and political dependency. Politics revolved, in the first instance, around village factions which usually reflected the agnatic rivalries inherent in Pakhtun society.[10] These factions, in turn, often formed wider political groupings by allying with one another across village boundaries. Factions were dominated by prominent individuals called Khans and *maliks*. Their position rested in part on land ownership and the economic resources it provided, but wealth alone could not ensure them of political power due to the Pakhtuns' egalitarian ethos. They also had to exhibit the personal qualities and behavior which the Pakhtuns expected of their leaders and the lower class non-Pakhtuns of their patrons.

Pakhtun factions served as the bedrock on which the Congress and Muslim League built throughout much of the Frontier, while the Pakhtuns' Khans and *maliks* provided them with one of their main sources of leadership. In the province's Pakhtun regions, each party was commonly identified at the local level with a single faction or with a combination of factions

10. For traditional Pakhtun politics, see Frederik Barth, *Political Leadership Among Swat Pathans* (London: The Athlone Press, 1968). A model of Pakhtun politics on the eve of British rule is included in Chapter 2.

that were traditional allies. This was unavoidable because nationalist issues were distant abstractions to the common villagers while factional disputes were the everyday realities of their political lives. As a result, many Pakhtuns joined political parties not out of an ideological commitment but to gain support in their factional conflicts. Even those men who made the transition to modern political organizers did not divest themselves entirely of their factional heritage. Rivals tended to join opposing parties even at the highest levels of the Congress and Muslim League.

The manner in which Pakhtun factions aligned themselves with political parties was influenced by the ways in which the British used and changed Pakhtun society before 1930. Therein also lies the explanation of why the Khudai Khidmatgars joined the Congress in the first place and why, at a later date, they did not switch to the Muslim League. The British had used selected members of the Pakhtuns' Khani elite as an informal extension of their administration. In return for government patronage, those Khans maintained order in the countryside, thereby relieving the authorities of a responsibility they could not handle with their limited resources. The men usually chosen for this privileged relationship belonged to the senior branches of the Pakhtuns' Khani lineages and tended to be the wealthier, more prominent individuals in their respective tribes and localities.

At the same time, colonial rule caused profound economic and social changes which undermined the influence of the very men the government chose as its associates.[11] Land settlements, irrigation projects, roads and railways, and the intrusion of market forces vastly enhanced the wealth of the Khani elite and economically differentiated it from other Pakhtuns to a degree previously unknown on the Frontier. By 1930, the government's allies, who benefited most from those changes, had largely transformed themselves into men whose status and power depended on their wealth and the support of the authorities. Freed from the restraint of social tradition, they tended to act in ways which alienated the other elements of Frontier society.

The Khans antagonized the lower class non-Pakhtuns by abandoning the role of patron in favor of a contractual economic relationship which increased their dependents' obligations while eliminating the reciprocal, paternalistic services they had once provided. An additional element of class tension was generated by the growth of a large body of Pakhtun tenants and laborers whose inferior status ran counter to their egalitarian traditions and history of landownership. The senior Khans also alienated the small landholding Pakhtuns and the other members of their own class by no longer conforming

---

11. My analysis of the changes which occurred in Frontier society is influenced by the work of James Scott, especially *The Moral Economy of the Peasant* (New Haven: Yale University Press, 1976); and Scott and Benedict Kerkvliet, "How Traditional Rural Patrons Lose Legitimacy: A Theory with Special Reference to Southeast Asia," in Steffen Schmidt, James Scott, Carl Lande, Laura Guasti, eds., *Friends, Followers and Factions. A Reader in Political Clientelism* (Berkeley: University of California Press, 1977), pp. 439-58.

to the behavioral norms expected of Pakhtun leaders. As men of wealth, they could coerce or buy support from reluctant followers; but by ceasing to act like Khans, they increasingly lacked the social legitimacy needed to sustain their leadership in Pakhtun society.

The erosion in their traditional standing became evident after World War I and accelerated with the onset of the world economic depression. As it occurred, popular sentiment shifted in favor of the factions opposing them. These were led by men whom Sir Olaf Caroe calls the small or junior Khans.[12] The label is appropriate, but only in a relative sense, because many of them were great landlords and men of high tribal status in their own right. As a generalization, these Khans tended to be less wealthy than their rivals and less traditionally prominent. Often, they were members of the cadet branches of the Pakhtuns' leading families and, as such, their rivals' junior cousins. These men had also profited from colonial rule but had adhered much more closely to the ideal of a Khan. Additionally, they had not been drawn as deeply into the government's network of patronage and, consequently, did not strongly identify themselves with the British.

By necessity, the challenge the junior Khans mounted against their rivals involved an assault on the government's authority. While the British recognized that their rule had altered Frontier society, they refused to modify their reliance on their local allies. Rather than introduce political reforms or broaden their informal base of support, they consciously chose in the 1920s to shore up the authority of the senior Khans.[13] This decision froze Frontier politics, leaving the junior Khans and their factional supporters without a legitimate means of pursuing their ambitions and grievances. In retaliation, they joined the Khudai Khidmatgar movement in 1930-31. Thus, factional and class disputes had fused with nationalist issues by 1930 in a pattern which identified the smaller, junior Khans as the champions of Pakhtun interests and the protectors of the lower classes, while their rivals bore the stigma of having betrayed their people to the British.

The Khudai Khidmatgars joined the Indian National Congress during the 1930 civil disobedience movement because of their common determination to achieve immediate independence through extralegal means. Once formed, their alliance endured because the Congress provided the Khudai Khidmatgars with indispensable assistance while tolerating their regional brand of nationalism. When the Muslim League turned its attention to the Frontier in 1936-37, therefore, it found itself cut off from the best organized, most dynamic political force in the province. This left the party with no choice but to build upon those elements which opposed the Khudai Khidmatgars for ethnic or factional reasons. In the Pakhtun countryside, the

---

12. Olaf Caroe, *The Pathans* (London: MacMillan & Co., 1958), p. 433; and "The End of British India," *Round Table*, No. 237, 1/70, p. 63.

13. PJ9/30. File 1344/21. Letter D.O. No. 941-R. 4/4/21. Sir John Maffey to Dennys Bray.

League had to depend upon the senior Khans despite the fact that they were no longer the dominant individuals in Pakhtun society and were stigmatized by their past association with the British. With these supporters, the party could not compete for the ethnic appeal in the Frontier. On the contrary, its Khani members left the League vulnerable to the Khudai Khidmatgars' repeated accusation that it was a party of traitors to the Pakhtun nation. Thus, the League made little effort after 1937 to represent itself as responsive to Pakhtun rights, preferring instead to challenge the Khudai Khidmatgars' ethnic nationalism with a strictly communal ideology.

As a result of its supporters and choice of tactics, the League could not compete with the Congress in the Frontier before 1946. It could not even capitalize on its control of the provincial government between 1943 and 1945, a situation made possible by the suppression of the Frontier Congress in the Quit India Movement. The party's fortunes in the province did not improve until the all-India communal deadlock deteriorated into wholesale violence in late 1946, producing a crisis which qualitatively altered the political environment in the Frontier and evoked a response reminiscent of a pattern which had occurred in earlier periods of Pakhtun history.

While nationalist politics in the Frontier revolved primarily around the question of ethnicity, religious sentiment cannot be entirely ignored. However weak their attachment to the broader Islamic community may normally have been in the face of their feelings of ethnic separateness, it did represent an alternative focus for Pakhtuns' loyalties. Islam was inextricably woven into the Pakhtun's culture. It provided them with moral and metaphysical precepts to guide their lives, ideals to which they could aspire, and holy men to revere. Ordinarily, religion did not enter into the Pakhtuns' factional conflicts, and the interpreters of Islam remained apart from their worldly feuds except when called on to use their moral authority as mediators. In periods of turmoil, however, Pakhtun politics often fused with religion.

With their deep-seated enmities, Pakhtuns needed some means of achieving unity when their collective interests were threatened. Islam provided the most effective cause around which they could rally whenever the threat could be plausibly construed in religious terms, for it represented a higher, spiritual order whose defense took precedence in their eyes over their mundane, material squabbles. Whenever the enemy could be identified as non-Muslims, or even as "bad" Muslims, Pakhtuns could be convinced to suspend their mutual hostilities and unite to fight for their faith. Historically, this had been the case even when the real issues at stake were political or economic rather than religious. The pivotal figure at such times was not the tribal leader, who was bound up in the Pakhtuns' worldly disputes, but the man of piety and religious learning who transcended tribal and factional considerations. His commanding power typically lasted only as long as the Pakhtuns' perception that a crisis existed; but while it did, it was sufficient to overcome the Pakhtuns' internal divisions and even their sense of separateness from other Muslims.

A comparable sequence of events occurred in 1946-47, when the Muslim League was transformed in the Frontier from an ineffectual political party into a religiously inspired mass movement through the catalyst of India's communal conflict.[14] In the last year before independence, the Frontier Muslim League exhibited two characteristics strikingly similar to the pattern outlined above. First, it became an umbrella organization for a wide range of groups and individuals who were normally at odds with one another but who managed to unite behind the millenial dream of Pakistan. Among these were many Pakhtuns who were bitter enemies. Second, the overwhelming majority of the province's religious leaders, many of whom had previously taken no part in politics, rallied behind the League. In particular, the party profited from the active support of men who were deemed to have acquired holiness either through their own pious devotions or by heredity from saintly ancestors. Some of these men rose to high offices in the League, but even those who did not, played a critical role in the party's success by helping to persuade Pakhtuns to give their universalistic religious identity temporary priority over their parochial ethnic and factional loyalties.

---

14. See Chapters 8-9.

# 2

# THE NORTH-WEST FRONTIER PROVINCE AND ITS PEOPLE

The North-West Frontier forms part of the transitional zone between India and Central Asia which extends from the Indus River to the Hindu Kush Mountains. From archaeological times, the region has been the primary route for the flow of people and ideas into the subcontinent, for India is surrounded on its other sides by relatively impenetrable natural barriers. Geography also guaranteed that the region became the focus of British imperial attention after its annexation in 1849. During the next one hundred years, the Frontier was the most volatile of India's borderlands. Across the Frontier, Afghanistan was the least tractable of India's neighbors, and beyond the Afghan buffer loomed the spectre of an expansionist Russia.

The British organized the lowland plains in the eastern third of the Frontier into settled districts with a regular administration but left the remaining mountainous tracts as autonomous tribal territory. At first, the Indian government treated the hill tribes as independent groups, nominally under the suzerainty of the Afghan *amir*. In time, it exerted an imperfect, *de facto* authority over them by means of political persuasion, economic incentives, and, when all else failed, military force. Its paramountcy over the area received formal recognition in 1893 with a treaty delimiting the Afghan kingdom's eastern border. The Frontier's settled districts were part of the Punjab in the 19th century. The Government of India formulated policy for the autonomous tribal areas but left its implementation primarily to the Punjab government. Lord Curzon ended this cumbersome division of responsibility on November 9, 1901, by consolidating the districts of Hazara, Peshawar, Kohat, Bannu, and Dera Ismail Khan into the North-West Frontier Province. The new province was administered by a Chief Commissioner, who was simultaneously made the Governor-General's agent for the tribal territory.

## The Geography of the Province

The North-West Frontier Province has a total area of 13,518 square miles.[1] Apart from Hazara, it lies west of the Indus River, and with the exception

1. The tribal territory covered another 25,147 square miles. *Census of India, 1931* (Pesha-

of the Isa Khel tract adjacent to Bannu and Kohat, it encompasses all the settled trans-Indus lands south to Dera Ghazi Khan. The administrative border between the NWFP and tribal territory skirts the foothills, or *daman* as it is locally known, of the Safed Koh and Suleiman Mountains. West of the Indus, the province consists of four basins separated by mountain systems of moderate heights. From north to south, they are the Peshawar Valley, Kohat basin, Bannu basin, and Derajat plain. East of the Indus, Hazara forms a transitional zone between northern Punjab and the mountains to its north and northwest.

The most important of these five physical divisions is the Vale of Peshawar. Except for the Sam Ranizai tribal area in the extreme north, the British first organized the Valley into a single district of 2,637 square miles and subdivided it into Peshawar, Charsadda, Nowshera, Mardan, and Swabi *Tehsils*. In 1937, the latter two, with an area of 1,094 square miles, were detached to form Mardan District, leaving Peshawar District with an area of 1,543 square miles.[2]

The core of Peshawar Valley consists of an alluvial plain watered by the Kabul River and its tributaries, which range in size from the Swat River down to *khwars* (drainage channels) which are dry much of the year. A small portion of this plain lies south of the Kabul River; the land between the Kabul and Swat Rivers forms a fertile *doaba*; and beyond the Swat River, the Hashtnagar-Yusafzai plain stretches over the greater part of the Valley. On its eastern side, the central plain ends at a ridge known locally as *sar-i-maira*,[3] beyond which the land drops to a narrow riverine plain along the Indus. In the other three directions, the central plain is bordered by foothills which give way to the barren, mountainous terrain of the tribal area. The foothill zone is not wide in the north and west, but in the south, it forms a broad outer band to the Valley, especially in Nowshera *Tehsil* where the desolate Khattak hills cover more than 350 square miles.

By any criteria, Peshawar Valley is the heartland of the North-West Frontier. Its river system and broad alluvial expanse give it an agricultural potential unmatched by any other part of the region, as can be seen from the figures in Table 1. Even before its annexation in 1849, the Valley had an extensive network of canals which compensated for its sparse annual rainfall of 13.2 inches.[4] The Government of India doubled its irrigated acreage with

---

war: Government Stationery and Printing, 1933), Vol. XV, Part II, Table 1. All references are to the NWFP as it existed prior to independence. The physical description of the province in this chapter is drawn from *Imperial Gazetteer. Provincial Series. North-West Frontier Province* (Calcutta: Superintendent of Government Printing, 1908), and David Dichter, *The North-West Frontier of West Pakistan* (Oxford: Clarendon Press, 1967).

2. *Census of India, 1931*, Part II, Table 1. Future references to Peshawar District in this chapter are to the district in its pre-1937 form unless otherwise specified.

3. The term, *maira*, is used for dry, unproductive land. *Sar-i-maira* means "ridge of barren land."

4. In 1868, 259,676 acres of the Valley were irrigated by private canals and wells. *NWFP*

**Table 1: Land Under Cultivation in the North-West Frontier Province in 1931**[5]

| | *Hazara* | *Peshawar* | *Kohat* | *Bannu* | *Dera Ismail Khan* | *Province* |
|---|---|---|---|---|---|---|
| Total area (in acres) | 1,925,760 | 1,665,503 | 1,729,920 | 1,086,720 | 2,221,440 | 8,651,520 |
| Cultivated acreage | 591,955 | 853,065 | 328,685 | 543,360 | 599,789 | 2,844,855 |
| % of total area cultivated | 27.0% | 51.2% | 19.9% | 50.0% | 27.08% | 32.9% |
| Irrigated acreage | 173,318 | 472,164 | 34,598 | 119,539 | 88,858 | 888,477 |
| % of total area irrigated | 9.0% | 28.4% | 2.0% | 11.0% | 4.0% | 10.3% |
| % of cultivated area irrigated | 33.3% | 55.4% | 10.5% | 22.0% | 14.8% | 31.2% |

5. Based on figures in *NWFP Gazetter. Peshawar District. 1931,* and *Census of India,* 1931, Part I, pp. 6-7.

three major irrigation schemes. Their impact was most dramatically felt in the Hashtnagar-Yusafzai plain, where large tracts of semi-barren land were converted into rich, productive farm acreage.[6] Out of 853,065 acres under cultivation in Peshawar in 1931, 472,164, or 55.4 percent, were irrigated.[7] All told, 51.2 percent of Peshawar's total area and 70.8 percent of its cultivable area was farmed in 1931, figures which none of the other districts in the province could match. Peshawar, in fact, contained 29 percent of the cultivated acreage of the NWFP and 52 percent of its irrigated land, even though it accounted for only 18.5 percent of its total area.

Peshawar's network of canals turned it into the granary of the NWFP before 1947. It accounted for the bulk of the province's main food staples, especially wheat and maize, and produced 90 percent of its primary cash crops (See Table 2).

Adding to its prosperity, the Valley lay along the main route from India to Afghanistan and Central Asia, with Peshawar city serving as the entrepot for both the legal trade and smuggling which took place across the border.

This economic base supported a larger population than any other region in the Frontier. In 1931, the 974,321 inhabitants of Peshawar District constituted 40.2 percent of the province's total population of 2,425,075.[8] Population density in the district was 369 per square mile, as compared to 179 for the NWFP as a whole; and among the province's sixteen *tehsils*, Peshawar and Charsadda ranked first and second in density with 613 and 464 per square mile respectively.[9] Peshawar also had a much larger urban component than the other districts. By the definition employed in the 1931 Census, the district contained the province's only city, Peshawar, and ten of its twenty-five towns.[10]

Peshawar enjoyed other advantages before 1947. Historically, the Valley had always been the political and administrative center of the Frontier. The British continued the trend by making it the center of their military establishment on the Frontier and by making Peshawar city the capital of the new North-West Frontier Province in 1901. To control the Valley, the British built a more elaborate administrative apparatus there than in the other districts of the province. They also invested more heavily in its infrastructure. By 1931, Peshawar contained three of the four government irrigation schemes in the NWFP, over 1,000 miles of road (a quarter of it paved), the province's main railroad link to the rest of India, and a good communication system by the

---

*Gazetteer. Peshawar District. 1897-98* (Compiled and Published under the Authority of the Punjab Government, 1898), Part II, Table II.

6. See Chapter 3 for a discussion of the changes produced by irrigation.

7. *NWFP Gazetteer. Peshawar District. 1931* (Lahore: Civil and Military Gazette, 1934), Part B, Table 18. The percentages have been computed.

8. *Census of India, 1931*. Part II, Table I. Percentage computed.

9. *Ibid.* Swabi, Mardan, and Nowshera ranked fifth, sixth, and eighth in population density.

10. *Ibid.*, Part II. Table IV.

**Table 2: Harvest (in Tons) in the North-West Frontier Province and Peshawar District, 1930–31**[11]

| *Crop* | *Total Yield in the NWFP* | *Yield in Peshawar* | *Peshawar Yield as a % of the Provincial Yield* |
|---|---|---|---|
| Wheat | 206,139 | 102,471 | 49.7 |
| Maize | 217,095 | 139,386 | 64.2 |
| Rice | 11,582 | 4,708 | 40.7 |
| Barley | 59,059 | 46,307 | 78.4 |
| Jowar | 10,261 | 7,610 | 74.2 |
| Sugarcane | 58,237 | 54,442 | 93.5 |
| Cotton | 1,936 | 1,686 | 87.1 |

standards of the time.[12] Finally, the Valley was the traditional cultural center of the Pakhtuns, while Peshawar city was the intellectual capital of the Frontier, the region's primary point of contact with Western influences, and the site of a disproportionate share of its educational institutions.

Kohat District contains 2,703 square miles of broken terrain divided among Hangu, Kohat, and Teri *Tehsils*.[13] Much of it is a tangle of barren ridges and ravines. Ranges of low hills run through the district in an east-west direction, creating a series of small, narrow valleys. The largest, the Kohat basin, is the smallest of the province's main plains. Drained by the Kohat *Toi* (River), the basin extends from the town of Hangu to the Indus but is no more than seven miles across at its widest. While most of it lies in Kohat *Tehsil*, it extends into Hangu *Tehsil* where it is called the Lower Miranzai Valley. The Upper Miranzai Valley slopes westward, with its streams draining into the Kurram River. Thal, its main town, is the gateway to the Kurram Agency and the strategic Peiwar Kotal Pass into Afghanistan.

Kohat's inhospitable terrain sustained less agriculture than any other district in the province before independence. Over 71 percent of its area was barren wasteland, and cultivation was limited in the remainder by poor soil conditions and a paucity of water. Only 10.5 percent of the cultivated land (or 2 percent of its total area) was irrigated, leaving most agricultural production vulnerable to an uneven and uncertain rainfall which averaged 16.2 inches annually.[14] This meant not only smaller harvests and more frequent crop failures but also a greater dependence than other districts on hardier, less desirable food grains.[15] Due to its precarious agricultural conditions,

11. Taken from *Report of the Season and Crops of the North-West Frontier Province for the Year, 1930-31* (Calcutta: Government of India Central Publication Branch, 1932), pp. xiii-xx. Exact figures for tobacco yields are not available, but almost all of the Frontier's production came from Peshawar as well.
12. See Chapter 3 for a further discussion.
13. *Census of India, 1931*, Part II, Table I.
14. See *supra*, Table 1, p. 15.
15. The district, for example, accounted for three-fourths of the province's *bajra* crop in

# North-West Frontier Province and Tribal Territories

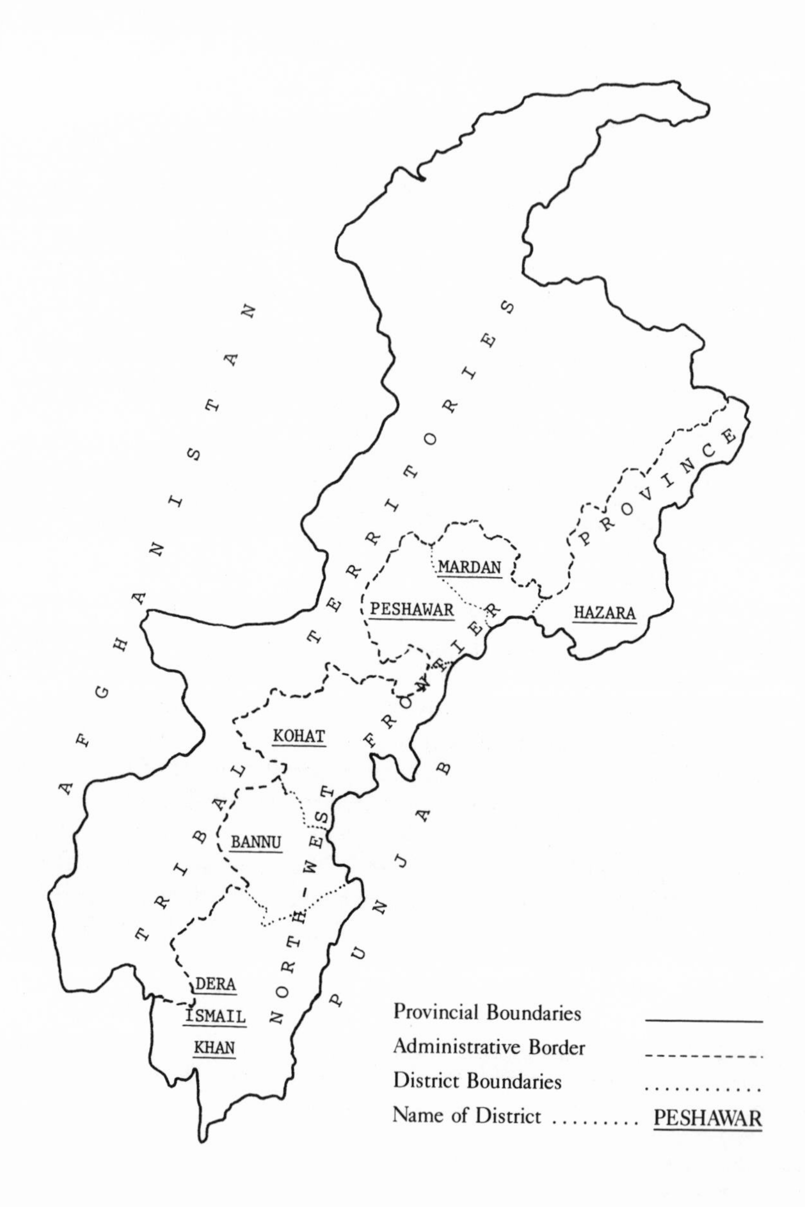

# North-West Frontier Province

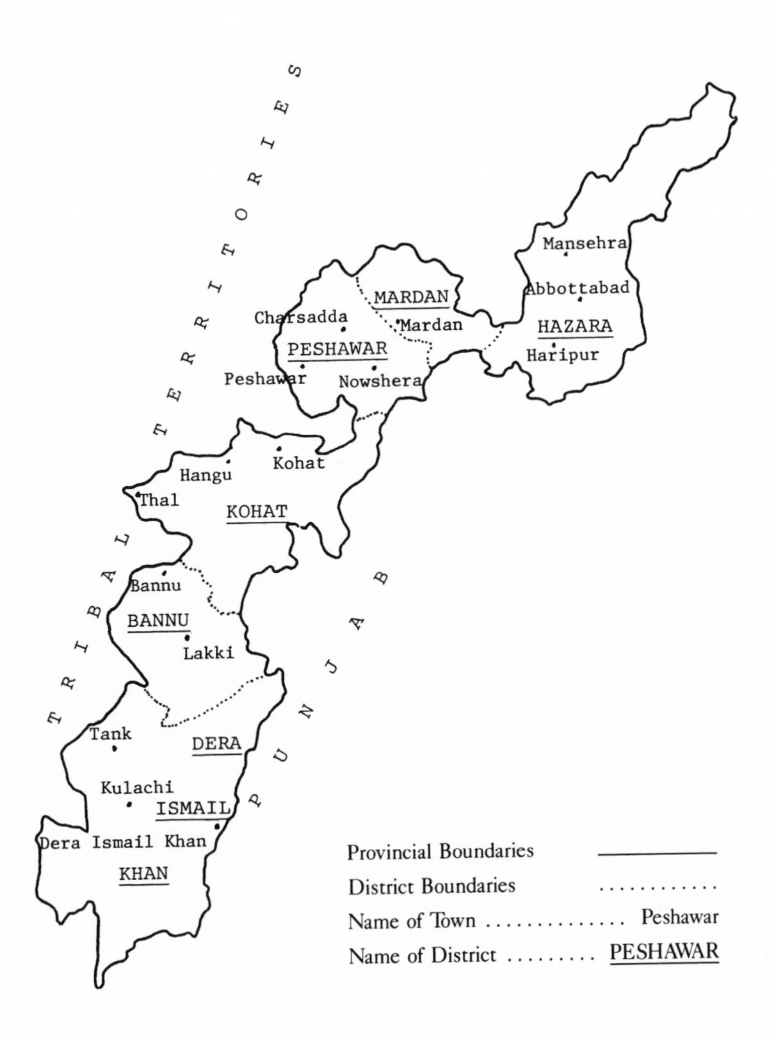

Kohat had only 236,732 inhabitants in 1931 and a population density of 89 per square mile, well below the provincial average of 179.[16] Even this was too much for the district to support, forcing many of its adult males to leave the district seasonally or for longer periods of time in search of work.

Bannu District forms a basin which is surrounded by mountains on all four sides. It covers 1,698 square miles and is divided into Bannu and Marwat *Tehsils*. It has only one major town, also called Bannu, which is the commercial and administrative center for the district and the adjoining tribal territory of Waziristan. In 1931, Bannu District contained a population of 270,301. Population density was only 159 per square mile, but in Bannu *Tehsil*, it was 350, the fourth highest among the NWFP's *tehsils*.[17]

With 50 percent of its land under crops and 22 percent irrigated, Bannu was the second most intensively cultivated area in the province.[18] Agriculture was disproportionately concentrated within Bannu *Tehsil* in the central flood plain between the Kurram and Gambila Rivers. Although the *doaba* has an area of only 270 square miles, or about one-sixth of the district, it contained more than two-thirds of the district's inhabitants and accounted for 60 percent of its land revenue before independence.[19] The prosperity of the *doaba* rested upon an extensive network of canals which largely predated British rule. The flow of the Kurram and Gambila, however, was too small to satisfy all irrigation demands in the area. Thus, the most prosperous and densely populated parts of the *doaba* lay in its extreme northwest around Bannu city, where the rivers could be tapped immediately on entering the basin.

In contrast to the fertile *doaba*, the remaining five-sixths of Bannu District—the outer half of Bannu *Tehsil* and all but a small portion of Marwat *Tehsil*—consists of sandy, poorly watered land. Agriculture in these areas was precarious and population light and dispersed. Except for some hill torrent irrigation (called *rodkohi*), which was limited by the unpredictability of the flood waters, cultivation depended on a rainfall which averaged 10.8 inches a year. Less than half of the region was farmed; harvest yields were low; and crop failures were common.[20]

Dera Ismail Khan, the southernmost district in the NWFP, is defined by the Derajat plain which is a natural part of the larger Indus Valley basin.

---

1931 and one-fourth of its gram but only one-eighth of its wheat and virtually none of its cash crops. Computed from *Report on the Seasons and Crops . . . , loc. cit.*

16. *Census of India, 1931*, Part II, Table 1.

17. *Ibid.*

18. See Table 1, *supra*, p. 15.

19. R.I.R. Glancy, *Final Report of the Second Regular Settlement of the Bannu District* (Peshawar: Commercial Press, 1908), p. 1 of the review by M.F. O'Dwyer. These figures could not have changed significantly after 1908 since the government undertook no major irrigation schemes.

20. *Imperial Gazetter*, p. 188, and Herbert Edwardes, *A Year on the Punjab Frontier in 1848-49* (Lahore: Printed under the authority of the Government of West Pakistan, 1963), Vol. 1, p. 259.

Thus, it is geographically oriented toward the Punjab and cut off from the rest of the NWFP. The district is the largest in the Frontier Province, with 3,471 square miles divided among Tank, Kulachi, and Dera Ismail Khan *Tehsils*. Physically, it consists of the *Kachchi* (the Indus River flood plain) in its eastern 20 percent and the *Daman* which includes the rest of its area. The district had a small population for its size. In 1931, it contained only 274,604 inhabitants and a population density of 79 per square mile, the lowest in the province.[21]

The Derajat is characterized by extreme heat and aridity. Average rainfall for the district as a whole is 9.8 inches. Tank, in the northwest, receives a little more, while the rest of the district receives much less. Before independence, the *Kachchi* was least affected by these conditions since it drew on the Indus for irrigation. In Tank, there was some irrigation from two perennial streams and some rain-fed agriculture. The rest of the *Daman* depended on *rodkohi* irrigation, which limited cultivation to the area immediately adjacent to the hill torrents and left three-fourths of the region unusable.[22] Due to these adverse natural conditions Dera Ismail Khan accounted for less of the province's total agricultural production than any other district except Kohat. Its main crops were wheat, which was grown in the *Kachchi*, and barley, gram and jowar, which were the basic crops of the *Daman*.[23]

Hazara, with its 3,009 square miles divided among Mansehra, Abbottabad, and Haripur *Tehsils*, is also geographically distinct from the rest of the NWFP. Although it lies east of the Indus, it was included in the province because it borders on tribal territory and Lord Curzon wanted to administer all relations with the hill tribes through one unit. The district contains three main plains arranged in a steplike manner north from the Punjab. The lowest and largest is the Haripur plain, which merges into the Potwar Plateau in the Punjab. It is followed by the Rash plain in Abbottabad *Tehsil* and the Pakhli plain in Mansehra. The rest of the district consists of mountainous tracts punctuated by narrow river valleys. Northern Mansehra forms an extension of the lesser Himalayas, while the eastern and western sides of the district consist of mountain systems which merge into Kashmir and the tribal territory respectively.

In spite of its mountainous nature, Hazara contained 670,227 inhabitants in 1931 and had a density of 223 per square mile. Abbottabad ranked second in total population and third in density among the province's *tehsils*.[24] The

21. *Census of India, 1931*, Part II, Table 1. Its *tehsils* ranked twelfth, fourteenth and sixteenth in density in the NWFP. Kulachi, with the lowest density in the province, contained only 48 people per square mile.

22. Dichter, *op. cit.*, p. 164.

23. *Report on the Seasons and Crops . . . , loc. cit.*

24. *Census of India, 1931*, Part II, Table 1. Haripur and Mansehra *Tehsils* ranked seventh and ninth in density respectively.

district depended mainly on rain-fed agriculture since the terrain limited irrigation to 9 percent of its total area. Hazara received an average of 43.8 inches of rain a year, enough to grow large crops of maize, rice, wheat, and barley.[25] The district, however, was not self-sufficient. With only 29 percent of its total area under cultivation, Hazara had to import food grain from Peshawar and the Punjab to meet the needs of its people.

## The Province's Population

The North-West Frontier is invariably thought of as the land of the Pakhtuns, from which follows the proposition that politics in the area were the singular expression of that ethnic group. These assumptions were accurate for the tribal area, but the NWFP did not have a homogeneous population, a demographic fact with a decisive influence on its nationalist history. Before 1947, the province contained a mixed population which will be simplified in this study into the three-way division of Pakhtuns, non-Pakhtun Muslims, and non-Muslims. Of the three, only the first is actually an ethnic community. The other two represent useful categories in a discussion of Frontier politics, but they were not cohesive groups. Instead, they consisted of a variety of tribes, castes, and in the case of the non-Muslims, religions.

Pakhtuns accounted for 37.32 percent of the population, non-Pakhtun Muslims 54.52 percent, and non-Muslims the remaining 8.16 percent.[26] These three groups were not evenly distributed throughout the NWFP. Pakhtun/non-Pakhtun differences set Hazara and Dera Ismail Khan apart from the other districts, as Table 3 indicates. By themselves, these figures do not fully demonstrate the division between Hazara and Dera Ismail Khan and the rest of the province. The distinction between Pakhtuns and other Muslims in Peshawar, Kohat, and Bannu was blurred by the large number of non-Pakhtuns who had been absorbed into Pakhtun society as tenants and artisans. The reverse had occurred in Hazara, with many Pakhtuns discarding their old ways for those of their non-Pakhtun neighbors. Deculturation was a less pronounced phenomenon in Dera Ismail Khan; however, patterns of migration had produced an internal boundary which demarcated Tank *Tehsil* in the northwest as distinctly Pakhtun and the rest of the district as heavily non-Pakhtun.[27]

Due to these cultural adjustments, language serves as a better indicator of the divisions in the NWFP than tribal or religious background. Pakhtuns and their dependents speak Pashtu, an East Iranian language which is an

25. Hazara produced 62.7 percent of the Frontier's rice, 34.3 percent of its maize, and 13.7 percent of its wheat. *Report on the Seasons and Crops . . . , loc. cit.*

26. *Census of India, 1931*, Part I, pp. 181 and 201. Christians formed .5 percent of the population. *Ibid.*, Part I, p. 187. Since they did not play a significant part in the independence movement, "non-Muslim" shall henceforth stand for the province's Hindus and Sikhs.

27. *Gazetteer of the Dera Ismail Khan District* (Lahore: Arya Press, 1884), p. 23.

**Table 3: Distribution of Pakhtuns and Non-Pakhtuns by District in 1931**[28]

| *District* | *Total Population* | *Pakhtuns* | *Percent of Total* | *Non-Pakhtun Muslims* | *Percent of Total* | *Non-Muslims* | *Percent of Total* |
|---|---|---|---|---|---|---|---|
| Hazara | 670,117 | 54,544 | 8.14 | 582,250 | 86.89 | 33,323 | 4.95 |
| Peshawar | 974,321 | 473,738 | 48.62 | 424,945 | 44.64 | 75,638 | 6.74 |
| Kohat | 236,273 | 148,089 | 62.68 | 70,347 | 29.77 | 17,728 | 8.55 |
| Bannu | 270,301 | 159,737 | 59.10 | 77,937 | 28.83 | 32,627 | 12.07 |
| Dera Ismail Khan | 274,064 | 69,005 | 25.18 | 166,702 | 60.82 | 38,356 | 14.00 |
| Total | 2,425,076 | 905,122 | 37.32 | 1,322,181 | 54.52 | 196,733 | 8.16 |

28. Compiled from statistics in *Census of India, 1931*, Part I, pp. 187 and 201.

**Table 4: Language Distribution by District in 1931**[29]

| *District* | *Pashtu Speakers* | *% of Population* | *Hindko Speakers* | *% of Population* |
|---|---|---|---|---|
| Hazara | 29,735 | 4.44 | 624,268 | 93.31 |
| Peshawar | 781,773 | 80.24 | 127,189 | 13.05 |
| Kohat | 186,290 | 78.85 | 35,755 | 15.13 |
| Bannu | 288,381 | 84.49 | 33,547 | 12.41 |
| D. I. Khan | 53,643 | 19.60 | 213,115 | 77.76 |
| Total | 1,339,882 | 55.25 | 1,033,874 | 42.63 |

integral part of their self-definition.[30] The great majority of those who do not speak Pashtu use dialects which can be grouped together under the rubric of Hindko. While differing among themselves, these dialects share a common derivation from Punjabi, an Indic language. Prior to 1947, Pashtu was the mother tongue of the overwhelming majority of the province's three central districts, while Hindko predominated in the other two. The religious minorities generally spoke Hindko as a first language, which meant that Pakhtun culture was even more pronounced among the Muslims of Peshawar, Kohat, and Bannu than the figures in Table 4 suggest.[31]

Ethnic differences cut across the North-West Frontier Province in a second direction, separating town from countryside. The province's major urban centers shared two common features—a disproportionate concentration of Hindus and Sikhs and, more generally, a strong non-Pakhtun character. As traders and merchants, non-Muslims naturally congregated in the Frontier's towns. Almost three-fourths of the NWFP's Hindus and over seven-tenths of its Sikhs resided in urban areas, accounting for 32.6 percent of the NWFP's urban inhabitants, or four times their percentage of its total population.[32] Their urban strength was even more pronounced in the southern districts where they formed 71 percent of Bannu city and 48 percent of Dera Ismail Khan city.[33]

29. Compiled from Ibid., Part I, pp. 176 and 178. A small percentage of each district spoke other languages such as Baluchi, English, Hindi, Kashmiri, and Persian.

30. Qayyamuddin, *Pakhtunwali* (Kabul: n.p., 1331 A.H.), p. 10. There are two dialects of Pashtu, a hard variant in the north and a soft variant in the south. One chief difference between them is whether a particular sound is pronounced 'kh' or 'sh.' This creates confusion in terminology. "Pakhtun" and "Pakhtunistan" become "Pashtun" and "Pashtunistan" in the south. "Pashtu" and "Peshawar" become "Pakhtu" and "Pekhawar" in the north. The terms used here are those most commonly found in the written literature on the Frontier.

31. No statistics exist for language distribution by religion. If one subtracts the figures for non-Muslims in each district from those for Hindko, a rough estimate can be obtained of Muslims whose mother tongue was Hindko.

32. *Census of India, 1941* (Delhi: Government of India Press, 1942), Vol. X, p. 20.

33. Computed from *ibid.*, p. 19.

Pakhtuns did not settle in towns even in the districts of their greatest concentration. In 1931, the Census officer reported:

> Many towns owe their existence and a great deal of their growth as well to immigrants not from neighbouring towns and villages but from outside the province altogether. To the vast majority of the inhabitants of the NWFP, town life presents few attractions. The link with the agricultural and rural elements in tribal life is a strong one and no general inclination towards the settled condition of town life has yet begun to develop.[34]

Peshawar city, for example, had been a largely non-Pakhtun enclave ever since the Pakhtuns conquered the surrounding valley. Mountstuart Elphinstone, the first European to describe it, wrote in 1808 that "the inhabitants of Peshawar are of Indian origin but speak Pushtoo as well as Hindkee. There are, however, many other inhabitants of all nations."[35] British rule sharpened the city's differences from the countryside by creating administrative, professional, and commercial opportunities which attracted additional non-Pakhtuns from other Indian provinces, especially the Punjab.

The Pakhtuns' poor representation in urban areas reflected their insistence that only agriculture and fighting were honorable occupations. As Elphinstone observed, they thought "it degrading to pursue the trades which assemble men in towns."[36] Commerce, crafts, and even government service were still frequently scorned 140 years later, sometimes in highly abusive language.[37] Pakhtuns believed that urban life styles were inherently inferior to their own and that anyone who settled in towns invariably adopted customs and mores which fell far short of the standards set by their own social code. These prejudices have diminished since independence, but many Pakhtuns still exhibit a contempt for city life which is apparent from the Pashtu term for urban dweller. *Khare* literally means a townsman, but it has been overlaid with strong pejorative connotations.

## The Pakhtuns

While ethnic and religious cleavages created enduring subdivisions in the NWFP's social life, the province did have an ascendant ethnic group. The Pakhtuns may have formed only two-fifths of its population, but they possessed a homogeneity which the province's larger non-Pakhtun population

34. *Census of India*, 1931, Part I, pp. 43-44.

35. Mountstuart Elphinstone, *Kingdom of Caubul* (Karachi: Oxford University Press, 1972), Vol. I, p. 74.

36. *Ibid.*, p. 332.

37. For example, see Muhammad Akbar Khadim, *Pakistan* (Peshawar: Manzur-i-Am Barqi Press, 1947), p. 200, or Allah Bakhsh Yusafi, *Sarhad aur Jad-o-Jehad-i-Azadi* (Lahore: Markazi Urdu Board, 1968), p. 66.

lacked. More significantly, they had controlled public affairs in the Frontier for more than four centuries. The allegiance of most Pakhtuns traditionally did not extend beyond family, clan, and tribe. Yet, however dimly perceived, they possessed a collective self-awareness of being distinct from other people and a feeling, as one Pashtu writer has put it, that they were "better than any other race."[38] Their chauvinistic pride was evident as early as the 17th century in the poems of Khushhal Khan Khattak. It made a strong impression on 19th-century Englishmen such as Elphinstone, who wrote: "Their clannish spirit diminishes their general patriotism but they all take a lively interest in the 'Nung du Pooshtanueh,' or honour of the Afghaun name. . . . "[39] In the 20th century, that spirit was manifested in the Pakhtun nationalism (or parochialism, depending on the observer's point of view) which became the central issue of the independence movement in the NWFP.

Theorists on ethnicity stress that members of an ethnic group single out one or a few of their common attributes as the decisive symbols of their separateness. For the Pakhtuns, the critical element has been kinship, the belief in a common descent through the male line. This conviction is embodied in comprehensive genealogical tables, called *shajras*, which trace their bloodline back to a single ancestor. Residing across one of the busiest crossroads in Asia's history, Pakhtuns do not actually come from a single stock; but the *shajras* affirm to their satisfaction, if not the scholar's, their essential ethnic purity. Once compiled some 400 years ago, the genealogies helped guarantee that end. For the most part, Pakhtuns have not grafted fictive branches on to their family tree.[40] This rule was much more closely observed in pre-British times, but it is still generally applicable today. Thus, the *shajras* define an essentially closed ethnic community. Other criteria are important, but in the first instance, a person must have a Pakhtun father to qualify as a true Pakhtun. As Elphinstone observed: "They are all very proud of their descent . . . they will hardly acknowledge a man for an Afghaun who cannot make his proofs by going back six or seven generations. . . . "[41]

Elaborate legends project the Pakhtuns' pedigree from their apical ancestor, Qais, back to Hebraic origins.[42] According to these myths, King Saul had a grandson, Afghana, whom David raised as a child and Solomon made the general of his armies. Nebuchadnezzar took his descendants to Babylon with

38. Qayyamuddin, *op. cit.*, p. 123.

39. Elphinstone, *op. cit.*, Vol. I, p. 328.

40. Frederik Barth, *Political Leadership Among Swat Pathans* (London: The Athlone Press, 1958). London School of Economics Monographs on Social Anthropology, No. 19, pp. 28-29. (Henceforth, Barth, *Political Leadership* . . . ) Regarding the *shajras*, see Olaf Caroe, *The Pathans* (London: MacMillan and Co., 1964), pp. 11-24.

41. Elphinstone, *op. cit.*, Vol. I, pp. 328-29.

42. Caroe, *op. cit.*, pp. 3-11.

the other Jewish people. When Cyrus liberated them, most migrated to Ghor but a few went to Mecca. A millennium later, one of the latter, the famous Arab general Khalid bin Walid, convinced Qais to travel to Medina to meet the Prophet. Qais adopted Islam, assumed the name of Abdur Rashid, and returned to Ghor to convert his people. While apocryphal at best, these stories reinforce the Pakhtuns' sense of distinctiveness by giving them a core of historical continuity extending into the distant past. Moreover, by associating them with the founder of Islam and great figures in the Jewish tradition, the legends mark them out as a historically special people. By their own reckoning, as Barth has written, "Pathans have no infidel past, nor do they carry in their history the blemish of defeat and forcible conversion."[43]

Before the British, the *shajras* held a much greater interest for Pakhtuns than as merely a semi-mythical charter of descent. Pakhtuns, as traditionally organized, had no permanent state institutions. Instead, their organization was derived from their principles of kinship as set forth in the *shajras*. These tables defined membership in a series of segmentary lineage groups which determined where one lived, who had rights in the land, what sort of community institutions evolved, and how people engaged in politics. In sum, descent provided the framework within which Pakhtuns conducted their lives, so the right to a place in the family tree was jealously guarded. Once the British constructed a formal government in the settled districts, the importance of kinship diminished, and with it the Pakhtuns' preoccupation with their *shajras*. Yet, even though genealogical assimilation became more acceptable, the principle, for the most part, remained that one must have a patrilineal connection with the community to be a Pakhtun.

Thus, the genealogies and myths have sustained the Pakhtuns' strong parochial sentiments down through the centuries because they were bound up with their social organization, economy, and politics. Further reinforcement was lent by the Pakhtuns' language, history, and values. Their language, which differs from those of their Indian neighbors, has nurtured a separate literary tradition with luminaries and literary forms uniquely its own. Their historical lore—the events they single out as important, and the men they honor as heroes—differs from, and sometimes is in conflict with that of India. For instance, the Mughals are viewed as ancient foes who overthrew the Pakhtuns' Lodhi and Suri dynasties and whose expansionary designs in the Frontier were vigorously resisted. Similarly, Ahmad Shah Abdali, a scourge in Indian history, is revered as the founder of their greatest empire.

Pakhtuns commonly encapsulate what differentiates them from others by referring to their system of values—*Pakhtunwali*, or simply *Pakhto*. Some observers have explained *Pakhtunwali* as a code of honor or chivalry, reducing

43. Frederik Barth, "Pathan Identity and Its Maintenance," in F. Barth (ed.), *Ethnic Groups and Boundaries* (Boston: Little, Brown and Co., 1969), p. 119. (Henceforth, Barth, "Pathan Identity . . . ")

it to the injunctions of *badal* (revenge), *melmastia* (hospitality), and *nanawati* (mediation). These are only the most striking of its prescriptions. *Pakhtunwali* is an all-embracing social code which embodies the Pakhtuns' customary laws, defines their ideals of conduct, and provides a normative yardstick for determining if an individual has the one attribute they most highly prize—*nang*, or honor. One Pakhtun writer has represented the code in the following sweeping terms: "*Pakhtunwali* is that *kalma* in which are embodied all those things—their national soul, historical greatness, and national traditions—which are considered basic and essential to their way of life."[44]

The significance of *Pakhtunwali* stemmed originally from the "stateless" nature of the Pakhtun society. In the absence of a formal government, *Pakhtunwali* assumed critical importance as an unwritten mechanism for regulating social behavior. It provided a relatively uniform ethos for the entire ethnic group and a set of norms which each of its members internalized as guides for his individual behavior. Even after the British gave the NWFP an elaborate legal system, *Pakhtunwali* still retained a vital role in the Pakhtuns' lives as a measure of whether a person was acting like a true Pakhtun. Anyone who flagrantly broke its rules forfeited his honor as a Pakhtun. As Barth notes:

> . . . Pathans have an explicit saying: "He is a Pathan who does Pashto, not (merely) who speaks Pashto"; and "doing" Pashto in this sense means living by a rather exacting code in terms of which some Pashto speakers consistently fall short.[45]

Finally, the Pakhtuns' separate consciousness is territorially rooted in a region they call *Pakhtunkhwa*. While it lacks boundaries in the modern sense of the term, *Pakhtunkhwa*'s core region has never been in doubt. It stretches from Qandahar in the south and west to the Indus in the east and Dir and Swat in the north. For centuries, leaving that area has carried the implication of moving into foreign lands, and from at least the 17th century, Pakhtuns have been exhorted by their political leaders and poets to defend its independence and integrity.[46]

Today, many Pakhtuns argue that their tribal background, social organization, culture, history, and sense of territoriality are proof of an age-old Pakhtun "nation." In many ways, this is a projection of modern concepts into the past. Nonetheless, Pakhtuns have undeniably had a pool of characteristics which encouraged the development of a separate identity well be-

---

44. Qayyamuddin, *op. cit.*, p. 10. For a discussion of *Pakhtunwali*, also see Charles Lindholm, *Generosity and Jealousy. The Swat Pukhtun of Northern Pakistan* (New York: Columbia University Press, 1982), Chapter 6.

45. Barth, "Pathan Identity . . . ," p. 119.

46. See D.N. Mackenzie (trans.), *Poems from the Divan of Khushal Khan Khattak* (London: George Allen and Unwin, 1965), pp. 92-94, 100-2, and 147-48; and Elphinstone, *op. cit.*, Vol. I, p. 258.

fore the 20th century and gave rise to an assertive ideology of Pakhtun nationalism during the independence movement.

## Pakhtun Social Organization

While the Pakhtuns' ethnocentrism shaped the major issues of the nationalist movement in the NWFP, their social organization and polity gave it structure. The remainder of this chapter, therefore, will examine the nature of Pakhtun society on the eve of British rule. It makes no pretense to deal with all Pakhtuns, only those living in the settled districts,[47] and even glosses over the substantial diversity which exists among them as a result of differing ecological influences and historical experiences. This, however, is unavoidable since its purpose is not to provide a comprehensive picture of how Pakhtuns lived but merely a model of their primary mode of organization in what became the NWFP. Most recent accounts of Pakhtuns draw heavily upon the example of the former tribal region of Swat, located north of Peshawar. This is an implicit acknowledgement of the influence of Frederik Barth's work, which is regarded even by his critics as a classic in modern anthropology. The following discussion is no exception to the general rule. Modifications, however, have been necessary to make Barth's analysis of a peripheral region of the Frontier, as it existed under unique historical conditions, relevant to the settled districts.[48]

Pakhtuns are not indigenous to the Frontier Province. They moved into it from the mountainous country of present-day Afghanistan, starting in the 15th century. The details of when, how, and why they came are obscure. Their own traditions portray them as conquerors, but Sir Olaf Caroe, for one, theorizes that they probably replaced the previous inhabitants peacefully over generations, absorbing many of them in the process.[49] Whether they established themselves by quick military victory or gradual encroachment, the results were the same. They gained control of the land and organized a political system which was virtually their exclusive preserve.

Pakhtuns belong to the category of peoples who have a segmentary tribal system. Centralized authority is absent in such a system. Instead, kinship provides the basic ordering mechanism for society. In the Pakhtuns' case, their *shajras* delimit a hierarchy of patrilineal descent groups, or lineages, each of which claims derivation from a single progenitor. Each is related to the others through blood ties, either real or fictive, as determined by the

47. Many Pakhtuns in the tribal areas displayed marked contrasts in their social organization. See Akbar S. Ahmed, *Millenium and Charisma among Pathans* (London: Routledge and Kegan Paul, 1976), Chapter 5.

48. Barth's work has come under strong challenge. See *ibid.*, and Talal Asad, "Market Model, Class Structure and Consent: A Reconsideration of the Swat Political Organization," *Man*, Vol. 7, no. 7, 3/72, pp. 74-94. Also see Lindholm, *op. cit.*, Chapter 3.

49. Caroe, *op. cit.*, p. 166.

position of its putative ancestor in the genealogical pyramid which spreads out from Qais, the presumed patriarch of all Pakhtuns. This form of organization can be visualized in family terms. Equivalent segments at one level in the hierarchy are part of a single unit at the next if their progenitors are sons of a common father. At the next higher level, the segment defined by the father fuses with those of his brothers into a unit tracing descent from the grandfather. This process continues up the family tree with each successive segment expanding in degree of inclusiveness until it encompasses the entire ethnic group in a single unit. Thus, an individual belongs simultaneously to a series of lineage segments ranging in size from his immediate kinsmen to the whole Pakhtun people.[50]

Among the more distant ancestors in the *shajras*, only Qais himself defines a group with any real significance, and its importance is confined to being the maximum unit of common Pakhtun identity. By their emergence into recorded history, the Pakhtuns already exhibited the main tribal configuration characteristic of them today. Larger lineage segments had been sloughed off as meaningful social and political units, although this had occurred sufficiently recently in some instances for them to remain a part of tribal memory.[51] Since then, there has been no lineage group bigger than the tribe with institutions for making and carrying out joint decisions. By the arrival of the British, moreover, even the tribe had ceased in many areas to have practical significance for Pakhtuns and had become merely a unit of identification and sentiment. In those cases, smaller descent groups, or *khels*, provided the framework within which their lives were organized.

As with other segmentary tribal peoples, Pakhtuns were distributed in a pattern which geographically replicated their lineage hierarchy. An individual's immediate neighbors were his brothers and close cousins; in other words, the members of his minimal descent group. Not only were their fields adjacent to one another, but they lived together as the sole Pakhtun inhabitants of a village, if it were small, or one of its *kandis* (wards), if it were large. Immediately beyond their lands were those of the next most inclusive unit in the hierarchy. In many places, its members inhabited a different *kandi* in the same village. This process was repeated up to the tribal level, where the major clans usually could be found adjacent to each other.

Pakhtuns monopolized the land over most of the Frontier, a right they claimed as the spoils of conquest. On acquiring possession of an area, a tribe permanently divided it into *tappas*, each of which was assigned to a specific *khel*.[52] Title was vested in the *khel* as a collectivity, while its mem-

50. For a good example of how this operates, see Akbar S. Ahmed, *Economic and Social Change in the Tribal Territories* (Karachi: Oxford University Press, 1977), pp. 14-16.

51. For example, according to tradition, Peshawar Valley was conquered by the Khakay and Ghoria Khel which subsequently split into their respective component tribes. Caroe, *op. cit.*, Chapter 12.

52. See Barth, *Political Leadership* . . . , pp. 64-68; James Spain, *The Pathan Borderland*

bers were entitled to shares, or *daftars*, in their joint estate. Access to land, in fact, was so intimately tied to membership in a lineage group that an individual who lost his *daftar* also lost his rights and status as a Pakhtun. The less productive parts of a *tappa* were set aside as *shamilat* (common lands), principally for grazing purposes. Utilization of the common lands was regulated by rights known as *inam*, which formed part of each Pakhtun's *daftar*. Productive areas were divided and periodically redivided in a process called *wesh*. At specific intervals of up to thirty years, the major descent groups within the *tappa* exchanged territory. Then the land was divided into smaller and smaller units among the segments at each succeeding level in the lineage hierarchy. At the lowest level, the portion allotted to a minimal descent group was divided among individual heads of household according to their *daftars*.

This complex system of land ownership and rotation was devised to preserve equality among lineage members, an ideal which was a legacy from the Pakhtuns' nomadic past.[53] In theory, the *wesh* prevented the concentration of land in a few hands, while economic differences which arose from families growing at varying rates were offset by carving additional plots out of the *shamilat*. In practice, various factors led to economic differentiation. Tribes often donated extra shares to individuals in return for special services; superordinate states, such as the Mughals and Sikhs, gave additional rights to prominent tribal leaders; *daftars* were freely alienable among Pakhtuns; and the forceable seizure of one man's land by another was not uncommon. Additionally, those who had larger land holdings could use their greater resources to obtain a greater share at the time of *wesh*. Finally, the compensatory mechanism provided by the common lands did not always work. A growing population meant there was a diminishing amount of cultivable *shamilat* to parcel out, and, even when there was enough, those individuals with disproportionate holdings were often adverse to seeing their economic and political dominance diluted by the distribution of additional common lands. Thus, the Pakhtun economy was not in a state of egalitarian equilibrium. A process of differentiation was already at work before the British, dividing Pakhtuns into large and small landholders and turning some of the latter into landless dependents. The Pakhtuns' strong normative emphases on equality and the *wesh* slowed the pace at which change occurred, but they did not entirely prevent it. To varying degrees, the different tribes departed from the Pakhtun ideal.[54]

---

(The Hague: Mouton and Co., 1963), pp. 80-84; and B.H. Baden-Powell, *The Indian Village Community* (London: Longmans, Green and Co., 1896), pp. 244-65.

53. Ahmed, *Millenium . . .*, p. 38; and Charles Lindholm, "Contemporary Politics in a Tribal Society: Swat District, NWFP, Pakistan," *Asian Survey*, Vol. XIX, no. 5, 5/79, pp. 486-87.

54. See Asad, *op. cit.*, for a theoretical explanation of how the class differentiation occurred.

The existence of a class structure becomes even more apparent on viewing Pakhtuns within the broader context of the society they dominated. Pakhtuns constituted only the upper stratum of the Frontier's population. The subordinate classes consisted primarily of the dispossessed remnants of earlier peoples or immigrants from outside the Frontier, who had been "naturalized by many generations of habitation in the country" and differed only slightly from Pakhtuns in customs and habits.[55] The rest were former Pakhtuns who had lost their *daftars*. The lower classes were all landless, a fact implicitly conveyed by the various terms used to describe them—*hamsaya*, *kamin*, *faqir*. As a result, they were dependent on the Pakhtuns who controlled the land and its produce. As H.W. Bellew wrote:

> None of these races, as a rule, have any position in the soil. They are all more or less vassals of the dominant Afghauns and compose the industrial population by whom are performed the cultivation of the soil, the tending of cattle and the various industrial arts.[56]

The link between landowner and those who worked for him was not solely economic but took the form of an open-ended association between patron and client. James Scott and Benedict Kerkvliet have defined that connection as

> an exchange relationship or instrumental friendship between individuals of different status in which the patron uses his own influence and resources to provide for the protection and material welfare of his lower status client and his family who, for his part, reciprocates by offering general support and assistance, including personal services to the patron.[57]

The relationship was clearly unequal, for the client gave much more than he received. Its harshness, however, was mitigated by the personal, almost parental, concern the Pakhtun patron showed for the client. The landlord assured his minimum physical needs by providing access to land and supplementing his share of the harvest with additional food, housing, and clothing. He also received assistance at important ritual events, such as marriages, financial aid in times of emergency, and protection in a society which could be quite hostile to the weak.

Clients not only served their patrons economically but followed them politically. Thus, politics were essentially a Pakhtun affair in which the lower

55. H.W. Bellew, *A General Report on the Yusafzai* (Lahore: Sang-e-Meel Publications, 1977), p. 183. Regarding the lower classes, see Barth, *Political Leadership* . . . , pp. 16-22, 42-52, and 68-70.

56. Bellew, *op. cit.*, p. 154.

57. James Scott and Benedict Kerkvliet, "How Traditional Rural Patrons Lose Legitimacy. A Theory with Special Reference to Southeast Asia," in Steffen Schmidt, et. al., eds., *Friends, Followers and Factions: A Reader in Political Clientelism* (Berkeley: University of California Press, 1977), p. 440.

class non-Pakhtuns were uninvolved except as they were mobilized through the patron-client tie. Among Pakhtuns, no such distinction between leader and follower can be easily made since they generally refused to recognize any difference in status among themselves. Each believed himself equal to, if not better than, all the rest, a situation not given to the emergence of strong and stable states. As Elphinstone observed:

> . . . in some rare cases, the Khaun establishes arbitrary power and acts without consulting any of the Jeergas [councils] under him. . . . But more frequently the chiefs are neglected and every sub-division, every quarter and even every family throws off its dependence on its superiors and acts according to its own interest or inclination.[58]

In the absence of an organized state, the Pakhtuns' segmentary lineage system provided the underlying structure for their politics. At the heart of Pakhtun politics were pervasive factional rivalries among landholders which are called *parajamba*. Since politics were localized and localities associated with lineage segments, the most intense enmities pitted close relatives against each other. Other types of rivalry existed, but the most prevalent consisted of competition among patrilineal cousins. This is called *tarburwali* in Pashtu. It was so common that *tarbur*, the word for first cousin, lost its purely kin connotation and assumed the meaning of an enemy among one's close cousins.[59]

The greatest source of contention among Pakhtuns was land and the major time of tension the *wesh* when it was redistributed. The further down the tribal hierarchy the process worked, the less predetermined and more open to dispute it became. At the lowest level, Barth writes:

> . . . the men must meet in a council of their small segment and devise a pattern of allotment through negotiation and compromise, or force. This is a type of issue uniquely suited to generate intense factionalism between collaterals; there is an overriding opposition of interests between such groups competing for the slightly better fields.[60]

Once the *wesh* was completed, the lands of close relatives bordered on one another, guaranteeing further disputes over field boundaries, irrigation rights, and damage done to one field by men or animals working in the next. Additionally, Pakhtuns commonly tried to expand their holdings by force and coercion. The most likely candidates for expropriation were one's patrilineal cousins, both because their lands were adjacent to one's own and because the Pakhtuns' ethos made their destruction a prime political objec-

58. Elphinstone, *op. cit.*, Vol. I, p. 216.

59. Frederik Barth, "Segmentary Opposition and the Theory of Games: A Study of Pathan Organization," *Journal of the Royal Anthropological Institute of Great Britain and Ireland*, Vol. 89, Part I and II, 1-12/59 p. 11. (Henceforth Barth, "Segmentary Opposition . . . ")

60. *Ibid.*

tive. Finally, inheritance served as another source of contention. No matter how clear the order of precedence among the deceased's relatives, ambiguous situations inevitably arose in which more than one person had a just claim to the patrimony. Even when succession rights appeared clear cut, close cousins still found grounds for fighting. As *tarburs*, the desire to injure one another often overrode considerations of equity, leading individuals to pursue vigorously the most tenuous of inheritance claims.[61]

These rivalries were institutionalized in the shape of factions which Pakhtuns called *gundis* or *dullahs*. As a rule, an individual belonged to the faction opposed to that of his *tarbur*. *Gundis* were not collections of equals. In a culture where the use of force was common, less powerful landholders often did not have the means or skill to defend their interests on their own. They consequently attached themselves to more forceful men as factional followers, pledging their loyalties in return for protection and other benefits. Thus, *gundis* centered around prominent individuals, or Khans. In Swat, Barth found that political alignments were defined solely in terms of those men.[62] In other parts of the Frontier, *gundis* had a permanent existence independent of any individual, but their leaders still played a pivotal role in deciding factional attitudes and activities.

Among a few tribes, individual families had hereditarily achieved positions of political prominence, often with the assistance of outside states. In the most extreme cases, some verged on being independent, petty rulers. More commonly, Pakhtun tribal chiefs were little more than first among equals, and such power as they did have was earned rather than inherited. Family background helped, but when a man's personal influence declined, his ancestry, however noble, could not prevent him from losing followers and power. The size of one's landholding was also important, but only because the more a Khan controlled, the more income he had at his disposal to maintain dependents, contract for the allegiance of other Pakhtuns, and in general, play the game of politics.[63] Land and wealth did not convey any inherent right to leadership. In fact, they were easily lost if a man did not demonstrate the personal qualities which Pakhtuns expected of their Khans. Above all, a Khan had to command respect. As Barth observes:

> . . . the intangible factor of prestige or reputation becomes a major source of authority, an important means by which a political pretender rallies supporters. The qualities are evaluated in terms of the polar opposites 'izzat,' honour, and 'sharm'—shame. The ideal personality of a leader is virile and impetuous, given to extremes rather than compro-

61. See Lindholm, *Generosity* . . . , Chapter 5, for a further discussion of the problems of inheritance.

62. Barth, *Political Leadership* . . . , p. 72. For the relationship of Khan and follower, see *ibid.*, Chapter 7; Lindholm also discusses the issue in *Generosity* . . . , Chapter 5.

63. Barth, *Political Leadership* . . . , p. 74.

> mise, sometimes unwise, but always brave. . . . Any insult, any action or condition which 'shames' a Pathan, requires him to defend his honour, if he is not to suffer permanent loss of respect and status.[64]

Thus, bravery, a gift for intrigue, vengefulness, a highly refined sense of honor, and a willingness to resort to violence were all necessary. Generosity and hospitality were also required, both because a miserly man was regarded as dishonorable and because a Khan had to spend lavishly to maintain the loyalty of his followers.

*Gundis* varied greatly in size. In some areas, their orientation was strictly local. Elsewhere, larger political groups emerged, usually as a result of local factions seeking outside assistance against one another. In Swat, this process reached its logical extreme with each *tappa* splitting into two opposing blocs.[65] These alliances usually had a long history, but unlike village factions, which were permanent entities, they had only a situational existence. According to Barth, "The alliance blocs . . . are called together to act with reference to each specific threat, but are otherwise inactive. . . ."[66]

Pakhtuns' commitment to their factions varied in intensity. In Swat, according to Barth, there were no moral or ascriptive constraints preventing a person from leaving his faction if he calculated that he could obtain a better deal elsewhere.[67] In other parts, a person's loyalties usually rested on more than a mere assessment of benefits and liabilities. Factional allegiances were widely viewed as a matter of honor; as one Pashtu journal has proclaimed: "It is against the principles of *Pakhto* for a man to leave his group. The Pakhtuns of old always remained steadfast in their loyalties."[68] Some even went to the extreme of holding *gundi* ties to be "stronger than blood."[69]

While factional conflict was the normal pattern of politics in the Frontier, it was not so deep-rooted that it could not be overcome when the members of a lineage group needed to cooperate against an external enemy. In this regard, Pakhtuns share a common characteristic with other segmentary tribal people. As Charles Lindholm observes: "The fundamental concept of the society is that all those related through a common male ancestor should stand together against outsiders."[70] *Tarburwali* itself conveys this principle, for the term has the secondary meaning that regardless of how deadly the enmity, if one's *tarbur* is attacked by an outsider, one should assist him as a

---

64. *Ibid.*, pp. 81-82.

65. *Ibid.*, p. 102-7 and 123-24.

66. *Ibid.*, p. 123. It also follows that "the territorial unit involved in a dispute (corresponding to a descent group council at a certain level of lineage segmentation) determines how large a part of the block will be mobilized." Barth, "Segmentary Opposition . . . ," p. 14.

67. Barth, *Political Leadership* . . . , p. 2.

68. *Pakhtun*, 9/14/45.

69. Elphinstone, *op. cit.*, Vol. II, p. 4.

70. Lindholm, "Contemporary Politics . . . ," p. 486.

matter of honor. Such alliances were at best temporary, existing relative only to the threat which called them into being. Otherwise, internal factionalism fragmented the descent group. Bellew captured this oscillation between co-operation and conflict when he wrote:

> Each tribe under its own chief is an independent commonwealth and collectively each is the other's rival, if not enemy . . . when undisturbed from without the several tribes are always opposed to each other; feuds, estrangements and affrays are of constant occurance. . . . Everywhere family is arrayed against family and tribe against tribe, in fact one way or another every man's hand is against his neighbor. Feuds are settled and truces patched up, but they break out afresh on the smallest provocation. . . . But when danger threatens from without, all family feuds and clan jealousies are at once forgotten and all unite to repel the common enemy.[71]

Lineage group cooperation was an ideal which was not always followed, for it conflicted with the even stronger commandment that one should be unforgiving and unremitting in his enmities. Since this sort of solidarity was difficult to achieve and often short-lived, a more dependable mechanism for uniting in times of crisis was needed. To meet this requirement, a single exception was made to the rule that non-Pakhtuns could only play a subordinate role in Frontier society. Although religious men usually had different ethnic roots, Pakhtuns treated them with deference and endowed some of them with a special political role. Their piety, learning, and presumed detachment from material concerns made them ideally suited both to act as mediators in the Pakhtuns' worldly quarrels and to unite them through appeals to Islam in times of extraordinary crisis.

Religious men do not form a single, homogeneous group in the Frontier. They perform a variety of duties, exhibit wide variations in demeanor, and receive varying degrees of respect. As a starting point, one can distinguish between two ideal-types—one being "legal, rational, formal, orthodox" and the other "pacific, mystical, informal, unorthodox."[72] The boundary between the two is not clear-cut and absolute. Nonetheless, they do point to a crucial division among Islamic religious leaders.

The interpreters of the rational, legalistic side of Islam are *mullahs* and *ulema*. It needs to be stressed that in the Frontier at least, most of these men also have some involvement with mysticism; however, their basic concerns are the formal ritual and the *Shariah*. "*Mullah*" is often generically used for any religious personage, but it specifically applies to a man who serves as a mosque attendant and administers to the common religious needs of his community. Most belong to the lower classes, for Pakhtuns consider their

71. Bellew, *op. cit.*, pp. 204-5.
72. Ahmed, *Millenium . . .*, p. 88.

position demeaning. Typically, they are badly trained, poorly paid, and little more than dependents on the most prominent Pakhtun landowners in their localities.[73] Ordinary *mullahs* are often respectfully called "*maulana*" or "*maulvi*." In a more restrictive sense, however, those titles are reserved for the *ulema* who are supposed to be experts in Islamic jurisprudence. Usually, an individual qualifies as an *alim* after an education at a *madrassah* or under the tutelage of a learned divine. Formal studies, however, are not essential. An *alim* can be self-taught provided there is a public consensus that his knowledge entitles him to the status.

*Mullahs* and *ulema* are viewed ambivalently in the Frontier. They are often stereotyped as hidebound conservatives wedded to a narrow vision of Islam and sometimes as avaricious, corruptible men.[74] Nonetheless, most are outwardly respected, and some are even regarded as saintly. Piety, exemplary personal conduct, and wisdom brings them honor and influence. Their authority, for the most part, is confined to the religious realm. Yet, as the voices of morality, rectitude, and learning, their opinions on their communities' affairs command attention. By and large, however, they have not been the ones to serve as unifiers. Those among them who have, moreover, earned the trust of Pakhtuns because of their spirituality rather than as a result of their occupational roles.

The importance of *mullahs* and *ulema* in Pakhtun society pales in comparison to that of men from the Sufi tradition. As J. Spenser Trimingham generalizes for all Muslims:

> Legalistic religion . . . had little to offer men's deeper needs. The legal religion fulfilled a social far more than a spiritual function, and it was the function of the [Sufi] orders to mediate to the ordinary man the inner aspects of Islam.[75]

Over the centuries, Sufism evolved from an individual quest for communion with God into highly institutionalized orders in which tombs (*ziarats*) and hereditary saints (*pirs*) were the focus rather than the mystical discipline itself.[76] Integral to this transformation was a change in the status of the Sufi master from merely a spiritually adept teacher to a *wali* (protege of God) with the ability to mediate between men and the divine. Once this occurred, as Trimingham observes, saint veneration became a central part of the Islamic mystic tradition.[77] Pakhtuns were affected by these develop-

73. Barth, *Political Leadership* . . . , p. 47; and Spain, *op. cit.*, p. 75.

74. The ambivalence can be seen in a common Swat insult: "You wife of a mullah." Barth, *Political Leadership* . . . , p. 47. It is also reflected in some of the Pakhtuns' proverbs. Jans Enevoldsen, *Sound the Bells, O Moon, Arise and Shine*! (Peshawar: University Book Agency, 1969), p. 35.

75. J. Spenser Trimingham, *The Sufi Orders in Islam* (London: Oxford University Press, 1967), p. 229.

76. See *ibid.*, Chapters 1-3 for a full discussion.

77. *Ibid.*, p. 26.

ments as much as other Muslims. Thus, while there continued to be numerous individual mystical seekers in the Frontier on the eve of British rule and *silsilahs* devoted to the propagation of the *tariqa* (codified rules of Sufism) remained influential, Sufism, and even Islam itself, was represented for the most part by *pirs* and *ziarats*. Moreover, as will be seen, it was the *pirs* who were best situated to fill the special political roles reserved for religious men in their society.

Like other Muslims, Pakhtuns believed not only that an individual can acquire holiness but also that his powers will pass to his descendants. This has led to the emergence of "saintly" lineages in the Frontier. Members of one such group, the Sayyids, are regarded as descendants of the Prophet Muhammad. The rest are subsumed under the label of *astanadar*, which literally means "one possessing a place."[78] There are four main types in the Frontier—*Pirs*, *Mians*, *Akhundzadas*, and *Sahibzadas*—with "*pir*" often being generically used for them all. As a rule, *Pirs* are of Pakhtun extraction, while *Mians* are not; *Akhundzadas* are descendents of learned scholars and *Sahibzadas* of saintly *mullahs*.[79] Not all *astanadars* were regarded as saints in the Frontier, nor was it necessary to be one to acquire a reputation for saintliness. Holiness in Islam must be proven through the display of spiritual qualities, even by descendants of an acknowledged saint. Many individuals who were neither Sayyid nor *astanadar* showed those characteristics, while most members of "saintly" lineages were not saints at all, for they had abandoned all religious pretensions and become indistinguishable in all but name from the Pakhtuns among whom they lived.

Thus, among all the men with names indicating a religious heritage, the number who were actual *pirs* was quite small. Their authority derived, in the first instance, from their inheritance of a special relationship with God and spiritual powers, or *baraka*. While all descendants of a holy man potentially had some special spiritual merit, his full sanctity and power passed down through the line of persons who succeeded him as the *sajjada nishin*.[80] On the basis of his reputation, a *sajjada nishin* attracted a following, the core of which consisted of *murids* (disciples) who took *baiat*, a formal vow of spiritual allegiance. An inner circle of *murids* withdrew from the world to devote themselves to spiritual pursuits under the *pir's* tutelage. A much larger number remained lay affiliates—members who had a formal but less exacting association with their spiritual preceptor.[81] A *pir* provided his *murids* with guidance, advised them on their personal lives, and was expected to use his mystical powers for their betterment. *Murids* gave their *pir* their complete

78. *NWF Province Gazetteer. Peshawar District. 1931* (Lahore: Civil & Military Gazette, 1934), Vol. A, p. 155.

79. *Ibid.*

80. The term literally means "sitting upon the prayer carpet." It is a title for a hereditary spiritual leader.

81. Trimingham, *op. cit.*, p. 27.

obedience in return, following his instructions implicitly out of a faith in his sanctity. Pakhtuns recognized the exalted position accorded to *pirs* in many of their proverbs. One adage relates, "Though a straw, the pir is still sufficient for his disciple," while another states, "Though the pir himself does not fly, his disciples would have him fly."[82]

Beyond the limits of his formal disciples, a *pir's* influence extended over all those who came to his ancestor's *ziarat* in search of worldly favors or salvation. A *ziarat* attracted regular devotees from its surrounding region, but the full extent of its appeal was evident only with the annual *urs* ceremony commemorating the death of the saint. On that occasion, pilgrims were drawn from a much greater distance. Many, if not most, of these people were not the *pir's* formal disciples but showed him reverence as the living representative of his ancestor. Finally, beyond those pilgrims, a *pir* could potentially exercise influence wherever he was known. His character and supposed powers generated deference and awe, and led Pakhtuns along with other Muslims to treat his opinions with respect.

Along with their aura of sanctity, the position of *pirs* in the Frontier rested upon their possession of an economic base which made them independent of Pakhtuns. Their *murids* gave them money and other presents, as did people who sought their spiritual intercession. As the keepers of their ancestors' shrines, they profited from the offerings people made at them in hope of acquiring merit or personal boons.[83] Additionally, hereditary religious men owned land. Pakhtuns deeded them property out of piety, in return for their services as mediators, and to separate feuding lineages. Their land, known as *seri*, was held permanently instead of being subject to the *wesh*. In some instances, it was substantial in size and dispersed over a wide area. Land not only vastly increased their wealth; it also provided them, as Barth discusses, with economic dependents and made them a potential force in the Pakhtuns' tribal affairs.[84]

Charismatic spiritual leaders played two unique, yet essential, roles in Pakhtun society. First, they served as mediators, men to whom Pakhtuns turned to compromise their disputes.[85] More dramatically, they assumed supreme political authority in situations which required Pakhtuns to submerge their differences and act for their common good. Some *mullahs* also served in this capacity, but those who did projected a strong aura of spirituality as Akbar Ahmed noted in the case of Swat: "These leaders were not—or no longer—the ordinary every-day village 'mullah' but were possessed men of charisma claiming supernatural powers or having such powers

82. Akbar S. Ahmed, *Mataloona* (Peshawar: Pakistan Academy for Rural Development, 1973), pp. 19 and 46.
83. Barth, *Political Leadership . . .*, pp. 57-59.
84. *Ibid.*, pp. 92-94.
85. *Ibid.*, pp. 96-99.

attributed to them. . . . "[86]

Provided they were serious enough, external threats to the integrity of Pakhtun society thrust men of *baraka* into prominence at the head of unified resistance by Pakhtuns. Their reputation for righteousness and indifference to worldly affairs gave them an aura of impartiality so far as the Pakhtuns' factional quarrels were concerned, making them acceptable as leaders in situations where tribal chiefs were not. Additionally, their presence infused the cause with a religious significance which inspired Pakhtuns to rise above their usual factious selves. Charismatic religious men invariably couched their calls to arms in Islamic terms. Appeals for *jihad* had a powerful attraction in their own right, but when issued by men with a special relationship with God, they acquired what amounted to a divine sanction and even seemed in some instances to portend the arrival of an Islamic millennium. Ahmed, for example, writes about one uprising against the British: "The ground was ripe for charisma and heightened suggestibility made men believe in extraordinary events and leaders of immense supernatural force."[87]

This pattern can be found recurring throughout the history of the Pakhtuns in the Frontier, even in situations where the enemies were other Pakhtuns or Muslims. For example, Lindholm observed that when the ruler of Dir Valley, who was a Yusafzai himself, invaded Swat Valley, it was usually a Sufi mendicant who rallied the Swat Yusafzai to drive him out.[88] Similarly, opposition to the Mughals, from Akbar to Shah Jahan, in the Peshawar region was organized largely by the charismatic, quasi-heretical leaders of the Roshaniyya movement.[89] In inter-tribal or intra-religious conflicts, leadership did not invariably come from the religious realm, for Pakhtuns could cooperate on a lineage basis. With the decline of the Durranis, however, the saintly model became particularly prevalent since the external powers with whom Pakhtuns had to contend were non-Muslim. Under these circumstances, it was much easier to appeal to religion, on which unanimity existed, while downgrading tribal loyalties. The enemy automatically became a threat to Islam, turning the confrontation into a *jihad* in which religious duty overrode factional enmities. In extreme cases, even the Pakhtuns' ethnic exclusiveness was overcome in the interest of Islamic unity. In the 1820s, for instance, Sayyid Ahmad Barelvi united a number of Pakhtun tribes with his Indian *mujahadin* against the Sikhs. Forty years later, his followers once more joined forces with Pakhtuns, this time against the British in the Am-

86. Ahmed, *Millenium* . . . , p. 108.

87. *Ibid.*

88. Charles Lindholm, "Models of Segmentary Political Action: The Examples of Swat and Dir, NWFP, Pakistan," in Stephen Pastner & Louis Flam, eds., *Anthropology in Pakistan: Recent Socio-Cultural and Archaeological Perspectives* (Ithaca: Cornell University South Asian Program, South Asia Occasional Papers and Theses No. 8, 1982), pp. 24-25.

89. See Caroe, *op. cit.*, Chapters 13-14.

bala campaign.[90]

Given this mechanism, tribal wars during the century of British rule regularly assumed a religious coloration. Their causes were usually secular, but since the enemy was Christian, they frequently took on the trappings of holy wars, with mystics or *pirs* at their head. For example, the *Akhund* of Swat led the Ambala *jihad*; the Mad *Mullah*, Hadda *Mullah*, and *Mullah* Sayyid Akbar instigated the 1897 uprisings; the *Haji* of Turangzai was prominent in every major Mohmand conflict after World War I; and the *Faqir* of Ipi maintained the banner of resistance in Waziristan from 1936 to independence.[91]

Ideally, the power of a charismatic leader was transitory, and he faded away with the crisis that called him forth. In fact, he often acquired a base of power during his moment of prominence that allowed him and his family to play a significant role in tribal affairs after it was over.[92] Even where this was the case, however, the unity which the religious crusade engendered inevitably disintegrated. Once the crisis ended, and in some cases even before, *parajamba* reasserted its divisive influence, or the tribesmen became suspicious that the religious leader was using the conflict to consolidate his power at their expense.[93] Yet, while the unity disappeared, the memory of the interlude of cooperation remained to reinforce the tendency for Pakhtuns to turn to religious intercession and leadership the next time a crisis occurred.

The social system described in this chapter has provided the framework within which politics in the Frontier have been played out for centuries. British rule produced major modifications, but none so radical as to prevent it from having a decisive influence on the independence movement. As in the rest of India, townsmen were the first to espouse nationalist ideas, but they were disqualified by the NWFP's urban-rural dichotomy from acting as a nationalist elite. That role fell to members of the rural Pakhtun gentry. With leadership of this kind, the general populace did not support either of the province's two main political parties purely on the basis of their ideologies or party programs. People's choices were shaped by factional considerations as well, to the point that party and *gundi* were for all practical purposes indistinguishable in many areas. While *parajamba* structured political alignments, Islam eventually overcame the divisions it created. Religious figures ordinarily played a secondary role in the nationalist movement, but when po-

---

90. *Ibid.*, Chapters 17 and 22.

91. For accounts of the role of religious figures in tribal wars, see Sir William Barton, *India's North-West Frontier* (London: John Murray, 1939); or Arthur Swinson, *North-West Frontier* (New York: Frederick Praeger, 1967).

92. In the most extreme case, a grandson of the *Akhund* of Swat established himself, with British help, as the ruler of Swat.

93. This happed to Sayyid Ahmad Barelvi, who united Pakhtuns around Peshawar Valley against the Sikhs only to have his position undermined by his Pakhtun supporters.

litical issues assumed an overriding religious coloration in 1946-47, charismatic individuals emerged to perform the same functions *pirs* and mystics in the Frontier had for centuries. By appealing to the Pakhtuns' universalistic religious identity, they temporarily united them internally and with other Muslims behind the demand for Pakistan.

# 3

# AGRARIAN CHANGE AND THE RISE OF NATIONALISM

The Pakhtuns' social organization helped shape the nationalist movement in two ways. As already suggested, it influenced who supported which political party and how the balance of power shifted from the Congress to the Muslim League. Equally important, the manner in which colonial rule affected Pakhtun society provided the impetus for the development of nationalism in the first place. On the one hand, political and financial necessity forced the British to form alliances with members of the Pakhtuns' Khani elite in order to govern the province. On the other, they pursued measures which dramatically altered the lives of the Frontier's inhabitants. Initially, these two facets of British policy were not in conflict. In the 20th century, however, economic and social changes undermined the acceptability of the allies of the British as leaders in Frontier society. Although the old political arrangements became outmoded, the British neither broadened their informal alliance system nor granted political reforms. Their refusal to adjust to the social changes they had set in motion alienated most Pakhtuns and produced the nationalist explosion of 1930.

This chapter will focus primarily on Peshawar Valley to show how changes in the Frontier's agrarian structure propelled Pakhtuns into the nationalist movement. The changes experienced by the NWFP as a whole are most clearly evident in the case of Peshawar since it was exposed most intensely to the disruptive effects of colonial rule and the market economy. Additionally, organized nationalist activity in the Frontier originated in the Valley. Thus, to speak of agrarian change as a precursor to the rise of nationalism is to look first and foremost at Peshawar.

## The Khani Alliance System

The British never had the resources to control the North-West Frontier Province on their own. From the start, they were compelled to construct a system in which the formal bureaucracy represented only the upper layer of government. At the local level, they created a quasi-formal extension of their administration by systematically coopting those men in tribal society with influence and power. Through a complex exchange of patronage for support, the government attached members of the landed elite to their rule and turned them into instruments for collecting taxes and ensuring peace in the countryside. In 1916, Sir George Roos-Keppel, the NWFP's Chief Commissioner, explained how this system initially operated:

> During the first seventy-five years of the last century the various authorities—Afghan, Sikh or British—took practically complete control of the cities but in rural areas there was little or no interference, as the Pathan system of the government of villages or groups of villages by local Khans, supported by landholding elders which the various conquerors found in existence, provided a rough but effective method of administration. Each Khan and his elders were responsible for the quota of land revenue due from his area . . . provided that he paid regularly which most did, there was practically no interference with internal affairs. The administration, policing and development of rural tracts was left entirely to the Khans, the local Governor confining himself to making main roads, etc., more with a view to military necessities than with any altruistic idea of benefitting the population. . . . [1]

In time, the colonial administration penetrated more deeply into rural society, but even as late as 1930, members of the bureaucracy did not regularly intervene in village affairs. At that level, Anil Seal's aphorism was still valid: "It might be the British who governed, but it was the Indians who ruled."[2]

There were sound political reasons for this system. British policies accelerated the preexisting tendency within Pakhtun society toward economic differentiation.[3] Thus, the Khani elite became much more than first among equals. This powerful landed gentry represented a potent force for stability or disorder which the government could not afford to ignore. Without the support of its members, the British hold over the NWFP would have been tenuous at best, no matter how strong an administration they might have constructed. By gaining their loyalty, the British ensured that the traditional sources of power and influence in the region reinforced their government.

Financial necessity also made a virtue out of using rural notables as the government's surrogates. Although the formal bureaucracy was not large, its cost always exceeded the revenues of the Frontier. In the 19th century, the Punjab government covered the deficit. With the formation of the NWFP in 1901, the Government of India assumed that responsibility. In succeeding years, the province's dependence on outside funding grew. In the 1901-02 fiscal year, the NWFP had a budget deficit of Rs. 38 lakhs; by 1929-30, it

---

1. RKP/3. Letter. 8/20/16.

2. Anil Seal, "Imperialism and Nationalism in India," in J. Gallagher, G. Johnson, and A. Seal, eds., *Locality, Province and Nation: Essays on Indian Politics, 1870-1940* (Cambridge: Cambridge University Press, 1973), p. 9.

3. See *infra*, pp. 55-58.

had risen to Rs. 254 lakhs.[4]

These financial strictures severely limited the number of employees the government could hire. This was true even in Peshawar which received more official attention than any other district. For example, in 1930, the Peshawar police force supervised 2,611 square miles, containing 974,321 people, and contended with one of the highest crime rates in India with only 2,318 men. Out of these, 1,105 were stationed in urban centers, and another 904 were assigned duties which kept them away from general police work. In other words, only 399 men dealt with most of the district on a regular basis.[5] They were stationed in twenty-six *thanas* (police stations) scattered throughout the Valley, and appeared in most villages only on periodic patrols or when called for specific reasons. In theory, the authorities could call on the large army contingents stationed in the district for help. In practice, they were reluctant to divert soldiers away from their ordinary military duties to civilian tasks for which they were not trained.

The peace-keeping staff demonstrates how thinly the formal bureaucracy was spread over the NWFP and how dependent it consequently was upon the assistance of non-officials to perform even its routine functions. Prominent local men helped the police investigate serious crimes, handled minor matters themselves, adjudicated village quarrels, and in general, bore the major responsibility for keeping peace in their localities. Their services were also vital to the collection of the land revenue, the first step of which consisted of village headmen, or *lambardars*, gathering the land tax from the actual assessees.

*Lambardars* received 5 percent of their collections for their work. More generally, the government's allies received their rewards in the form of patronage rather than pay. Foremost among the diverse benefits the government dispensed were financial rewards given out of the land revenue. The British either absolved individuals from a portion of their taxes or assigned them revenue or cash grants. In the first regular revenue settlements, the amounts disposed of in this way ranged from 27.6 percent in Peshawar to 56.7 percent in Kohat.[6] The percentage dropped with succeeding settlements, but by 1930, it was still substantial. In the case of Peshawar, some 2,900 men received grants and remissions totalling Rs. 1.45 lakhs.[7] Government officials were quite frank about the political purpose of these measures. Commenting on Dera Ismail Khan, M.F. O'Dwyer, the Revenue Commissioner of the Punjab, wrote in 1907 with satisfaction:

---

4. *Report of the North-West Frontier Subjects Committee, 1931* (Calcutta: Government of India Central Publications Branch, 1931), p. 18.

5. *NWF Province Gazetteer, Peshawar District. 1931* (Lahore: Civil and Military Gazette, 1934), Part B, Table 47. (Henceforth, *1931 Gazetteer)*

6. Lal Baha, *N.-W.F.P. Administration Under British Rule, 1901-1919* (Islamabad: National Commission on Historical and Cultural Research, 1978), p. 143ff.

7. Computed from *1931 Gazetteer*, Part A, p. 261.

> The liberality shown in the past and the present Settlement in the matter of assignments has borne good fruit. There is no other district on the frontier where Government can count on such prompt and willing assistance both from chiefs and people whether in internal administration or in the event of transborder complications.[8]

The provincial authorities also invested their village surrogates with a panoply of administrative, judicial, and police powers; appointed members of their families to the provincial bureaucracy; and enhanced their prestige with titles, such as *Nawab* or *Khan Bahadur*, or lesser honors, such as *kursi nishini* (the right to sit in the presence of a magistrate). They even manipulated the Pakhtuns' traditional life by restricting the right to erect *hujras* (guest houses), which were the accepted centers of village affairs, to men of their own choosing.[9] Finally, they added to the status of those they favored simply by treating them with deference and making them the mediators between the state and the general populace.

Through this conscious use of patronage, the British sought to coopt the NWFP's notables and give everyone of standing some interest in the colonial regime. As pragmatic administrators, the British did not select their allies on any *a priori* basis but dealt with whoever was powerful at the local level. Since conditions varied from region to region, the background of the privileged Khans varied markedly. A definite pattern only emerges on examining the Frontier Province on a tribe-by-tribe and village-by-village basis. The men who were the most heavily patronized tended to have the biggest landholdings in their localities, the greatest social status, and initially at least, the strongest political standing. Many belonged to the senior lineages in their tribe and clan. Thus, it is possible to generalize that the government's allies were the large or senior Khans, provided it is understood that they are only being compared with Pakhtuns in their immediate vicinity.[10]

## The Reforms Controversy

Neither the system described above nor the type of men the British chose as allies were unique to the NWFP. Throughout British India, the government had developed the same sort of links to the dominant men in rural society. What was distinctive was the Frontier government's adherence to this

8. H.N. Bolton, *Settlement Report of Dera Ismail Khan District* (Lahore: Civil and Military Gazette Press, 1907), p. ii of Review of M.F. O'Dwyer.

9. Inayatullah and O.M. Shafi, *Dynamics of Development in a Pakistani Village* (Peshawar: Pakistan Academy for Rural Development, 1963), p. 5.

10. In Swabi *Tehsil*, for example, few of the Khans owned large estates since almost everyone was a small landowner. In Mardan and Charsadda, in contrast, the cadet branches of Khani families owned vast estates but were not heavily patronized since their senior cousins were even more well-to-do.

informal system long after it had been modified elsewhere. While constitutional changes had expanded the level of popular participation in the government of other provinces by 1930, no reforms were implemented in the NWFP before 1929 when, with great reluctance, the government made a minority of the seats on the Peshawar Municipal Committee elective.

Contrary to nationalist assertions that the government was determined to keep the province *sarzamin be-ain* (a land without law), serious consideration was given to changing the province's political system before 1930. Nothing, however, materialized due to deep-seated British misgivings, simple government inertia, and the complications of communal politics. Above all, the Frontier's strategic location and turbulent history of tribal wars made popular government seem singularly inappropriate to the British. As the Simon Commission analogized: "The inherent right of a man to smoke a cigarette must necessarily be curtailed if he lives in a powder magazine."[11] Before 1930, moreover, policymakers saw little urgency in the reforms issue. In their estimation, the demand for self-government emanated from a small, politically ineffectual segment of the urban intelligentsia, who could be easily controlled. The Khans appeared to retain their political vitality, and the province's vast rural majority seemed content to follow their leadership. Finally, opposition from the Frontier's Hindu and Sikh minorities had turned reforms into a communal issue. The minorities' objections and the authorities' reluctance fed on one another, making the problem more intractable with the passage of time. The government pointed to communal antagonisms as a reason for denying the NWFP even the most modest form of self-government afforded to other provinces. This, in turn, encouraged minority intransigence by implying that they held a veto over constitutional change.

The reforms controversy first developed in the early 1910s. Most Hindus and Sikhs had opposed the formation of the NWFP because it cut them off from the Punjab's large non-Muslim population. Their experience during the province's first decade aggravated their sense of insecurity. Educated Muslims pressed for a greater share of government jobs which had previously been a minority preserve; Muslim indebtedness to Hindu moneylenders generated communal antagonisms; crime rose sharply; and a major communal riot occurred in Peshawar city in March 1910. To escape these conditions, the minorities called for the province's reunification with the Punjab.[12] They justified the merger on two grounds. First, Lord Curzon had called the NWFP an experiment which could be altered if the need arose. Accordingly, minorities insisted that decreased governmental efficiency and their own personal insecurity proved that the experiment had failed and

11. PP, 1929-30. Vol. XI. Cmd. 3589. "Report of the Indian Statutory Commission," Vol. II, p. 103.

12. *Report of the North-West Frontier Enquiry Committee and Minutes of Dissent by Mr. T. Rangachariar and Mr. N.M. Samarth* (Delhi: Government Central Press, 1924), pp. 34-37. (Henceforth, *Bray Committee Report*).

should be abandoned. Second, Curzon had assured the province's inhabitants they would not suffer politically from their new situation, yet the Frontier had been denied any representative institutions under the Morley-Minto reforms of 1909 while the Punjab had been granted limited self-rule. This, the minorities claimed, constituted a breach of promise which could be rectified most expeditiously by once more making the NWFP a part of the Punjab.

The minorities' proposal elicited outright hostility from Pakhtun leaders who did not wish to be part of a predominantly Punjabi province. It also failed to win sympathy in official quarters where the province was universally judged a success. On the contrary, policymakers were debating whether to give the NWFP a measure of self-government. The deciding voice belonged to Chief Commissioner Roos-Keppel who argued against any change on the grounds that the province was unaffected by the nationalist currents which made reforms essential elsewhere and that a council was unlikely to give advice as frankly and honestly as could be obtained through informal consultations with the Frontier's leading citizens.[13] Due to his opposition, the Montagu-Chelmsford scheme rejected any devolution of power in the province and held out only the vague promise of an appointed advisory body at some unspecified future date.

Pakhtun participation in the *Hijrat* and Khilafat movements drastically changed the thinking of Roos-Keppel's successor as Chief Commissioner, Sir Hamilton Grant. In December 1919, Grant urged the Viceroy to sanction an advisory council as soon as possible to pacify public opinion. While his initial request was not approved, he won both the Viceroy's backing and the Secretary of State's tentative approval for a far more meaningful change by the end of his term of office—a Legislative Council with some elected seats and powers approximating those conceded to other provinces.[14] With these assurances, he announced on February 28, 1921, shortly before he left the province, that the NWFP would be given some sort of representative institutions.[15]

Grant's promise was never fulfilled, for he was replaced as Chief Commissioner by Sir John Maffey, a hardliner on the question of reforms. Maffey recognized that political changes had left the government's position in the NWFP insecure, but his solution was to reinvigorate its old network of Khani alliances. On April 4, 1921, he wrote the Foreign Secretary of the Government of India:

> I find absolutely no interest or enthusiasm on the subject [of reforms] in the people with whom I have discussed the project, and those are

13. PJ9/19. No. 973/R. Notes by Sir George Roos-Keppel, 10/15/20 and 10/25/20.
14. LCP/23. No. 854a. Letter, 12/24/19. Also PJ9/30. No. 1344/21. Letter D.O. 1226-Public, 3/3/21. For the correspondence on the question of reforms, see PJ9/19.
15. GP/26. Speech at a Provincial Durbar on 2/28/21.

> the people who still count in this province. I daresay if I were to ask the opinion of the agitators, I might hear something different. But I think you will agree with me that what I have to do in a Province of this kind is to maintain the conservative element and to strengthen it. . . . This province may want reform but to my mind it wants reforming backwards, i.e., in view of the vital strategic and political considerations involved, we ought rather to put back the clock and revive the powers of the great Khans and Arbabs. In this way the province would fulfill its role of being a roof to the rest of India and not a constant source of danger.[16]

Maffey's attitude was not the only reason for the Government of India's retreat from reforms. Minority demands for reunification with the Punjab had increased after World War I in direct proportion to the possibility of reforms. There was very little difference of opinion on the issue within the Hindu and Sikh communities. Even confirmed nationalists who agitated for self-rule for India as a whole wished to deny it to the Frontier.[17] The minorities were concerned that their economic and cultural interests would suffer under representative government. In addition, tribal raiding into the districts of Bannu and Dera Ismail Khan had reached chronic proportions by 1919 in the wake of an uprising in Waziristan. Over the next three years, there were 686 raids which created a deep-seated fear among the minorities over their physical safety.[18] They were convinced not only that they were the tribesmen's primary targets but also that their Muslim neighbors were conspiring with the raiders.

Under these circumstances the minorities reacted sharply to Grant's public assurances of reforms. Even Maffey's subsequent statement that representative institutions were impossible for the foreseeable future did not satisfy them.[19] Since the British had not heeded their repeated pleas for reunification with the Punjab, minority leaders turned to Indian Hindu politicians for help. The province's Muslims were forced to counter by calling on their own coreligionists. Indian politicians, however, did not confine themselves to the merits of the local controversy. Instead, they complicated the issue by concentrating on its wider implications and turning it into one of the total package of issues dividing Muslims and Hindus in India.

On July 21, 1921, Sir P.S. Sivaswami Aiyer introduced a resolution in the Indian Legislative Assembly proposing the judicial merger of the Punjab and NWFP and the formation of a committee to determine if total administrative union should follow.[20] The Government responded with an *ad hoc*

16. PJ9/30. No. 1344/21. Letter D.O. No. 941-5, 4/4/21.
17. For example, see *Frontier Advocate*, 10/30/28.
18. PS12/23. File 99.
19. CLAD, 1926. Vol. VII, Part III, 3/18/26, p. 2732. Diwan Chand Obhrai, *The Evolution of North-West Frontier Province* (Peshawar: The London Book Co., 1938), p. 97.
20. CLAD, 1921. Vol. II, 9/21/21, p. 726.

committee under Sir Dennys Bray, the Foreign Secretary, which was charged to consider reforms as well as Aiyer's proposals. The Indians on the committee split along communal lines. The English members joined the Muslims to write a majority report which favored constitutional reforms. The Hindus argued at great length that the Frontier would be better governed as part of the Punjab, but no matter how they tried to mask it, their differences with the majority were obviously communal.[21] Bray later recalled that the committee "blazed a communal trail from one end of our Frontier journey to another."[22] The issue also generated a heated communal debate, and a straight communal vote, in the Punjab legislature. Alarmed by the controversy's divisiveness, the Government of India took refuge in inaction. It procrastinated until 1925 before announcing it would not merge the two provinces but simultaneously stated that it did not intend to act upon the Bray Committee's recommendations on reforms.[23]

The dispute, nonetheless, did not fade away. Throughout the 1920s, Muslim politicians continued to treat it as one of the prerequisites for breaking India's Hindu-Muslim impasse. The Muslim League passed a resolution in May 1924 pointing to "the immediate and paramount necessity of introducing reforms in the N.W.F. Province and of placing the province in all respects in a position of equality with other major provinces of India."[24] In 1927, the demand surfaced again as part of the Delhi Proposals which Muhammad Ali Jinnah formulated as a basis for Hindu-Muslim cooperation, and two years later, it became part of his Fourteen Points.

The Indian National Congress temporized on the question until 1927. Its leaders sympathized with the Frontier minorities, but they refrained from saying so since that would have been inconsistent with their constitutional demands for the rest of India.[25] After the appointment of the Parliamentary Statutory Commission (Simon Commission) in November 1927, party leaders finally came out in favor of reforms as part of their effort to enlist Muslim support for an Indian statement on the next installment of reforms. The search for an India-wide consensus foundered over other, irreconcilable differences, but the change in the Congress' attitude toward the Frontier was permanent.

At the provincial level, Muslims continued to petition for representative institutions. Frontier authorities periodically explored the idea of elected local committees, but regularly drew back, pleading that communal strife

21. *Bray Committee Report*, p. 22. Also see the minutes of dissent for the Hindus' position on reforms.

22. CLAD, 1926. Vol. VII, Part II, 2/16/26, p. 1326.

23. *Ibid.*, 1926. Vol. VII, Part III, 3/19/26, pp. 2767-68.

24. Syed Sharifuddin Pirzada, ed., *Foundations of Pakistan* (Karachi: National Publishing House, 1970), Vol. I, pp. 578 and 580.

25. Interviews with Mian Jafar Shah and Amir Chand Bombwal.

would follow.[26] Finally, in November 1929, they made eight of the twenty seats on the Peshawar Municipal Committee elective and set voter qualifications at a level enfranchising 4 percent of the city. The fact that the government considered this a generous concession and the maximum allowable until repeated elections in Peshawar proved that the public had acquired political maturity is indicative of its general resistance to reforms.[27]

## Agrarian Change in Peshawar Valley

As the 1930s began, the government still adhered to the policy Sir John Maffey had laid down a decade earlier: reforms were to be avoided, or at least postponed as long as possible, and in their place, the government was to rely on its Khani allies. In many parts of the NWFP, however, agrarian changes had eroded the social legitimacy of the pro-government Khans and undermined their ability to fulfill their end of the imperial bargain. This was especially true in Peshawar Valley, the heartland of the province. Peshawar experienced a marked growth in wealth under the British, but prosperity was not shared equally by all its inhabitants. The benefits of change accrued mainly to a small privileged elite, within which the larger Khans prospered the most. Along with their growing wealth, they ceased to act in the manner expected of Pakhtun leaders. By doing so, they antagonized the other elements of the Valley's population—the smaller Khans who were their competitors for power, the smallholding Pakhtun majority, and the lower class artisans and tenants. Social tensions were already evident by the early 1920s. With the onset of the international depression, they became acute. In these circumstances, the long run consequences of Maffey's policies were disastrous in that they isolated the government from all but a narrow circle of ineffectual men and their immediate dependents, while the rest of the population extended its opposition to the senior Khans to their British patrons as well.

Even before the British, Pakhtun society was changing. Thus, the model presented in Chapter 2 is only an ideal-type to which the various tribes in Peshawar more or less conformed on the eve of colonial rule. The extent to which they did had a significant impact on where nationalism first developed in the Valley. The Mughals, Durranis, and Sikhs had all brought the area south of the Swat River under their direct authority, primarily because it contained Peshawar city and the strategically important route to Kabul. They had been much less intrusive north of the Swat, exercising only a loose suzerainty over the tribes of the Charsadda, Mardan, and Swabi. This pat-

26. PP, 1929-30. Vol. XI. Cmd. 3568. "Report of the Indian Statutory Commission," Vol. I, p. 324.

27. *Ibid.* and PJ9/57. Telegram 5-S, 1/1/32.

tern of political control caused the tribes in the two parts of the Valley to evolve differently; in particular, it led to a sharp contrast in the status and power of their leaders. North of the Swat River, Hugh James, a settlement officer in the 1850s, observed:

> [The leaders are] simple patriarchal chiefs with limited powers who appear to have been nothing more than leaders in war and agents for the clan in their transaction with their neighbours. . . . The share of the khan in the hereditary possession of the community was not larger than that of his brethren, nor his privileges greater than to secure for him the semblance of a rude chiefship.[28]

In contrast, among the tribes to the south, he noted:

> . . . much of this independence has been lost by the assistance afforded to the chief men by government in reducing their clansmen to a subordinate position; they have not, indeed, lost the peculiar characteristics of the Afghan communities, but these had become fainter; and the will of the Chief in many cases superseded that of the brotherhood.[29]

It was not coincidental that the tribes of Charsadda, Mardan, and Swabi were the first to espouse the nationalist cause. Since they had come closest to the egalitarian paradigm of Pakhtun society, the changes which occurred under the British constituted a more radical departure from their traditions than for others in the Valley. This was especially so since their *tehsils* were the most profoundly affected by the economic changes accompanying colonial rule. Consequently, those tribes were the least willing to accept the leadership of the government's Khani allies once they ceased to act as proper chiefs and objected most intensely to the decision to prop up their position in Pakhtun society.

Agricultural production in Peshawar Valley expanded dramatically under the British. The total area under cultivation grew from less than 750,000 acres to 847,197 in 1929-30.[30] More importantly, the amount of irrigated acreage rose sharply with the construction of three major canal systems. The Kabul River Canal, which was completed in 1907, watered 48,105 acres in Peshawar and Nowshera *Tehsils* in 1930. The Lower Swat Canal was opened in 1885 and by 1930, irrigated 161,320 acres in Charsadda and Mardan. The more ambitious Upper Swat Canal, which was opened in 1914, watered 209,009 acres in 1930—principally in Charsadda and Mardan—and potentially commanded another 110,000 acres.[31]

---

28. Hugh James, *Report on the Settlement of the Peshawur District* (Lahore: Published by Authority of the Punjab Government, 1865), p. 103.

29. *Ibid.*, p. 103.

30. *Gazetteer of the Peshawar District, 1883-84* (Compiled and Published under the authority of the Punjab Government, 1884), Table 2. (Henceforth, *1883 Gazetteer*). Also *1931 Gazetteer*, Part B, Table 1.

31. *1931 Gazetteer*, Part B, Table 24.

**Table 5: Land Usage and Irrigation (in Acres) in Peshawar Valley**[32]

| | *1868–69* | *1929–30* | *Percent Change* |
|---|---|---|---|
| Total cultivated area | 750,511 | 845,197 | + 12.62 |
| Irrigated area | | | |
| Private works | 259,676 | 154,632 | – 40.45 |
| Government works | ---- | 423,368 | --- |
| Total | 259,676 | 578,000 | + 122.59 |
| Unirrigated area | 490,835 | 267,197 | – 45.56 |

A comparison of land usage in 1868-69, the earliest year for which statistics are available, and 1929-30 offers a rough measure of the changes produced by irrigation (see Table 5). Due to the unpredictability of the rains, any area which was not reached by canals produced, at most, a single crop each year. Single cropping was also common on a substantial percentage of privately irrigated fields.[33] The government canals, therefore, permitted a much more systematic and intensive exploitation of the land. Larger areas were brought under regular cultivation for the first time, and wherever the government works reached, double cropping became routine.

These developments disproportionately affected Charsadda and Mardan, as Table 6 shows. By 1931, the percentage of their total area which was irrigated significantly exceeded that in any other *tehsil*. All told, over four-fifths of cultivation in Charsadda and over three-fifths in Mardan depended on canal waters. Most of the irrigation was supplied by the Swat River Canals which transformed the semi-barren Hashtnagar-Yusafzai plain into rich farmland. They commanded over nine-tenths of the irrigated land in Mardan and two-thirds in Charsadda. Swabi was also affected by the expansion of irrigation, although not as dramatically as its neighbors. The Upper Swat Canal watered about 18 percent of its cultivated area in 1931. Additionally, Swabi accounted for two-thirds of the well irrigation in the Valley.[34]

As irrigation spread, hardier and coarser cereals were replaced by higher quality foodgrains and cash crops. For example, while the acreage devoted to millets and barley dropped by more than 55 percent between 1873-74 and 1930-31, maize acreage rose by 300 percent, sugarcane by 360 percent, and

32. Compiled from *1883 Gazetteer*, Table 2 and *1931 Gazetteer*, Part B, Table 1. Percentages computed. Government works included District Board Canals.

33. According to government classification, *Nahri* I was privately irrigated land bearing two crops a year and *Nahri* II, one crop. In 1874-75, 38 percent of all canal lands was *Nahri* II. Computed from figures in *Gazetteer of Peshawar District, 1897-98* (Compiled and published under the authority of the Punjab Government, 1898), p. 193. (Henceforth, *1897 Gazetteer*)

34. *1931 Gazetteer*, Part A, p. 206.

**Table 6: Percentage of Land Irrigated in Peshawar Valley in 1931**[35]

| | *District* | *Peshawar* | *Charsadda* | *Mardan* | *Swabi* | *Nowshera* |
|---|---|---|---|---|---|---|
| Percent of area irrigated | | | | | | |
| of total area | 28.4 | 31.4 | 56.0 | 38.9 | 18.7 | 8.4 |
| of cultivated area | 55.4 | 66.6 | 80.5 | 61.8 | 30.3 | 32.0 |
| Percent of area irrigated by government works | | | | | | |
| of total area | 18.7 | 6.5 | 37.9 | 36.6 | 7.9 | 6.6 |
| of cultivated area | 36.5 | 13.8 | 54.4 | 58.1 | 17.6 | 24.9 |
| of irrigated area | 66.0 | 20.5 | 67.7 | 93.4 | 58.1 | 78.0 |

tobacco by 289 percent.[36] The total area planted with wheat remained relatively constant, but yields increased because an improved variety of seed which was more vulnerable to fluctuations in water could be used on canal lands.[37] Once again, Charsadda, Mardan and Swabi were affected the most by these changes. For example, out of 40,743 acres planted with sugarcane in 1930-31, 52.7 percent were in Charsadda and 21.6 percent in Mardan. Similarly, out of 10,352 acres of tobacco, Swabi contained 58.6 percent, Mardan 27.3 percent, and Charsadda 11.5 percent.[38]

The shift to higher quality crops reflected an expanding production for market. This trend would not have developed without major improvements in Peshawar's transportation system. By 1901, the Valley was crossed by paved roads and railways which linked its strategic extremities—the Kohat, Khyber, and Malakand Passes—with its main urban centers and the rest of India. In the 20th century, these routes were upgraded and supplemented by a network of roads which connected the major towns and villages in the Valley. By 1930, Peshawar contained 85 miles of railroad, 270 miles of paved road, and 732 miles of unpaved road. Only sixty years earlier, it had only had 52 paved miles and 466 rude, unpaved miles of road.[39]

The Valley had always grown more than its inhabitants consumed. Before the first government canal was opened, British officials estimated in 1878 that Peshawar had a net export surplus in foodgrains alone of 2.25 lakh maunds (9,225 tons).[40] In the early years of British rule, most of the surplus went to the immediately adjoining tribal areas, Hazara, Kohat, and northwest Punjab. As transportation improved, Peshawar was drawn into a much wider market system governed by world economic forces. The bulk of its export production continued to be surplus foodgrains, especially wheat and

35. Computed from the figures in *ibid.*, Part B, Table 18 and Part A, p. 206.

36. Computed from *ibid.*, Part B, Table 19 and *1883 Gazetteer*, Table 20.

37. *1931 Gazetteer*, Part A, p. 183. The new seed, Pusa No. 4, was introduced in 1916.

38. Computed from *ibid.*, Part B, Table 19.

39. *Ibid.*, Part B, Table 1 and *1883 Gazetteer*, Table 2. For a description of transportation developments, see Baha, *op. cit.*, pp. 107-131.

40. *1897 Gazetteer*, p. 213. A maund is 82 lb.

maize. Sugarcane and tobacco accounted for a much smaller portion, but in terms of value per acre, they were the Valley's most important cash crops. Vegetables and fruits were a close third. While some of these perishables were exported (particularly melons), they were mainly grown for local, urban consumption.[41]

In the absence of adequate statistics, the growing agricultural trade can only be inferred. Beyond the expansion of total output, two measures suggest the magnitude of that growth. First, the Valley's three main towns—Peshawar, Nowshera, and Mardan—developed into major agricultural markets, while many villages, especially those with railroad stations, emerged as local trading centers. Mardan, for example, became the chief market for the northern half of the Valley and the adjoining tribal areas after 1900. As a result, its population grew from only 2,766 in 1881 to 26,279 in 1931.[42] Second, bullock carts, which were used principally for the transport of agricultural commodities from village to market, increased steadily in number until trucks began to replace them in the 1920s. In 1868-69, the government counted only twenty of them in the district. Their number rose to 4,062 in 1919-20 before falling off to 3,111 in 1931-32. The decline in the 1920's was offset by a substantial rise in the number of motor vehicles from 446 in 1919-20 to 2,697 in 1931-32.[43]

Commercial agriculture did not promote a broad-based growth in individual prosperity. By 1930, the Valley contained three identifiable economic strata: a Khani elite whose members owned a major share of the land but did not cultivate it themselves; a smallholding yeomanry of Pakhtun owner-cultivators; and a large class of tenants, laborers, and artisans. In part, chance determined who became wealthy. People with land along the new canals suddenly found themselves with highly productive property. In some instances, as Louis Dane observed in 1897, the change was so great as to raise "ordinary maliks to the wealth and status of khans."[44] Geographic good fortune alone, however, cannot account for the stratified society which developed in the Valley. Colonial policies either directly or indirectly led to the concentration of land in the hands of the Khani elite.

After annexation, the British caused a revolution in property rights by eliminating the *wesh* and replacing the concept of a *daftar* with permanent rights in specific pieces of land. Ownership was stripped of all ethnic and tribal restrictions, and in theory at least, land became a freely saleable commodity. The immediate practical consequences of these changes were limited. In the early years of British rule, when subsistence farming was still widespread, comparatively little property changed hands, and its value stayed at a relatively low level. Between 1868-69 and 1890-91, for example,

41. NWFP. Bundle 30. S.No. 1009. Misc 2/1. Letter No. 282-Revenue.
42. *1931 Gazetteer*, Part A, p. 175 and Part B, Table 7.
43. *Ibid.*, Part B, Table 1 and *1897 Gazetteer*, pp. 194-97.
44. *1897 Gazetteer*, p. 133.

the average sales price fluctuated between Rs. 33 and Rs. 36 per acre.[45] With the growth of commercial agriculture, however, land became a prized and actively traded commodity, especially since there were few alternative investments available. Between the mid-1890s and mid-1920s, 20 percent of the Valley's agricultural lands changed hands, and the average sales price rose to levels that varied from Rs. 171 in Mardan *Tehsil* to Rs. 503 in Peshawar *Tehsil.*[46]

The bigger landowners were best able to respond to the opportunities of commercial agriculture. In addition to having more acreage, they had the capital needed to grow cash crops. Their greater resources also permitted them to play the market—to hold produce for higher prices rather than selling immediately after the harvest and to switch crops in response to fluctuations in prices and demand. Smallholders, in contrast, operated within much narrower constraints—less land, fewer capital resources, and more urgent cash needs—which often forced them to sell off their property or contract debts. Most sales occurred among agriculturists, with the more prosperous, bigger owners being the most frequent buyers.[47] Contrary to the prevailing stereotype that all moneylenders were Hindu, the large Pakhtun landowners conducted a substantial portion of the business of lending in Peshawar Valley. It offered them a high return on investment—higher, in fact, than any other type of business venture—and a means of controlling the agricultural operations of their clients for their own benefit. It also created the possibility of acquiring more property at concessionary rates or through foreclosure.

While all of the Valley experienced some economic stratification, British policies created special conditions in Charsadda and Mardan. Under the traditional Pakhtun system of land ownership, parts of a tribe's holdings were set aside as *shamilat* for grazing or other common purposes. The British converted these lands into individually owned property during the summary settlements of the 1850s.[48] Wherever traditional shares were clearly delineated, they governed the division. In many areas, however, rights in the *shamilat* were either vague in character, or the Pakhtuns intentionally obscured them in an effort to minimize their tax burdens. In those cases, the settlement officers usually assigned ownership to the leading men in the tribe.[49] Louis Dane reported in 1897:

> The unusually large holdings in Mardan and Charsadda are due to the fact that enormous areas of waste in those tahsils were recorded as the property of the leading men. . . . Thus in Charsadda, nearly the whole

45. *Ibid.*, p. 238.

46. *1931 Gazetteer*, Part A, pp. 192-93. For a breakdown of sales prices by revenue circle, see NWFP. Bundle 30. S.No. 1009. Misc. 2/1.

47. *1931 Gazetteer*, Part A, p. 192.

48. James Spain, *The Pathan Borderland* (The Hague: Mouton and Company, 1963), pp. 82-83.

49. *1897 Gazetteer*, p. 301.

> of the Maira Circle except Tangi-Barazi, 4,200 acres of cultivation, is held by 20 owners and 39 owners hold 31,586 acres or 34 percent in the Nahri Circle. In Mardan no less than 43,763 in the Maira Circle are held by four men. . . .[50]

Initially, this arbitrary division had little significance since the common lands were of marginal economic value. Thirty years later, however, the opening of the Lower Swat Canal turned 150,000 acres of wasteland into a valuable asset to those who had so casually acquired ownership. The government tried to rectify this injustice by redistributing the *shamilat*, but it was only partially successful due to the confusion in rights produced by the lapse of time, the resistance of the Khans who had title, and the government's own reluctance to be too thorough since those Khans were the men on whom it relied in the countryside.[51] Thus, the Khani elites of Charsadda and Mardan were left with large tracts of productive acreage which were not theirs by traditional right. They also retained substantial amounts of the former *shamilat* which were still unirrigated and barren but which would be similarly transformed by the Upper Swat Canal thirty years later.

The Swat Canals touched off a speculative boom which furthered the process of land concentration.[52] Shortly before they opened, wealthy Khans bought up lands which were due to be irrigated at low prices or acquired title from their weaker neighbors through pressure and fraud. Once the canals started operating, further transfers occurred as many small owners sold off part of their holdings to raise the capital to develop the rest. Still others disposed of their property along the canals because it was far from the land they had traditionally cultivated and they did not feel they could work both.[53]

By the mid-1920s, the smallholding Pakhtun majorities in both Charsadda and Mardan were confined mainly to small plots in those areas cultivated before the British, while the Khani elite dominated the new canal tracts. In Charsadda, for example, most of the Muhammadzai, the *tehsil's* main tribe, were concentrated in the Sholgirah area. By 1926, 52 percent of the holdings there were less than ten acres large, and the average had dwindled to three acres per owner. On the less populated, former *shamilat*, in contrast, 79 percent of the land irrigated by the Upper Swat Canal and 53 percent by the Lower Swat Canal was owned in holdings of fifty acres or more.[54] All told,

---

50. Louis Dane, *Final Report of the Settlement of Peshawar District, 1898* (Lahore: Civil and Military Gazette Press, 1898), p. 15.

51. *1897 Gazetteer*, p. 301.

52. For example, as much as 28 percent of the land irrigated in Charsadda by the Lower Swat Canal changed hands within a short period after its completion. Dane, *op. cit.*, p. 16.

53. F.V. Wylie, *Assessment Report of the Charsadda Tahsil of the Peshawar District* (Calcutta: Government of India Central Publication Branch, 1926), p. 29. (Henceforth, Wylie, *Charsadda Report*). Also, NWFP. Bundle 30. S.No. 1009. Misc. 2/1. Note on the Mardan Assessment Report. O.K. Caroe.

54. Computed from Wylie, *Charsadda Report*, p. 50.

43.6 percent of the land in Mardan and 50.1 percent in Charsadda was held in estates of fifty acres or more by 1930.[55]

The revolution in property holdings had far-reaching social consequences. The old economic system had been geared towards maintaining equality among Pakhtuns and a relatively benign Pakhtun dominance over non-Pakhtuns. Under the British, the ethnic distinction between Pakhtun landowner and non-Pakhtun dependent began to break down, and the patron-client bond gave way to a more contractual tie between employer and employee. Among Pakhtuns, wealth and government support replaced personal character and attentiveness to social obligations as the basis of prestige and power. All three changes, and the resulting social tensions, were strongest where the large Khans were involved, for they departed the most from the ideal of a Pakhtun chief.

Peshawar's population grew steadily under the British. From an estimated 450,099 residents in 1855, it expanded to 592,674 by the first census in 1881, 788,707 in 1901, and 974,321 in 1931.[56] Percentage-wise, Peshawar *Tehsil* grew the least since it was already densely populated before the British. Mardan and Charsadda grew the most under the dramatic impact of the Swat River Canals.[57] While a natural increase contributed to the growth, the greater part resulted from immigration, with the adjacent tribal territory providing the single largest source of migrants.[58] Mohmands, and to a lesser extent tribesmen from Bajaur and Afghanistan, descended from their barren, mountain homes in large numbers to settle as tenants and laborers, particularly in Charsadda and Mardan where they formed the bulk of the population working the new canal tracts.

These tribal migrants injected a new element into class relations in Peshawar. Previously, most of the lower classes had been non-Pakhtun. With few, if any, horizontal ties, their loyalties and attachments were oriented vertically on an individual patron-client basis toward members of the Pakhtun elite. Some Pakhtuns had been absorbed into the lower classes, but in their case, movement had been individual, with the person involved losing his rights and status as a Pakhtun once he lost his land. Stripped of his former social connections, he had no choice but to conform to the pattern of dependency expected of non-Pakhtuns. For the Mohmands, in contrast, movement was collective rather than individual and essentially spatial rather than social.

55. Computed for *ibid.*, pp. 3 and 50; and F.V. Wylie, *Assessment Report of the Mardan Tahsil of the Peshawar District* (Calcutta: Government of India Central Publication Branch, 1926), pp. 3-4 and 38. (Henceforth, Wylie, *Mardan Report*)

56. 1897 Gazetteer, p. 92 and *1931 Gazetteer*, Part B, Table 50.

57. Between 1868 and 1931, the population of the district increased by 86.24 percent. The increase by *tehsil* was: Charsadda, 88.73 percent; Mardan, 182.09; Swabi, 64.88; Peshawar, 42.54; and Nowshera, 140.54. Computed from *1897 Gazetteer*, p. 96 and *1931 Gazetteer*, Part B, Table 50. The figure for Nowshera is misleading since part of the increase resulted from the transfer of the Khwarra-Nilab tract from Kohat to Peshawar District in 1895.

58. See *1931 Gazetteer*, Part B, Table 8.

They retained their distinctive tribal identity, cohesion, and organization for acting jointly. They could count upon support from their tribal kinsmen back in the hills and could return in the last resort to their ancestral homes rather than submit to treatment they regarded as demeaning.

These factors gave the Mohmands an independence vis-à-vis their landlords which other tenants and artisans lacked and led to tensions wherever they settled. In part, the conflict simply reflected tribal animosities between the Mohmands and the dominant tribes among which they resided. Also, while the Mohmands retained the egalitarian outlook so characteristic of Pakhtuns, they were confronted with landlords who treated them as inferiors. As F.V. Wylie explained:

> The Khans are . . . inclined to look upon a tenant as a kamin—after the old hamsayah tradition—and try to exact small degrading services from him which the Mohmand as free Pakhtuns of full status refuse to render. The tenants by way of retaliation indulge in wholesale dishonesty at the division of the crop.[59]

More fundamentally, the Mohmands wanted to own the land they worked not only for its economic benefits but also because ownership was essential for validating their claim to recognition as Pakhtuns. Rather than purchase property, they commonly tried to undermine the rights of their landlords by paying as little rent as possible and seizing *de facto* control of the land. The resulting conflict was exacerbated by the tendency of many landowners to view their property in strictly economic terms. In other words, at the very time the Mohmands were trying to minimize their rents, their landlords were seeking to maximize their return from their property with the least personal involvement in the agricultural process.[60]

The attitude of the Mohmands' landlords was reflective of a more general change in class relations. The patron-client bond of pre-British times began to unravel into a more impersonal economic connection devoid of the social services landlords had once provided their dependents. As the old system of rural relations broke down, the underlying resentments of the less privileged surfaced, for there was little to ameliorate the exploited nature of their position without the paternalistic concern their landlords had once shown. Necessity perpetuated their dependence on their landlords, but to the degree that the relationship came to be defined by economic criteria, it lost its legitimacy in the eyes of the lower classes.

This trend was most pronounced in Charsadda and Mardan, especially on the estates of the large Khans. By 1926, 70 percent of Charsadda and 52 percent of Mardan were farmed by tenants-at-will subject to whatever terms the landlord wished to exact.[61] A growing proportion paid fixed cash rents which

---

59. Wylie, *Charsadda Report*, p. 19.

60. *Ibid.* and Wylie, *Mardan Report*, p. 16.

61. NWFP. Bundle 30. S.No. 1009. Misc 2/1. Notes on the Charsadda and Mardan Assessment Reports. O.K. Caroe.

imposed all the risks of crop failure and fluctuating market prices on their shoulders. In Charsadda, only 5 percent of the land was let out on cash terms in 1896; in 1926, the figure had risen to 27 percent. While the increase was not as steep in Mardan, 16 percent of the *tehsil* was cultivated on cash rents by 1926.[62] Cash rents went hand in hand with a system of leasing which became prevalent in the new canal areas. Leasing permitted the landlord to derive a constant and usually high income from his estate while shifting responsibility for its management to middlemen and freeing himself from all non-economic obligations to his tenants.[63] Landowners also moved toward an impersonal economic relationship with artisans and laborers. F. V. Wylie wrote in 1926: "Times are changing and status is yielding place to contract in the village economy—cash wages being much more commonly paid than was formerly the case."[64] The benefits of the wage system to the landowners were similar to those of cash rents. They were fixed, usually at a rate advantageous to the employer, and specific, obligating him to no more than the agreed upon sum, as opposed to the open-ended responsibilities of a patron.

By the 1920s, the class tensions spawned by these changes were evident to government officials. As Peshawar's Collector in 1926, Olaf Caroe wrote:

> Though there are faults on both sides, the chief fault is probably to be found in the owners, and particularly with the large owners, who lease their lands on cash rents in order to avoid all trouble. The great prevalance of leases is a very distinguishing feature of the Shah Nahri [government irrigated] areas of the Peshawar District. . . . It is one of the reasons why big owners have become rent-receivers and why tenants finding the cash demand too heavy return again to the hills. It also inevitably introduces the middleman. It removes the owners from all immediate personal interest in cropping and improvements and thus weakens their control and influence. It is a contributing cause to the difficulty experienced in realising Government dues.[65]

Not all landowners had tenant trouble. Smaller Khans faced some lower class discontent, but they continued to act sufficiently like patrons to prevent a rupture. As Caroe suggested, it was the larger Khans, and especially those in the new canal tracts, who had the most serious problems. By ceasing to fulfill the paternalistic duties expected of patrons, the large Khans turned their tenants and artisans into a disaffected pool of potential recruits for any opposition to their authority. In Charsadda, Mardan, and, to a lesser degree, Swabi, the lower classes tended to shift their allegiance to the factions of the smaller Khans. Thus, when those men joined the Khudai Khidmatgars for

62. *Ibid.*
63. Dane, *op. cit.*, p. 16 and Wylie, *Charsadda Report*, p. 28.
64. Wylie, *Charsadda Report*, p. 40.
65. NWFP. Bundle 30. S.No. 1009. Misc 2/1. Note on the Charsadda Assessment Report. O.K. Caroe.

reasons of their own, they brought most of the three *tehsils*' tenants and artisans into the nationalist movement with them.

The large Khans' relations with other Pakhtun landowners—both the smallholding majority and the junior members of the Khani elite—also degenerated as they ceased to act in the manner expected of them and thereby lost the respect normally given a Pakhtun chief. The change is captured in one of the many derogatory names used to describe them, *Dode Bacha*, which suggests someone who willingly sacrifices his honor to pursue a life of material well-being by disregarding the Pakhtun social code.[66] Instead of cultivating a following in the traditional manner, the large Khans depended on their ability to buy or coerce support and upon the deference they received from acting as intermediaries for the government. Until 1930, these proved sufficient to maintain their leadership in Pakhtun society but at the cost of generating pervasive resentment which ultimately found an outlet in the Khudai Khidmatgar movement.

The nationalist movement also fed upon the discontent arising from the weakening of community institutions and the strong social cohesion they had once engendered. For example, the importance of the Pakhtuns' lineage hierarchy declined as colonial rule usurped many of its former functions. Land was no longer distributed on a kinship basis, and as has already been shown, the principle of economic equality receded into a utopian ideal. While the British eliminated clan ownership of *tappas*, they had permitted joint ownership of specific estates by small tribal brotherhoods to continue. The trend, however, was for cosharing tenures to give way to outright individual possession. In 1878, less than a fifth of all holdings were *bhaiachara* tenures—the mark of individual property rights. In 1931, the figure had risen to almost three-fourths.[67] Once more, Charsadda and Mardan led the way among the Valley's five *tehsils*.

Even residency patterns changed under the British. Before 1849, villages were organized by descent groups, with the members of a *khel* living in the same ward. After annexation, many Pakhtuns spread out from their original settlements to new hamlets or to individual residences near their lands. The Khani elite took the lead in this process, especially in the new canal tracts.[68] As population dispersed, the social bond maintained by residential proximity loosened; descent groups declined in importance; and the Khans were able to reduce the social pressures they faced by geographically distancing themselves from their fellow tribesmen.

For the small landholder, the disintegration of his community institutions and the change in Khani behavior meant a loss of standing in tribal affairs. Before the British, when personal character counted for more than economic

---

66. Interview with Abdul Akbar Khan.

67. Computed from Dane, *op. cit.*, p. 15 and *1931 Gazetteer*, Part A, p. 241.

68. *1897 Gazetteer*, p. 134; NWFP. Bundle 29. S.No. 995. Rev 1/7. Letter No. 1223. 3/29/25.

standing and when community affairs were decided in *jirga* (council) where everyone had an equal say, there was greater scope for the individual Pakhtun to exercise political and social influence. After annexation, economic differentiation and government intervention vastly increased the power of the Khans and altered the very basis on which social influence rested, all at the expense of the small landholders. This reinforced the economic grievance which they felt on seeing the land and wealth of the Khani elite expand while their own resources were squeezed by population pressure, land fragmentation, credit problems, and the uncertainties of the market economy.

For the junior Khans, the situation was more complex. They profited from colonial rule almost as much as their rivals, and many became enormously wealthy by local standards. Despite these similarities, they conformed more closely to traditional Khani norms than their rivals. As the large Khans withdrew from their traditional role, they left a void which the smaller Khans were happy to fill. By behaving like a Khan should, those men acquired legitimacy in the eyes of the smallholding Pakhtuns and lower classes. This augmented their prestige, offset their rivals' economic advantages and government patronage, and allowed them to build strong factional followings. By the 1920s, the smaller Khans were the most dynamic political force in the Peshawar countryside. They were prevented, however, from capitalizing on their greater effectiveness by the government's determination to maintain their rivals as the dominant rural elite. That policy, more than anything else, alienated them from British rule. It froze a polity formerly characterized by fluidity into a mold where government anointment rather than personal capacity was the key to social leadership. This left the smaller Khans with no option but to seek outside support to overcome their rivals' government support. They turned to the Khudai Khidmatgar movement, for its demand for immediate independence offered the possibility of eliminating the one remaining impediment in the way of their becoming the dominant figures in Pakhtun society.[69]

Social tensions were already evident in Peshawar Valley by the early 1920s, but official support for the large Khans and the generally low level of political activity after the collapse of the Khilafat movement bought another decade of tranquility. At the end of the 1920s, however, the conflicts which had been brewing below Peshawar's surface calm came to a boil. The ensuing political eruption resulted in part from the acceleration during the decade of the changes already discussed in this chapter. Additionally, the Valley was hard hit by the world economic crisis, crop failures, and a new land revenue settlement. The combination created a general atmosphere of unrest which made Peshawar a fertile area for nationalist efforts.

Having been drawn deeply into the world market economy, the Valley was hurt badly by the international depression. Commodity prices dropped pre-

---

69. Caroe, *op. cit.*, p. 432.

cipitously, and export markets for agricultural crops shrank. For example, wheat, which had commanded as much as Rs. 5/8/- per maund early in the 1920s, sold for Rs. 3/10/- in 1929 and only Rs. 2/-/- the next year. Similarly, maize fell from a high of Rs. 4/12/- per maund to Rs. 1/4/- and *gur* from Rs. 8/1/- to Rs. 5/13/-.[70] Land values plummeted in tandem with produce prices,[71] and a credit squeeze which had begun in 1922 with the extension of the Punjab Land Alienation Act to the district became acute. By forbidding the transfer of property from agriculturists to non-agriculturists, that act had rendered land worthless to Hindu and Sikh moneylenders as collateral. As a result, loans became less attainable; interest rates rose; and indebtedness increased. The depression constricted credit even further by drastically reducing the capital agricultural lenders could devote to moneylending and by making land, the one asset farmers could use as collateral, less valuable.[72]

Even with the exorbitant rates which resulted from the credit squeeze, cultivators in the Valley had no choice but to contract more debt since the falling prices did not give a return sufficient to cover their expenses.[73] This was particularly true of those heavily committed to cash crops which involved higher production costs. Many smallholders did not survive this crisis. Landlords were also hurt, but the situation was not critical for most of them since they found it easier to obtain more credit. Additionally, many shifted part of their problems to the lower classes by pressing their tenants for full payment of fixed rents, reducing wages to their artisans and laborers, and even more ruthlessly eliminating the services they had once provided their dependents.[74] Not all Khans behaved in this manner. Those who reacted most aggressively to the depression tended to be the men who had moved the furthest from the ideal-type of a Khan—in short, the larger landlords on whom the British relied. By doing so, they increased the animosities the lower classes felt toward them and accelerated the erosion in their tribal influence.

As if man-made problems were not enough, Peshawar was beset by climatic misfortunes in the late 1920s.[75] The winter *rabi* wheat crop of 1928 was off 31 percent due to poor rains. The next summer, excessive rain and flooding hurt the sugarcane and cotton crops. The rains faltered once more in September 1929, causing a serious reduction in agricultural output. Charsadda and Mardan were especially hurt by poor sugarcane crops. The decline in output, coupled with a fall in *gur* prices, had serious economic im-

70. *1931 Gazetteer*, Part B, Table 19.
71. *Ibid.*, Part A, p. 193.
72. *Ibid.*, Part A, p. 213.
73. *Ibid.*
74. For example, wages fell to pre-1920 levels. *Ibid.*, Part A, p. 210.
75. NWFP. Bundle 65. S.No. 1954. Rev 35/43; and *Administration Report of the North-West Frontier Province, 1928-29*, p. iv and vii.

plications. As the Charsadda *Tehsildar* warned: "In this Ilaqa land revenue and other expenses are defrayed from the income of 'Gur'."[76]

Unfortunately for the British, the onset of the depression coincided with a new revenue settlement which revised the tax rate upward by an average of 22 percent.[77] Charsadda, Mardan, and Swabi were singled out for the largest increases. Their assessments rose 30, 28, and 24 percent respectively, while the tax burden in Peshawar and Nowshera *Tehsils* was raised only 16 and 11 percent respectively.[78] Even without the economic collapse, the revenue enhancement would have been ill-received in the Valley which had a long history of tax resistance.[79] In 1928-29, for example, only 81 percent of Peshawar's revenue was collected; in contrast, over 97 percent was realized in the rest of the province. That year, the district accounted for 97 percent of the NWFP's total arrears and three-fourths of all coercive measures taken to force payment.[80]

During the prosperity that prevailed before 1929, British officials had insisted that the poor revenue collections did not reflect an inability to pay.[81] Even after the economic crisis began, they saw no reason to change their opinion until the civil disobedience campaign made revenue remissions politically expedient.[82] The tax hike proved particularly damaging to their authority, for it channelled the general malaise produced by the depression into a concrete, understandable grievance against a little-loved target. Their adamant rejection of any modification in the increase, in turn, increased the receptiveness of the rural population to the nationalist rhetoric and made an already unsettled political situation much more volatile.

---

76. NWFP. Bundle 65. S.No. 1954. Rev 35/43. Report dated 5/2/30.

77. *1931 Gazetteer*, Part A, p. 253.

78. *Ibid.*

79. Dane, *op. cit.*, p. 31.

80. Computed from *Report on the Administration of Land Revenue, Land Records and Agricultural Estates under the Court of Wards and the Alienation of Land Act in the North-West Frontier Province for the Year 1928-29*, pp. 3 and 7.

81. For example, see NWFP. Bundle 30. S.No. 1009. Misc. 2/1. Note on the Mardan Assessment Report.

82. NWFP. Bundle 65. S.No. 1954. Rev 35/43. Letter No. 1080-R.A. 5/21/30; and Note by Agricultural Officer.

# 4

# EARLY NATIONALISM AND THE CIVIL DISOBEDIENCE CAMPAIGN OF 1930

Historians and politicians alike often use precise dates to impose order on events which are complex and drawn out. Such is the case with the independence movement in the North-West Frontier Province which is often said to have started with the Peshawar riots of April 23, 1930. By that date, Frontier politics had already undergone a long historical evolution which shaped the province's involvement in Indian nationalism. Before 1930, political activism was confined primarily to Peshawar Valley, and interest in all-India issues, such as the Rowlatt agitation or Khilafat movement, was limited mainly to the nationalists in Peshawar city. The rural activists, who were young men from the *tehsil* of Charsadda, concentrated instead upon local ethnic concerns and in the process laid the foundations for the eventual emergence of a strong Pakhtun nationalist movement. Their parochial orientation did not change until the end of the 1920s when issues which touched upon their Pakhtun interests combined with the influence of Indian nationalism to prompt them to organize the Khudai Khidmatgars and prepare for civil disobedience.

The agitation of 1930 was intense and widespread in the NWFP. Its main center was in Peshawar Valley where the Congress assumed virtual control of Peshawar city for nine days, while the Khudai Khidmatgars paralyzed the government over much of the surrounding countryside for more than two months. The southern district of Bannu was the second major area of nationalist resistance. There, a coalition of urban politicians, tribal *maliks*, and religious leaders sustained the agitation for the better part of four months by involving an ever-widening number of rural inhabitants.

Civil disobedience caught the provincial authorities by surprise. Their first line of defense, their Khani allies, was immediately and totally ineffectual in Peshawar and Bannu, thereby demonstrating the fallacies and costs inherent in Sir John Maffey's policy of propping up the Khans at the expense of other elements in Pakhtun society. Contingency plans for coping with the agitation were lacking, and before they could be developed, the government's problems were compounded by the intervention of tribesmen around the rim of Peshawar Valley and in Waziristan. It took until the end of the summer for the government, with major assistance from the military, to re-establish its control over both Peshawar and Bannu. While a semblance of order was henceforth maintained through sheer repression, the intensity of the agitation forced the authorities to reassess their view of the province's future. The failure of their Khani allies and the obvious depth of popular opposition convinced them to reverse their position on reforms and press for the rapid introduction of democratic institutions in the North-West Frontier Province.

## The Beginnings

In the decade after its creation in 1901, the NWFP began to respond to the nationalist feelings stirring other parts of India. These embryonic beginnings barely disturbed the province's political calm, but they established patterns whose influence can be traced forward to when the nationalist movement emerged in its fully developed form. A segment of the intelligentsia in Peshawar city espoused all-India causes, while some of the landed elite of Charsadda *Tehsil* began to organize around regional ethnic issues.

The first Peshawaris to be drawn into nationalist politics were Hindus, some of whom had attended the Congress' annual sessions well before the NWFP was formed. The Bengal partition propelled a younger generation into politics.[1] Some of them returned from the 1906 Calcutta Congress to organize a Provincial Congress Committee in February 1907. The infant party was suppressed three months later and its leaders detained. After their release, they embraced revolutionary ideas and means, although never very effectively. They were sufficiently innocuous that the government took no action against them before World War I. The few young Muslims in Peshawar city who showed any interest in nationalist politics in the pre-war years were mostly graduates from Aligarh or colleges in Lahore.[2] They started a Frontier Muslim League in 1912 but attracted little public support due to the opposition of their more conservative elders. The young Muslims were preoccupied with pan-Islamism and the defense of Turkey. One of their leaders, Qazi Abdul Wali, even fought for the Sultan in the Balkans. As a result, the government suppressed the party at the start of World War I and either arrested its leaders or forced them to abandon politics.

1. Interview with Amir Chand Bombwal. Also see *Frontier Mail*, 4/23/67; and Allah Bakhsh Yusafi, *Sarhad aur Jad-o-Jehad-i-Azadi* (Lahore: Markazi Urdu Board, 1968), pp. 69-70. (Henceforth, Yusafi, *Sarhad aur . . .*)

2. See RKP/1. Letter, 8/25/12. Abdul Qaiyum to Roos-Keppel; and Letter, 9/6/12. Roos-Keppel to H. Wheeler. Also see Lal Baha, *N.-W.F.P. Administration Under British Rule, 1901-1919* (Islamabad: National Commission on Historical and Cultural Research, 1978), pp. 212-3 and 227; and Irshad Javed, "Sarhad men Tehrik-i-Azadi ke Qafila Salar," *Khatun*, Vol. 2, No. 22, 8/14/73, pp. 2 and 14.

Fazl-i Wahid, the *Haji* of Turangzai, was the first major figure in the rural areas to turn from armed resistance to new political methods.[3] The descendant of a Muhammadzai *pir*, he had moved to the Mohmand tribal area as a young man and participated in the 1897 tribal wars. After returning to Charsadda in 1908, he spent his time trying to convince Pakhtuns to abandon non-Islamic customs and to settle their disputes according to the *Shariah* rather than blood feuds or English law. He also founded a number of *madrassahs* to impart a purified version of Islam to Pakhtun children. His activities in Charsadda came to an end in 1915 when he fled to the tribal territory on the assumption that he was about to be arrested and instigated a succession of tribal wars against the government.

While the *Haji* of Turangzai was a *pir* in the traditional sense of the term, he used his spiritual authority in a manner novel for his times. His *madrassahs* served as rudimentary political centers as well as religious bodies. Similarly, while he presented his reforms in a traditional religious idiom, he also began to arouse the Pakhtuns' ethnic consciousness and touched off a Pashtu cultural renaissance. One of his *murids*, Fazl Mahmud Makhfi, in fact, is considered the founder of Pakhtun nationalist poetry.[4] Most of the *Haji's* immediate disciples were religious men, but he also found political followers among the younger members of the landed Muhammadzai elite of Charsadda. Foremost among them was Abdul Ghaffar Khan, who later became the central figure in NWFP politics.[5]

The NWFP was politically quiet during World War I, but in the years that followed, the province's apparent isolation from Indian political currents came to an end. While the province did not respond to Gandhi's call for a *hartal* against the Rowlatt Act, the Punjab disturbances, in the words of Sir George Roos-Keppel, "united all in hatred of British rule."[6] By May 1919, the Indian crises combined with trouble in Afghanistan to produce a volatile situation in Peshawar. *Amir* Amanullah had ascended the Afghan throne in late February under the suspicion that he had connived in the murder of his father. To consolidate his authority, he decided to go to war with the British empire. In preparation, his agents made contact with anti-government forces in the NWFP. The provincial government reported:

> A Committee of Union and Progress was formed in Peshawar City, the members of which in consultation with the Afghan Postmaster and sub-

3. For the Haji of Turangzai, see Muhammad Nowshervi *Mujahid Sarhad. Jangnama Haji Bahadur Sahib Turangzai* (Peshawar: Sadiq Brothers, n.d.), pp. 4-25; and Muhammad Amir Shah Qadri, *Tazkira Ulema-o-Mushaikh Sarhad* (Peshawar: Azim Publishing House, 1964), Vol. I, pp. 207-9.

4. Abdul Akbar Khan, *Karavan-i-Azadi. Manzil Avil. Safarnama-i-Russi Turkestan, 1920-21* (Peshawar: n.p., n.d.), pp. 7-8.

5. All published accounts of his early life are based on his reminiscences. See Abdul Ghaffar Khan, *My Life and Struggle* (Delhi: Hind Pocket Books, 1969), pp. 4-14 and 19-39.

6. LCP/22. No. 283. Letter, 5/5/19. Roos-Keppel to Lord Chelmsford.

> sidized with Afghan money, stirred up all the most violent elements in the City and despatched emissaries to the surrounding villages to preach resistance to Government. Efforts were made with some initial success to promote union between Hindus and Muslims and to establish panchayats to decide civil and criminal disputes, so the litigants should abstain from attendance at Government Courts of Law.[7]

War began on May 4th, but plans for an agitation—a planned uprising in the words of Roos-Keppel—in Peshawar were forestalled when troops surrounded the city on May 8th. The Afghan agents were seized, and the leaders of the Committee of Union and Progress were arrested and deported to Rangoon. The success of British arms against the Afghans and martial law cowed most of rural Peshawar, although people submitted reluctantly according to Roos-Keppel:

> The agitation of the last month was so skillfully conducted and had so much money behind it that the whole country is poisoned . . . large numbers hate us with such bitterness that they would welcome even an invasion if they saw a chance of getting rid of us.[8]

Force was used against only a few villages, most notably Utmanzai in Charsadda *Tehsil* where Abdul Ghaffar Khan helped organized protest meetings.[9]

By the time the government lifted martial law at the end of 1919, the Frontier had been embroiled in the Khilafat controversy. Khilafatists in Hazara stirred up anti-government sentiment in the rural areas of Mansehra *Tehsil* and the adjoining tribal area until the government jailed their leaders in June 1920.[10] A Khilafat Committee was founded in late 1919 in Bannu city and quickly spread to the surrounding countryside where it won support from members of the Bannuchi tribal elite.[11] Its leaders were arrested in March 1920 and again in May 1922, but the party survived throughout the 1920s to become the core of a broader-based Congress movement in 1930 in the district.

While other districts were drawn into the Khilafat agitation, Peshawar was the main center of activity. By the summer of 1920, the Valley was deeply affected by the call for a *hijrat* (exodus) from India. Muslim ideologues postulated that British hostility toward Turkey had turned India into *dar ul-harb* (land of war), making it religiously incumbent on Muslims to migrate to a

7. *Administration Report of the North-West Frontier Province for 1919-20*, p. i. For further information, see LCP/22.

8. LCP/22. No. 351. Letter, 5/13/19. Roos-Keppel to Lord Chelmsford.

9. LCP/22. No. 542. Telegram 1502-R, 5/30/19. Chief Commissioner to Private Secretary to the Viceroy.

10. GP/25. Letter, 9/20/20. Grant to Lord Chelmsford; and *Report on the Administration of the Border of the North-West Frontier Province for the Year, 1920-21*, p. 3.

11. Gul Ayub Khan Saifi, *Bannu aur Waziristan Tarikh* (Peshawar: Shahin Printing Press, 1969), pp. 224-33.

*dar ul-salam* (land of peace) where Islam could flourish. Due to its close proximity, Afghanistan became the goal of most of the *muhajirs* (emigrants).

As the main staging area for their departure, Peshawar Valley received "the concentrated essence of the Hijrat Movement," according to Sir Hamilton Grant, Roos-Keppel's successor as Chief Commissioner.[12] He reported:

> . . . hundreds of peasants are flocking daily into Peshawar to join the emigration, and there is a general unrest affecting all classes. One of the worst signs is that the country people are taking no interest in agriculture. . . . Apart from the Peshawar City, the area most affected is the Charsadda Sub-Division, particularly the Doaba and Hashtnagar tracts; two-thirds of the Patwaris in that area have resigned their appointments . . . and even the wealthy Khans are depressed and distracted.[13]

More *muhajirs* left Peshawar than any other part of India, in part because of their ethnic affinities with and geographic proximity to the Afghans. The government estimated that 21,000 people entered Afghanistan by mid-August; over 18,000 were from the NWFP, and 13,000 of them were from Peshawar.[14] The organizers of the migration consisted mainly of *mullahs* and nationalists like Abdul Ghaffar Khan who led one group of *muhajirs* himself. Peshawar city politicians, in contrast, confined themselves to providing logistical support. The migration collapsed in mid-August when Amanullah refused to accept more Indians for fear they would disrupt his country. Only a few of the *muhajirs* stayed in Afghanistan. Most returned home where they resumed possession of their former property with the government's help.

After the *hijrat* ended, a new Khilafat Committee was created in Peshawar city. Factional disputes paralyzed the movement until the end of 1920 when Indian Khilafat leaders reformed the Provincial Committee with Abdul Ghaffar Khan as a compromise president.[15] The reconstituted party forged a close working relationship with a new Frontier Congress which was formed in December 1920. The Khilafat movement found only minimal support in rural Peshawar, even among Abdul Ghaffar Khan's associates in Charsadda who sympathized but kept their distance to ensure government tolerance of their own activities. Since it was not broadly based, little force was needed to subdue the movement in Peshawar. Selective arrests, beginning with Ab-

---

12. PJ6/1701. No. 15. Memo 2090-R, 7/27/20. Grant to A.N.L. Carter.

13. *Ibid.*

14. PJ6/1701. No. 37a. Telegram 661, 8/13/20. Viceroy to Secretary of State. For further information on the movement, see *Report on the Administration of the Border of the North-West Frontier Province for the Year, 1920-21*, p. 2. Also, Abdul Akbar Khan, *op. cit.*, pp. 26-27 and Yusafi, *Sarhad aur* . . . , pp. 213-36.

15. Allah Bakhsh Yusafi *Sarhadi Gandhi se Mulaqat* (Peshawar: Manzur-i-am Barqi Press, 1939), pp. 22-24. (Henceforth, Yusafi, *Sarhadi Gandhi* . . . )

dul Ghaffar Khan in December 1921, brought its activities to an end and left it an organization in name only. (Even Abdul Ghaffar Khan severed his ties with the Khilafatists after his release from prison in 1924 to devote his time to purely rural, Pakhtun causes.) Interest in the Frontier Congress also ebbed until it was annexed to the Punjab PCC (Provincial Congress Committee) in 1923.

Except for Abdul Ghaffar Khan, the Charsadda nationalists were politically inexperienced youths, rebellious *kasharan* (young men) of the Muhammadzai and Mian elite with little standing in the province's public life. Nonetheless, they represented the mainstream of Frontier nationalism, for their Charsadda-based movement evolved into the Khudai Khidmatgars in 1930. In the aftermath of the *hijrat*, the Charsadda activists found an outlet for their nationalist feelings in social work. They drew their inspiration primarily from the memory of the *Haji* of Turangzai, with the all-India noncooperation movement providing a secondary impetus. Institutionally, their movement consisted of a social reform organization, called the *Anjuman-i-Islah-ul-Afaghania* (Society for the Reform of the Afghans), and a number of unaccredited *Azad* (Free) schools. Their leaders have claimed a network of branches distributed throughout the province.[16] By all indications, however, their movement was confined largely to Charsadda *Tehsil*. All the *anjuman's* officers were from there as were most of its executive committee. Few of the men who would later turn the Khudai Khidmatgars into a mass movement in the rest of Peshawar were associated with the *anjuman*, while it had virtually no support at all in the other parts of the province.[17]

The *Azad* schools were, for the most part, *ad hoc* bodies which were strapped for funds, lacked qualified staff, and had no fixed curriculum. According to a 1922 government report, " . . . no regular scheme of instruction appears to be followed. Schools open, exist for a few months and then close. Their pupils have then to shift for themselves. . . . "[18] The exception to this pattern was the original school in Utmanzai, which was affiliated with Jamia Millia in Delhi and prepared its pupils for the matriculation exam of the Punjab University. The main goals of even that *Azad* school, however, were to offer instruction in Islam, foster Pashtu culture, and promote a sense of ethnic self-awareness and pride.

Besides running the *Azad* schools, the members of the *Anjuman-i-Islah-ul-Afaghania* engaged in a wide gamut of activities. Like the *Haji* of Turangzai, they wanted "to cleanse society of bad customs; to create a real Islamic love and brotherhood amongst the people; . . . to teach the Pakhtun nation their responsibility of serving Islam."[19] They placed particular emphasis on

---

16. Interviews with Abdul Akbar Khan, Mian Jafar Shah, and Mian Abdullah Shah.

17. Interviews with Pir Shahinshah, Muhammad Ramzan Khan, Muhammad Zarin Khan, and Sayyid Ashiq Shah.

18. *Report on Public Instruction of the North-West Frontier Province for the Year, 1922-23*, p. 23.

19. *Pakhtun*, 10/28.

ending the practice of feuding which they held to be morally debilitating and the primary impediment to Pakhtun unity. They tried to make trade respectable in Pakhtun eyes and to break the Hindu and Sikh monopoly over Peshawar's commerce.[20] The *anjuman* also encouraged the Pashtu revival started by the *Haji* of Turangzai. A host of serious literary figures emerged out of its ranks, including some who have made major contributions to modern Pashtu literature.

One of the enduring nationalist myths is that the *anjuman* was a purely social movement with no political objectives or ambitions. Although they outwardly concentrated on uplifting Pakhtuns, Abdul Ghaffar Khan and his associates remained committed political activists. Social reform and political action were inseparable in their minds, for they regarded British rule as the root cause of the economic and social evils plaguing Pakhtun society. Thus, ending colonial rule remained one of their foremost objectives. For example, under the original masthead of their journal, *Pakhtun*, were the lines: "Years of a slave in servitude are nothing as compared with a single hour of freedom spent even in the agonies of death." The movement's true accomplishment, in fact, lay in the political realm. While it failed to purify Pakhtun society, it nurtured the Pakhtuns' sense of ethnic nationalism and provided an incipient organizational structure on which later political parties would build. The *Anjuman-i-Islah-ul-Afaghania* disappeared with civil disobedience in 1930, but in a sense, it paved the way for its own demise by contributing to the Frontier's political awakening.

## Prologue to Civil Disobedience

In November 1928, the Simon Commission visited Peshawar on a fact-finding mission and brought in its wake a flurry of meetings, deputations, and processions. The small group of politicians in the Frontier Khilafat Committee and the Congress conducted a brief, ineffectual protest on the day of its arrival, but they were alone in their hostility. Everyone else wanted to register his opinions and demands. Even many Hindu Congressmen who objected to the commission for all-India reasons cooperated with it to protect their local interests.[21] The province's senior Khans asked for a legislature with two-thirds of its members appointed, on the assumption that the Chief Commissioner would nominate them to those seats. The urban Muslim intelligentsia demanded reforms equal to those of other provinces. Hindus, who saw no means of safeguarding their interests in a democratic system, argued against any change from the status quo. Sikhs, who formed only

20. Abdul Khaliq Khaliq, *Azadi Jang. Silidili au sa Auridili* (Peshawar: Idara-i-Ishaat Sarhad, 1972), p. 41; and Yusafi, *Sarhadi Gandhi* . . . , p. 37.

21. *Frontier Advocate*, 10/30/28. For a nationalist account of the protest against the commission, see Yusafi, *Sarhad aur* . . . , p. 458.

1.75 percent of the province, demanded 25 percent of the seats in any future legislature.[22]

The Simon Commission touched off a political reawakening in the North-West Frontier Province. Since the collapse of the Khilafat movement, public interest in all-India issues had subsided, and the amount of political organizing had been minimal. In the final two years of the decade, in contrast, politics acquired a new urgency. Previously dormant groups were mobilized into the public arena, and efforts at party building resulted in a level of organization which was minimal by the standards of other provinces but which placed Frontier politics on a qualitatively different footing from before. Without this groundwork, the province's response to civil disobedience in 1930 could not have been as intense or widespread as it was.

While Frontier politics ran parallel to those in the rest of India, they were not motivated by identical concerns. Few of the province's inhabitants were ready to challenge the government over all-India issues. Frustration over the lack of self-government proved a powerful argument among the politically sophisticated intelligentsia, but reforms, like the problem of India's future, were not an issue capable of galvanizing the province as a whole. Since the vast majority of the Frontier's people were insular in outlook, it took local grievances to estrange them from the government. The underlying source of the new political spirit was the tension social and economic change had produced in the province. Nationalists, like Abdul Ghaffar Khan, capitalized on the antagonisms Pakhtuns felt toward the senior, pro-government Khans to win public support. For example, he told audiences that "they could expect nothing from the Khans, Arbabs and Zaildars whose only desire was to shake hands with the Sahib Bahadurs and to secure employment for their sons."[23] Additionally, the onset of the depression created an atmosphere of discontent which made people receptive to nationalist propaganda. Beyond these general stimuli, the Pakhtuns' political interests were aroused by issues which impinged directly upon their ethnic and religious feelings.

Concurrent with India's drift toward civil disobedience, Afghanistan passed through a period of political instability.[24] When Shinwari tribesmen rebelled against *Amir* Amanullah in November 1928, the army joined the insurgents, thereby leaving Kabul undefended. Bacha-i Saqao, a Tajik outlaw, seized the capital and turned back the *amir's* attempts to regain his throne. Amanullah went into exile in May 1929, but his cousin, General Nadir Khan, captured Kabul in October 1929 with the aid of tribal levies from Waziristan. While these events had few repercussions in India as a whole, they had a

---

22. Diwan Chand Obhrai, *The Evolution of North-West Frontier Province* (Peshawar: London Book Co., 1938), pp. 124-26.

23. Isemonger Report, p. 14.

24. Louis Dupree, *Afghanistan* (Princeton: Princeton University Press, 1973), pp. 449-61.

profoundly unsettling influence in the Frontier Province. Pakhtuns were deeply concerned about what happened across the border in a way they were not about events in India. Afghanistan was still the paramount symbol of their past glories, political aspirations, and sense of honor as a people. The *Anjuman-i-Islah-ul-Afaghania*, for example, used the royal Afghan emblem on the cover of its journal, *Pakhtun*, until 1930. Its leaders spoke of Pakhtuns and Afghans as forming one nation and metaphorically called the Afghan *amir* their king. In one article, its general-secretary, Mian Ahmad Shah, addressed Amanullah:

> All Pakhtuns are the children of one set of parents. Anywhere there are Pakhtuns, they are your brothers. You have to care for them all. . . . Stretch out your benevolent hand to all of them. You are the shepherd of these people.[25]

Nationalists in the Frontier Province turned the crisis in Afghanistan into a political issue. They started by hinting that the Government of India had some hand in the revolt and eventually declared that it had "fostered and instigated the rebellion" to replace Amanullah with a more pliant *amir*.[26] When Nadir Khan conquered Kabul, politicians treated his triumph as a Pakhtun victory over the British. Abdul Akbar Khan, the president of the *Anjuman-i-Islah-ul-Afaghania*, wrote in *Pakhtun*:

> Any man with a brain and a heart cannot but be elated by the recent conquest of Kabul. Every Muslim, every Pakhtun, and even every human being can have no greater moment of happiness than now when the Pakhtuns have restored their honor, their lost throne, and their looted wealth. They have frustrated the evil designs of troublemakers and criminals with their valor. The Pakhtuns have sacrificed their lives for this cause. They have revealed to the world that Pakhtuns are a living nation. They can be proud of the fact that they have preserved their honor.
>
> Pakhtuns should not take this event as unique and unusual. The Kabul revolution was not an unusual occurrence . . . any king who has disobeyed the British even slightly, who has shown any rebelliousness, or who has tried to be free from their slavery has been treated like Amanullah Khan. But now the Pakhtuns are aware of the situation and recognize the devilish deceit, cunning, and villainy of the British.[27]

Abdul Ghaffar Khan held the conquest up as an inspirational model:

> This is an example for you, the Pakhtuns of the Frontier, to abandon your petty differences, become united and break the shackles of slavery. . . . We need to join the war for the freedom of India and rid our-

25. *Pakhtun*, 7/29. For other examples, see *ibid.* 8/28, 11/28, and 5/29.
26. FR 4/29(I).
27. *Pakhtun*, 11/29.

> selves of the shame that an alien nation rides our backs. Then we may say with pride that we are able to stand shoulder to shoulder with free nations.[28]

Provincial politicians tried to aid the Afghans by creating a medical mission under the auspices of the Red Cresent Society.[29] The government reluctantly agreed to the idea, but Nadir Khan did not. He turned down the offer of help, thereby forcing the mission's cancellation. Although it never went to Afghanistan, the mission had an important by-product in that the campaign to create it helped politicize Pakhtuns. More specifically, the campaign marked a turning point for the *Anjuman-i-Islah-ul-Afaghania* whose leaders henceforth devoted themselves to overtly political work. Another unintended, but lasting effect of their efforts on behalf of the mission was to give them valuable contacts throughout the province upon which they would later draw in preparing for civil disobedience.

While the turmoil in Afghanistan touched on the Pakhtuns' ethnic sensitivities, the Sarda Act aroused their religious feelings. The act, which was passed by the Indian Legislative Assembly in September 1929, made it punishable for anyone to arrange a marriage if the bride was less than fourteen and the groom less than eighteen.[30] The new law encountered a storm of hostility in the NWFP on the grounds that it infringed upon the sanctity of the *Shariah* and violated Muslims' religious freedom. In addition, it was falsely alleged to invade the privacy of women by requiring pre-marital medical examinations to ensure compliance with its provisions. Protests against the Sarda Act brought many more moderate Muslims into alliance with the province's nationalists in the last months of 1929. Public expressions of resentment diminished in 1930, but the law remained a festering source of discontent which the nationalists exploited to rally popular support.

Organizationally, the first step in the province's political reawakening occurred when the politicians who had gathered in Peshawar to demonstrate against the Simon Commission formed a Provincial Congress Committee (PCC) on November 17, 1928.[31] Whereas earlier Frontier Congresses had been Hindu parties, the new PCC was intercommunal. The balance was best symbolized by its provincial officers. In 1929, its president and vice-presidents were Muslims, while its general-secretary and treasurer were Hindus. The next year, a Hindu became president and a Muslim general-secretary.[32] The party was formed from the top down, causing Jawaharlal

---

28. *Ibid.*

29. FR1/29(II), FR3/29(I), FR5/29(I), FR6/29(I), and FR7/29(II). Also, Yusafi, *Sarhad aur. . .*, pp. 473-75.

30. N.N. Mitra (ed.), *Indian Quarterly Register, 1929* (Calcutta: Annual Register Office, 1929), Vol. I, p. 167.

31. AICC File G-86, 1928. Letter, 11/18/28. C.C. Ghosh to AICC General-Secretary; and Letter, n.d. Paira Khan to AICC General-Secretary.

32. AICC File P-28(i), 1929. Inspection Report. Sardul Singh Caveshar, 6/26/29.

Nehru to complain in July 1928: "... your Provincial Congress Committee is a superstructure without any basis... there is no district Congress Committee functioning properly."[33] It also failed to meet its membership quota of 2,000, the minimum necessary to secure affiliation with the All-India Congress Committee (AICC). It claimed to have done so in December 1929, but the largest number of members for which it submitted substantiation was only 567.[34]

Despite its organizational failings, the Frontier Congress replaced the Khilafat Committee as the main vehicle for the province's urban nationalists. By 1929, the All-India Khilafat Committee had turned into just another Muslim party whose communal preoccupation did not speak to the needs of its Frontier adherents. As a result, Khilafatists in Kohat and Bannu transferred their loyalties to the Congress once district branches were started in the summer of 1929. Most of the Peshawar Khilafat Committee, including its senior leaders, maintained dual membership in the two parties but worked primarily for the Congress. A minority preferred to remain pure Khilafatists, although they too showed a readiness to cooperate with the Frontier Congress on specific issues.[35] One other urban party, the *Anjuman-i-Naujawanan-i-Sarhad* (Association of the Youths of the Frontier), was started in February 1929 by a small group of radical Peshawaris. Its stated purpose was "the organising through the youth of the province of the labourers and peasants against the curse of the capitalists and Imperialism."[36] In spite of its quasi-Marxian rhetoric, first priority was given to winning independence through a joint effort with Congress.

The Frontier Congress was an urban party with a little appeal to the province's agrarian Pakhtun majority. Both provincial and all-India Congress leaders looked to Abdul Ghaffar Khan to help them overcome this limitation.[37] While he attended the annual meetings of the Congress in Calcutta in 1928 and Lahore in 1929 as a member of the All-India Congress Committee and served as the PCC vice-president in 1928-29, Abdul Ghaffar Khan did not consider the Congress the appropriate party for Pakhtuns. Instead, he and his associates created a new organization—the Frontier *Zalmo Jirga*, or Afghan Jirga, as it became better known—on September 1, 1929. The *Anjuman-i-Islah-ul-Afaghania* supplied the new party with its officers. Abdul Abkar Khan was chosen as president and Mian Ahmad Shah as general-sec-

33. AICC File P-28(i), 1929. Letter P28(i)/2299, 7/1/29. Nehru to NWFPCC Secretary.

34. *Congress Bulletin*, No. 14, 10/5/29, p. 155; and No. 16, 12/26/29, p. 183. AICC File P-30 (ii), 1929. Letter 277, 9/7/29. Abdur Rahman Riya to J. Nehru.

35. FR7/29(I), FR1/30(I), and FR1/30(II). Also Yusafi, *Sarhad aur...*, pp. 489-90. Interviews with Mian Jafar Shah and Rahim Bakhsh Ghaznavi.

36. FR9/29(II). Also see GoI File 465, 1930.

37. AICC File G-86, 1928. Letter, 9/18/28. C.C. Ghosh to J. Nehru; and AICC File P-28(i), 1929. Inspection Report. Sardul Singh Caveshar, 6/26/29. Also see Khaliq, *op. cit.*, p. 57.

retary. The party's goal was succinctly stated to be "complete independence for India,"[38] but it gave first priority, as Mian Ahmad Shah later explained, to representing Pakhtun interests in that cause:

> Most people in the villages do not understand the Khilafat and Congress. . . . They think they are tricks and traps of the Indians. For these reasons, most of our brothers are not part of the Congress and Khilafat. Having considered the problem, we deemed it essential that we form our own national party. . . . The *Zalmo Jirga* is not against the Congress and Khilafat. It is ready to support them in the cause of freedom. It can involve people who are beyond the reach of the Congress and Khilafat.
>
> The second reason for the *Zalmo Jirga* is that our province needs its own party. The Congress and Khilafat Committee are Indian parties. Hindus, Sikhs, and Muslims in this province have sacrificed for those committees. They have given funds and gone to jail, but at the time of reforms the Frontier was excluded. All our sacrifices were swept away by the tide of indifference. Now the Viceroy is considering Dominion Status for India, but we are ignored. The leaders of India exploit us for their own ends and do not give us any benefits. Yesterday Afghanistan was in flames. Our Pakhtun brothers were being massacred. We went door to door for them, but no one in India sent us a penny even though they have taken thousands from us. Why is this so? It is because we do not have our own party. We should come together and think about our own interests. We should stand on our own feet. No one else is going to help us.[39]

Shortly after the party's formation, the Afghan Jirga's organization was radically altered by the creation of a quasi-military body of volunteers called the Khudai Khidmatgars (Servants of God) in November 1929. Sarfaraz Khan of Utmanzai became their first *Salar-i-Azam* (Commander-in-Chief). Abdul Ghaffar Khan later claimed that the Khudai Khidmatgars were meant to be a social movement but that the British forced them into politics.[40] His claim may be discounted, for the Afghan Jirga's orientation was strictly political and the Khudai Khidmatgar's formation was part and parcel of its preparations for a confrontation with the government. By chance, the volunteers adopted a burnt-red color for their uniforms since ordinary white showed dirt too easily. From this, they acquired the popular name of *Surkh Posh*, or Red Shirts, which the British seized upon as proof of their "Bolshevik" character.[41]

Although its organizers conceived of the Afghan Jirga as provincial in scope, it started, like the *Anjuman-i-Islah-ul-Afaghania*, with a strong Char-

---

38. *Pakhtun*, 10/29.
39. *Ibid.*, 1/30.
40. Abdul Ghaffar Khan, *op. cit.*, pp. 95-96.
41. GoI File 11/III/30. Letter 2/46/PC, 6/12/30. Norwef to Home Department.

sadda bias. More than fifty of the party's seventy founders were residents of that *tehsil*, and most of the others came from the nearby town of Mardan. The rest of the province had only scattered representation, most of which consisted of men working or studying in Peshawar rather than in their home districts.[42] To broaden the party's base, Abdul Ghaffar Khan, Abdul Akbar Khan, and Mian Ahmad Shah conducted a series of tours throughout the province.[43] In November, they visited the towns and some of the larger villages in the three southern districts. Over the next four months, they concentrated on the rural areas of Peshawar and the adjoining Malakand Tribal Agency. Then, Abdul Ghaffar Khan embarked on another tour of the southern districts in the company of Congress leaders at the end of March.

These efforts produced a level of political mobilization previously unknown in the Frontier Province. The Afghan Jirga established a network of party branches in Charsadda, Mardan, and Swabi *Tehsils* by enlisting members of the Khani elite as local organizers. In the southern districts, it gained only scattered adherents, but its leaders did develop a cooperative relationship with the local political organizations. Wherever they went, Abdul Ghaffar Khan and his associates coordinated party plans and shared the public platform with Congress and Khilafat leaders. To symbolize their common purpose, the Afghan Jirga named three prominent politicians in Kohat and Bannu to its central council.[44] The Afghan Jirga also established close ties with the all-India Congress leadership. At the Lahore Congress in December 1929, Abdul Ghaffar Khan promised to work on behalf of the party and committed the Afghan Jirga to participating in its civil disobedience campaign.[45] In the succeeding months, the Congress deferred to him in preparing for the agitation in the NWFP because of his commanding political reputation and his control of the only rural party in the province.

The Frontier authorities were remarkably complacent in the face of mounting nationalist activity. Following celebration of the "Independence Day" on January 26, 1930, the Chief Commissioner, Sir H. N. Bolton, wrote the Viceroy that he saw no reason to prosecute Congress leaders and dismissed the Khudai Khidmatgars as insignificant.[46] Three months later, he was still confidently assuring Lord Irwin on April 19th that "the tranquility prevailing here is largely due to the level-headed loyalty of the people of this province."[47] His administration finally reacted on April 22nd after nationalists announced that picketing of liquor stores would begin the next day to

---

42. For a partial list of participants, see *Pakhtun*, 10/29. Interviews with Muhammad Ramzan Khan and Ali Asghar Khan.

43. Isemonger Report, pp. 13-14.

44. *Ibid.*, pp. 16-17.

45. *Ibid.*

46. GoI File 88, 1930. Letter, 2/2/30. Bolton to Home Secretary; and Telegram 64-P, 2/2/30. NWF Peshawar to Home Department.

47. HP/24. No. 143. Telegram 261/P, 4/19/30. Bolton to Viceroy.

coincide with the arrival of a Congress enquiry committee into the Frontier Crimes Regulations. The committee was barred from the province, and arrest warrants were issued for eleven city politicians. Nine were seized at home on the morning of April 23rd, but the other two, Ghulam Rabbani Sethi and Allah Bakhsh Barqi, had already gone to the Congress office, thereby setting the stage for the upheaval which made the day a milestone in the independence movement in the North-West Frontier Province.

## Civil Disobedience in Peshawar Valley

As the single most dramatic event in the NWFP's nationalist history, the April 23rd riots have been the subject of intense controversy. Two investigations in May 1930 provided the basic versions from which all later accounts begin. Two judges, Shah Muhammad Sulaiman and H. R. Panckridge, investigated the riots for the government. They aimed for accuracy in reconstructing the events of April 23rd since the government needed to know what had happened in order to be prepared for similar occurrences in the future. The Congress' enquiry committee, which was chaired by Vithalbhai Patel, operated under quite different constraints. Its purpose was to rally support for the civil disobedience campaign by showing that the public had acted peacefully while the government had been needlessly and intentionally brutal.[48] Although less accurate, the Patel Report had a more profound political impact than the report prepared by Sulaiman and Panckridge. By reinforcing popular beliefs about the riots, it influenced public opinion in favor of civil disobedience and helped to create heroes, martyrs, myths, and symbols which politicians have exploited ever since 1930.

According to Sulaiman and Panckridge, a hostile crowd prevented the police from taking Sethi and Barqi to the Kabuli Gate *thana* (police station). The two men proceeded to the station on their own, accompanied by the crowd which remained in the surrounding bazar after they went inside. Informed that the crowd could not be controlled, the Deputy Commissioner, H.A.F. Metcalfe, entered the bazar with four armored cars. The vehicles were met by a barrage of bricks, and a despatch motorcycle rider, who had accompanied them against orders, was killed. In the turmoil, at least one of the armored cars ran over people congregated near the *thana*. The crowd set fire to one car, while mechanical failure disabled a second. Their crews were assaulted on leaving the vehicle, and Metcalfe was knocked unconscious on the steps of the *thana*. On recovering, he ordered one of the remaining ar-

48. Non-violence has become passé in the NWFP since independence. In this spirit, some local historians contradict the Patel Report and substantiate key elements of the government's case by describing how the Peshawaris retaliated against the government with force. Farigh Bukhari, *Bacha Khan. Abdul Ghaffar Khan ke Savanah Hayat* (Peshawar: Niya Maktuba, 1957), pp. 111-12; and Khaliq, *op. cit.*, pp. 67-68.

mored cars, which had also come under assault, to open fire. The crowd temporarily dispersed, only to reform and build a barricade from which to attack the armored car furthest into the bazar. Troops sent to protect the vehicle were themselves attacked and forced to open fire to scatter the crowd and people on surrounding roof-tops. Sulaiman and Panckridge estimated crowd casualties at thirty killed and thirty-three wounded, but they conceded that their figures were probably incomplete.[49]

The Patel Report disputes almost every detail in the government's account. It contends that there was no disturbance outside the Congress office and that the crowd at the *thana* had started to disperse peacefully when the armored cars recklessly rushed into the bazar, crushing a dozen people or more. The motorcyclist died after falling beneath one of the cars, while the armored car caught fire for unknown reasons; the allegation that the crowd was responsible was "an afterthought to serve as a cover for the unjustifiable firing by the authorities."[50] The report conceded that Metcalfe was hit by "a piece of stone" but charges:

> . . . the Deputy Commissioner had perpetuated a most shocking piece of inhumanity . . . and he perhaps saw no escape out of it except by giving the happenings of the 23rd April the form of a serious riot and painting the crowd in the blackest possible colour.[51]

Regarding the second firing, the report states that the crowd had wanted only to collect its dead and wounded and, in fact, had agreed to disperse if the armored cars and troops were removed. When the authorities refused, it stood its ground non-violently while troops shot and bayonetted people for four hours. The report puts the known dead for the day at 125 and states that the actual total was undoubtedly much higher.

While the riots were limited to one locality, their repercussions were widespread and profound. They pushed the general public in Peshawar city into open opposition to the government and fueled a movement in the surrounding countryside which paralyzed the administration in three of Peshawar's five *tehsils*. Along the Peshawar border, tribesmen were induced by sympathy for the nationalists and the apparent collapse of British authority to take up arms against the government. The conflict reached such proportions that Lord Irwin wired the Secretary of State in August: "The whole of Peshawar District as far as Attock must be considered in [a] state of war."[52]

Troops patrolled the streets of Peshawar on April 24th, but that evening two platoons of the 2/18th Royal Garhwali Rifles refused to enter the city "on grounds that they would not fire on their people."[53] The Garhwalis' dis-

49. Sulaiman-Panckridge Report, p. 27.
50. Patel Report, p. 16.
51. *Ibid.*, p. 17.
52. GoI File 255/V, 1930. Telegram 2665-S, 8/11/30. Viceroy to Secretary of State.
53. PJ6/1897, 1930. No. 1987. Telegram 1255-S, 4/22/30. Home Department to Secretary of State.

obedience caused provincial administrators to panic and question the reliability of all Indian soldiers.[54] They, therefore, withdrew all soldiers from the city hoping that influential private citizens could pacify its inhabitants instead. The stratagem misfired due to the intense anti-government feelings aroused by the riots. For the next nine days, the Congress had *de facto* control of the city.[55] While its volunteers maintained order, apprehended criminals, and manned the city gates, its leaders used the sudden absence of authority to expand its organization, proselytize in nearby villages, and correspond with tribal leaders in search of support. The police, the sole remaining representatives of authority in the city, were unable to restrain the party. As the government admitted, "in so far as they are functioning at all, [they] are doing so on sufference."[56]

By first projecting an image of brutality and then of paralysis in the city, the administration fueled the anti-British campaign in the countryside where major segments of the populace were already restive and the Afghan Jirga had a rudimentary organization with which to channel their alienation into coordinated activity. Civil disobedience began with the arrest of the leaders of the Afghan Jirga—Abdul Ghaffar Khan, Abdul Akbar Khan, Mian Ahmad Shah, and Sarfaraz Khan—on April 23rd en route to Peshawar to investigate reports about the riots. In the evening, the Afghan Jirga's central committee reaffirmed its commitment to civil disobedience, appointed new officers, and ordered Mian Abdullah Shah and Mian Jafar Shah underground to assume day-to-day direction of the agitation.

Civil disobedience plunged much of Peshawar Valley into turmoil. Volunteers paraded daily in military formation; meetings drew audiences as large as 10,000 people; and liquor and foreign cloth stores were subjected to constant picketing. Sir Steuart Pears, Bolton's successor as Chief Commissioner, later wrote Lord Irwin:

> Peshawar District itself, as far as the Charsadda, Mardan and Swabi Tahsils were concerned, was being overrun by bands of 'red shirts', holding meetings everywhere and moving across country to different centres everyday. . . . Revolutionary cries and seditious speeches were universal and obviously even the law-abiding part of the population was being worked up into a ferment. . . . I am afraid that in these three Tahsils the minor officials of all departments of our civil administration were terrorised and ceased to function.[57]

Government and village officials resigned as a result; revenue collections stopped; regular police activity ceased; and courts were supplanted by nationalist *jirgas*.

---

54. HP/24. No. 162. Telegram C.R./16, 4/26/30. Bolton to Viceroy.

55. See PJ6/1897, 1930. No. 1970, 2050, and 2105; FR4/30(II) and FR5/30(I); and Aziz Javed, "1930 aur Sarhad. Hissa 3," *Khatun*, 1/28/73, p. 9.

56. PJ6/1897, 1930. No. 2105. Telegram 1320-S, 5/1/30. Home Department to Secretary of State.

57. HP/24. No. 301. Letter, 6/12/30. Pears to Viceroy.

The administration's collapse in Peshawar was as much a function of its own failures as of popular animosity. The security forces it had on hand were insufficient to maintain order, and army reinforcements were delayed by the absence of proper contingency planning. Both the lack of manpower and planning resulted from the government's antiquated system for controlling the province's rural areas. Civil disobedience exposed the bankruptcy of relying exclusively on the senior Khans after they had lost their social legitimacy. As British officials recognized in retrospect, the attempt to "bolster up the Khans at the expense of everyone else was more responsible than any other single event for the Red Shirt agitation. . . ."[58] The decision drove the lesser Khans, ordinary Pakhtuns, and lower classes, all of whom were antagonistic toward the senior Khans, into the nationalist agitation. In turn, civil disobedience removed the prop on which the senior Khans depended by undermining the government's authority and thereby left them incapable of performing the very role for which the British had maintained them at such a political cost.

Patterns of dominance and subordinance in Pakhtun society carried over to the nationalist movement. Leadership at all levels came mainly from the Pakhtun elite, and *parajamba* determined that it consisted mostly of men from the junior branches of Khani lineages. The rank-and-file consisted predominantly of small Pakhtun landholders and members of lower classes. One government report stated:

> The directors of the movement in each tappa and subordinate village were Pathans. . . . As the executive force to carry out their orders, they enrolled villagers, many of whom were either landless or 'kamins' of the menial classes, under commanders who were given various ranks from 'Commander-in-Chief' to 'Captain.'[59]

Support from the Khani elite was the key to the success of the movement. Although Charsadda, Mardan, and Swabi appeared to form a solid "red" belt, the response of their tribes varied according to the extent to which members of their landed elite joined the Khudai Khidmatgars. In Charsadda, for example, the party was strongest in Hashtnagar, the home area of its Muhammadzai and Mian founders. Its influence dropped off among the Gigiannis and more so among the Mohmands whose tribal elders served as a partial brake on the agitation.[60] Similarly, in the Baizai area of Mardan, it drew its strength from the Khattaks due to support from members of the tribes' dominant family. In contrast, the Utman Khels and Yusafzais remained comparatively quiet because their leaders abstained from the movement.[61]

---

58. CP/5 p. 10.

59. *NWF Province Gazetteer. Peshawar District, 1931* (Lahore: Civil and Military Gazette, 1934), Vol. A, p. 95.

60. FR4/31(II).

61. Interviews with Mian Shakirullah and Muhammad Zarin Khan. Also, PJ7/17. Part I. No. 2878. Report of the tour of the Guides Cavalry. Captain C.W. Free.

Civil disobedience was loosely structured in Peshawar. Some officials claimed that the Afghan Jirga had a cellular organization based on a communist model.[62] In fact, they were reading a sophisticated party structure into a situation more nearly corresponding to the absence of organization. Lines of authority quickly became confused as the movement's rudimentary infrastructure was inundated by new members. The campaign was conducted largely by the quasi-military Khudai Khidmatgars whose numbers grew so rapidly that shortly after the agitation began they exceeded those of their parent organization.[63] Pears observed:

> . . . there were several organisations grouped generally under this (Red Shirt) name in the Charsadda and other Tahsils. The original organisation was Abdul Ghaffar's 'Afghan Youth League'. . . . Subsequently, ancillary organisations seem to have sprung up from unspecified sources; they all correspond to the National Volunteers of Congress, but they were known by different names, i.e., 'Khudai Khidmatgaran' in Charsadda, 'Razakaran' (Volunteers) in Mardan and Swabi and 'Qaumi Khidmatgaran' (Tribal Servants) in Nowshera.[64]

In fact, the volunteers' development was even more piecemeal than Pears suggested. While they had been conceived as a centralized force with a military chain of command, they emerged as a loose series of semi-independent village units among which there was only a minimum of integration.

Although civil disobedience was conducted by a local organization, it was part of the all-India non-cooperation movement. Whereas the Afghan Jirga had informally coordinated its plans with the Congress prior to April 23rd, its leaders felt compelled by early May to seek a closer alignment. Congress leaders had initially been surprised by the intensity of the agitation in Peshawar. Gandhi even disavowed it at first because he thought that non-violence had not been maintained.[65] Any doubts about the Afghan Jirga's overtures, however, were quickly lost, for the Congress position was enhanced in its campaign against the government by the strong participation of the strategically located and overwhelmingly Muslim populace of the Frontier.

Khudai Khidmatgar leaders have represented their affiliation with the Congress as a desperate necessity forced on them by Indian Muslims. Abdul Ghaffar Khan has told one biographer:

> While we were kept in jail, the tyrannical Government indulged in inhuman oppression. Mian Jafar Shah and Abdullah Shah who had come

62. See GoI File 11/III, 1930. Letter 2/46/P.C., 6/12/30. Norwef to Home Department.
63. Estimates of their size range from 25,000 to more than 100,000. These figures are all

> for an interview and had acquainted us with the situation in the Frontier Province, were requested to visit Lahore, Delhi and Simla, to inform the Muslim League leaders about the people's plight and seek their help in at least acquainting the outside world with the situation in the Frontier. In a couple of months they came again for an interview with us. They told us that the Muslim League leaders did not want to help us because we resisted the British. They were not prepared to oppose the Britishers, they wanted to fight the Hindus. We had not joined the Congress till then. As a drowning man tries to catch hold of any straw—being thwarted by the Muslim League—we requested the two colleagues to seek help from the National Congress.[66]

This explanation grew out of the party's later political need to neutralize allegations that it had sold out to the Hindus. In the context of 1930, it would have been highly incongruous for the party to turn first to the Muslim parties for help. While the Afghan Jirga and Congress had similar political goals and a history of cooperation, the Muslim parties were weak and fragmented, objected to immediate independence, and condemned civil disobedience. In fact, according to Mian Abdullah Shah and Mian Jafar Shah, their only contact with their jailed colleagues occurred in mid-May. During secret meetings in the Gujrat jail in the Punjab, the need for some form of link to the Congress was treated as a foregone conclusion, with the discussion focusing on the terms to be sought. The envoys then went to Allahabad to negotiate the alliance. Neither consulted with Muslim politicians until after the pact was signed.[67]

The alliance provided that the Afghan Jirga would act under the Congress' general direction while retaining its separate identity. Its relationship to the Frontier Congress was left unclear, but the Congress leaders agreed in principle to give it overall responsibility for the movement in the NWFP. They also promised the Afghan Jirga immediate financial aid, assured it that they would not enter into a separate agreement with the government, and pledged themselves to fight for the NWFP's right to equal status with other Indian provinces in all future reforms.[68]

By the time the Congress-Afghan Jirga alliance was signed, the situation in Peshawar had been complicated by still another factor—unrest in the neighboring tribal areas. Civil disobedience aroused the tribesmen's sympathies for their ethnic kinsmen in the Valley, adding one more grievance to their already long list against the government.[69] The economic depression,

66. Quoted in D.G. Tendulkar, *Abdul Ghaffar Khan* (Bombay: Popular Prakashan, 1967), p. 75.

67. Interviews with Abdul Akbar Khan, Mian Abdullah Shah, and Mian Jafar Shah. 1930. No. 6.

68. *Ibid.*

69. See *Report on the Administration of the Border of the North-West Frontier Province for the Year, 1929-30*; and ID, 1930. No. 6.

the civil war in Afghanistan, and the Sarda Act had left them in a state of unrest. Each tribe also harbored its own grudges against the authorities. Some Afridis, for example, were dissatisfied with the government-imposed settlement of a Shia-Sunni conflict in the Tirah, while the Upper and Lower Mohmand clans were embroiled in an on-going feud over the latter's government subsidies. Finally, the initial success of civil disobedience spawned wild reports that the British were about to abandon the NWFP and even leave India. Many tribesmen were eager to capitalize on the situation to settle old scores with the government and engage in a little looting besides.

Despite their protests to the contrary, provincial politicians played upon the tribesmen's sympathies, grievances, and avarice in an effort to draw them into the conflict.[70] The first to heed the nationalists' call was the *Haji* of Turangzai, who brought a *lashkar* (tribal army) of Upper Mohmands down to the edge of Peshawar District at the end of April. Other tribesmen around Peshawar were slower to react, but by May, intelligence reports pointed to the probability of trouble in Bajaur to the northwest and, more ominously, among the Afridis to the west.[71]

Thus, the provincial authorities were simultaneously confronted by the first of May with grave challenges on three fronts—Peshawar city, rural Peshawar, and the adjoining tribal areas. Compounding the crisis, Bolton suffered a nervous breakdown and left the province on April 30th.[72] Pears, his replacement, did not reach the province until May 10th. In the interim, Courtney Latimer, the Revenue Commissioner, acted in his place, with assistance from Sir Evelyn Howell, the Indian Government's Foreign Secretary, whom Lord Irwin had sent to Peshawar on April 29th.

Latimer acted first to bring Peshawar city, the seat of government, under control.[73] The Congress was declared illegal on May 3rd. The following morning, troops sealed off the city, reoccupied it in force, imposed severe curbs on all activity for twenty-four hours, and arrested Congress activists. This overpowering show of force ended most overt signs of political resistance. Meetings and demonstrations were no longer staged, and the public appeared to revert to its normal preoccupations. Popular resentment, however, flared into the open again on May 31st when an English soldier accidentally killed two Sikh children and wounded their mother.[74] Although he was summarily tried and sentenced to placate public opinion, the children's funeral procession turned into a political demonstration which clashed with troops. Unlike the April 23rd riots, these disturbances had no further repercussions, for security was too tight and the nationalists' forces too depleted

70. PJ6/1897, 1930. No. 2139, 2422, 2589, 2620, and 2740; ID, 1930. No. 18 and 26.

71. See ID, 1930. No. 17, 18, 19, and 20.

72. HP/24. No. 178b. Letter, 5/3/30. Bolton to Viceroy; and No. 176c. Letter, 4/30/30. Mrs. E. Bolton to Viceroy.

73. FR 5/30(I); and PJ6/1897, 1930. No. 2313 and 2332.

74. FR5/30(II).

after a month of repression. Peshawar thereafter remained quiet, with the exception of sporadic picketing in the fall, thereby allowing the authorities to withdraw all soldiers from the city by July.

While Peshawar city was comparatively quiet after May 4th, the government's peacekeeping force was too small to end the agitation in the countryside. Moreover, its intelligence system no longer functioned. Until military and additional police units were deployed, the agitation could not be contained, and until its intelligence network was reactivated, the government did not know how to use the forces it had on hand. The necessity of operating in strength was driven home once more in Mardan *Tehsil* on May 30th.[75] A crowd interfered with the arrest of the Afghan Jirga leaders in the village of Takar and then accompanied them toward the *tehsil* headquarters. A small party of police and troops stopped it at the village of Gujar Garhi but could not disperse it without using force. In the ensuing melee, an English police officer was killed. Three days later, police and troops surrounded Takar; fighting broke out; and several villagers were killed.

During May, 1,222 Additional Police were recruited, and another 100 mounted men were obtained on loan from the *Wali* of Swat. But, as Pears later observed, he "could not have done anything with civil force alone, even if they had been five times as numerous as they were."[76] Preoccupied with tribal hostilities, the military could not transfer sufficient units to civil duty until June. While waiting for reinforcements, Pears concentrated his resources on the worst trouble spots.[77] Military units were despatched to the Shabqadar border region to deal with the Mohmand tribal threat. Other troops occupied Utmanzai on May 14th, a day after the Khudai Khidmatgars were declared illegal, and kept the village under partial blockade until the end of the month. Although the Afghan Jirga headquarters were closed, its leaders escaped to Charsadda, from which they continued to direct their campaign with impunity.

The task of piecing together a picture of the Khudai Khidmatgar movement was also problematical. Pears wrote that for two weeks after he took office on May 10th, he found "it very difficult not only to ascertain exactly what the situation was in the Peshawar District and adjacent areas but even to obtain the materials on which to frame an opinion."[78] Even after information started to flow in again, the authorities remained uncertain as to how the movement was organized. These doubts shaped their strategy. Pears explained to Lord Irwin on June 12th: "The general line of policy—in fact the only line I could take in view of the obscurity which surrounded the origins

75. *Ibid.* For the nationalists' version, see Sohbat Khan Takar, *Pakistan aur Khan Abdul Ghaffar Khan, al-Maruf Badshah Khan* (Peshawar: Shahin Printing Press, 1970.), pp. 93-96.

76. HP/24. No. 301. Letter, 6/12/30. Pears to Viceroy.

77. ID, 1930. No. 19 and 20; and PJ6/1897, 1930. No. 2452, 2563, and 2740. Also Isemonger Report, p. 23.

78. HP/24. No. 301. Letter, 6/12/30. Pears to Viceroy.

and basis of this furious agitation—was to hunt for the organisers and 'bottle them up.'"[79]

By the end of May, the government started to implement a three-stage strategy to split the agitation into smaller geographic segments, clamp down on its center at Charsadda, and then act against the remaining areas of unrest piecemeal. This approach attacked the nationalists at their weakest point, their poor organizational integration. The military first manned key roads, bridges, and ferries and imposed strict controls over travel in the Valley. Without the freedom of movement they had previously enjoyed, the nationalists' loosely structured, decentralized organization started to lose its coherence. On June 1st, troops placed Charsadda and the adjoining villages of Babra and Prang under a strict blockade.[80] All movement and communication in and out of the three villages were stopped for nineteen days until inhabitants surrendered political activists, furnished intelligence, and signed undertakings to abandon the agitation. When Utmanzai showed signs of resuming direction of the campaign, a military cordon was thrown around it on June 15th for another eight days.

Troops also started to act against villages in Mardan, but then the third stage of the government's plan had to be deferred. Pears explained why in mid-June:

> The rural problem . . . has been complicated by tribal risings on the border of the district. These risings . . . have been closely connected with the disturbed conditions of the district. In their turn the presence of such tribal gatherings on the border have aggravated district unrest. The two factors often act and react on each other, and the tribal risings have delayed the action required to deal with the rural situation by demanding the urgent attention of the authorities to problems outside the district itself.[81]

There was virtually no coordination among the tribes. They rose individually, which reduced the gravity of the total crisis but prolonged its effects. Pears complained that "as soon as we have weathered one storm here, we seem to have had to face another."[82]

The *Haji* of Turangzai's *lashkar* had grown to about 2,000 men by the end of May in spite of aerial bombardments.[83] It remained along the border until late June, but the presence of troops and the refusal of the Lower Mohmands to allow it passage through their territories prevented it from invading the district. The *Haji* finally withdrew on June 25th after Lower Mohmand *ma-*

---

79. *Ibid.*

80. FR6/30(II).

81. FR6/30(I).

82. HP/24. No. 301. Letter, 6/12/30. Pears to Viceroy.

83. For the Mohmand situation, see ID, 1930. No. 21, 23, and 26; and PS12/23. File 5. No. 3982, 4004, and 4355.

*liks* agreed in a face-saving gesture to press his demands with the government. In the meantime, the *Faqir* of Alingar, another anti-British religious figure, had mobilized a second tribal force in Bajaur with the aid of emissaries from Peshawar.[84] Utman Khel tribesmen, numbering over 1,500, filtered into Charsadda *Tehsil* where they established contact with local nationalists in early June. Air action stopped the flow of men, but it took ground troops to drive out those already in the district.

By the end of May, the primary center of tribal opposition to the government shifted south to the Afridis. It was an axiom of British policy that the Afridis were the most important Pakhtun tribe since they could mobilize thousands of men close to Peshawar city, the nerve center of India's border defenses, and astride the Khyber Pass. When they rose, as happened in 1897 and 1919, they threatened border security in a way that other tribes could not. By the start of June, pro-Kabul *mullahs*, who were in regular contact with Peshawar politicians, gathered a *lashkar* of 1,200 men on the edge of Peshawar District.[85] The tribesmen penetrated into the district on the night of June 4th, and some actually reached the outskirts of Peshawar city before being driven out of the district on June 5th.

Once the tribal situation had stabilized in mid-June, the authorities created two military-police columns to mop up the remaining areas of Khudai Khidmatgar activity.[86] One started in Charsadda *Tehsil* on June 18th by dispersing the Utman Khel *lashkar* near Tangi. It then moved through Mardan *Tehsil* and the adjacent Sam Ranizai tribal area before disbanding on June 27th. The second worked its way through Swabi *Tehsil* between June 19th and 27th. Both columns followed the same tactics. The troops surrounded a new village each day before dawn. The political officer attached to the column entered the village with the police, made arrests, confiscated political literature and party records, and extracted a collective pledge that the village would abstain from further participation in the agitation. In some villages, the *hujras* of the leading activists were also demolished. The entire column then withdrew to prepare for the next village the next day.

These operations reasserted government control in the last nationalist strongholds. Equally important in the eyes of the authorities, their Khani allies resumed responsibility for the day-to-day maintenance of order in the countryside after two months of having been intimidated and immobilized. The police henceforth served as a back-up force to handle situations the Khans could not contain, while the military reverted to its normal duties. While the nationalists thereafter remained on the defensive, their activities

84. For the Bajaur situation, see ID, 1930, No. 23; PS12/23. File 3. No. 3784 and 3910; and PJ6/1897, 1930. No. 3022.

85. For the Afridi situation, see ID, 1930. No. 21, 22, and 24. Also, PJ6/1897, 1930. No. 3138, 3219, and 3260; and GoI File 255/V, 1930.

86. FR6/30(I) and FR6/30(II). For the procedures followed by the columns, see NWFP. Swabi Column.

did not cease altogether. A make-shift organization was pieced together under secondary party workers who were less skillful and decidedly less influential than the arrested men they replaced. Without a strong organization, the nationalists could not recreate a sustained agitation in the face of the government's countermeasures. Each time they tried, their efforts were disrupted, forcing them to regroup on an even more reduced and clandestine basis. By the fall, civil disobedience had for all purposes degenerated into periodic episodes of picketing in Charsadda and Peshawar city. Each lasted only ten to twenty days, depending on how long it took the police to arrest the available supply of volunteers.

While the other three *tehsils* threw off government control for two months, Peshawar and Nowshera responded much less aggressively to the agitation. The government, therefore, left them out of its plans to break up the Khudai Khidmatgars on the assumption that once the rest of the Valley was subdued, they could be pacified with a minimum of official intervention.[87] This policy showed signs of succeeding until August when it collapsed under the impact of another Afridi invasion.

After their first attack had failed, the Afridis had engaged in two months of intra-tribal maneuvering before trying again.[88] Pro-government *maliks* initially blocked an attempt to raise a new *lashkar*, but when they failed to win political concessions from the Khyber Political Agent, the militants once more gained the upper hand. By August 7th, 6,000 men had gathered on the Khajuri Plain adjoining Peshawar District. After two nights, 2,500 of them had evaded the troops deployed along the border and slipped into the district.[89] Additional men were funnelled across the border on succeeding nights to keep up the raiders' strength. The tribesmen brought the administration in Peshawar *Tehsil* to a standstill for twelve days. The Government of India reported on August 15th:

> They at one time succeeded in cutting off all communications with Peshawar, and one party forced its way into the Supply Depot where it did considerable damage before being driven out. They have also made several attempts in small parties by night to enter the city and cantonment. . . . Their total strength is now reported to be about 1,200—moving about rapidly in gangs from 50 to 200 strong among the ravines and walled gardens and villages round Peshawar City. Military action is being taken against them; but decisive action is difficult at the present season, when crops are high. . . .[90]

People in Peshawar *Tehsil* treated the tribesmen as allies and gave them food, shelter, and information. Some even joined their bands, leading the govern-

87. FR7/30(I).

88. See ID, 1930. No. 25, 26, 29, and 30.

89. ID, 1930. No. 32; and GoI File 255/V, 1930. Telegram 2710-S, 8/18/30. Viceroy to Secretary of State.

90. GoI File 255/V, 1930. Press Communique, 8/15/30.

ment to consider shelling several of their villages.[91] On August 16th, martial law was declared in Peshawar District, and within three days, the military cleared the district of the remaining raiders. Martial law remained in force until the end of the year, although the authorities used its powers sparingly.

Following the Afridi invasion, various tribes continued hostilities, but the fighting shifted away from the province to the tribal area.[92] The Afridis fought on until October 1931 before they were brought to terms, while Sunni tribesmen in the Kurram Agency and adjoining parts of Afghanistan attacked military outposts and the Shia Turi tribe in August and September 1930. The other tribesmen around Peshawar curbed their anti-British feelings. Some of the Orakzais had decided on August 9th to invade Kohat, but news of the Afridis' defeat caused them to abandon their plans as impolitic. Still suffering from earlier losses, the Mohmands and Bajaur tribes did not respond to the renewed calls of the *Haji* of Turangzai and *Faqir* of Alingar for war, while the tribes in the Kohat Pass flatly resisted all attempts to draw them into the conflict.

## Civil Disobedience Outside of Peshawar Valley

Next to Peshawar, civil disobedience was most intense in Bannu. The agitation began in the town of Bannu but won an immediate following among the Bannuchis in the Kurram-Gambila *doaba*. The Wazirs in the outlying areas of Bannu *Tehsil* were politicized as the campaign progressed, but the Marwats in the southeastern half of the district remained quiet under the restraining influence of their Khans. Civil disobedience also touched off some trouble in the adjacent tribal area of Waziristan, although it was not as serious as the conflict around the rim of Peshawar.

The Congress, rather than the Afghan Jirga, organized the agitation in Bannu. The Bannu Congress was unique among Frontier parties in 1930 in that it bridged the province's urban-rural division. It began in July 1929 as an urban, inter-communal alliance under the leadership of educated professionals, but it quickly acquired a strong rural base by inheriting the network of allegiances the Khilafat Committee had assembled among Bannuchi *maliks* and religious leaders in 1919-20. The alliance between the urban, largely Hindu intelligentsia and the rural tribal *maliks* was not as incongruous as it might seem. As C.H. Gidney, the Deputy Commissioner, explained:

> In Bannu there is less cleavage between the Muhammadan urban and rural population than perhaps in any other district in the Province. There are few of the more influential urban Muhammadans who do not

---

91. *Ibid.*, Telegram 12-L, 8/10/30. NWF Peshawar to Foreign Department.
92. See PS12/23. Files 3, 5, and 8. Also, ID, 1930. No. 33 and 35.

> own land outside, and many of them have, therefore, a strong rural connexion and influence.[93]

Some of the Muslims in the town were actually tribal *maliks*. Others were linked to them through kin and tribal ties while sharing professional interests with the rest of the town's educated elite.

As in Peshawar, the composition of the nationalist forces in rural Bannu was influenced by the government's alliance with the landed elite. *Parajamba* (factionalism) was rampant among the Bannuchis, as Englishmen had observed from the time of Herbert Edwardes.[94] By identifying with the senior *maliks*, the government antagonized their rivals, with the result, as Gidney reported, that "practically in each case [village] the leader of the Congress movement has belonged to the faction opposed to the Bannuchi Khan."[95]

Bannu's religious leaders constituted the other source of the Congress' rural strength. Religious men were particularly influential among the Bannuchis and historically had played an active role in their tribal affairs. With the latent religious content of the nationalist issues, the Congress had no difficulty in recruiting a majority of them even before civil disobedience began.[96] As long as tribal *maliks* directed the party, religious men played a secondary part in the movement. Once the Congress *maliks* were arrested, however, they assumed control of the agitation, and significantly changed its complexion in the process. As long as Bannuchis dominated the Congress, it had little appeal among the Wazirs. Religious leaders were able to transcend those tribal identifications and thereby attracted Wazirs on a significant scale.

The government, then, was faced with an agitation with three layers of leadership, each associated with a successively wider sphere of activity: the urban nationalists with the district town of Bannu; the Bannuchi tribal *maliks* with the Kurram-Gambila *doaba*; and the religious leaders with the whole of Bannu *Tehsil*. As soon as the authorities eliminated one, the next assumed control of the campaign, spreading it over a broader geographic region and rendering it more difficult to contain.

District authorities first directed their punitive measures against the party's urban cadre, with very little effect.[97] The arrest of Ram Singh, District Congress Secretary, on April 8th was followed by daily processions and meetings in defiance of a ban on political activity; a complete *hartal* was observed on April 16th; and picketing of liquor stores began on April 20th. By the arrest of the last important urban leader, Habibullah Khan, on April

93. Gidney Memorandum.

94. Herbert Edwardes, *A Year on the Punjab Frontier in 1848-49* (Lahore: Printed under the authority of the Government of West Pakistan, 1963), Vol. I, p. 62. Also Gidney Memorandum.

95. Gidney Memorandum.

96. *Ibid.*

97. FR4/30(I) and FR4/30(II).

20th, Bannuchi villagers had started to appear at meetings and on picket lines in the town. After that date, leadership was exercised almost entirely by rural tribal *maliks* who confined the agitation to the town for the next three weeks but recruited their forces from the surrounding Bannuchi villages. On May 14th, troops occupied Bannu and closed the local political offices. In retaliation, Congress leaders imported more Bannuchis who brought the town's normal life to a halt for three days. Gidney reported:

> The presence of so large a number of villagers within the city was clearly dangerous and steps were at once taken to eject them. Further arrests were also made of the leading Congress leaders, all of them Muhammadans of the rural area. These arrests were made by combined parties of Police and Military. . . . In order to control the situation in the city and to prevent the influx of villagers into it the gates were closed. In this way control was reasserted and on the 19th May the 'hartal' was called off and the shops re-opened.[98]

In the next six weeks, the agitation was carried on throughout the Kurram-Gambila *doaba* on a decentralized basis by men with strong *gundi* (factional) ties at the local level. The government aggravated matters by cementing the relationship between traditional and national politics, as Gidney explained:

> . . . the enlistment of the active assistance of the Khans in suppression of the movement merely served to intensify faction-feeling, with the result that in many cases meetings were organised with the primary, if not, in some cases, the sole object of discrediting the Khans.[99]

By late June, the authorities had seemingly defeated civil disobedience among the Bannuchis, only to discover that *mullahs* had taken over the agitation and turned it into a religious confrontation. Gidney later recalled:

> The boycott of the courts was advocated as a step towards securing the introduction of Shariat law, while the picketing of liquor shops was enjoined as a religious duty upon all true believers of the Qoran. The [slogan] 'freedom of the Qoran' was unscrupulously exploited as a more general stick with which to beat Government. . . . The Wazir is just as ignorant and because of his ignorance and superstition just as priest-ridden as the Bannuchi and in both these backward communities the Mullahs found a fertile field for the dissemination of sedition.[100]

Bannuchis began to picket in the town of Bannu again, causing Gidney to close its gates and restrict entry until August 26th. In the countryside, *mullahs* kept civil disobedience alive in the Bannuchi villages and recruited

98. Gidney Memorandum.
99. *Ibid.*
100. *Ibid.* Also FR7/30(II) and ID, 1930. No. 32.

new supporters among the Wazirs. To stem the spreading unrest, punitive police posts were established in the most visibly pro-Congress villages; all government weapons distributed in Bannu *Tehsil* for village defense were recalled; licenses for privately owned rifles were revoked; and a magistrate toured the countryside with a squadron of police to prevent meetings and arrest people carrying arms.

These measures restored order among the Bannuchis by August but not among the Wazirs. *Mullahs* Fazli Qadir and Abdul Jalil, with an armed escort of up to one hundred black-shirted volunteers, had worked actively among the Jani Khel and Bakka Khel Wazirs since mid-June.[101] Under government pressure, the *maliks* of those clans expelled them from their territories on July 29th, but the *mullahs* only moved into the Hathi Khel Wazir country where they found support among the tribal elite. When that clan's *maliks* ignored government orders to arrest the *mullahs* and their backers, the military was called in. On August 24th, troops and Frontier Constabulatory were sent to break up a gathering at Spin Tangi. While civil officials negotiated with *Mullah* Fazli Qadir to secure the crowd's peaceful dispersal, a British captain set off a pitched battle. According to official accounts:

> Captain Ashcroft and eight other ranks were killed while ten were wounded. In the fighting which ensued some forty of the Mulla's party were killed and a number wounded. Seventy persons were also arrested. The Mulla himself died subsequently of wounds.[102]

In the manner of the Peshawar riots, nationalists represented the Hathi Khel incident as proof of the government's barbarity.[103] Once again, their version of the clash lacked factual accuracy but reflected popular beliefs. In the long run, therefore, the incident helped to politicize people in Bannu and draw them into the nationalist movement. The immediate consequences, however, were quite the opposite. Civil disobedience fell off sharply in the wake of the fight at Spin Tangi.[104] Thereafter, the appearance of troops, or even the threat of their use, prevented demonstrations. The number of times they were actually needed were few. Backed by the public's renewed respect for the government's power, pro-government *maliks* increasingly turned opinion against the agitation in the *tehsil.*

Civil disobedience produced unrest across the administrative border in Waziristan. Tribal hostilities fed on local conditions—the impact of the depression, dissension over the government's tribal allowances, and the af-

---

101. PS12/23. File 2. No. 7104. Memorandum 148-S.T., 8/30/30. Gidney to Secretary to Chief Commissioner.

102. FR8/30(II).

103. See, for example, *The Frontier Tragedy*. Reprinted in *Frontier Mail*, 9/26/65.

104. GoI File 121/II, 1931. Telegram 152/L, 9/14/30. NWF Peshawar to Home Department; and Telegram 155/L, 9/15/30. NWF Peshawar to Home Department. Also FR9/30(I) and (II).

tereffects of the revolution in Afghanistan in which the Wazirs and Mahsuds had provided the backbone of Nadir Khan's army.[105] But it is doubtful if these conditions would have touched off a conflict without the added impetus of the agitation. As it was, only a minority of the tribesmen engaged in any fighting and only under intensive pressure from tribal leaders and nationalist emissaries. Even before April 1930, provincial politicians had been in contact with tribal dissidents. Abdul Ghaffar Khan, for instance, is reputed to have sent Mahsud leaders letters urging them to prepare in case the province needed their assistance to throw off British rule.[106] Once civil disobedience began, numerous nationalist agents entered Waziristan. The most active was *Mullah* Muhammad Yusaf, alias the Bannuchi *Mullah*, who had been the Assistant Secretary of the Bannu Congress and claimed to be the envoy of Abdul Ghaffar Khan and Gandhi.[107]

Militants in Waziristan never intervened directly in the conflict in Bannu District because they were unable to win the general support of their tribes.[108] They mounted only a series of minor attacks on military posts and pro-government tribesmen in the tribal territory itself. In May, elements of two Wazir clans unsuccessfully assaulted the army post at Datta Khel. In July, it was the turn of the Mahsuds. Two *lashkars* representing sections of eight clans blew up bridges and besieged military posts for a few days but melted away when a troop column was despatched through their territory. Tribal *maliks* blocked subsequent efforts to incite the two tribes, and once the government restored its authority in Bannu after the Hathi Khel incident, interest in the nationalist movement subsided.

Among the Pakhtun districts, Kohat alone conformed to the authorities' expectations during the civil disobedience campaign. The Khani elite kept the rural populace quiet with minor police assistance, while the towns were the scene of a superficial and short-lived agitation which the authorities easily suppressed. Unlike either of its neighbors, Kohat was unprepared for civil disobedience. The Congress was confined to a Kohat city, while the Kohat Afghan Jirga was a paper entity without real popular support. A number of factors combined to mitigate against Kohat's politicization.[109] In the town of Kohat, the memory of a riot in 1924 blocked inter-communal cooperation between Muslim and Hindu nationalists and led most of the influential citizens to oppose any political organizing, lest it lead to further vio-

---

105. ID, 1929. No. 38 and 39. Also, PS12/23. File 1. No. 6498. Memorandum 665-S, 5/29/30. Griffith to Secretary to Chief Commissioner.

106. PS12/23. File 1. No. 6498. Memorandum 751, 5/7/30. Political Agent, S. Waziristan to Griffith; and No. 7715. Memorandum 309-S, 9/27/30. Political Agent, S. Waziristan to Griffith.

107. PS12/23. File 1. No. 7715; and PJ6/1897, 1930. No. 2740, 4755, and 5175.

108. For the conflict in Waziristan, see PS12/23. File 2. Also, Obhrai, *op. cit.*, pp. 85-88.

109. Best Memorandum; PS12/23. File 1. No. 6879. Memorandum 635-S, 8/28/30. D.C. Kohat to Secretary to Chief Commissioner.

lence. In the countryside, the government's Khani allies, and especially the *Nawab* of Teri who was the hereditary chief of the Kohat Khattaks, could still fulfill the policing duties the authorities assigned to them. Unlike Khans in Peshawar and Bannu, their prestige had not been irrevocably undermined, and they were not so bitterly divided that the nationalists could exploit *parajamba* to build a rural following. Economic conditions also retarded political organizing in the district. As the major military recruiting ground in the NWFP, Kohat contained a heavy concentration of families with some connection to the army. This created an atmosphere of goodwill toward the military which extended to the government as well. In addition, since most of Kohat was uncultivable, employment in the military, police, or bureaucracy was an economic necessity which made people reluctant to challenge the authorities.

Without a conducive political climate, civil disobedience in Kohat was brief and ineffectual. Demonstrations began in the town of Kohat after Abdul Ghaffar Khan's visit in late March, but their impact was so negligible that for three weeks after the Peshawar riots, the district authorities countered them only "by word of mouth and through reputed influential local gentry."[110] When demonstrations continued, the Congress was declared illegal on May 11th. The next day troops surrounded the town, while police and Frontier Constabulary arrested nationalist organizers and closed the Congress headquarters. The troops and police were withdrawn after one day, but when picketing resumed on May 16th, the town was cordoned off and reoccupied for four days. Thal was subjected to similar treatment on May 13th-14th, Hangu on May 15th, and the village of Darsamand on May 21st. These measures effectively ended nationalist protests in Kohat.

Civil disobedience aroused even less interest in the predominantly non-Pakhtun districts of Hazara and Dera Ismail Khan than in Kohat. M.E. Rae, Hazara's Deputy Commissioner, reported in September:

> No disturbance in the proper sense of the word occurred in the Hazara District at all. The Congress activity commenced on "Independence day" (26 January 1930) and continued to 16th June when the Congress Committee closed its office at Haripur and hauled down the National Flag. The only occurrences approaching the nature of a disturbance were hartals which occurred in Abbottabad and Haripur on 2nd and 6th May and the picketing of liquor shops at Haripur which commenced on 6th June and ended a few days afterwards. These events were entirely due to the activities of a few persons associated with the Congress and ceased when action was taken against those persons.[111]

---

110. Best Memorandum. Also see, FR5/30(I) and PJ6/1897, 1930. No. 2452, 2589, and 2711.

111. PJ7/17, 1931. Part I. No. 1423. Memorandum 1001-S, 9/6/30. Lt.-Col. M.E. Rae.

The nationalist campaign in Dera Ismail Khan initially involved only a small segment of the Hindus in the district town.[112] The picketing of liquor stores began on April 29th, but generated so little public interest that the authorities ignored it until late May when an incipient alliance emerged between Hindu and Muslim politicians. Then, police and Frontier Constabulary occupied the town on May 30th, closed the local political offices, and arrested fourteen activists. Troops blockaded the town for four more days until its citizens promised to abstain from further demonstrations, a promise they kept for the duration of 1930.

## Civil Disobedience and Reforms

In the short run, both the provincial and central authorities saw no alternative to suppressing the nationalist agitation. It immediately mattered less that people liked the government than that they obeyed it. Both, however, realized that order which depended solely on coercion was costly and in the long run, inherently unstable.[113] A permanent peace could only be achieved when the people accepted the government as legitimate. For the Government of India, the problem had an added dimension. Even though Indian Muslim leaders felt that their Frontier coreligionists were misguided in joining hands with the Congress, they bitterly denounced the government's authoritarian methods in the province. To defuse their anger and prevent the NWFP from becoming a catalyst for a general Muslim-Congress alliance, Delhi placed great importance on detaching the Frontier from the agitation.

Various schemes were advanced to pacify the Frontier.[114] Many consisted of tinkering with the administration to stamp out corruption, bureaucratic indifference, and abuse of power by petty officials. To alleviate agrarian hardships, Pears recommended a reduction of 20 percent in the land revenue for the 1930 *kharif* crop and the diversion of funds earmarked for other projects into *taccavi* loans. Theorizing that the religious antagonism aroused by the Sarda Act was the chief cause of the public's alienation, the provincial administration urgently, but to no avail, pressed for its suspension. Most attention, however, was devoted to expediting reforms. Suddenly, representative institutions no longer seemed unsuitable for the NWFP; they appeared imperative if the government were to conciliate the province and particularly its Muslim intelligentsia. From its all-India perspective, the central government also considered constitutional concessions as the best way to appease

112. PJ7/17, 1931. Part I. No. 1423. Memorandum 42-C, 9/18/30. Major W.K. Fraser-Tytler; FR4/30(II), FR5/30(II), and FR6/30(II); and PJ6/1897, 1930. No. 2826 and 2967.

113. FR6/30(II). Also HP/24. No. 200. Letter, 5/13/30. Viceroy to Pears.

114. See, Gidney Memorandum; GoI File 422, 1930. Note by E.B. Howell, 6/2/30; GoI File 275KW, 1930. Telegram 1652-S, 5/23/30. Home Department to Secretary of State; PJ6/1897, 1930. No. 2150 and 2754; and GoI File 255/V, 1930. Telegram 2302-S, 7/16/30. Foreign Department to Chief Commissioner.

Muslim opinion over the Frontier. Lord Irwin even asked the Secretary of State in early May to intervene with Sir John Simon to see that nothing in his forthcoming report "hurt Muslim feelings unnecessarily regarding their general position and particularly the NWFP."[115]

While the two governments agreed on the need for reforms, Pears cautioned against hasty promises on the grounds that the government had to proceed with care if it were to avoid unsettling security along the border. He also looked on Muslim pressure for reforms as self-serving:

> I must confess to a suspicion that in the minds of some highly placed Mussalman politicians there is really a desire to have an announcement (almost equivalent to a fait accompli) to be used as a counter in their bargainings with other parties.[116]

Delhi, however, not only wished to mollify the men Pears mistrusted but desired the very end he denigrated—the improvement of the Muslims' position vis-à-vis the Hindus. It also reasoned that the prospect of reforms would give Muslims an incentive to help pacify the NWFP.[117] Lord Irwin, therefore, overruled Pears and publicly endorsed reforms in an interview with a deputation of Punjab Muslims on June 4th:

> I am fully convinced of the importance which the people of the Province attach to constitutional advance and realise the desire of your community in general that a Province which is predominantly Muslim should not be denied the means of self-expression. . . . I can assure you that so far as I and my Government are concerned, when making recommendations on this subject to His Majesty's government, the natural claims of the Province in the constitutional field will be viewed with sympathy. . . .[118]

In light of the province's sudden militancy, the Government of India found the recommendations published in the Simon Commission Report in late June wholely inadequate. Under its proposals, the NWFP was offered only a forty-man council—half appointed and half indirectly elected by Khans, ex-soldiers, and local governing bodies—with powers roughly akin to those in the Morley-Minto reforms. According to a government despatch dated September 20th:

> A discontented frontier province would be a serious threat in the rear of any army operating in the defense of India. We would be reluctant, therefore, to adopt a form of constitution for the North-West Frontier

115. HP/24. No. 203. Letter, 5/13/30. Viceroy to G. de Montmorency.

116. GoI File 275KW, 1930. Letter, 5/27/30. Pears to E.B. Howell.

117. GoI File 206, 1930. Note by H.W. Emerson, 5/26/30. Also, GoI File 275KW, 1930. Telegram, 5/31/30. Home Department to Chief Commissioner.

118. GoI File 275KW, 1930. Viceroy's reply to address by the deputation of Muslim *Zamindars* of the Punjab, 6/4/30.

which would fall so far short of provincial expectations.[119]

Pears suggested, and Delhi endorsed, the idea of a legislative council in which 51 percent of the members would be chosen by direct election. They further agreed that the chief executive officer of the province should be a Lieutenant Governor instead of a Chief Commissioner and that he should appoint two ministers, one of whom would be a non-official. Finally, they recommended that the classification of subjects should follow that in other provinces, with the exception that matters relating to tribal affairs and imperial defense should be reserved to the center.[120] The Round Table Conference liberalized these proposals slightly in 1931, recommending that the elected element in the proposed legislature be raised to twenty-six out of forty and that at least one of the ministers be an elected representative.[121] These recommendations were accepted by the government and became the positive program with which it tried to induce Frontier nationalists to be more moderate once the NWFP was released from the straitjacket of political repression.

119. PP, 1930-31. Vol. XXIII. Cmd 3700. Government of India Despatch on Proposals for Constitutional Reforms, 9/20/30. p. 75.

120. *Ibid.*, p. 333; and PP, 1930-31. Vol. XXIV. Cmd 3712. Letter 3305-P, 8/28-29/30. Chief Commissioner, NWFP, pp. 332-36.

121. PP, 1930-31. Vol. XII. Cmd 3778. "Indian Round Table Conference. 12th November 1930-19th January 1931, Proceedings," p. 378.

# 5

## NON-COOPERATION, 1931-1934

While the tumult of the preceding spring had given way to a relative political calm by the end of 1930, a strong undercurrent of popular animosity nonetheless remained. Recognizing this, the provincial authorities supplemented repression with promises of reforms in an effort to soften popular opposition to their rule. Given time, their strategy might have worked, but before it could be fully tried, the Government of India undercut it on March 5th in the interest of a settlement with the Indian National Congress. The terms of the Gandhi-Irwin truce were extended to the NWFP over the strenuous objections of the Frontier government, freeing the Khudai Khidmatgars from political restrictions.

Abdul Ghaffar Khan and his associates concurred with the provincial authorities in not seeing the truce as a step toward the peaceful resolution of India's political problems. They treated it, instead, as a chance to rebuild their movement and prepare for a new showdown with the British. The Khudai Khidmatgars were quickly revived in Peshawar Valley and then extended into the province's southern districts. However, the movement's commitment to Pakhtun interests precluded it from appealing to non-Pakhtuns. Most seriously, its ethnic character helped precipitate a conflict with the province's urban nationalists for control of the Frontier Congress, which ended with the Khudai Khidmatgars firmly in charge of the party but with an important element of the 1930 nationalist coalition alienated from the independence movement.

Alarmed by the revival of the Khudai Khidmatgars, the provincial authorities quickly abandoned any hope of turning the Gandhi-Irwin truce into a permanent political peace. Throughout 1931, they asked for permission to suppress the Frontier nationalists, only to be turned down by the central government on the grounds that any step of that kind would destroy its accommodation with the Indian National Congress, an eventuality it was not yet ready to consider. Protected by this umbrella, the Khudai Khidmatgars produced an intense political ferment in the Frontier Province and especially Peshawar Valley. The authorities could only respond with ordinary legal restraints, which were ignored with increasing frequency, and plan for the day the truce collapsed. That occurred at the end of the year once the failure of the Second Round Table Conference convinced the Government of

India that a peaceful settlement with the Congress was not possible. Given a free hand, the Frontier authorities swiftly and systematically cracked down on the Khudai Khidmatgar movement and thereafter maintained a strict vigilance against any form of nationalist activity. As a result, the nationalists were unable to mount an agitation even remotely comparable to that of 1930. Officially, civil disobedience continued until March 1934, but for all practical purposes, it amounted to little more than a symbolic statement of defiance against British rule.

## The Khudai Khidmatgar Revival

On January 25, 1931, Gandhi and the members of the Congress Working Committee were unconditionally released from jail. Since Abdul Ghaffar Khan was not included in the amnesty, the Khudai Khidmatgars feared that the government intended to omit the NWFP from any agreement it reached with the Congress. In protest, they organized the first large-scale demonstrations in the province in five months. These culminated with a mass protest in Utmanzai on February 21st which clashed with the police, leaving two dead and ninety-seven injured.[1] The fears of the nationalists were not unwarranted. During the bargaining which led up to the Gandhi-Irwin Pact, the Frontier authorities urged the Viceroy to exclude their province from its terms. They were overruled, however, when Gandhi made the Frontier's inclusion a precondition for an all-India settlement.[2] Even then, Sir Steuart Pears balked at freeing the Khudai Khidmatgars. While the central government withdrew its repressive ordinances on March 6th and ordered the release of all political prisoners, Pears only lifted the restrictions on the Provincial Congress. Summoned to a conference in Delhi three days later, he subsequently recalled:

> His Excellency, Lord Irwin, pointed out that the Pact with Gandhi would be nullified unless it included the Frontier Province in its scope, and for this reason I agreed that I must face the very real menace of the renewal of the Red Shirt movement in the hope which was held out to me that the Pact with Gandhi might lead to such an improvement of the political situation in the rest of India as would ultimately react on this Province.[3]

1. See FR1/31(II), FR2/31(I), and FR2/31(II); and PJ7/17, 1931. Part I. No. 571, 677, and 989.

2. According to Mian Jafar Shah, he learned from Sir Abdul Qaiyum, the NWFP's representative in the Central Assembly, that the provincial authorities had convinced the Viceroy not to release the province's political prisoners. He relayed the information to Gandhi who told Lord Irwin that the Congress would reject any settlement that excluded the Frontier. Interview with Mian Jafar Shah.

3. PJ7/17, 1931. Part I. No. 2506. Letter 678/S.S., 4/27/31. NWF to Foreign Department.

On March 10th, therefore, he removed the ban on the Khudai Khidmatgars. The same day, Abdul Ghaffar Khan was released from Gujrat jail in the Punjab.

Putting aside his suspicions, Pears issued a statement welcoming the settlement and calling on the people of the NWFP to work with him to obtain the same rights as other Indians. The Afghan Jirga leaders ignored his appeal, for they viewed the truce as only a temporary, tactical halt in India's struggle for freedom. Working on the premise that the truce would end sooner rather than later, they set out to enlist the maximum number of members in the shortest possible time. Their party's organization was left in disarray and its chain of command so confused that its leaders often could not exercise effective control over its subordinate branches.[4] They could not even be sure of the size of their party, since membership lists, when kept at all, were never up-to-date.

Party leaders concentrated first on Peshawar Valley, the movement's core region. Their appeal for members received an immediate and enthusiastic response in the nationalist strongholds of 1930. By late March, recruiting, drilling, and processions were in full swing again in Charsadda, Mardan, and Swabi. In mid-April, for example, Captain C.W. Free of the Mardan Guides reported that more than half of the people from the town of Mardan to Katlang were "red or red backers" and that the nationalists were equally strong elsewhere in Mardan *Tehsil*.[5] Next, the movement penetrated into those parts of the Valley where it had won little support the previous year. Within two months, it had established an extensive party network among the Khalils and Bara Mohmands of Peshawar *Tehsil* and acquired a strong foothold among the Akora Khattaks, the largest tribe in Nowshera *Tehsil*.[6] Khudai Khidmatgar activity also resumed in the Sam Ranizai tribal area which was geographically an extension of the Valley but administratively part of the Malakand Agency.[7] The government had refused to lift political restrictions there on the grounds that the truce applied only to the settled districts. Regarding this as a breach of the Delhi Pact, the nationalists simply ignored the government's ban and organized on a clandestine basis in the area. Pears wanted to react strongly to their activity, but he was overruled by the Government of India which feared that he might provoke a confrontation with the Khudai Khidmatgars which would jeopardize the entire Gandhi-Irwin Pact.[8] Consequently, conditions in Sam Ranizai were allowed to

---

4. PJ7/17, 1931. Part II, No. 3475. B.C.A. Lawther, Deputy Inspector-General of Police, Intelligence Branch. Report on the Red Shirts; also ID, 1931. No. 25.

5. PJ7/17, 1931. Part I. No. 2878. C.W. Free. Report on the Mardan Tour of the Guides Cavalry. Also, FR3/31(II) and FR4/31(I).

6. FR3/31(II), FR4/31(I), and FR4/31(II).

7. See ID, 1931. No. 13, 15, and 19; FR 3/31(II) and FR4/31(I). PJ7/17, 1931. Part I. No. 2071, 2506, and 2661; and PJ7/17, 1931. Part II. No. 3232.

8. PJ7/17, 1931. Part I. No. 2427. Telegram, 5/4/31. Foreign Department to Chief Commissioner; and Telegram 763-L, 4/17/31. Chief Commissioner to Foreign Department.

continue unchanged for the rest of 1931 to the satisfaction of neither side. Unrestricted nationalist activity was not permitted, but the government could not eradicate the movement there entirely.

As the nationalist movement revived in Peshawar, the Khudai Khidmatgars assumed a prominent public profile, while the Afghan Jirga receded in visibility and importance. By April 15th, the NWFP's Inspector-General of Police conservatively estimated, 12,575 regular Khudai Khidmatgars had been enlisted in the Valley, and large numbers of additional people were active in the movement on a part-time basis.[9] The Afghan Jirga lagged far behind in numbers, and most of its members were simultaneously Khudai Khidmatgars. This organizational transformation was not wholly unexpected, for the Afghan Jirga had been envisioned as a series of small decision-making bodies, while the Khudai Khidmatgars had been created as a mass cadre to implement their directives. Additionally, the volunteers simply enjoyed greater popularity, as symbolized by the ubiquitous use of red clothing throughout the Valley in 1931. Finally, Abdul Ghaffar Khan turned them into his personal power base. Although he held no official title, he was the Khudai Khidmatgars' undisputed leader, a position he solidified by making his maternal nephew, Rab Nawaz Khan, their *Salar-i-Azam* (Commander-in-Chief). Due to his commanding position in the Frontier movement as a whole, the volunteers became an autonomous body, which received advice from the regular party wing, but took its orders from its own leaders.[10]

The nationalist movement in 1931 once more reflected the class divisions in Peshawar society. The majority of the rank-and-file were artisans and tenants, leading Pears to warn that the movement was "in danger of assuming the character of a mass organisation of the poorer and needier classes."[11] Few men from the lower classes occupied positions of party authority, and their numbers steadily declined at each higher level in its hierarchy. Leadership came primarily from the landed Pakhtun gentry, to which the lower classes deferred for reasons of economic power, social status, and tradition. As before, *parajamba* was a primary determinant of who supported and opposed the movement. In a review of 1931, the provincial administration observed:

> The movement . . . has done much to embitter social relations. Locally, the most important stimulus is to be found in village factions and animosities. A picture of this tendency may be seen in almost any village of the district where the movement is strong.[12]

---

9. PJ7/17, 1931. Part I. No. 2661. Note by J.H. Adam, 4/27/31. There was only one membership form for both the Afghan Jirga and Khudai Khidmatgars, which meant that technically everyone belonged to both.

10. Interviews with Abdul Akbar Khan, Amin Jan, Sher Dil Khan, and Sayyid Ashiq Shah.

11. FR3/31(II).

12. GoI File 4/7, 1933, p. 5.

The Valley's junior Khans provided the backbone of the nationalist movement. Opposition came from the once ascendant senior Khans, who still found it impossible to act in unison. The authorities hoped that their opposition presaged the emergence of an anti-nationalist coalition in the countryside, but that expectation did not materialize in 1931.[13] Mutual jealousies, an individualism which precluded their working within a formal party, and the taint of their past association with the government prevented them from mounting a credible challenge to the Khudai Khidmatgars.

Due to the enmity of the senior Khans, the nationalist Khans associated themselves rhetorically with the masses against their own class. Abdul Ghaffar Khan referred to the Khans as slaves of the British and promised that once independence was achieved, "the kamins would be equal with the Khans, there would be no difference between rich and poor."[14] The authorities seized upon this propaganda as proof of their lingering suspicion that the Frontier nationalists were communists:

> It seems clear that while Abdul Ghaffar and Abdul Akbar dominate the Central Committee of the Youth League, the trend of their policy will become increasingly Communist. This explains why their agitation is marked by race-hatred and class-hatred and by promises of redistribution of wealth, particularly of land, among all workers whether Pakhtun or Kamin.[15]

Abdul Ghaffar Khan and his associates, however, had no intention of introducing radical measures which would destroy their own economic power and social standing. Their rhetoric was predicated upon a redefinition of a Khan which narrowly limited the term to those in the Pakhtun elite who supported the government. Thus, its object was political, not social or economic—to discredit their Khani opponents and solidify their own support among their lower class constituents.

The Khudai Khidmatgars extended their field of operations in May to the NWFP's three southern districts where the nationalist cause had elicited little public interest since the Gandhi-Irwin Pact. On May 10th, Abdul Ghaffar Khan embarked on a two-week tour of the south which had its most striking results in Kohat. Since the old Kohat Congress was an urban, essentially non-Pakhtun caucus with few ties to the countryside, Abdul Ghaffar Khan bypassed it to create a new, rural-dominated Khudai Khidmatgar-Congress party.[16] First, he concentrated on the district's Khattak area, overcoming the

---

13. FR5/31(I) and FR/5/31(II); also ID, 1931. No. 16, 18, and 23.

14. PJ7/17, 1931. Part I. No. 2661. B.C.A. Lawther. Record of Speeches made by Abdul Ghaffar Khan since his release. 4/27/31.

15. PJ7/17, 1931. Part I. No. 2874. Letter 793/S.S., 5/6/31. NWF to Foreign Department.

16. FR5/31(I) and FR5/31(II); also ID, 1931. No. 19 and 21. While the district party officially assumed the Congress label, it was also called the Afghan Jirga or Khilafat Committee at times. Most commonly, it appeared under the rubric of "Khudai Khidmatgar".

opposition of tribal elders. He then moved to Hangu *Tehsil* where he organized among the Bangash and Orakzai, using the local Khilafat Committee as the nucleus of his party.

After his departure, his lieutenants in the district mobilized a powerful following among the Khattaks. In late June, the Intelligence Bureau reported:

> Khattak country is going red with great rapidity. . . . The chief leaders . . . claim to have enlisted many thousands of volunteers. There is no doubt that their efforts have met with an unexpected and widespread success. Village to village recruiting tours are being carried out and audiences have increased enormously in size; opposition on the part of Maliks and pensioners to the movement is half-hearted and the Nawab of Teri, its chief enemy, is losing his influence day by day as the acknowledged, if unpopular leader of the Khattaks.[17]

From their Khattak base, moreover, the nationalists threatened to link up with their Bannu compatriots to form "a solid block of 'red country' on both sides of the common border" whose influence, the authorities feared, would spread into neighboring Waziristan.[18] In Hangu *Tehsil*, in contrast, the Congress-Khudai Khidmatgars were confined to the Upper Miranzai Valley, while few members were enrolled in the country between the towns of Hangu and Kohat.[19] In the town of Kohat, itself, the movement was visibly weaker than in the countryside. The factors which had retarded its growth there the previous year still applied—the memory of the 1924 communal riots and the restraining influence of the city's traditional leaders. In addition, the urban-rural division, which had blocked the Congress' expansion into the countryside in 1930, had a limiting effect on its spread in the opposite direction in 1931.

The nationalists organized around local issues while minimizing their propaganda against the government toward which the people, with their extensive association with the army, retained favorable feelings. In the Khattak area, for example they concentrated their attacks on the *Nawab* of Teri, absorbing the factional network among the tribal elite which was opposed to the *Nawab*. By focusing on the *Nawab*, moreover, they tapped a reservoir of popular antagonism since virtually everyone in Teri *Tehsil* was affected by his right to traditional taxes which amounted to Rs 12,000 per year. In addition, a fraction of everyone's land revenue (-/1/16 out of every rupee) was given to the *Nawab* in recognition of his superior proprietary rights to the *tehsil*.[20] The nationalists' position was also strengthened throughout the district by

17. ID, 1931. No. 25.
18. FR6/31(I).
19. ID, 1931. No. 25.
20. VC, 1938. Vol. I, File 44. No. 18. D.O. Letter G.H.-89, 3/23/38. Cunningham to Viceroy.

support from religious leaders who told the public that the movement's aim was to defend Islam.[21]

Abdul Ghaffar Khan's tour also stimulated renewed activity in Bannu. Meetings, processions, and picketing became common; recruitment picked up; and Congress branches were reorganized in the villages of Bannu *Tehsil*. The Bannu Congress, however, was unable to sustain this tempo for long.[22] Activity began to subside in June, and Kohat displaced Bannu as the nationalists' secondary center in the NWFP. Although Bannu city served as the focal point of district politics, the countryside remained the nationalists' main source of strength. Since the Bannu Congress already possessed a rural base, Abdul Ghaffar Khan did not create a new party structure as he did in Kohat. He did not even start a Khudai Khidmatgar branch because Bannu had an indigenous volunteer force, the Black Shirts, who had gained wide public recognition the previous year. The District Congress was simply designated as the Bannu equivalent of the Afghan Jirga, while the Black Shirts became the district's Khudai Khidmatgars.

The party's core region continued to be the Kurram-Gambila *doaba* where Bannuchi *maliks* provided it with a following whose loyalty rested as much on *gundi* attachments as nationalist sentiments. In contrast, the party made little headway among the Marwats due to the continuing hostility of their tribal elders. The situation was almost identical among the Wazirs. Only the Hathi Khel showed any nationalist sympathies, and they responded because of the animosities created by the bloodshed of August 1930. The rest of the tribe rejected the nationalists' overtures, in part because their *maliks* opposed the Bannu Congress and in part because the Bannuchis, with whom they had a history of enmity, reasserted their dominance over the party after the Delhi Pact.

In Dera Ismail Khan, as in Kohat, the center of nationalist activity shifted from the district town to the countryside in 1931. After Abdul Ghaffar Khan's visit, an Afghan Jirga-Khudai Khidmatgar branch was created in Tank *Tehsil*. The other two *tehsils*, with their high proportion of non-Pakhtuns, proved less receptive to the movement and its appeal to Pakhtun nationalism. Nationalist activities in Tank became inextricably entwined with factional politics which revolved around the enmity between the *Nawab* of Tank and the Kundi tribe, with both sides competing for the loyalties of the Bhittani tribesmen.[23] The Dera Ismail Khan Afghan Jirga drew its leadership from the Kundis' leading family, the Khans of Gul Imam. To win Bhittani support, it deemphasized nationalist rhetoric in favor of parochial issues such as the tribe's dispute with the Nawab of Tank over the water of the Zam, the main stream in the *tehsil*.

21. FR7/31(II).
22. FR5/31(II), FR6/31(II), and FR8/31(I). Also ID, 1931. No. 21.
23. ID, 1931. No. 20 and 28; FR6/31(I) and FR6/31(II); and *Lahore Tribune*, 7/17/31.

The fact that Abdul Ghaffar Khan did not go to Hazara during his May tours was not a matter of chance. Cultural and ethnic differences left the district's predominantly non-Pakhtun population unsympathetic to his movement.[24] After months of labor, Congress workers from Peshawar city aroused modest public interest in Mansehra, the *tehsil* with the largest number of Pakhtuns, only to have it disappear when political gatherings were banned in the village of Baffa, the local nationalist center, in July. An Afghan Jirga branch was also opened in Abbottabad, but it never grew into a significant political force due to the town's non-Pakhtun character.

By the summer of 1931, then, a resurgent nationalist movement existed in every district save one. This alone alarmed the authorities, but what made the Khudai Khidmatgars seem so ominous was their intransigence. Their leaders viewed the Gandhi-Irwin Pact as a temporary truce, an interlude before a final showdown with the government. Rather than seek compromise, therefore, they exploited the protection of the settlement to whip up popular enthusiasm for the day civil disobedience resumed. As in 1930, their impact was most pronounced in Peshawar Valley. Demonstrations, meetings, drilling, and marching kept the countryside in a constant state of excitement. Picketing, coupled at times with forceful interference, harassed liquor and foreign cloth merchants and unsettled the Valley's market centers. Attempts to persuade government officials to resign their posts gave way in some areas to social ostracism. As disruptive as these activities were, they were overshadowed in the government's estimation by the nationalists' exploitation of agrarian unrest and their attempts to undermine the criminal justice system.

The depression was at its severest in 1931. Agricultural prices reached their nadir, and the credit shortage became acute. Capitalizing on these conditions, the nationalists in Peshawar mounted a concerted campaign against the land tax. They did not openly urge people to default, but their agitation for remissions of 50 percent or more produced those results. Collections precipitously declined, first in their Hashtnagar (Charsadda *Tehsil*) and Baizai (Mardan *Tehsil*) strongholds and then, as their movement spread, elsewhere in the Valley. Land revenue and water rate arrears, which stood at ten lakhs of rupees in February, increased in spite of remissions to well over twenty-one lakhs by September. Collection rates were cut to less than one-third of normal, and in addition, the nationalists undermined the traditional means of recovering arrears by enforcing boycotts of auctions held to sell defaulters' property.[25] In the rest of the province, by comparison, the economic situation was just as bad, yet collections remained at their usual levels since a political drive was not mounted against revenue payment.[26]

24. FR7/31(II) and FR8/31(II).

25. PJ7/17, 1931. Part I. No. 2874. Memorandum 590-P.A., 5/5/31. Deputy Commissioner, Peshawar, to Secretary to Chief Commissioner; and No. 778. Letter 86-S, 10/12/31. Chief Commissioner to Foreign Secretary; ID, 1931. No. 30.

26. FR6/31(II).

Immediately after the Delhi settlement, Khudai Khidmatgars in Peshawar also started to interfere with the police and courts. At first, they encouraged people not to volunteer information about crimes, but by summer, they had adopted more aggressive means to frustrate the authorities. They sporadically prevented police from seizing wanted men, tried to free arrested criminals, intimidated witnesses into remaining silent, and even disrupted court proceedings.[27] In some instances, they preempted the whole criminal justice system by bringing cases before nationalist *jirgas*. The maintenance of law and order had always depended heavily upon popular cooperation and specifically upon the ability of the government's Khani allies to police the countryside. The police were simply too few in number to cope on their own. In the face of the growing political excitement, the senior Khans once more proved incapable of performing their part of their bargain with the government, while popular respect for the police and colonial courts diminished. Crime, therefore, increased sharply over 1930, which had itself been a disturbed year. At the end of June, the government reported a 15 percent rise in all types of crime over the preceding year, while murders were up 29 percent, burglaries 19 percent, and dacoities 73 percent.[28]

These conditions confirmed the provincial authorities skepticism about the Gandhi-Irwin truce. After six weeks of mounting nationalist activity, they started to lobby for an end to the settlement. From the end of April, Pears and his subordinates repeatedly pressed for permission to use strong, punitive measures on the grounds that the Khudai Khidmatgars were a menace to the peace and security of India's borders. For example, Olaf Caroe, Peshawar's Deputy Commissioner, contended in a memorandum dated May 4th:

> The effect on this District of the Delhi Pact and of the license necessarily given to the forces then released has been to retard the machinery of District Administration to so dangerous an extent that recovery cannot be expected without a radical alteration of policy. In other words, big sums of revenue arrears . . . will have to be written off as irrecoverable and a permanent increase in heinous crime must be expected if steps are not taken to chain or remove those who desire to profit by the present malaise . . . the ordinary processes of law are not sufficing and will never suffice to restore authority unless accompanied by measures which will show the determination of Government to control subversive activities.[29]

---

27. For instance, see GoI File 4/7, 1933, pp. 6 and 9-12; FR6/31(II) and FR8/31(II): and ID, 1931. No. 11.

28. FR6/31(II).

29. PJ7/17, 1931. Part I. No. 2874. Memorandum 590-P.S., 5/5/31. Deputy Commissioner, Peshawar, to Secretary to Chief Commissioner. Also see, *ibid.*, No. 2506 and PJ7/17, 1931. Part II. No. 3147, 3452, and 3704.

The Army General Staff took a similar line, bluntly urging that the "Red Shirt Organisation be stamped out without further delay."[30]

The Government of India vetoed these proposals on the grounds that the problems of the NWFP could not be treated in isolation. In a message to Pears on July 23rd, the Foreign Department explained:

> Abdul Ghaffar Khan's arrest and prosecution whether initiated inside or outside NWFP would almost certainly create a situation where general action against Red Shirt organisation would be unavoidable . . . [and] it seems quite certain that general action against Red Shirt movement would cause immediate break with Gandhi on grounds peculiarly favorable to him.[31]

It concluded, therefore, that no action could be sanctioned. If the truce had to end, it wanted the blame to fall unmistakably on the Congress. Despite the unequivocal nature of its position, the provincial authorities continued to press Delhi to reconsider. Pears even telegraphed the outline of a plan for suppressing the Khudai Khidmatgars in reply to the Foreign Department's July 23rd message.[32]

In lieu of the decisive measures it desired, the provincial government applied Section 144 of the Criminal Procedure Code to large areas of every district except Hazara to curb political activity.[33] Wherever the evidence warranted, political workers, with the exception of Abdul Ghaffar Khan who enjoyed an absolute immunity from arrest, were prosecuted under ordinary laws. Fines and punitive police posts were also imposed as collective punishment on villages whose nationalists committed illegal acts. Revenue officials were instructed to use force to collect the land tax, arrest defaulters, and seize their property.

These measures reduced the general level of political activity in Peshawar Valley but at the cost of increasing the nationalists' intransigence. The Khudai Khidmatgars treated each new restriction and punitive act as a violation of the Delhi Pact. By July, Abdul Ghaffar Khan started to threaten to "recommence war against the Government" on the grounds that the truce had become a farce.[34] Conditions proved to be more tractable in the other districts where the nationalist protest was fueled mainly by local issues. The government had few problems in Hazara since the district's non-Pakhtun inhabitants were indifferent to the Khudai Khidmatgars. In the three southern

30. BP. "The Red Shirt Movement in the NWFP," p. 5.

31. PJ7/17, 1931. Part II. No. 3812. Letter 325(i)-F/31, 7/23/31. Foreign Department to NWF.

32. PJ7/17, 1931. Part II. No. 3812. Telegram 1993-L, 7/27/31. Chief Commissioner to Foreign Department.

33. See PJ7/17, 1931. Part II. No. 3147, 3632, 3803, 4342, and 4658. Section 144 prohibited all meetings and processions, except of a religious nature, for a period of up to two months.

34. FR7/31(I).

districts, judicious concessions on local grievances, selective arrests, fines, and Section 144 caused political activity to subside by September.[35] The government was also helped by communal rioting which began in Dera Ismail Khan city on August 12th with a quarrel between a Hindu shopkeeper and Muslim customer and spread to the other towns in the district.[36] These disturbances diverted public attention in Dera Ismail Khan from nationalist questions and alienated its Hindu population from the Muslim-dominated nationalist movement, especially since Khudai Khidmatgars played a prominent part in the rioting in some places. The minorities in Bannu and Kohat also became less receptive to the nationalist campaign for fear that it might lead to communal violence in their own districts.

The Government of India assisted the NWFP administration by asking Gandhi to restrain Abdul Ghaffar Khan. It pointed out to him that it might otherwise have to sanction a repressive policy in the Frontier. While warning that the Delhi truce would collapse if the Khudai Khidmatgars were suppressed, Gandhi repeatedly urged Abdul Ghaffar Khan to refrain from provoking the authorities.[37] His counsel had a moderating effect on the Frontier leader, for the two had established a close personal relationship which resembled that between a *pir* and his *murid*. Like a religious disciple, Abdul Ghaffar Khan implicitly accepted the virtue of Gandhi's teaching, copied his personal behavior, and placed great reliance on his political advice.

## Factionalism Among the Frontier Nationalists

In early May, Mian Abdullah Shah and Mian Jafar Shah resigned from the Afghan Jirga. Motivated by personal grievances, their defections had few repercussions, but they did foreshadow more serious conflict within the Frontier nationalist movement. Dissension developed as the Afghan Jirga and Indian National Congress tried to place their association on a sound organizational basis. Their pact in 1930 had laid down only the broad principles governing their cooperation, creating an amorphous arrangement which functioned satisfactorily only as long as civil disobedience subordinated questions of party position and power to the need for unity. Once civil disobedience was suspended, the alliance's ambiguity raised two interrelated questions which became the focus for organizational disputes: What should be the relationship between the Afghan Jirga and the old Provincial

35. FR8/31(II) and FR9/31(I).

36. "Report of the Enquiry Committee of the Rioting that Occurred in Dera Ismail Khan City on the 12th August 1931," *Government Gazette*, 7/1/32. For their political impact, see PJ7/3891. No. 4540, 4066, and 5248; and FR8/31(II).

37. PJ7/17, 1931. Part II. No. 3147. Telegram 1619-S, 6/29/31. Foreign Department to Secretary of State. Also ID, 1931. No. 25; and GoI File 303, 1931. Telegram 888-L, 6/18/31. Chief Commissioner to Foreign Department. D.G. Tendulkar, *Abdul Ghaffar Khan* (Bombay: Popular Prakashan, 1967), pp. 91-92, 105, and 114-18.

Congress Committee (PCC), and should the Afghan Jirga merge into the Indian National Congress?

The Frontier's urban and rural nationalists had always had an ambivalent relationship. Ethnic and cultural differences produced intrinsically divergent outlooks. Additionally, the urban nationalists felt intellectually superior due to their much higher levels of education, while the rural movement contained a strong streak of anti-intellectualism.[38] These factors alone would have created tensions between the Khudai Khidmatgars and the PCC. In combination with the dispute over organizational precedence, they led to an urban-rural schism in Peshawar, Kohat, and Dera Ismail Khan. The urban-rural alliance of 1930 only remained intact in Bannu, where the ethnic cleavages between town and countryside were not as sharp.

The eventual outcome of the conflict was never in serious doubt since the Indian National Congress' position in the NWFP depended upon its ties to the Khudai Khidmatgars. The PCC, by comparison, contributed little to its strength, as one Congress emissary wrote Nehru: "... the PCC shows a lot on paper, but Abdul Ghaffar Khan's [party] shows practical results."[39] The Peshawar city politicians who dominated the PCC, nonetheless, refused to be consigned to a secondary role in what they considered their own party. They argued that the Khudai Khidmatgars did not accept the Congress ideals, were exploiting the alliance for parochial and communal ends, and threatened the Delhi Pact with their militancy.[40] Underneath, however, their objections stemmed from their personal loss of power.

For three months after the Delhi Pact, Khudai Khidmatgar leaders were too busy rebuilding their own party to institutionalize their ties to the Congress. Coordination between the two parties continued on an informal, unstructured basis. The members of the PCC objected to this arrangement since it deprived them of authority over the rapidly expanding rural movement. When private attempts at mediation failed, Dr. C.C. Ghosh, the PCC President, forced the issue on May 14th by declaring publicly:

> I am much pleased to note that... responsible leaders of the Afghan Jirga now avowedly declare that their league is a part and parcel of the Indian National Congress and that the Khudai Khidmatgar are Congress volunteers. So far this confession lacks confirmation. I have made a thorough search through the Provincial Congress records and am of the opinion that this organisation has no constitutional connection whatsoever with the Congress and has never followed the instructions of the FCC....[41]

---

38. Interviews with Pir Bakhsh Khan and Abdul Ghani Khan. Allah Bakhsh Yusafi, *Sarhadi Gandhi se Mulaqat* (Peshawar: Manzur-i-Am Barqi Press, 1939), p. 72.

39. AICC File P-17, 1931. Letter, 10/5/31. Bal to Nehru.

40. AICC File P-17, 1931. "Report of Devadas Gandhi on the NWF Province," and ID, 1931. No. 24.

41. *Lahore Tribune*, 5/14/31.

In conclusion, he offered to resign his office in favor of Abdul Ghaffar Khan to facilitate the Afghan Jirga's merger into the Congress. Ghosh's offer was presented as a principled sacrifice for the good of the nationalist cause, but it was actually a strategy by which the old Congressmen sought to gain control over the rural nationalists. Since only the party presidency would have changed hands, Abdul Ghaffar Khan would have presided over a party executive dominated by Peshawar city politicians. The Peshawaris anticipated that he (and his movement) would thereby become bound by the will of their PCC majority.[42]

Abdul Ghaffar Khan declined Ghosh's proposal and nominated Mian Ahmad Shah, the Afghan Jirga's General-Secretary, in his place. After he was elected PCC President on May 31st, Mian Ahmad Shah tried to dictate to the PCC since he recognized that he would be outvoted if democratic procedures prevailed. He insisted that since he represented the province's major party, the Frontier Congress should submit unquestioningly to his authority. The Peshawar Congressmen, led by Ali Gul Khan and Pir Bakhsh Khan, the PCC Vice-President and General-Secretary respectively, not only refused but tried to give orders to the Khudai Khidmatgar volunteers.[43] Within three weeks, both sides tried to read the other out of the party.[44] Mian Ahmad Shah expelled Pir Bakhsh Khan and several other Peshawaris from the PCC on June 19th, and packed the committee with his own rural partisans. The old Congressmen retaliated six days later by meeting in a rump session and deposing him as PCC President. Abdul Ghaffar Khan persuaded both sides to rescind their expulsions at the end of June, but he could not mediate the fundamental issues dividing them since he was identified with one of the parties in the dispute. For the next six weeks, the PCC remained bitterly split and paralyzed.

The Peshawaris' relations with the Khudai Khidmatgars grew even more embittered as their rural rivals encroached upon their urban power base. The Khudai Khidmatgars moved into the city in June, with Dr. Khan Sahib, Abdul Ghaffar Khan's elder brother, serving as their chief organizer. They bypassed the Congress altogether and set up their own organization which quickly enlisted more members than the PCC had. The Khudai Khidmatgars found a ready-made constituency among Peshawar's Pakhtun laborers, who were disposed towards its ethnic nationalism, and especially among handcart operators who were angered by taxes which made their ordinarily marginal businesses precarious.[45]

Unable to compete on their own, the urban Congressmen looked to the Congress High Command for help. In June, they persuaded an emissary of

---

42. Interviews with Pir Bakhsh Khan and Amir Chand Bombwal. Also FR6/31(I).

43. FR6/31(I), and FR6/31(II); also ID, 1931. No. 26. For the new PCC officers, see *Lahore Tribune*, 6/31/31.

44. FR6/31(II), FR7/31(I) and *Lahore Tribune*, 7/1/31 and 7/2/31.

45. FR6/31(I), FR6/31(II), and PJ7/5612, 1931. No. 5612. Letter 1290-A, 10/26/31. O.K. Caroe to Dr. Khan Sahib.

the Working Committee to report on the potential political and communal dangers of the Khudai Khidmatgars. The next month, they prepared a report of their own which concluded that the independence movement would suffer rather than gain from the Khudai Khidmatgars.[46] Gandhi sent his own son, Devadas, to the NWFP on July 27th to assess the situation. The Peshawaris first tried to convert him to their side. When it became clear that he favored Abdul Ghaffar Khan, they telegraphed the AICC that he was biased and untrustworthy.[47] Devadas stressed the strength of the Khudai Khidmatgars in his report and their commitment to non-violence. He discounted the old PCC's objections as primarily the result of jealousy:

> The Congressmen find work taken out of their hands by the Khudai Khidmatgar movement which has taken everything by storm. They are reluctant to join the movement on grounds of prestige as also because they do not regard it as a Congress movement.[48]

In conclusion, he stated that the open friction between the two parties was detrimental to the nationalist movement in the Frontier and recommended that they be consolidated into a single Provincial Congress organization.

The Working Committee arranged the merger with representatives of both parties at the AICC meetings in Bombay in early August. The terms of the union, however, only prolonged the dissension due to their ambiguous wording.[49] The Working Committee had stated that while the new organization would be the Provincial Congress Committee, it could also be called the "Provincial *Jirga*." The old PCC argued that the party should be known as the Congress Committee, with *jirga* appended in brackets. The Afghan Jirga wanted the names in the reverse order. This was more than a semantic issue. It was a question of who should merge with whom. Members of the party that was dissolved would have to apply for admission in the other. Members of the one that remained intact would have the power to scrutinize the applications and run the new organizational elections. Acting unilaterally, the Afghan Jirga's Central Council directed its branches on August 23rd to hold new elections to the PCC. The urban Congressmen protested since the order deprived them of any further voice in the party. A second issue arose over the location of the party's offices, a point on which the Working Committee had taken no position. The Afghan Jirga Council voted to locate them in Utmanzai. The old PCC appealed this decision as well, hoping to keep them in Peshawar city where its strength relative to its rival was greatest.

---

46. GoI File 4/7, 1933, p. 6. Also, FR6/31(II) and ID, 1931. No. 25.
47. ID, 1931. No. 31.
48. AICC File P-17, 1931. "Report of Devadas Gandhi on the NWF Province."
49. The Bombay accord is quoted in Tendulkar, *op. cit.* pp. 111-12. For the controversy, see AICC File P-17, 1931; FR9/31(I) and FR9/31(II); and ID, 1931. No. 37.

The question which brought the dissension to a head concerned the authority of Abdul Ghaffar Khan. The Working Committee had decided that he should "shoulder the burden of leading the Congress movement in the Province."[50] With this mandate, Abdul Ghaffar Khan demanded that the old Congressmen resign from the PCC in early September. When they refused, on the grounds that he did not have the authority he claimed, he simply removed them. The old PCC asked the High Command for a ruling on the legitimacy of his actions and, in the interim, continued to function as a separate body. Abdul Ghaffar Khan, in turn, wrote to Sardar Patel, the AICC President, that the time had come for the Congress to choose between the two parties since he could no longer work with the old Congressmen.[51] While waiting for an answer, he once more demanded that the Peshawaris resign. When they still refused, the Khudai Khidmatgars took the issue to the streets. Repudiating an agreement the PCC had just reached with city merchants, they started to picket Peshawar's cloth stores on September 16th, including Dr. Ghosh's *swadeshi* shop.

With compromise no longer a possibility, the Congress Working Committee sided with Abdul Ghaffar Khan.[52] At the start of October, Sardar Patel delegated to him sole authority to reconstitute the PCC and ordered the old Congressmen to follow his orders. Abdul Ghaffar Khan dissolved both organizations on October 15th and appointed provisional officers drawn primarily from his adherents. Out of twenty-four members in the new PCC, only five had belonged to the old Congress. In contrast, Charsadda *Tehsil* alone provided six of its members, while another five were Afghan Jirga workers from Mardan. The rest were Afghan Jirga supporters from the outer districts. In protest, the entire old Peshawar Congress leadership, twenty-one men in all, resigned from the party.[53]

The Bombay accord also brought longstanding tensions within the rural movement itself into the open. Abdul Akbar Khan and Mian Ahmad Shah, who had served as president and secretary of the *Anjuman-i-Islah-ul-Afaghania* and Afghan Jirga, considered themselves the equals of Abdul Ghaffar Khan, but they had found themselves increasingly deprived of power after the Delhi Pact as he consolidated his own political position.[54] Their organizational base, the Afghan Jirga, had been downgraded in favor of his Khudai Khidmatgars. Their authority had been undercut by his reliance on other associates, most notably Qazi Attaullah, Amir Muhammad Khan of Mardan, and his relatives, Dr. Khan Sahib and Saadullah Khan. Mian Ahmad Shah

50. Quoted in Tendulkar, *op. cit.*, p. 112.

51. AICC File P-17, 1931. Letter, 9/9/31. Abdul Ghaffar Khan to Sardar Patel.

52. FR10/31(I). Also, AICC File P-17, 1931. Letter, 10/23/31. Paira Khan to Nehru.

53. AICC File P-17, 1931. Letter, 10/10/31. For the new PCC members, see *ibid.*, Letter, 10/16/31. Saadullah Khan to AICC General-Secretary.

54. FR6/31(II) and FR8/31(II); ID, 1931. No. 26. Also, Interview with Abdul Akbar Khan.

had also been offended by Abdul Ghaffar Khan's less than wholehearted support during his own dispute with the PCC. The Bombay agreement rendered these personal grievances acute by concentrating party power solely in Abdul Ghaffar Khan's hands. The two men also opposed the merger on principle.[55] They feared that Pakhtun interests would be ignored within the Congress. As a separate party, they believed the Afghan Jirga could maintain its leverage over the Congress since it could always strike out on its own if its needs and desires were disregarded. They were also apprehensive that their party might be religiously discredited by being identified too closely with the Congress. As it was, the party's opponents had already started to attack its members as Hindu agents and traitors to Islam.[56]

The two men broke away from Abdul Ghaffar Khan in mid-September and started their own Afghan Jirga, which they claimed was the true spiritual heir to the original Pakhtun movement. After the split, the two attacked Abdul Ghaffar Khan in the press. Abdul Akbar Khan, for instance, wrote in *Zamindar*, a Lahore newspaper, that "the blunders that have been committed by that worshipper of Hindus, Abdul Ghaffar Khan, by subjecting the Khudai Khidmatgars to the control of the Congress . . . [have] destroyed the future of the Muslims and Afghans."[57]

No other important leader and few members of the rank-and-file left the party with Abdul Akbar Khan and Mian Ahmad Shah.[58] Nor was their subsequent campaign to discredit their former colleagues successful, for Abdul Ghaffar Khan's personal reputation was at its zenith and the Khudai Khidmatgars' identification with Pakhtun interests was too strong to be open to question. In the long run, therefore, their defection had little effect on the Frontier Congress. The resignation of the old Congressmen proved more damaging since it significantly diminished the support the nationalist movement received from the Frontier Province's urban and non-Pakhtun residents.

After the dissension with the Peshawaris came to a head, the Frontier Congress still managed to enlist a substantial number of new members in Peshawar city, but the composition of the recruits demonstrated the inherent limitations imposed by its Pakhtun character.[59] Most of its members in the city were Pakhtun laborers and handcart peddlers. Few non-Pakhtuns, particularly those belonging to the city's predominantly non-Pakhtun, educated elite, supported the party after the Afghan Jirga-PCC split. Elsewhere, the party's lack of appeal to non-Pakhtuns was most vividly demonstrated by Abdul Ghaffar Khan's tour of Hazara in early November. Few new members

55. Interview with Abdul Akbar Khan.
56. FR5/31(I).
57. Quoted in FR9/31(II).
58. FR10/31(II).
59. PJ7/5612, 1931. No. 5612. Letter 1290-A, 10/26/31. O.K. Caroe to Dr. Khan Sahib. Interview with Pir Bakhsh Khan.

were enrolled; some meetings had to be cancelled due to local opposition; and those that were held were poorly attended, even in Mansehra *Tehsil* where the number of Pakhtuns was greatest. Abdul Ghaffar Khan was himself partly to blame, for he treated his audiences in a condescending manner. He maligned Punjabis although the district had largely adopted their culture, and he insisted on speaking Pashtu although few people in his audiences could understand it. At one stop, for example, he patronizingly told his listeners:

> . . . when we will have our Self-Government, we will have everything in pushto. . . . Therefore, I say that try to learn your mother tongue. . . . As you have forgotten pushto so you are no longer Pathans. . . . I say that the Pathans of Hazara have forgotten the language and lack the morals which a Pathan possesses.[60]

In a larger sense, however, it was Abdul Ghaffar Khan's message which rendered him ineffectual. His insistence on Pakhtun rights and values reflected the uncompromising ethnocentric core of his party. Few of Hazara's non-Pakhtun and deculturized Pakhtun inhabitants could be expected to respond favorably to his repeated declaration: "This country belongs to a Pathan [sic] and the Pathans will rule over it, and nobody else has a right to govern it."[61]

## The Collapse of the Gandhi-Irwin Compromise in the North-West Frontier Province

The last four months of 1931 were marked by a general expectation in the Frontier that a second round of civil disobedience was imminent. This anticipation, however, did not translate into stepped-up activity uniformly throughout the province. When the authorities spoke of conditions bordering on open rebellion, or the nationalists of popular resistance to British rule, they were generalizing from the conditions in Peshawar. The rest of the province witnessed a moderating trend in its politics.[62] The nationalists' strength in Dera Ismail Khan had been dissipated by arrests, Section 144 orders, and communal rioting. The Bannu Congress could not expand beyond its Bannuchi base. It failed to appeal to the Marwats and Wazirs, while the religious minorities withdrew from nationalist politics due to communal fears. In Kohat, the nationalists had reached the limits of their growth in the countryside by August, while political activity in Kohat city subsided after the Dera Ismail Khan riots and the defection of the old Congressmen from

60. Quoted in PJ7/5612, 1931. No. 917. Letter 299-P.S., 1/19/32. NWF to Foreign Department.

61. *Ibid.*

62. FR9/31(I), FR9/31(II), and FR11/31(II).

the movement. Making a virtue of necessity, the Kohat Congress issued instructions to its members in early September to abstain from further activity until the outcome of the Round Table Conference in Great Britain was known.[63]

The rising tempo of Peshawar politics was directly related to the fading hopes for the Round Table Conference. Neither the Khudai Khidmatgars nor the Frontier authorities had paid more than lip service to the Delhi Pact, for neither viewed compromise as possible or even desirable. Both had tolerated the stalemate the settlement had created only because the Congress and Government of India had insisted that all peaceful avenues be exhausted before reverting to force. At the end of August, Gandhi sailed for Great Britain where he spent two fruitless months at the Round Table Conference. As the news from London pointed increasingly toward its failure, the Frontier nationalists' impatience with the Delhi Pact grew and, correspondingly, their readiness to abide by it diminished.

In Peshawar city alone, there were twenty-seven major processions, nine large public meetings, and one *hartal* in September and October. Khudai Khidmatgars picketed cloth and liquor shops continuously, intimidated some into closing, and imposed fines on others for remaining open. They also tried to disrupt the trials of men indicted for political crimes and initiated a campaign to withhold payment of municipal taxes.[64] In the countryside, the Khudai Khidmatgars largely paralyzed the civil administration. Resignations from the subordinate ranks of the bureaucracy increased. The police operated with great difficulty since they lacked public support. Revenue collections continued to decline. In the Daudzai *tappa* of Peshawar *Tehsil*, the Khudai Khidmatgars openly set up a parallel tax system to collect the land revenue at reduced rates and funnel it into their treasury. Elsewhere, they were more circumspect, counselling people to contend that they could not, rather than would not, pay. The results, however, were still the same. Collections never rose above half the level of assessment during the fall.[65] The Khudai Khidmatgars also started agitating against the use of canal water on the grounds that the *abiana* (water rate) was too high. While few farmers could do without canal irrigation, the campaign did lead to a drastic reduction in popular willingness to pay the *abiana*.[66]

The government's attitude also hardened with the impasse in London. Before he left India, Gandhi warned that the Congress would treat any action against Abdul Ghaffar Khan or his movement as grounds for reviving

63. FR9/31(II).

64. PJ7/17, 1931. Part II. No. 5410. Telegram 1221-L, 10/28/31. Chief Commissioner to Foreign Department. FR10/31(I) and FR10/31(II).

65. FR11/31(II) and PJ7/5612, 1931. No. 5740. Letter 2867-9-P.S., 11/13/31. NWF to Foreign Department.

66. For the agitation against the use of canal waters, see ID, 1931. No. 45, 46, and 47.

civil disobedience.[67] Sir Ralph Griffith, who became Chief Commissioner on Pears' accidental death in September, nonetheless continued his predecessor's campaign for action against the Khudai Khidmatgars. His persistence began to pay off when the Government of India instructed him on September 25th to prepare contingency plans in case coercive measures became necessary.[68] Until that day came, however, it ordered him to deal with the nationalist campaign as best he could under the existing laws. The measures he could take, however, had lost their utility. He relied primarily upon Section 144 of the Criminal Procedure Code to ban political gatherings. At first, the Khudai Khidmatgars maintained the appearance of observing Section 144 by taking advantage of a loophole allowing religious meetings. Gatherings were held in mosques and given a religious coloration. By November, however, even this veneer had worn thin, and Abdul Ghaffar Khan had begun to urge his audiences to defy the orders altogether.[69]

The Second Round Table Conference ended in failure on December 1st, removing the last rationale for the Delhi settlement. So far as many Congressmen were concerned, the outcome of the conference demonstrated the uselessness of relying on negotiations to achieve their objectives. In the Frontier, as in other parts of India, events rapidly moved toward a confrontation. Abdul Ghaffar Khan conducted one last tour through Peshawar Valley in the last two weeks of December, holding meetings and reviewing Khudai Khidmatgar processions in deliberate defiance of orders prohibiting public gatherings under Section 144 of the Criminal Procedure Code. Griffith once more asked, on December 10th, for permission to suppress the Khudai Khidmatgars. In addition to his old arguments about deteriorating law and order, he cited the promise which Prime Minister Ramsay MacDonald had made at the close of the Round Table Conference that the NWFP would be given reforms equal to those enjoyed by other provinces as soon as possible. He argued that it would be impossible to implement constitutional changes unless he was allowed to stamp out the Khudai Khidmatgars and restore the government's authority.[70] This time the Government of India gave its consent because the failure of the Round Table Conference seemed to have destroyed the last chance for a peaceful settlement with the Congress.[71]

On December 20th, the Province Jirga (FPCC) officially rejected any po-

---

67. PJ7/17, 1931. Part II. No. 4501. Telegram 2307-S, 9/14/31. Foreign Department to Secretary of State.

68. PJ7/17, 1931. Part II. No. 5013. Telegram 2418-S, 9/27/31. Foreign Department to Chief Commissioner.

69. FR11/31(I).

70. PJ7/5612, 1931. No. 5861. Telegram 3133-S, 12/18/31. Foreign Department to Secretary of State.

71. PJ7/5612, 1931. No. 5905. Telegram 1/C, 12/18/31. Foreign Department to Chief Commissioner.

litical reforms short of complete independence.[72] Abdul Ghaffar Khan, along with his brother, Dr. Khan Sahib, was instructed to decline an invitation to a provincial *durbar* at which the governor planned to announce his plans for reforms. Instead, he was asked to go to the AICC meeting set for December 29th in Bombay to seek permission to renew civil disobedience. Confident of a positive reply, the party scheduled a mass meeting for January 1, 1932, to commence the agitation. Griffith decided to act first, as he explained in a telegram to the Government of India on December 22nd:

> I must impress upon Government of India that I now consider the situation critical. Failure to anticipate Red Shirt action, as proposed, will probably lead to successful launching of calculated Red Shirt campaign, which cannot but gather momentum once launched.[73]

The government's crackdown began on December 24th. It removed the Frontier Congress' leadership, depleted its rank-and-file, and overawed the general public. Only scattered and ineffectual underground nationalist cells survived, precluding the possibility of civil disobedience on the scale of 1930.

The rapidity with which the authorities regained control of events was a mark of the thoroughness of their preparations. The contrast with their unpreparedness and complacency in April 1930 could not have been more complete. Ten months of intensive efforts at gathering intelligence gave Griffith's administration a detailed picture of the Frontier movement. It had a list of almost 4,000 wanted men by December 1931, graded according to their importance.[74] Arrests began on the night of December 24th after the Government of India had issued three emergency ordinances applicable to the NWFP and declared both the Frontier Congress and Khudai Khidmatgars illegal. Abdul Ghaffar Khan, Dr. Khan Sahib, Saadullah Khan, and Qazi Attaullah of Mardan, the four top nationalist leaders, were arrested under Regulation III of 1818 and deported to prisons in northern India without trial. The next morning the assault on the Khudai Khidmatgars' strongholds began in earnest.

Civil disobedience had caught the government without a coherent strategy or adequate security forces in 1930. In 1931, detailed contingency plans existed, and the necessary manpower was assembled and briefed in advance. Six "civil disorder" columns were formed in Peshawar Valley, each consisting of a large body of police backed by a contingent of troops.[75] One was

72. FR12/31(II).

73. PJ7/5612. No. 5973. Telegram 27-C, 12/12/31. Foreign Department to Secretary of State.

74. Interview with Sir Olaf Caroe.

75. *Ibid.* For information on the columns' operations, see FR12/31(II), FR1/32(I), and FR1/32(II); and PJ7/5612, 1931. No. 6066, 22, 124, and 225.

deployed in Peshawar city; the others were dispatched to the Valley's five *tehsils*. All six began operations on Christmas day according to a timetable specifying which villages to search and when. They were also given tactical instructions which reflected the lessons learned in 1930. The troops invested each village before dawn. The police then conducted a house-to-house search to arrest nationalist leaders, seize their party records, close their offices, and collect revenue arrears. Elsewhere in the province, the government created columns as the need arose.[76] One was formed in Kohat to operate around the district town after a clash between Khudai Khidmatgars and troops left fourteen dead and thirty wounded on December 26th. Another was mobilized before the year's end to restore order in the Miranzai Valley, and a third was sent through Khattak country. Police dealt with the Congress in the town of Bannu without military assistance, but when civil disobedience started to spread to the Bannuchi countryside, a column was despatched to the region. The authorities in Dera Ismail Khan employed a column only in Tank *Tehsil*, while in Hazara, the regular security forces dealt with the nationalists without military assistance.

By the end of January, arrests totalling 5,697 had disrupted the Khudai Khidmatgar movement's infrastructure and eliminated its leadership from the central council down to the village branches.[77] Except during the provincial legislative elections in April 1932, civil disobedience in Peshawar henceforth consisted of sporadic, localized disturbances. Outside the Valley, the last signs of open defiance disappeared altogether. A further indication of the change in the political climate was the record revenue collection made in January. Part was recovered by force, but most people simply started to pay their back taxes on seeing that the government would no longer tolerate evasion. This trend continued throughout the rest of the 1931-32 fiscal year, which ended with 85.31 percent of the total demand being realized, a dramatic rise from the 48 percent collected the year before.[78]

The authorities started to let up on their sweeping use of force in February. The "civil disorder" columns were disbanded and the emergency ordinances withdrawn in all districts except Peshawar, where they were used sparingly for the rest of the year. The number of political arrests declined sharply. By the end of January, 2,616 people had been seized under the ordinances and 3,081 under regular laws. During the rest of the year, only 63 more were detained under the ordinances, while 2,254 were jailed under regular laws.[79] The government, moreover, started to release political pris-

76. FR12/31(II) and FR1/32(I).

77. Compiled from FR12/31(II) and FR1/32(II).

78. *Report on the Administration of Land Revenue, Land Records and Agriculture Estates under the Court of Wards and the Alienation of Land Act in the North-West Frontier Province for the Year 1931-32*, p. 2. The collections in January totalled Rs. 745,000.

79. Compiled from the figures in FR1/32(I) through FR12/32(II).

oners. One-third were freed by March and more than three-quarters by the end of the year.[80] Many of the freed men had served out their sentences, but almost one-third won early parole by apologizing for their past activities and posting security against future activity.[81] Many of their colleagues at large also petitioned to disassociate themselves from the nationalist movement.

Remembering the gravity of the tribal situation in 1930, Griffith's administration paid close attention to the reaction across the administrative border to civil disobedience. It depended primarily upon the tribal *maliks* to maintain peace, but just in case they failed, it also placed military units on alert.[82] Few of the tribesmen, in fact, were aroused by the renewed political conflict in the province. The Afridis had only come to terms with the government in October 1931 and were in no mood to resume fighting. The Wazirs, Mahsuds, Orakzais, and Kurram tribes were also reluctant to aid the nationalists aid. Overt hostility was shown only by the Mohmands and tribes of Bajaur.[83] The *Haji* of Turangzai raised a *lashkar* of over 1,000 Upper Mohmands in the closing days of 1931, but internal dissension, the threat of air reprisals, bad weather, Ramzan, and the refusal of the Lower Mohmands to cooperate all contributed to its dispersal by January 15th. With the encouragement of the Khudai Khidmatgars, the *Haji* of Turangzai reassembled his tribal army in March and gained support from both the Mohmands in Afghanistan and the tribesmen of Bajaur. The *lashkar*, however, was diverted into a traditional tribal feud. The Upper and Afghan Mohmands turned against the Lower Mohmands, who received government subsidies for protecting the administrative border, on the pretext of opening the road to the settled districts.[84]

Besides purely repressive measures, the provincial administration tried to rally public support to its side. Aid was forthcoming without solicitation from its old allies, the province's senior Khans, and from Hindu and Sikh businessmen. Therefore, the government's propaganda was primarily designed to win over the intelligentsia which had been hostile to it in 1930. The authorities emphasized their commitment to reforms and their inability to proceed with them in the face of the Khudai Khidmatgars' campaign. Sir Ralph Griffith set the tone on December 26, 1931, when he publicly declared:

---

80. *Report on Police Administration in the North-West Frontier Province for the Year Ending December 31, 1932*, p. 2. FR12/32(II).

81. By October, 2,709 people had apologized. GoI File 5/7/32. Diary No. 9112/32-Pol., 11/24/32. Total arrests in the same period were 7,966.

82. Interview with Sir Olaf Caroe.

83. See ID, 1932. No. 1, 2, 4, and 5.

84. Government threats forced the *lashkar* to disband in June. The following year, the government had to intervene militarily to protect its Mohmand allies. The campaign lasted until April 1935, involved over 30,000 troops, and cost Rs. 50,000,000. A.H. Byrt, "The Indian North-West Frontier Under Modern Political Conditions," *Journal of the Royal Central Asian Society*, Vol. XXVIII, Part III, July 1941, p. 285.

> Abdul Ghaffar Khan and his lieutenants have persistently rejected the path of constitutional advance. . . . They have deliberately used the Delhi Settlement to organize a movement, the success of which would not only cause chaos in the province but would make impossible any scheme of constitutional reforms . . . the local Administration with full support of the Government of India has been compelled to take measures to bring the movement under full control and to restore to the province conditions in which the new constitution promised by the Prime Minister can be introduced with the minimum of delay. To this, the Chief Commissioner had pledged himself and his officers, but it is clear that . . . in order to bring that promise to fruition it is necessary to restore order and respect for law.[85]

The intelligentsia, which was urban-based and heavily non-Pakhtun, responded to this appeal. Its members had been largely estranged from the Congress by the ascendancy of Abdul Ghaffar Khan's party. They were, moreover, eager for reforms, for they considered themselves the logical men, by virtue of their education, to sit in the proposed legislature and exercise the powers it was to receive.

The only part of the NWFP where the Khudai Khidmatgars were too firmly entrenched to be quickly subdued was Peshawar Valley. Although they had been severely weakened, the Khudai Khidmatgars there still possessed the vitality to mount a campaign against the April elections to the new Legislative Council. They characterized the reforms as a political sham and anti-Islamic, and told the rural populace that the government would use the voting as a sign of public support for everything from its repressive methods to increased taxes.[86] During the five days of polling, which started in Peshawar on April 7th, the Khudai Khidmatgars convinced many voters not to cast their ballots. They also blocked access to the polling booths, stoned vehicles carrying voters, tried to wreck polling stations, and assaulted candidates and government officers monitoring the elections. The climax came in Mardan on April 12th:

> Huge demonstrations took place at Katlang, Hoti-Mardan, Kalu Khan and Rustam, and it is estimated that about 30,000 persons must have taken part. . . . There was no fire-arms, but most of the men were armed with lathis. There was a great deal of stone throwing. Twenty-one members of the police force and many of the voters received injuries. . . . The crowd was most violent at Kalu Khan where the agent of one of the candidates is reported to have been seized and tied to a tree.

---

85. GoI File 4/7, 1933. Statement by Chief Commissioner, 12/26/31, pp. 27-28.

86. "The First Elections in the North-West Frontier of India," *Journal of the Royal Asian Society*, Vol. XXI, Part I, January 1934, p. 66. The article contains the firsthand observations of the author, a candidate. Though unsigned, the article was written by Mian Ziauddin.

> The police had to fire a few rounds at Katlang, at Mayar near Hoti and at Kalu Khan.[87]

The nationalist campaign sharply curtailed voting in the Valley. Out of the seven rural constituencies which were contested, the turnout in four was below 16.5 percent and in two others around 40 percent.[88] In the rest of the province, in contrast, the elections proceeded normally.

Although the boycott proved that the Khudai Khidmatgars were still a potent force in Peshawar, it did not herald a return to the popular ferment of the preceding two years. Peshawar Valley was never completely pacified before the Khudai Khidmatgars abandoned civil disobedience in 1934, but government vigilance kept their activities at a low level after the elections. The authorities gradually deprived them of their remaining leadership. With the arrest of Abdul Malik, the Provincial "Dictator," on September 26, 1932, all of the movement's original underground organizers, none of whom were major political figures, had been captured.[89] They were replaced by men of even less political stature and ability. When top party leaders detained in Haripur jail tried to smuggle instructions out to their colleagues, prison surveillance was tightened to stop them. The government also arrested Congress agents from other parts of India who, disguised as employees of reputable businesses, served as conduits for information, orders, and funds between the provincial and all-India party leaders.[90] At the village level, the government relied primarily on its Khani allies to prevent open nationalist activity, and when meetings or demonstrations did occur, it reacted strongly with arrests and fines.

The government's success in smothering civil disobedience can be measured by the Khudai Khidmatgars' response. Increasingly, government pressure drove them to organize activities at night or in places inaccessible to the police, and even those expedients frequently failed to prevent detection and retribution. By 1933, civil disobedience had become so singularly ineffective that its continuation made little practical sense. Its value lay only in being a statement of defiance—that no matter how complete the physical repression, intellectual and spiritual opposition to British rule could not be eliminated. In this vein, the underground party leaders declared on December 25, 1932: "Even if the Government hangs us, we shall continue Civil Disobedience (non-violent warfare) until the time when the Government agrees to all the demands of Mohatma Gandhi and Khan Abdul Ghaffar Khan."[91] The agitation continued fitfully until Gandhi suspended mass civil disobedience in May 1933. His announcement disabled the remnants of the

87. FR4/32(I).

88. PJ9/57. No. 1916(c). Letter 11330-Reforms, 5/4/32. Chief Secretary, NWFP, to Home Department.

89. See FR5/32(I), FR6/32(I), FR7/32(I), and FR9/32(II).

90. For instance, see FR6/32(I) and FR7/32(I).

91. AICC File P-16, 1932. Weekly Report from Peshawar District, 12/28/32.

Frontier movement, creating a split between the central committee which was ready to abide by the decision and dissidents who felt betrayed.[92] The differences were temporarily composed and demonstrations fitfully resumed, but dissension over the party's future reemerged by the fall.

The issue was ultimately resolved with the wholesale release from jail of high-ranking party officials in late 1933.[93] A consensus existed among those men that civil disobedience had become counterproductive and served only to stiffen the government's determination to prevent their party from reviving in any form. Rather than condemn themselves to a perpetual political limbo, they wanted to redirect their energies into constitutional channels where they hoped to win what they had failed to achieve through non-cooperation. Their view prevailed in March 1934 when the Frontier Congress accepted the Indian National Congress' decision to abandon civil disobedience for legislative politics.[94]

The provincial authorities, however, remained skeptical about the nationalists' intentions. From May 1933, when it became evident that the Indian National Congress would regain the right to act freely, they had lobbied for an indefinite retention of the ban on its Frontier branch. The events of 1930-31 had left the indelible impression that the Khudai Khidmatgars were fanatics who could not be allowed any latitude. "Red Shirtism," they told the Government of India, "was an excess—an 'abscess' on the body politic, the elimination and continued absence of which alone makes normal growth possible."[95] It was their pessimistic view that even if the Congress abandoned civil disobedience, the Khudai Khidmatgars would undo the hard-won peace achieved since 1931 on the first sign of government relaxation, embark on a socially disruptive campaign against the Khans, engulf the tribal area in turmoil, and unsettle relations with Afghanistan. In short, the provincial authorities argued, the Khudai Khidmatgars would recreate the conditions of 1930-31, when "the slightest unforeseen contingency might have led to bloodshed such as has hardly been seen in India since the beginning of British rule."[96] The Government of India accepted the provincial authorities' position, even though it realized that it would invite public criticism by doing so. When it lifted the ban on the Congress in July 1934, it retained the notification against its NWFP branch.

---

92. FR6/33(II), FR8/33(I), FR8/33(II), and FR11/32(II).

93. In July 1933, the province still had 1,600 political prisoners. They were freed at an accelerated rate until only 134 remained in April 1934. GoI File 4/7, 1933. Note, 7/1/33. M.G. Hallett. GoI File 4/4/34. Telegram No. 116-S, 4/11/34. Norwef, Peshawar, to Home Department.

94. FR3/34(I).

95. GoI File 11/1/34. Letter 338-S, 7/6/34. A.J. Hopkinson, Chief Secretary, NWFP, to Home Department.

96. GoI File 4/7, 1933. Letter No. 821-PS, 5/19/33. O.K. Caroe, Secretary to the Governor, NWFP, to Home Department.

The provincial authorities were equally adamant that Abdul Ghaffar Khan had to be kept out of the NWFP.[97] The central government deferred to their wishes on this point as well, externing Abdul Ghaffar Khan and Dr. Khan Sahib from the NWFP and Punjab on their release from Hazaribagh Central Jail in Bihar on August 27, 1934. In his first public appearance after his release, Abdul Ghaffar Khan gave a speech in Patna which the Bihar provincial authorities considered seditious. However, they did not prosecute him since they did not wish to seem vindictive by arresting him so soon after he had been freed. The Government of India took a sterner view. It instructed all the provinces to monitor his activities closely and prosecute him on the first occasion he said anything falling within the definition of sedition.[98] On December 7th, he was arrested in Bombay for a speech he had made in late October to the Indian Christian Association. He stated at his trial that he had not meant to break the law and apologized if he had done so unwittingly. Nonetheless, he was found guilty of inciting people against the government and sentenced to prison for two more years.[99]

By the time Abdul Ghaffar Khan was released again, conditions in the NWFP had changed significantly. The provincial legislative council had functioned for four years, giving the province a strong taste for legislative politics. Further, the Frontier Congress had been revived with the expressed intention of contesting the upcoming elections to the provincial assembly promised under the 1935 Government of India Act.

---

97. GoI File 4/4/34. Note, 4/23/34. H.G. Haig, Home Member of the Government of India.

98. Tendulkar, *op. cit.*, pp. 165-70.

99. *Ibid.*, pp. 186-92 for the speech and pp. 195-205 for the trial.

# 6

# THE START OF PARTY COMPETITION, 1932-1939

Repression represented only one side of the government's policy after 1931. Even before civil disobedience had resumed, the provincial administration had been preparing reforms in hopes of persuading people to adopt a more moderate brand of constitutional politics. The first installment of reforms was inaugurated in April 1932 with the election of a legislature which functioned through 1936. The new legislature paid little attention to nationalist issues, focusing instead on communal questions which embittered relations between the province's Muslims and minorities. Outside the legislative halls, as well, the issues and personalities which had dominated public life in 1930-31 were temporarily eclipsed because of political repression. Even after civil disobedience was called off in 1934, the provincial authorities remained deeply suspicious of the Frontier Congress and allowed it to resume public activity only gradually and begrudgingly, out of a recognition that they needed its support if the new reforms then being planned were to succeed.

The 1935 Government of India Act gave the North-West Frontier Province its first popular government in 1937. After the governor tried unsuccessfully to patch together a non-Congress coalition, the Frontier Congress, under Dr. Khan Sahib's leadership, assumed office. Over the next two years, party leaders used their control of the government, as well as their revitalized organization, to promote the interests of their supporters, the junior Pakhtun Khans and lower classes, at the expense of the province's senior Khans. Under this concerted attack, the senior Khans turned to the Muslim League. They were joined by the province's non-Pakhtuns who were alienated by the Congress' strong espousal of Pakhtun interests. Before World War II, however, the League was weak, badly organized, dominated by Khans who had lost their traditional social influence, and dependent upon a communal rhetoric which was ineffective in the face of the Frontier Congress' powerful appeal to Pakhtun nationalism.

## The 1932 Legislative Council

The NWFP was raised to the status of a Governor's province under the reforms of 1932 and given a legislature consisting of twenty-eight elected representatives (twenty-two Muslims, five Hindus, and one Sikh), six appointed officials, and six appointed non-officials. The Governor (formerly Chief Commissioner) appointed two ministers who sat in the council but did not serve at its will. An elected minister directed the affairs of the "nation-building" departments, while an official, called the Executive Councillor, handled law and order, finance, land revenue, and the administrative establishment. Tribal policy remained a central subject under the direct control of the Governor who served as the Agent to the Governor-General.

The elections to the legislature passed off smoothly in the second week of April 1932, except in some Peshawar constituencies, allowing the Reforms Officer to state that "the percentage of voting . . . compares most favourably with any province in India."[1] In the absence of the Congress, there was no organized party in the elections, which fragmented into twenty-eight separate races with little or no bearing on one another. Restrictive property qualifications limited the electorate to four percent of the population and ensured a legislature dominated by conservative, wealthy men.[2]

The non-Muslims who were elected espoused a sectarian philosophy characterized by a distrust of Muslims and a presentiment that the legislative council would prove disastrous for their communities. The preference of the minority voters was best illustrated by the race in Peshawar where *Rai Sahib* Mehr Chand Khanna, the Provincial Hindu *Sabha* leader, received a three-to-one majority over C.C. Ghosh, the former PCC President.[3] Khanna, a banker and urban landowner, had run as a defender of Hindu interests, while Ghosh had downgraded communal questions and campaigned as a representative of Congress opinion in a province where the Congress was identified with the Pakhtun community. Similarly, *Rai Sahib* Rochi Ram, a wealthy government contractor and the President of the Dera Ismail Khan Hindu *Sabha*, scored an easy victory over Bhanju Ram Gandhi, another former Congressman, in Dera Ismail Khan. Nationalist alternatives were absent in the other minority constituencies and the leading candidates fought the elections over who could best protect their communities from the province's Muslim majority.[4]

In the two urban Muslim constituencies, Pir Bakhsh, the former PCC General-Secretary, and Malik Khuda Bakhsh were elected on the basis of

---

1. *Report on the Legislative Council Elections in the North-West Frontier Province for the Year 1932* (Peshawar: Manager, Government Stationery and Printing, 1932), pp. 2-4. See PJ9/57. No. 1916(c) for the electorate and percentage voting in each constituency.

2. PJ9/57. No. 1485(c). Telegram 5-S, 1/1/32. Reforms Department to Secretary of State.

3. *Lahore Tribune*, 3/20/32; PJ9/57. No. 1916(c). Letter 11330-Reforms, 5/4/32. Chief Secretary, NWFP, to Home Department.

4. The winners included *Rai Sahib* Ishar Das Sahni, the largest timber merchant in the province, and *Rai Bahadur* Karam Chand, another banker in Peshawar City. PJ9/57. No. 1916(c). Letter 11330-Reforms, 5/4/32. Chief Secretary, NWFP, to Home Department. See Stephen Rittenberg, *The Independence Movement in India's North-West Frontier Province, 1901-1947* (New York: Columbia University. Ph.D. dissertation, 1977), Appendix I for an analysis of the elections among the minorities by constituency.

their nationalist reputations. In the rural Muslim constituencies, in contrast, one's nationalist credentials mattered less than the status of one's family and the strength of one's *gundi*. All the successful candidates were members or agents of the dominant elite in their constituencies, as were most of their opponents.[5] The victors included two hereditary *Nawabs* and one appointed for life, two *Arbabs*, three other individuals from families of tribal chieftains, one religious leader, and seven men of high tribal status. In selecting the council's nominated non-officials, the governor reinforced its conservatism by appointing five Muslims with strong traditional standing.[6]

Local considerations dominated the campaign in all constituencies. Tribal divisions or factional alignments determined the outcome in some, while religious issues materially influenced the results in others.[7] Most typically, the elections pitted the families who were the wealthiest and had the highest tribal status in a constituency against each other.[8] Three men associated with the nationalist movement were elected, but in each case, family and faction had a more important bearing on the outcome than voters' patriotism. For example, Habibullah Khan's record as a former Vice-President of the Bannu Congress was of secondary importance in his election. He was victorious principally because he had the backing of one of the two *gundis* into which the Marwat tribe was divided. Similarly, Abdul Qaiyum Khan of Safaida captured a seat in Hazara due to personal feuds and religious controversies which split the strength of the leading Swathi Khans in his constituency.[9]

After the council convened, its members coalesced into four groups.[10] Nationalist opinion was represented, rather tepidly, by the eight members of the *Azad* Party, with Malik Khuda Bakhsh as their leader. Nine Khans formed the Liberal Party, while a combination of nine professionals and Khans created the Progressive Party. The seven Hindus and Sikhs banded

5. Rittenberg, *op. cit.*, Appendix I.

6. *Ibid.*

7. For information on tribe and faction, see the examples of the constituencies of Hazara Central, Hazara East, Inner Mansehra, Nowshera, and Bannu South in *ibid.* Religion was a factor in three constituencies: Outer Mansehra, Nowshera, and Kohat West. *Ibid.*

8. For instance, *Arbab* Abdur Rahman Khan, who belonged to a collateral branch of the titular chiefs of the Daudzai tribe, was elected in the Doaba-cum-Daudzai constituency in Peshawar over two of the most prominent Khans in his tribe, Khalil-ur-Rahman of Khatki and Mughal Khan of Jogani. *Ibid.* For other examples, see the constituencies of Hashtnagar, Mardan, and Dera Ismail Khan East.

9. See *ibid.* Also, interviews with Habibullah Khan and Ghulam Rabbani Khan. The third individual with nationalist associations was Abdul Hamid Khan who belonged to the leading family of the Kundi tribe in Dera Ismail Khan. He won in the NWFP Landholders constituency where the electorate consisted of the wealthiest landowners (and some of the staunchest opponents of nationalism) in the districts of Hazara, Kohat, Bannu, and Dera Ismail Khan. Rittenberg, *op. cit.*, Appendix I and PJ9/57. No. 1485(c). Telegram 5-S, 1/1/32. Reforms Department to Secretary of State.

10. *Administration Report of the North-West Frontier Province, 1932-33*, p. 19.

together into the Minorities' Party. These parties had no organization beyond the council halls, no ideology, and little party discipline. The government could count on the support of all but the *Azad* Party on questions relating to the nationalist movement and the Muslim parties on communal issues.

The council's first major legislation extended the emergency ordinances issued to combat the nationalist agitation. The authorities were reluctant to dispense with the ordinances, even though the need for them had abated by October 1932, but they found them an embarrassment at a time when they wanted to show their readiness to accommodate moderate political opinion. They resolved their dilemma by incorporating the ordinances' extraordinary powers into the Public Tranquility Bill while reassuring the council that they would be used sparingly:

> It is not the intention of Government to use these powers except in cases of absolute necessity or to any further extent than is imperatively called for in the interest of the public peace. Their motive in introducing this legislation is in no way to interfere with constitutional methods of advancement but solely to ensure, to the best of their ability, peace and prosperity among all sections of the population of the North-West Frontier Province.[11]

These assurances satisfied most of the council. *Maulvi* Nur Bakhsh expressed the prevailing opinion when he insisted the measure was necessary because the Khudai Khidmatgars were "inimical to the best interests of the Frontier people."[12] The *Azad* Party tried to dilute the bill's provisions but without success. On October 25, 1932, it passed almost intact by a vote of twenty-seven to eight.[13]

While the government subsequently had to answer a steady stream of questions on politics in every legislative session, nationalist questions took a backseat in the council to communal bickering over patronage, education, and economic reforms. The pattern was set on the council's first working day, May 18, 1932, when *Nawab* Sir Sahibzada Abdul Qaiyum, Minister for Transferred Subjects, and C.H. Gidney, Executive Councillor, responded to a series of questions on communal representation in the administration.

Government employment had long been a focus of contention. Hindus and Sikhs had acquired a preponderance of the positions in the administrative services prior to World War I due to their greater education.[14] The British

11. *North-West Frontier Government Gazette*, 10/11/32.

12. *Lahore Tribune*, 10/27/32.

13. LCD, Vol. II, No. 9, 10/25/32, pp. 777-78. Only a few sections of the act were ever used. They were applied in Peshawar District from 1933 to September 1937 and in Hazara in 1935-36.

14. HM File No. 1b. "Summary Statement of the Hindu Minority of the North-West Frontier Province." See Lal Baha, *N.-W.F.P. Administration Under British Rule, 1901-1919* (Islamabad: National Commission on Historical and Cultural Research, 1978), Ch. VII for an account of educational developments in the province through World War I.

started to redress the communal balance after the war, but at a pace which satisfied no one. Muslims found the rate of change too slow, while the minorities were alarmed by any reservation of jobs on a communal basis. The position of Hindus and Sikhs in 1932 ranged from underrepresentation in some government departments to a majority in others, but overall, they still occupied between 20 and 30 percent of the total posts in the administration.[15] These facts, however, counted for less during the legislative debates than the subjective impressions of the members of the Legislative Council (MLCs). The minorities viewed their portion of the services as small and shrinking, while the Muslims considered it much too large. The minorities anticipated that the Muslim MLCs would try to speed up the pace at which they were being displaced, while the Muslims wanted to use the council to win what they regarded their fair share of administrative jobs.

At the heart of the dispute were two questions: What should be the communal composition of the administration and how should positions be filled? The minorities remained deliberately vague on the first, saying only that their percentage should reflect their education, economic importance, and loyalty to the empire instead of their numbers. On the second, they asked for safeguards against discrimination and recommended that most recruitment be by competitive examination.[16] Such a procedure would have ensured heavy Hindu and Sikh representation since it placed a premium on education, an area in which they excelled. For precisely that reason, Muslim MLCs denounced recruitment by exams as "a sugar-coated pill of communalism."[17] They wanted the services divided on a strict communal basis with quotas conforming to population percentages.

The issue of jobs never provoked a major council debate. Instead, there was constant skirmishing over the communal proportions of specific departments. Usually, these clashes were instigated by the representatives of the minorities who were convinced that their communities were being eliminated from public service but felt powerless to do anything more than monitor recruiting practices and complain of victimization. Muslims raised the issue less frequently, but they showed how drastic a change they wanted when they did. In October 1932, *Maulvi* Nur Bakhsh urged that the Agriculture Department be reserved for Muslims since they were the province's farmers. The next spring, Ghulam Rabbani Khan demanded more Muslim appointments in the Irrigation Department on similar grounds, even though they already held over three-quarters of its posts.[18] The controversy gener-

15. The estimate is based on the statistics revealed in the question periods in LCD, Vol. I and II.

16. LCD, Vol. VIII, No. 5, 3/9/35, p. 172.

17. LCD, Vol. II, No. 2, 10/12/32, p. 164. For the Hindu position, see HM File No. 1b. "Summary Statement of the Hindu Minority of the North-West Frontier Province." Also, Diwan Chand Obhrai, *The Evolution of North-West Frontier Province* (Peshawar: The London Book Co., 1938), p. 278, and LCD, Vol. II, No. 2, 10/12/32, pp. 156 and 170.

18. LCD, Vol. II, No. 1, 10/10/32, pp. 3-4; and Vol. III, No. 7, 3/20/33, p. 491.

ated verbal acrimony but few practical results. A prima facie case can be made that the communal balance in some departments was altered, but the non-Muslims' percentage in the administration as a whole did not drop appreciably. A list of employees in the Transferred Departments shows that they still occupied 469, or 21.24 percent, of the 2,162 posts in November 1935.[19]

In addition to their fears over jobs, the minorities were apprehensive that the Education Department, on Sir Abdul Qaiyum's orders, would financially discriminate against their communities. The NWFP had three colleges, of which Islamia College in Peshawar had been founded by Muslims, under Sir Abdul Qaiyum's leadership, and Vedic Bharatriya College in Dera Ismail Khan by Hindus. Islamia regularly received grants ten times larger than V.B. College, in large part because it had been designated as the province's science college. The minorities did not object to it having the science program, but they did complain that V.B. College was being unfairly deprived of funds so that Islamia could be lavishly financed.[20] They also suspected that Sir Abdul Qaiyum had devised a discriminatory policy for pre-college education, even though non-Muslim private schools received two-thirds of the government's grants-in-aid.[21] They were certain he was guilty of favoritism in distributing scholarships since the minorities' proportion was smaller than their percentage of the educated inhabitants of the province.[22] (It was, however, larger than their percentage of the NWFP's total population.)

These financial issues were often ambiguous since they involved the manipulation of statistics. They did not, therefore, evoke the same sort of visceral reaction among the minorities as the removal of certain subjects from the province's educational curriculum. Sir Abdul Qaiyum ordered in March 1933 that the Sanskrit post in Peshawar Government High School be abolished, explaining that the decision had been pending when he became minister and that he had endorsed it only after determining that a sufficient number of students were not interested in the subject to warrant its continuation.[23] Mehr Chand Khanna, nonetheless, accused him of turning the school into a Muslim institution and attacking "Hindu culture of which Sanskrit is the main foundation."[24]

The Sanskrit dispute was a dress rehearsal for a much more bitter controversy. As part of an effort to rationalize the province's school system, an administrative circular was issued in October 1935, making Urdu or English the mandatory language of instruction from the third standard in govern-

19. Figures computed from statistics in LCD, Vol. IX, No. 3, 11/3/35, pp. 79-83.
20. LCD, Vol. III, No. 5, 3/17/33, p. 233; and No. 11, 3/25/33, pp. 781 and 794.
21. LCD, Vol. III, No. 5, 3/17/33, pp. 242; and No. 7, 3/20/33, pp. 506-7.
22. LCD, Vol. VIII, No. 2, 3/6/35, p. 24.
23. LCD, Vol. III, No. 11, 3/25/33, p. 794.
24. *Ibid.*

ment-aided schools for girls. A transition period of five years was allowed, after which any school not complying would forfeit government support. Non-Muslims denounced the order since it prevented education in Hindi and Gurmukhi, even though it had been unanimously recommended by a committee which included two minority MLCs and did not bar the teaching of Hindi and Gurmukhi as second languages. A similar order, moreover, had already been implemented in boys' schools without protest.[25] The circular hardly seemed, therefore, to warrant the reaction it provoked. But to the non-Muslims, it symbolized their sense of having been victimized by reforms and their fears that the future would only get worse. Ganpatrai, a Frontier Hindu serving as the Secretary of the All-India Hindu *Mahasabha*, expressed their feelings in an open letter to the government:

> This is, to say the least, the climax of Muslim communalism which has overwhelmed the administration of the Frontier Province under the present regime ever since the reforms were unceremoniously introduced during the Round Table Conferences. These memoranda forecast the fate of the Hindu and Sikh minorities in that Province when full Provincial Autonomy will be introduced under the new Government of India Act.[26]

Having turned the circular into the embodiment of their grievances and fears, the minorities' fight for its rescission became bitter and uncompromising. A Hindi-Gurmukhi Defence Committee was formed under the leadership of the minority MLCs, which orchestrated a flood of protests and petitions from Frontier groups, messages of support from organizations in the rest of India, deputations, marches, and *hartals*. All the minority MLCs boycotted the legislature beginning in the fall of 1935 on the grounds that the circular was "a grave menace and a direct challenge to our religion and culture . . . [and] will constitute an intellectual oppression of the worst kind."[27]

The campaign provided an outlet for the minorities' pent-up frustrations and feelings of victimization, but on balance, it contributed to the very force they feared, Muslim hostility. Most politically aware Muslims, including Frontier Congressmen, were antagonized by the issue. They suspected, as the *Khyber Mail* stated, that the protest had a more sinister objective than the mere withdrawal of the circular:

> It appears that the real struggle is not between Urdu and Hindi and Gurmukhi. . . . It is rather a political struggle against the much criticised reforms to which the Hindu and Sikh minority in the NWF Prov-

25. *Lahore Tribune*, 10/25/35 and 11/13/35; and *Khyber Mail*, 1/5/36.
26. *Lahore Tribune*, 10/30/36.
27. LCD, Vol. IX, No. 1, 11/4/35, p. 15. For a description of the agitation, see Obhrai, *op. cit.*, pp. 266-71.

> ince do not yet seem to have reconciled themselves. They fought tooth and nail against the introduction of the first installment of reforms and succeeded in obtaining privileges to which their population strength did not give them a right. . . . Now perhaps they want to repeat their experiment on the eve of the advent of Provincial Autonomy.[28]

For its part, the government considered the protest an irrational outburst over a routine bureaucratic measure and refused to make any concessions.[29] The circular, therefore, remained in effect until politics intervened in 1937 when Sir Abdul Qaiyum rescinded the order in return for minority support for a ministry he had formed under the new Government of India Act.[30]

When jobs and education were not at issue, economics injected communalism into the legislature's proceedings. The two sides found themselves in an adversarial relationship since the province's agriculturists were almost all Muslim while non-Muslims were mainly traders and moneylenders. Measures beneficial to one community commonly carried costs for the other, even when the connection was not intended. For instance, Muslim MLCs offered a non-official resolution in October 1932, calling for a 50 percent remission in the land revenue.[31] The minorities opposed the motion for fear that the government would compensate for the lost revenue by raising the income and excise taxes which fell disproportionately on their communities.

The most heated exchanges over economic issues occurred over three bills the administration introduced in 1934 to protect agriculturists from moneylenders and give them debt relief.[32] The Usurious Loans Amendment Bill fixed a ceiling of interest which varied from 12 to 25 percent. The Regulation of Accounts Bill required moneylenders to send their debtors clear statements of what they owned at regular intervals. The Redemption of Mortgages Bill provided for the summary settlement of mortgages of less than Rs. 1,000 on holdings of less than thirty acres.

These bills were the focus of a yearlong communal debate before they were finally passed in March 1935. Although they strongly supported the measures, many Muslims considered them too modest. *Maulvi* Nur Bakhsh, for example, introduced a non-official resolution in March 1934 to "rescue zamindars from village moneylenders." He told the council:

> They [moneylenders] don't advance money to earn simple interest only. They don't even care for the early recovery of their advances. In advancing money, their chief object is to get him [the zamindar] entangled in such an extent that he may not be able to disengage from their clutches for generations. . . . What should be done to assist the zamin-

28. *Khyber Mail*, 1/19/36.
29. *Lahore Tribune*, 11/13/35.
30. *Ibid.*, 11/12/36 and 7/4/37.
31. LCD, Vol. II, No. 4, 10/18/32.
32. LCD, Vol. V, No. 2, 3/7/34, pp. 84-86.

dars? There is no remedy excepting cancellation of all previous loans.[33]

Non-Muslims condemned the bills for allegedly making a scapegoat out of an already oppressed minority business community.[34] They argued that the repeal of the Punjab Land Alienation Act, which prohibited the transfer of land to non-agriculturists, would much more effectively aid agriculturists, restore their credit, and drive down interest rates since Hindu and Sikh moneylenders would then be able to accept property as collateral for loans. Such a step would also be morally defensible, they contended, since it would restore the non-Muslims' right to own land instead of punishing them for conditions which were not their fault.[35]

## The Revival of the Frontier Congress and the 1937 Elections

From 1934, the reemergence of the Frontier Congress increasingly diverted public interest away from the Legislative Council. Since the party remained technically illegal, the speed and manner in which it reasserted itself depended upon the government's good will. The provincial authorities slowly, and only with considerable misgivings, relaxed their restrictions on the party in the interest of securing its cooperation in the new reforms granted under the 1935 Government of India Act. Thus, the three years before the 1937 elections were characterized by the Congress probing to determine, exploit, and expand the imprecisely defined limits on its activities, while the authorities closely monitored its efforts to ensure that it did not exceed what they regarded as proper political bounds.

Tempted by the vacuum created by the government's suppression of civil disobedience, a group of Peshawar city nationalists, led by Pir Bakhsh, briefly bid in the spring of 1934 for the party power they had lost in 1931. Their attempted coup failed when Gandhi declared that no new organization would be formed without Abdul Ghaffar Khan's consent.[36] Leadership passed in his absence to his recently freed lieutenants who acted with great caution to avoid renewed repression. Instead of reconstructing a formal party organization, they initially worked informally and under the cover of non-political causes to reestablish the network of political ties which had made the Khudai Khidmatgars so formidable.

When the government ignored these low-keyed activities, they decided to test its receptivity to a more formal party effort in September 1934 by putting up a candidate for a bye-election to the Legislative Council in Dera Is-

33. LCD, Vol. V, No. 7, 3/13/34, pp. 310-12.

34. For a sample of the minorities' arguments, see LCD, Vol. V, No. 4; Vol. VI, No. 14; and Vol. VIII, No. 8 and 9.

35. LCD, Vol. VI, No. 1, 11/2/34, pp. 40-41.

36. FR5/35(II), FR6/34(I), FR7/34(II), FR8/34(I), and FR8/34(II).

mail Khan.[37] The election officer rejected his papers because he had been imprisoned in 1932, but the provincial government reversed the decision in keeping with its policy of encouraging Congress participation in constitutional politics. Although the party refused to resume campaigning, its leaders found the episode encouraging since it established that Congress candidates would be tolerated in future elections. They, therefore, went ahead with plans, formulated in August 1934 at the first meeting of provincial leaders since 1931, to contest the provincial seat to the Central Legislative Assembly. Dr. Khan Sahib, the party's candidate, could not campaign in person since he had been barred on his release from prison in late August from entering the NWFP. The Frontier Congress was also hampered by its ambiguous legal standing which prevented it from mounting an open and organized campaign. Nonetheless, Khan Sahib decisively defeated his two opponents in the November 1934 polling—Seth Ram Das Bagai, who ran on the Hindu Mahasabha ticket, and Raja Haidar Zaman Khan, who stood as a Muslim alternative to the Congress at Sir Abdul Qaiyum's request. His victory was due largely to his party's popularity, but *parajamba* also played a part.[38] Many Khans who had no sympathy for the Congress nonetheless supported him out of a greater dislike for Sir Abdul Qaiyum.

Due to his elected status, the government permitted Khan Sahib to return to the NWFP in May 1935, tour the province, and address meetings sponsored by the Congress. These were precedents which the party interpreted as meaning that it could begin to work openly again as long as its activities remained temperate. Backed by his brother's prestige and a commission from the High Command, Khan Sahib ended the party's decentralized management and informal organization. He called for the creation of "Parliamentary Boards" from the local to the provincial level, ostensibly to prepare for the elections to the new provincial assembly planned under the 1935 Government of India Act. In actuality, these boards were intended to perform all the functions of Congress Committees, only under a different name since the FPCC was still illegal. A Provincial Parliamentary Board was formed in Utmanzai on November 10, 1935, and District Boards were organized in every district by 1936; but few subordinate boards were ever established, except in Peshawar.[39]

The Provincial Parliamentary Board used local body elections in 1936 to test its new organization. When all seven of its candidates for the Mardan Municipal Committee were defeated in February, the board abandoned the

37. *Lahore Tribune*, 9/15/34 and 9/19/34.

38. Allah Bakhsh Yusafi, *Siyasiyat-i-Sarhad ke Intiqai Manazil* (Karachi: Muhammad Ali Educational Society, 1972), pp. 25-26. For the election results, see *Lahore Tribune*, 11/18/34.

39. The Province Parliamentary Board consisted of Muhammad Ramzan Khan (DIK), President; Ram Singh (Bannu), Secretary; Pir Shahinshah (Kohat); Dr. Khan Sahib (Peshawar); Amir Muhammad Khan (Mardan); and Mehdi Zaman Khan (Hazara). Mardan subdivision was made a separate district in 1937.

strategy of restricting its nominations to men with nationalist credentials.[40] Thereafter, it sought to broaden its base by attracting influential non-Congressmen in localities where the party was not strong. This approach was rewarded in October with victories in twenty-eight of the thirty-five seats on the Peshawar District Board.[41] It subsequently became the basis for selecting candidates to the new Provincial Assembly.

Under the 1935 Government of India Act, dyarchy was replaced by provincial autonomy. The governors remained the provincial chief executives, but all provincial subjects were transferred to ministers who served at the will of popularly elected assemblies. The NWFP was given the same reforms as other provinces, although the governor, in his capacity as the Agent to the Governor-General, still retained sole control over tribal policy. Elections for a fifty-man provincial assembly (thirty-eight Muslims, nine Hindus, and three Sikhs) were scheduled for February 1937. Franchise requirements were significantly lowered, swelling the electorate to a quarter million voters, or about 14 percent of the population.[42]

The Provincial Parliamentary Board formed a three-man subcommittee of Khan Sahib, Qazi Attaullah, and Ram Singh in November 1936 to dispense Congress tickets. They chose thirty-eight candidates, of whom thirty were Muslim and the remaining eight were Hindu.[43] In twelve constituencies where they could not find a strong candidate, the Congress ran no one rather than dissipate its resources. These included all three Sikh and both landlord constituencies, while another three were in Hazara where the party had always been weak. The election officer rejected the papers of the party's nominees in two constituencies in Mardan (which had been made a separate district in 1937), and the party itself suspended its campaign in two more—one Muslim and one Hindu—although too late to remove its candidates from the ballot.[44] Thus, the Congress had only thirty-four active candidates in twenty-seven of the thirty-eight Muslim constituencies and seven of the nine Hindu constituencies.

Twenty-two of the Congress' nominees were longstanding party members and had been imprisoned in the 1932 civil disobedience campaign. In addition to Dr. Khan Sahib, these included many of the founders of the Afghan Jirga and Frontier Congress as well as their most prominent organizers in each district.[45] Another four nominees had been prominent in the Afghan

40. FR2/36(II). Also see GoI File 24/13/36. Note on the revival of the Red Shirt movement.

41. FR10/36(II).

42. *Lahore Tribune*, 1/31/37. For franchise qualifications, see Obhrai, *op. cit.*, p. 275.

43. PP, 1937-38. Vol. XXI. Cmd 5589. "Returns Showing the Results of Elections in India, 1937."

44. They were the urban Hindu seat in Peshawar and the rural Muslim seat in Tank.

45. See Rittenberg, *op. cit.*, Appendix II for the background of the Congress candidates. For example, the Congress candidates for the four seats in Kohat were Pir Shahinshah, the

Jirga or Congress in 1930 but had resigned during the factional conflict between the two parties in 1931.[46] Finally, ten nominees who had had little or no previous association with the party were given tickets because they were stronger candidates than any Congressmen in their constituencies. Two, for example, were MLCs from wealthy Pakhtun families, while another two were related to the *sajjada nishin* of Rajuya, an influential *pir* in the southern part of Hazara.[47]

Among the party's Muslim nominees, even those with strong nationalist credentials tended to be distinguished as well by belonging to the Pakhtun landed elite. The Afghan Jirga-Congress movement had, from its inception, been controlled by junior Khans, men from influential families but not the most senior in their tribe or locality. The Congress candidates in 1937 typically came from the same background. For example, *Arbab* Abdul Ghafur Khan, the fiery nationalist organizer in Peshawar, belonged to a collateral branch of the hereditary chiefs of the Khalil tribe, while Amir Muhammad Khan, the Congress leader in Mardan, was a cousin of the Khan of Hoti, one of the two hereditary chiefs of the Kamalzai Mandanr Yusafzai.[48] Even a man like Abdul Aziz Khan, whom the British dismissed as insignificant because he was not wealthy, belonged to a family of social influence—a junior branch of the Zaida Khans who were the dominant family among the Aba Khel Mandanr Yusafzai, the largest tribal group in his Mardan constituency.[49]

The Congress officially started its election campaign in November 1935 with the formation of the Provincial Parliamentary Board. Its leaders were cautious at first, and their meetings were small, infrequent, and temperate in tone.[50] When the government did not seem to take notice, they convened larger gatherings and in the spring started to revive the practices of wearing red uniforms and marching in military formation. Their rhetoric also grew more bold, harkening back to themes they had emphasized in 1930-31. They once more began to refer to British rule as slavery which people had to resist at all costs and to denounce the province's Khans as reactionary, exploitative, and anti-national. Mixed in with these condemnations were promises of dramatic changes if the Congress won—of greater political freedom and a reshaping of the province's economy. Some speakers even went so far as to

---

PCC President in 1931; Muhammad Aslam Khan, the district commander of the Khudai Khidmatgars; and Muhammad Afzal Khan and Ghulam Haidar Khan who were respectively the leading nationalist workers among the Khattaks and Bangash, the district's two main tribes.

46. Mian Jaffar Shah had been one of Abdul Ghaffar Khan's earliest political associates, and Sayyid Qaim Shah was a leader of the Afghan Jirga during the 1930 civil disobedience campaign. Dr. C.C. Ghosh had been the President of the PCC and Bhanju Ram Gandhi, a prominent Congress leader in Dera Ismail Khan in 1930.

47. Rittenberg, *op. cit.*, Appendix II.

48. *Ibid.*

49. *Ibid.* and PR, No. 9.

50. GoI File 40/1/36. Note on electioneering activities of the Khudai Khidmatgars, p. 9.

promise that the large Khani estates would be broken up and the land distributed among their tenants.[51]

The authorities monitored the party's campaign with rising apprehension but initially hesitated to intervene for fear of turning people against the elections. They finally reacted in the summer of 1936 when the Congress called for a mass meeting on July 3rd. Political gatherings were banned in Peshawar Valley under Section 144 of the Criminal Procedure Code, and the Deputy Commissioner summoned party leaders to his office to warn them that the government would not tolerate the revival of Khudai Khidmatgar tactics.[52] At almost the same time, Abdul Ghaffar Khan, on his release from prison in Bombay on June 26th, was barred from the NWFP and Punjab because provincial authorities feared he would make peaceful elections impossible by creating a "quasi-Fascist movement" given to "fanaticism, intimidation and violence."[53] When these measures failed to restrain the Congress, the government prosecuted some of its campaign workers and asked the central government in September for permission to take even sterner measures. The Home Secretary of the Government of India turned down the request. He doubted there were any legal grounds for further prosecutions, and more important, he feared a hardline policy would embarrass the government throughout India.[54] The provincial authorities, therefore, had to confine themselves to issuing another warning, an action which had no appreciable effect on the Congress' campaign.

The Frontier Congress faced stiff opposition in both the Muslim and non-Muslim constituencies. Its main adversaries among the minorities banded together in the Hindu-Sikh Nationalist Party on November 11, 1936.[55] The new party was a loose electoral coalition with no organizational base of its own. It drew its support from those segments of minority opinion which regarded the NWFP's communal problems as the election's paramount issue. Its members tended to be wealthy, conservative businessmen and professionals whose political sympathies lay with the province's Hindu and Sikh *Sabhas*. They viewed all Muslims, Congress and non-Congress, as inherently untrustworthy. In their estimation, the majority community would use the wide powers granted by the 1935 Government of India Act for communal ends, just as they believed it had manipulated the more limited reforms of 1932.

The Hindu-Sikh Nationalists believed that the minorities' only hope lay in presenting a united front in the new assembly.[56] If no Muslim group could

51. GoI File 24/11/36. Enclosure A. Note on Congress Parliamentary Board's speeches during 1936.

52. FR7/36(I).

53. GoI File 24/11/36. Series II. Memorandum 1713-PC/684(112) P.S., Part I, 5/6/36. A.J. Hopkinson to Home Department.

54. GoI File 40/3/36. Letter 40/3/36-Pol., 9/21/36. M.G. Hallet to A.J. Hopkinson.

55. Obhrai, *op. cit.*, p. 308. *Lahore Tribune*, 11/12/36. See Rittenberg, *op. cit.*, Appendix II for the men it chose as nominees.

56. Interviews with Amir Chand Bombwal and G.D. Khera.

form a government on its own, they intended to barter their votes for ironclad communal guarantees, and even if a purely Muslim ministry were created, they still believed that as long as they were united, it could not ignore them without risking conflict with the governor who had a special responsibility to look after the interests of minorities under the 1935 Act. The party, therefore, ran candidates in every Hindu and Sikh constituency except one where it supported an independent.[57] Its strategy, however, was defeated by the lack of consensus among the minorities. All Hindus and Sikhs did not accept its hostile view of Muslims or see the need for the unity toward which it logically pointed. A sizeable segment of opinion was swayed by nationalist sentiments and sided with the Congress. Even those who shared the new party's political views did not necessarily concede its claim to be the sole legitimate representative of their communities. Dissident *Singh Sabhas* ran candidates for all three Sikh seats; men with *Sanatan Dharm* affiliations ran in seven Hindu constituencies; and individuals personally at odds with the party's leaders ran as independents or threw their support to other non-Congress candidates.[58]

The Congress' opponents in the rural Muslim constituencies were predominantly Khans who relied upon family ties, factional alignments, and tribal affiliations to win electoral support. As a consequence, their sense of shared interests was exceedingly weak. Sixty-six Khans stood as candidates in thirty-five constituencies, testimony in itself to their disunity.[59] They and their supporters were so fragmented by enmities and intrigues that many found the thought of a Congress government more tolerable than the success of each other. As Sir Ralph Griffith observed: "One Khan at enmity with another will do all in his power to spoil the chances of success of his enemy."[60] Two loose blocs of Khans did emerge during the campaign, but personal hostilities prevented their cooperation.[61] One group, primarily from Hazara, united behind Sir Abdul Qaiyum. His past disdain for the Khani class and his modest family origins made him anathema to the Khans who coalesced around *Nawab* Sir Muhammad Akbar Khan, the Khan of Hoti. The two blocs were temporarily reconciled in December 1936, but within a month the rapprochement unraveled, in large part, as Griffith explained, because Sir Abdul Qaiyum "continued to back Red Shirt candidates who happen to be opposed to individuals of the Khanate class personally obnoxious to him."[62]

The election campaign also marked the Muslim League's first serious foray into Frontier politics. It had attempted to start a provincial branch as

57. The independent was Sardar Ajit Singh of Kohat who ran in the Southern Districts (Sikh) constituency. He joined the Hindu-Sikh Nationalists after the elections.

58. PR No. 3, 11/9/36.

59. PR No. 6, 1/12/37.

60. PR No. 3, 11/9/36.

61. *Ibid.*

62. PR No. 6, 1/12/37 and No. 3, 11/9/36.

early as 1934, but without success since it could not find a constituency.[63] The Congress had preempted the one organized Muslim body in the countryside and the most appealing issue, Pakhtun nationalism, while the non-Congress Khans had seen little to be gained from abandoning their political individualism. Thus, the League modestly concentrated in 1936 on gaining a foothold among the province's urban Muslim intelligentsia. Muhammad Ali Jinnah named Pir Bakhsh and Malik Khuda Bakhsh of the *Azad* Party, and Allah Bakhsh Yusafi and Rahim Bakhsh Ghaznavi of the Peshawar Khilafat Committee to the All-India Muslim League Parliamentary Board in May.[64] Neither party, however, was capable of serving as the nucleus for a Provincial Muslim League. The Khilafat Committee was moribund, while the *Azad* Party was a legislative coalition whose sole justification had been to act as a surrogate for the Frontier Congress while it was banned. Every effort to expand its organization had been stymied by the Congress which ate away at its membership until it was little more than an urban rump of two. In addition, Pir Bakhsh and the Khilafatists were bitterly at odds due to factional disputes within Peshawar city politics.[65]

Jinnah spent a week in Peshawar in October 1936 in an attempt to salvage something from the elections. He unsuccessfully sought both an association with the Frontier Congress and the support of Sir Abdul Qaiyum before settling upon an eighteen-man Parliamentary Board with Pir Bakhsh as convenor.[66] Jinnah weighted its membership in favor of urban politicians, especially Peshawaris, out of recognition that the League would have little influence for the time being among the rural 85 percent of the province. Nearly half of its members were chosen without their consent, an indication that its creation was largely a face-saving exercise. The board, in fact, never functioned. Six of its members joined the Congress and another four ran for the assembly as independents.[67] Even Pir Baksh and Malik Khuda Bakhsh found the *Azad* Party label preferable to the League.

Polling took place between February 1 and February 10, 1937, with 179,529 people, or 72.8 percent of the electorate, voting. Turnout was highest in the rural Muslim constituencies and lowest among the Sikhs. The Congress won nineteen seats, while the Hindu-Sikh Nationalists captured six and the *Azad* Party two. The remaining twenty-three successful candi-

---

63. Interviews with Mian Ziauddin and Pir Bakhsh Khan.

64. *Lahore Tribune*, 5/22/36.

65. Interviews with Pir Bakhsh Khan and Rahim Bakhsh Ghaznavi.

66. *Lahore Tribune*, 10/2/36 and 10/24/36.

67. Abdul Ghafur Khan and *Arbab* Abdur Rahman Khan, *Azad* MLCs, received Congress tickets. Abdul Qaiyum Khan Swathi, *Azad* MLC, withdrew from the election in favor the Congress candidate. Hakim Abdul Jalil, Khair Muhammad Jalali, Malik Amir Alam Awan, and he rose to high positions in the Congress. Abdul Hamid Khan Kundi ran as an independent with Congress support. Muhammad Abbas Khan, Muhammad Jan Khan, and *Arbab* Muhammad Sharif also ran as independents. The first became a minister in the Khan Sahib government in September 1937. The second joined the Congress after the elections.

dates had no party affiliation.[68] These results showed that the Frontier Congress had overestimated its popularity while undervaluing the abiding strength of the traditional loyalties on which its opponents drew. Both of its urban candidates lost, a reflection of the province's rural-urban dichotomy. In Peshawar and Mardan, the party won all ten of the seats it contested and would have taken the other two had its nominees not been disqualified. Even there, however, family and faction influenced the outcome of the voting. Five of the successful Congressmen belonged to junior branches of the dominant families in their tribes, and three of them defeated their *tarburs*.[69] Three others were also members of prominent families in their tribes, while a fourth belonged to a clan of influential *Mians*.[70] In the rest of the province, where tribal and factional loyalties were much stronger, the Congress was victorious in only one-third of the fifteen seats it contested. It captured one seat each in Kohat, Bannu, and Dera Ismail Khan, but five of its top leaders in those districts were defeated in close races in which factional or religious issues rather than nationalism proved decisive.[71] Ironically, the party did better in non-Pakhtun Hazara, capitalizing on unique religious factors to win two seats.[72] The Hindu and Sikh results exposed the sharp philosophical split among the minorities. The Hindu-Sikh Nationalists' contention that they represented minority opinion was seriously weakened when it won only six seats, but the Frontier Congress could hardly substantiate its counterclaim that the minorities had confidence in its communal impartiality, for it managed to capture only four.[73]

While less conclusive than they had hoped, the election results left Congressmen optimistic that they would be asked to form the first popular ministry in the history of the Frontier Province. They were the largest party in the new assembly and the only organized one among its Muslim majority.

---

68. PP, 1937-38. Vol. XXI. Cmd 5589. "Returns Showing the Results of the Elections in India, 1937," p. 12. The turnout for the Muslim seats would have been higher except for the Congress boycott of two races in Mardan where its candidates had been disqualified. See Rittenberg, *op. cit.*, Appendix II for a description of the elections in each constituency.

69. They were *Arbab* Abdul Ghafur Khan, Muhammad Zarin Khan, Amir Muhammad Khan, *Arbab* Abdur Rahman Khan, and Abdul Aziz Khan. See Rittenberg, *op. cit.*, Appendix II.

70. Abdul Ghafur Khan of Prang, Dr. Khan Sahib, and Muhammad Samin Jan Khan were members of the Muhammadzai tribe. Mian Jafar Shah belonged to a collateral branch of the family of the *sajjada nishin* of Kaka Khel.

71. Rittenberg, *op. cit.*, Appendix II. The five constituencies were Hangu, Kohat, Teri North, Bannu East, and Kulachi.

72. Pir Muhammad Kamran belonged to the family of the *sajjada nishin* of Rajuya whose disciples were concentrated among the Jaduns, the largest tribe in the constituency. Faqira Khan won in Lower Pakhli (Mansehra *Teshil*) where the election turned on the affiliation of his opponent, Ghulam Rabbani Khan, to the Ahmadiyya sect. Interviews with Sardar Bahadur Khan and Ghulam Rabbani Khan.

73. PP, 1937-38. Vol. XXI. Cmd 5589. "Returns Showing the Results of the Elections in India, 1937," p. 12. See Rittenberg, *op. cit.*, Appendix II for the race in each constituency.

Sir George Cunningham, the new governor, however, held all the suspicions of British officials about their party and perfunctorily dismissed their claims, even though the situation among the other members of the Legislative Assembly (MLAs) was, in his own words, "chaotic."[74] The Frontier Congress could not force him to reconsider by putting together a legislative majority of its own because of the equivocation of the Congress Working Committee over whether to accept office.[75] The Working Committee did not make any decision until March 26th, by which time Cunningham had helped to wield the non-Congress MLAs into a coalition. Then, it came out against forming ministries because the Viceroy would not promise that the governors would not use their special powers under the Government of India Act to overturn ministerial decision.

Shortly after the elections, Sir Abdul Qaiyum managed to bring fourteen MLAs together to form the United Muslim Nationalist Party, despite the existence of serious personal and factional disputes among them. Six Hazara MLAs formed the Democratic Party for the sole purpose of obtaining a ministership, while the two *Azad* representatives and one other Muslim remained independent. Even with direct help from the governor, Qaiyum managed to lure only two of the Democrats into his party in the ensuing months.[76] Cunningham, nonetheless, asked him to form a ministry on March 16th and then ordered the officers in the permanent administration to lobby for support on its behalf. He told them that "any official who did not help the ministerial party was being disloyal to me."[77] When Qaiyum failed to form a coalition with the Hindu-Sikh Nationalists, the governor mediated a settlement; and when the entire, shaky enterprise threatened to collapse over who should be a minister and how their portfolios should be divided, he arbitrated among the conflicting claims.[78]

A weak ministry of Sir Abdul Qaiyum, Saadullah Khan, and Mehr Chand Khanna was sworn in on April 1st, but before the assembly could meet, defections reduced its supporters to a minority of twenty-one. Cunningham, therefore, confined the first legislative session to a two-day ceremonial gathering.[79] No official legislation was considered, and four adjournment resolutions and a no-confidence motion were ruled out of order by either Cunningham or his appointee as acting assembly speaker, Abdul Majid Khan. The only business the assembly conducted was the election of parliamentary officers. The Congress sponsored non-Congressmen to solidify the anti-

74. CD, 3/6/37; also, PR No. 10, 3/8/37.

75. For the Congress' changing position on the question of forming ministries, see V.P. Menon, *The Transfer of Power in India* (New Delhi: Longmans Orient, 1968), pp. 53-55.

76. CD, 3/13/37.

77. CD, 3/22/37.

78. CD, 3/28/37 and 3/29/37; and LP/117. No. 205 and 220. For the terms of the pact with the Hindu-Sikh Nationalists, see *Lahore Tribune*, 7/4/37.

79. LP/118. No. 331b. Letter, 5/26/37. Cunningham to Linlithgow.

ministerial forces. Conscious of its weakness, the ruling coalition did not oppose Malik Khuda Bakhsh for Speaker; but it ran Malik-ur-Rahman Kiyani for Deputy Speaker against Muhammad Sarwar Khan (Democrat) and lost by twenty-nine votes to nineteen, thereby exposing its inability to control the assembly without the governor's help.[80]

Qaiyum was unable to improve his position in the five months before the next assembly session, even with the active assistance of Cunningham and the permanent administration.[81] By September, moreover, the impasse between the Congress and the Viceroy over the formation of ministers had been resolved, leaving the Frontier Congress free to consolidate its anti-ministerial coalition into a governing majority of its own. On September 3rd, the Congress passed a no-confidence motion against Sir Abdul Qaiyum, twenty-seven votes to twenty-two, with the support of four Democrats, two ex-Hindu-Sikh Nationalists, and two independents. Four days later, Dr. Khan Sahib formed a ministry which included Qazi Attaullah and Bhanju Ram Gandhi of the Congress and Muhammad Abbas Khan of the Democrats.

Since the sole justification for Qaiyum's coalition had been to share power, it quickly disintegrated after he fell. The Hindu-Sikh Nationalists welcomed the new government: "With its antecedents of sacrifice, service and fair play, the Congress Party, we feel, can be safely relied on to protect the rights and interests of minorities."[82] Ishar Das Sahni, Khanna's rival in the Hindu-Sikh Nationalists, and five United Muslim Nationalists formed the Nationalist Party and promised to support the Congress' constructive programs.[83] Two deaths, including Qaiyum's, and two successful election petitions further depleted the non-Congress ranks. The Congress won three of the four resulting bye-elections and gained another vote when a United Muslim Nationalist switched sides.[84] Thus, by the time the assembly reconvened in March 1938, thirty-one MLAs sat on the government benches—twenty-four Congressmen (including two ex-Hindu-Sikh Nationalists), four Democrats, and three independents. The opposition consisted of eight United Muslim Nationalists, six Nationalists, and four Hindu-Sikh Nationalists. Subsequently, the opposition Muslims coalesced into the Frontier Muslim League, and Ishar Das Sahni returned to his old party.

The Congress never lost the upper hand in the assembly before resigning of its own volition in November 1939. Its position was in jeopardy in the fall 1938 and spring 1939 sessions, but Khan Sahib averted defeat on both occa-

80. Two Hazara MLAs in Qaiyum's party voted for Muhammad Sarwar Khan, which accounts for the decrease in the number of the ministry's backers from twenty-one.

81. LP/118. No. 331b. Letter, 5/26/37. Cunningham to Linlithgow; No. 337. Letter, 5/29/37. Cunningham to Linlithgow; and No. 287. Letter, 6/22/37. Linlithgow to Cunningham.

82. *Lahore Tribune*, 10/12/37.

83. *Ibid.*, 9/18/37.

84. *Ibid.*, 3/2/38, 3/3/38, and 3/5/38. GR/41. No. 1, 1/10/38.

sions by reasserting party discipline among the Congress MLAs and offsetting desertions by non-Congress supporters through new accommodations with opposition members.[85] More important, the opposition was too divided to offer a realistic alternative. A bitter communal atmosphere precluded any agreement between Muslims and minorities; Khans and urban politicians were at odds; and the Khans themselves were fragmented by factional and personal enmities. Many simply concluded in the manner of Saadullah Khan, the Muslim League leader, that "the Opposition was not cohesive enough to make it worthwhile trying to turn out Congress."[86]

## The First Khan Sahib Ministry

Once in office, the Frontier Congress did not challenge the existing governmental structure as the authorities had feared, not even the laws which it had once anathematized as pillars of British imperial repression.[87] Its ministers, in fact, tried to add to the government's powers to deal with communal violence. They passed the *Goondas* Bill in September 1939 which allowed precautionary externment from the province, *in camera* trials, and the denial of legal assistance and the right of appeal to the accused.[88] The main objective of the Khan Sahib ministry was to alter the political balance within Frontier society by dismantling the informal system of alliances the British had used to govern the region. The British had frozen Pakhtun society into a mold in which their allies, the senior Khans, retained an ascendant position even after they had lost their social legitimacy. This had been the major reason why their rivals within the Pakhtuns' landed elite had joined the Khudai Khidmatgars in the first place. On coming to power, the Congress systematically set out to strip the senior Khans of their powers and perquisites and to transfer the government's patronage and support to its own Khani supporters.

The ministry first abolished the position of Honorary Magistrate, through which the British had invested a select group of non-officials, mainly Khans, with judicial powers. Next to go were the last nominated seats on the local governmental bodies, positions which had usually been filled by pro-government Khans.[89] The Khans lost still another instrument of power when the ministry terminated the *naubati chaukidari* system under which every vil-

85. LP/73. No. 12. Letter D.O. GH-249, 10/31/38. Cunningham to Linlithgow. LP/74. No. 1. Letter D.O. GH-1, 1/5/39. Cunningham to Linlithgow. GR/42, No. 21, 11/9/38.

86. CD, 11/11/38.

87. When Abdur Rab Nishtar introduced a bill to repeal parts of the so-called "repressive" acts, Khan Sahib privately opposed the bill. While he felt politically unable to kill it in the assembly, he did not protest when Cunningham denied it certification. LP/72. No. 16. Letter D.O. GH-79, 3/15/38. Cunningham to Linlithgow.

88. LAD, Vol. 6, No. 1, 9/14/39, p. 112 and No. 11, 9/28/39, pp. 1040 and 1071.

89. GR/40. No. 12, 10/9/37 and GR/41. No. 2, 1/24/38.

lager, except government employees, had to take turns as an unpaid night watchman or provide a replacement. The system had long been a source of popular resentment since the dominant senior Khans had turned the watchmen into unpaid personal retainers.[90] In the land revenue administration, the ministers abolished the position of *zaildar*, an intermediary employed in parts of Peshawar and Dera Ismail Khan. They also gave serious thought to replacing the province's 7,425 *lambardars*, who collected the land revenue, performed minor police duties, and acted as official village headmen, with government officials.[91] The ministry regarded the *lambardars*, who were appointed on a hereditary basis from among the leading men in each village ward, as politically hostile to the Congress, a perception which was largely accurate given the *lambardars'* former dependency on the British for their position and the fact that *lambardars* who had actively favored the Congress in 1930-31 had been removed from office. Their position was saved only by the ministers' fear of disrupting revenue collection and by the governor's strong objections to their elimination.[92]

In making these reforms, the ministry was not acting strictly out of political motives. These measures all contributed to greater government efficiency and fairness.[93] Nonetheless, their impact was primarily political in that they eliminated some of the institutions the senior Khans had formerly used to maintain their dominance in Pakhtun society and, more important, signalled that the old order was changing.

Khan Sahib's government also struck at the economic benefits the British had given their Khani supporters. Besides *zaildari* fees, it wiped out all but seventy-five of the province's 700 *zamindari inams* (revenue grants given in return for a variety of services) and suspended the practice of nominating sons and relations of influential Khans to administrative jobs.[94] In March 1938, the Congress passed the Teri Dues Regulations Repealing Bill to abolish a 1902 act legitimizing the *Nawab* of Teri's right to collect cesses totalling more than Rs. 12,000 per annum from the people of Teri *Tehsil* (Kohat).[95] The bill also ended *haq taluqdari*, an assessment levied in recognition of the *Nawab*'s superior proprietary rights to the *tehsil*. Cunningham originally felt the ministers had exceeded their authority in passing the bill, but they insisted that they would resign if he denied it certification.[96] A compromise was finally reached in July 1938 to revise the bill to eliminate the cesses,

90. GR/41. No. 2, 1/24/38; and *Pakhtun*, 10/9/46.

91. CP/5, Part II, p. 3; GR/41. No. 10, 5/26/38; GR/42. No. 1, 1/9/39; GR/43. No. 11, 6/9/39; and GR/44. No. 3, 7/7/39.

92. CP/5, Part II, p. 3.

93. Cunningham acknowledged that many of the reforms were also in the best interest of the province. *Ibid.*, Part II.

94. LP/75. No. 17. Letter GH-94, 4/19/40. Cunningham to Linlithgow; and GR/41. No. 2, 1/24/38.

95. LP/72. No. 18. Letter D.O. GH-89, 3/23/38. Cunningham to Linlithgow.

96. *Ibid.* Also LP/72. No. 29 and 35; and CD, 5/3/38, 5/4/38, and 5/26/38.

which were the people's main grievance, and to leave *haq taluqdari*, which was the governor's primary concern, untouched.

In handling their administrative responsibilities, the ministers also made no attempt to hide their favoritism toward their own supporters. They gave party members preferential treatment in the distribution of patronage jobs, permits for firearms, and *taccavi* (agricultural improvement) loans and allocated public works money with an eye toward their advantage. In granting revenue remissions in Peshawar Valley in March 1938, they put an acreage limit on who was entitled to relief which effectively excluded many of the senior Khans who tended to have larger landholdings.[97] Critics repeatedly accused the ministers of favoring their supporters and punishing their opponents in the press in the placement of government ads, a lucrative, and for many papers, crucial source of revenue.[98] In addition, Khan Sahib and his colleagues commonly expedited bureaucratic action on requests and complaints of Congressmen while acting with less aclarity on the problems of their rivals.[99] More generally, by relying upon Congress Khans for advice and help in the countryside, the ministry signalled that they, rather than the senior Khans, had become the privileged intermediaries between the people and the government.

The ministry most seriously threatened the senior Khans by exploiting the province's agrarian unrest. Tenant problems plagued most landlords to some degree, but they were most serious on the larger estates, owned, in the main, by non-Congress Khans. By 1930, the old patron-client ties between the big landlords and their tenants had been replaced in many areas by a contractual, economic relationship in which the former tried to extract as much rent as possible without providing any of the reciprocal services which had once made their demands acceptable to their dependents. The tenantry retaliated by withholding rents, challenging their landlords' rights to the land, and supporting the Congress. As Cunningham explained:

> . . . for many years they [the Khans] have been striking too hard a bargain with their tenants and have made no effort to earn their affection or respect. They have, in consequence, lost their following and the discontent of their tenants has been exploited by political organisations.[100]

While individuals in the Congress also fit this pattern, the problems of the Congress Khans, as a whole, were not as severe since they had retained many of the attributes of traditional patrons rather than seeking to maximize their economic profits.

---

97. GR/41. No. 7, 4/9/38.
98. For example, see LAD, Vol. 4, No. 4, 11/8/38, pp. 376-403.
99. PJ8/588. Collection 117-C-3. "Working of Congress Ministries in the Provinces. Reports by Governors," p. 5.
100. GR/43. No. 16, 8/23/38.

Landlord-tenant relations became even more tense after the 1937 elections. The Frontier Congress had raised expectations during the campaign by promising everything from the cancellation of existing arrears in rent to the redistribution of the land to those who tilled it.[101] Party leaders, in fact, never favored structural reforms in land ownership since that would have been ruinous for the entire Khani class, including themselves. Instead, they sought to manipulate tenants' grievances in a selective manner designed to consolidate their support among the lower classes while hurting only the non-Congress Khans. Since the tenantry was pro-Congress, it seemed possible at first to minimize the problems of the Congress Khans through party adjudication while aggravating those of their opponents through governmental action and a strident anti-Khani rhetoric.

During their first year in office, the ministers, especially Qazi Attaullah, could be counted on to support tenants in any conflict with their landlords. This encouraged many tenants to neglect their obligations to their Khans and to give the resulting disputes a political coloration. The situation became most acute in Charsadda *Tehsil*, with its longstanding problems between the Muhammadzai landlords and Mohmand tenants. By May 1938, non-Congress Khans were realizing as little as 25 percent of their rents in comparison to 80 percent or more in previous years.[102] They felt unable, moreover, to retaliate with evictions because of the government's hostility. In the one instance where a Muslim League landlord actually tried, Congress leaders intervened to frustrate him.[103]

In the midst of this growing unrest, the ministry pushed the Agricultural Debtors' Relief Bill through the assembly in the fall of 1938. Hindus and Sikhs, including those in the Congress, unanimously opposed the bill because it hurt their communities' interests as moneylenders.[104] Outwardly at least, Muslim opinion was just as solidly in favor of its passage. These reactions led people to view the bill in strictly communal terms, whereas it was, in fact, carefully crafted to further the Congress' campaign against the senior Khans as well. The main provision cancelled loans incurred by agriculturists before October 1, 1937. This, in itself, hurt many of the senior Khans who were actively engaged in moneylending. Additionally, "agriculturist" was defined in such a way as to exclude the largest landlords of the NWFP, most of whom were senior Khans, from the benefit of the bill.[105] Finally, the bill contained a clause discharging rent arrears incurred by tenants

101. GoI File 24/11/36. Enclosure A. "Note on Congress Parliamentary Board's Speeches during 1936." Also FR9/38(II).

102. CD, 5/26/38. Also GR/41. No. 10, 5/26/38.

103. FR5/38(II); GR/41. No. 10, 5/26/38; and *Pakhtun*, 6/21/38.

104. LAD, Vol. 4, No. 8, 11/14/38, p. 697. Also GR/42. No. 14, 7/23/38; GR/43. No. 2, 1/22/38; GR/43. No. 7, 4/9/39.

105. Erland Jansson estimates that about 700 were excluded. Erland Jansson, *India, Pakistan or Pakhtunistan* (Uppsala: Studia Historica Upsaliensia, No. 119, 1981), p. 80ff.

before October 1, 1937. This provision also disproportionately hurt the senior Khans, even those who qualified under the bill's definition as agriculturists. Provided that a landlord's tenants were not too far behind in payment, his loss in rents was offset by his own debt relief. This was the case for most Congress Khans since their party had used its influence with the tenants to ensure that they did not seriously fall behind in the payment of their rents. The non-Congress Khans, in contrast, lost the right to significant amounts of rent from tenants who had fallen into arrears, in large measure as a result of the Frontier Congress' deliberate encouragement.[106]

The Agricultural Debtors Relief Bill marked the high point of the Frontier Congress' pro-tenant policy, for party leaders had come to realize by its passage that there was no airtight formula for limiting *kisan* disputes to non-Congress estates. Congress Khans also had restive tenants, many of whom were encouraged to press their own grievances by the success with which other tenants defied their landlords. Again, this was most true in Charsadda and Mardan *Tehsils*, the party's core regions.[107] The Congress Khans who were affected put class interests above party needs and pressed the ministry for action to curb tenant demands. The ministers also became disenchanted because agrarian unrest threatened revenue collection.[108] The Khans who had difficulty in collecting their rents tended to fall behind in their revenue payments, and many other landowners followed suit in the generally unsettled atmosphere generated by the agrarian disputes. By September 1938, revenue receipts were four lakhs below normal, and in Peshawar alone, almost 60 percent of the land revenue and water rates for the summer crop was outstanding.[109] The ministers at first wanted to use force only against the big landlords, but the magnitude of the financial crisis ultimately compelled them to apply coercive measures against Khans and tenants alike.[110]

The change in their policy became apparent with an agitation in Mardan against the *Nawab* of Toru, whom Cunningham called a "notoriously bad landlord."[111] In July 1938, he had resumed lands from tenants who were in default in the village of Ghalladher. When the tenants, with support from the Congress Socialists, tried to cultivate their old fields, the police arrested them for trespassing, thereby touching off a two-month *satyagraha* campaign. Khan Sahib tried to find a peaceful solution, while party leaders ordered the Congressmen involved to abandon the agitation. When those steps

106. PJ8/588. Collection 117-C-3, p. 1

107. Interviews with Abdul Akbar Khan and Mian Jafar Shah.

108. GR/41. No. 12, 6/24/38. Also see GR/42. No. 18, 9/23/38.

109. *Ibid.*

110. GR/42. No. 16, 8/23/38 and No. 20, 10/22/38, and CD, 10/20/38. Also, interview with Mian Jafar Shah.

111. GR/42. No. 15, 8/8/38. For information on the agitation, see GR/42. No. 16, 8/23/38 and No. 17, 9/3/38; *Khyber Mail*, 9/9/38 and 9/16/38; and Farigh Bukhari, *Bacha Khan, Khan Abdul Ghaffar Khan ke Savanah Hayat* (Peshawar: Niya Maktuba, 1957), pp. 169-72.

failed, the party censured the Socialists, and Khan Sahib broke the agitation by force.[112] Similar firmness was displayed in June 1939 when Mohmand tenants at Muftiabad in Charsadda *Tehsil* resisted eviction. Abdul Ghaffar Khan denounced the *kisans* for wanting "to tear the [Pakhtun] nation into pieces," and Khan Sahib ordered the arrest of the tenants and their Congress supporters, including his own son, Obeidullah Khan.[113]

## The Reorganization of the Frontier Congress

The change in the ministers' policies on agrarian issues did not mean that the campaign of the Frontier Congress against its Khani opponents stopped. The non-Congress Khans not only had to worry about the continued hostility of the government but also about the Congress' powerful party organization. While the ministry was unfriendly, it was at least removed from daily village life. The party organization, in contrast, had a network of local branches identified with their rivals, and the resources the Congress Khans obtained from the party—money, allies, and prestige—gave them as much of an edge in village politics as the more remote support they received from the ministry.

While the Frontier Congress had been able to organize on a limited scale since 1934, its efforts had been hampered until August 22, 1937, when Sir Abdul Qaiyum lifted all restrictions on its political activities and allowed Abdul Ghaffar Khan to return to the province.[114] These measures removed the lid on years of pent-up political energies. For some party partisans, they created an opportunity to renew working for nationalist goals; for others, a chance to use the party to pursue personal ambitions or factional interests. For all, they signalled the enthusiastic return to the political arena. The Provincial and District Parliamentary Boards, which were created to contest the elections, were converted into Congress Committees; new party branches were formed from the *tehsil* down to the local level; and the Khudai Khidmatgars were revived as the party's volunteers. By early 1938, the Frontier Congress had built a party organization which Cunningham felt was "practically unassailable in the rural areas."[115] Primary village branches numbered 386 by March, in contrast to 81 a year before. Approximately 20,000 Khudai Khidmatgars had been enlisted in the same period, and by June, their numbers doubled or tripled again.[116] The number of dues-paying Con-

112. GR/42. No. 17, 9/3/38. FR9/38(II).

113. *Pakhtun*, 7/21/39; and GR/43. No. 11, 6/9/39 and No. 12, 6/23/39.

114. FR8/37(II).

115. GR/41. No. 1, 1/10/38.

116. GR/41. No. 11, 6/8/38 and No. 5, 3/10/38. The Khudai Khidmatgars did not keep accurate membership rolls. They claimed 60,000 members, but the government considered that figure inflated by one-third.

**Table 7: Congress Membership in 1938 and 1939**[117]

| | *Congress Members* | | *Percent of Total Membership* | | *Membership per 1,000 Inhabitants* | |
|---|---|---|---|---|---|---|
| *District* | *1938* | *1939* | *1938* | *1939* | *1938* | *1939* |
| Hazara | 1,148 | 1,720 | 6.25 | 7.22 | 1.44 | 2.13 |
| Mardan | 7,562 | 6,008 | 41.09 | 25.21 | 12.76 | 11.86 |
| Peshawar | 7,000 | 9,351 | 38.04 | 39.32 | 8.22 | 10.99 |
| Kohat | 1,353 | 1,794 | 7.35 | 7.52 | 4.68 | 6.17 |
| Bannu | 600 | 3,568 | 3.26 | 14.95 | 2.03 | 12.06 |
| D. I. Khan | 730 | 945 | 4.01 | 3.95 | 2.45 | 3.17 |

gressmen was also substantial, although considerably fewer than the Khudai Khidmatgars—18,398 in 1938 and 23,815 in 1939[118]—partly because the Khudai Khidmatgars had no dues and partly because they were a Pakhtun movement while the Congress was seen as having alien origins.

As Table 7 indicates, the party revived most quickly in Peshawar Valley where it had always been strongest and where the rudiments of an organization had survived the years of government repression. Peshawar and Mardan provided four-fifths of the party's members in 1938 and had the highest ratio of members to district population. By the next year, the party had measurably improved its position in Bannu and Kohat, but the Valley still accounted for two-thirds of all Congressmen. Membership figures also indicate that the Frontier Congress remained a party of Pakhtuns. Not only was recruitment weakest in the non-Pakhtun districts of Hazara and Dera Ismail Khan, but within those districts, Tank and Mansehra, the *tehsils* with the largest number of Pakhtuns, accounted for a disproportionate share of the party's members.[119]

The Frontier Congress also retained its decidedly rural complexion after 1937. In 1938, 27 percent of dues-paying Congressmen lived in towns and in 1939, 31 percent.[120] When the membership of the Khudai Khidmatgars, who were overwhelmingly recruited from the countryside, is included, those figures drop well below the urban percentage in the province's population.[121] A disproportionate number of urban Congressmen were Hindu, and many of its urban Muslim members were Pakhtuns who had migrated to the towns in search of work.[122] Thus, the party continued to display a decided inability

117. AICC File G-46, 1938; and File G-54, 1939.

118. *Ibid.*

119. *Ibid.*

120. Assuming that the number of Khudai Khidmatgars was at least 40,000, the percentage of urban members in the movement, as a whole, was no more than 6.8 percent in 1938 and 11.5 percent in 1939. Computed from *ibid.*

121. Computed from *ibid.*

122. *Ibid.* and interviews with G. D. Khera and Mian Jafar Shah.

to win support from the non-Pakhtun Muslims who formed the great majority of the NWFP's urban Muslim population.

The Frontier Congress developed three striking organizational characteristics after its revival which it would retain for the rest of the independence movement. It was dominated by Abdul Ghaffar Khan, even though he held no official position in the Provincial Congress Committee (PCC). The Khudai Khidmatgars maintained a high degree of autonomy from the regular side of the party, and finally, the party, as a whole, enjoyed a semi-autonomous status within the Indian National Congress.

Abdul Ghaffar Khan's power rested on two institutional bases. First, he controlled the Khudai Khidmatgars, the more popular wing of the party.[123] Second, he served as a member of the All-India Congress Working Committee. Congress leaders routinely deferred to him on questions relating to the Frontier and framed their orders to the PCC in accordance with his wishes. They also gave him discretionary authority over the major portion of the financial subsidy they gave the provincial party. Since the Frontier Congress depended on that subsidy for the greater part of its finances, Abdul Ghaffar Khan, as Cunningham observed, could "call the tune as he pays the pipers."[124] Ultimately, however, his ascendancy rested on his unmatched popularity among the Pakhtuns. His commanding character evoked strong personal loyalties from Pakhtuns throughout the NWFP, especially since he increasingly emphasized his role as a moral leader rather than as a politician. Other party leaders, by comparison, were men of less imposing stature, who had local power bases but did not command a wider following in their own right.

Although factionalism was endemic in the Frontier Congress, it rarely involved Abdul Ghaffar Khan. The only serious challenge to his position came from Ghulam Muhammad Khan of Lundkhwar, a Khan among the Baizai Khattaks of Mardan District, who served as the PCC President in 1938.[125] There was no ideological basis for the rift, no burning issues to divide the two men. The conflict was purely a struggle for power in which Ghulam Muhammad, who lacked the influence and prestige of Abdul Ghaffar Khan, was badly mismatched. Despite his position as the official head of the Frontier Congress, Ghulam Muhammad could count on the votes of only about one-third of the members of the PCC, and most of his supporters were urban politicians or socialist dissidents. In short, he failed to attract serious support from the key party figures who dominated its organization in the countryside.[126]

Ghulam Muhammad alienated Abdul Ghaffar Khan and other party leaders by unsuccessfully asserting his right as PCC President to issue binding

---

123. GR/41. No. 10, 5/26/38; GR/41, No. 11, 6/8/38; and GR/42. No. 22, 11/21/38. Interviews with Abdul Akbar Khan and Mian Jafar Shah.

124. GR/42. No. 20, 10/22/38. Also see GR/40. No. 14, 11/9/37; and GR/41. No. 8, 4/23/38.

125. GR/42. No. 15, 8/8/38; and GR/43. No. 3, 2/9/39. Also see Allah Bakhsh Yusafi, *Sarhadi Gandhi se Mulaqat* (Peshawar: Manzur-i-Am Barqi Press, 1939), pp. 8-9.

126. Interviews with Abdul Akbar Khan and Muhammad Zarin Khan.

orders to the Khudai Khidmatgars and the Khan Sahib ministry.[127] In retaliation, he was denied reelection in January 1939 as PCC President and passed over in the selection of the NWFP's representatives to the All-India Congress Committee (AICC). His fight with the established powers in the party, however, did not end with these defeats, for he allied himself with Subhas Chandra Bose, the Congress President in 1938-39, and turned his faction into the Frontier Forward Bloc.[128] This tied him to the losing side in the factional struggle taking place in the Congress' central councils. When Bose resigned in April 1939, Ghulam Muhammad's last source of influence within the party disappeared.

The Frontier Forward Bloc attacked the party's leaders over economic issues in the months that followed in an effort to compensate for its lack of organizational power by winning over the membership at large. The PCC countered by amending its constitution on September 25th to prohibit the formation of any party within the Frontier Congress except the Khudai Khidmatgars.[129] Party leaders intended to use the amendment to justify disbanding the Frontier Forward Bloc and expelling Ghulam Muhammad, but the political crisis created by the start of World War II intervened. In the interest of party unity, they embraced Ghulam Muhammad as one of their own on the understanding that he would cease to challenge their authority. Nonetheless, they were careful to exclude Ghulam Muhammad from any position of power within the party organization, and one year later, they finally revoked his membership in the Congress on the grounds he had started once more to criticize their leadership.[130]

The Frontier Congress after 1937 showed the same organizational dichotomy that had characterized it in 1931. The Khudai Khidmatgars, who were theoretically the party's volunteers, constituted an autonomous body parallel to the regular party structure.[131] Their officers sat on the Congress Committees coinciding with their territorial responsibilities, and cooperative relations were further assured by the frequently close family ties between the leaders of the two sides of the party.[132] However, the volunteers did not receive their orders from the Congress Committees. The Frontier Congress

127. GR/42. No. 23, 12/9/38 and Yusafi, *op. cit.*

128. Interview with Muhammad Zarin Khan. GR/43. No. 3, 2/9/39.

129. See correspondence in AICC File P-16, 1939. Also *Lahore Tribune*, 10/8/39 and 10/12/39.

130. FR11/40(II) and interview with Muhammad Zarin Khan.

131. AICC File P/22, 1934-35. Interviews with Amin Jan Khan, Sher Dil Khan, and Hasan Gul Khan.

132. For instance, Muhammad Yakub Khan, the *Naib Salar* of Bannu, was the younger brother of Muhammad Aslam Khan, who served as the DCC President for many years. Mehr Dil Khan served as *Naib Salar* of Mardan, while his cousin, Amir Muhammad Khan, was the DCC President. Abdul Hanan Khan, the Hangu *Tehsil* General, was the cousin of Ghulam Haidar Khan, the Congress leader in the *tehsil*. Generally, the younger man served in the Khudai Khidmatgars and the older on the regular side of the party.

constitution stated: "The Khudai Khidmatgar party which exists in the province shall obey the orders of the Congress (AICC) for the achievement of the Congress objectives, but it will be independent in its management."[133] In practical terms, this clause vested sole control in Abdul Ghaffar Khan since he was the arbiter of Frontier affairs in the AICC. The Working Committee also guaranteed his authority by channeling its subsidy to the volunteers directly through him without reference to the PCC.

The Khudai Khidmatgars were organized in a quasi-military fashion.[134] Abdul Ghaffar Khan held no rank but set policy and appointed their official head, the *Salar-i-Azam*. (To reinforce his personal authority, he initially reappointed Rab Nawaz Khan, his maternal nephew, to that position.) The Khudai Khidmatgars' organizational chart laid out a well-ordered hierarchy with a fixed ratio of officers at every level of its organization. On paper, each district was headed by a *Naib Salar* (deputy commander) and subdivided into successively smaller units commanded by generals, colonels, and majors. At the village level, or *kandi* (village ward) if membership were large enough, the Khudai Khidmatgars were supposed to be headed by captains, with a set number of lieutenants, NCO's, and ordinary volunteers under them. In practice, the organization of the volunteers barely approximated this model. Recruitment was haphazard; membership varied widely from region to region and over time; and officers at every grade tended to appropriate higher ranks than they deserved. Discipline was never as strong as the by-laws demanded, and many individuals' involvement consisted of little more than periodically putting on a red uniform for party meetings. These shortcomings notwithstanding, the Khudai Khidmatgars were the most powerful force in Frontier politics, for they had no rivals in terms of their numbers, popularity, or ability to mobilize large numbers of people on short order.

Because "Khudai Khidmatgar" was a more familiar and popular name, party leaders tended to use it instead of the Congress label. Over wide areas of the NWFP, in fact, the Congress Committees were called civil *jirgas*, as if they were merely an adjunct of the Khudai Khidmatgars.[135] The preference for an indigenous name reflected the party's unique position in the Indian National Congress. As Ghulam Muhammad Khan explained:

> A gulf exists between the Congress and the Khudai Khidmatgar movement, and they are not one. In this connection Khan Abdul Ghaffar Khan . . . has gone so far as to state that they are not Congressmen but have an alliance with the Congress and could sever their relations with

133. AICC File P-23 (Part I), 1938, p. 15.

134. AICC File P/22, 1934-35. Interviews with Amin Jan Khan, Sher Dil Khan, and Hasan Khan.

135. Interviews with Abdul Akbar Khan and Amin Jan Khan. Also see FR8/37(II) and FR11/37(I).

the Congress at any time as they liked.[136]

The support of the Frontier was an increasingly valuable asset to the Congress as the rest of India polarized along communal lines; yet its strength there depended on its ties to the provincial party and not on its own popularity. Congress leaders, therefore, allowed the Frontier Congress much wider latitude than other provincial parties. As long as it abided by their decisions on vital political questions concerning India as a whole, they were ready, though by no means pleased, to let it function without strict supervision and pursue its regional brand of nationalism. The FPCC not only acted without their prior approval on many provincial matters but often without even keeping them informed.[137] It also took liberties with the Congress constitution, such as when it unilaterally raised the number of its AICC members and delegates to the annual Congress session in 1938 or chose its 1938 and 1939 AICC representatives in a manner contrary to party rules.[138] Both actions in 1938 won the High Command's grudging indulgence, but Subhas Chandra Bose insisted upon new elections of AICC members in 1939 because his ally, Ghulam Muhammad Khan, had been denied a fair chance at one of the positions. Even then, it took months of correspondence and a threat to bar the Frontier's representatives from the AICC before the PCC complied.[139]

The Frontier ministry also demanded and received special treatment, as Sir Arthur Parsons, the NWFP's acting governor, explained to the Viceroy in September 1939: "In the past Congress headquarters had always given him [Khan Sahib] and his party much more rope than other Ministries."[140] Khan Sahib enjoyed this freedom because he was answerable to provincial colleagues rather than all-India leaders. This allowed him to pursue policies with which the High Command was, at times, openly dissatisfied.[141]

## The Founding of the Frontier Muslim League

The Frontier Congress offered a sharp contrast in the late 1930's to the Frontier Muslim League, which was weak, disorganized, and without an appealing ideology. The Frontier League's activities, shape, and very existence were not so much of its own making as a reaction to its rival. The latter's policies spawned the Frontier League and defined the pool of its potential members—the groups which were alienated or simply ignored by

136. *Lahore Tribune*, 10/8/39. Also see GR/41. No. 2, 1/24/38.

137. AICC File P-16, 1938. Letter, 2/29/38. Nehru to Abdul Ghaffar Khan.

138. See correspondence in AICC File P-16, 1938; and File P-16, 1939.

139. AICC File P-16, 1939. Telegram, 4/24/39. Abdul Jalil to AICC General-Secretary.

140. LP/74. No. 56. Telegram 26-T, 9/29/39. Parsons to Linlithgow. Also see GR/41. No. 8, 4/23/38; GR/41. No. 11, 6/8/38; GR/42. No. 17, 9/3/38; and GR/42. No. 20, 10/22/38.

141. GR/41. No. 10, 5/26/38; and GR/42. No. 22, 11/21/38.

the Congress. They also determined the issues it espoused and the tactics it adopted. The growth of the Frontier League, in short, was not an independent phenomenon but a response to its more powerful rival.

The League's first venture into the NWFP in the 1937 election campaign had produced no lasting results. It established a foothold in the province only after Sir Abdul Qaiyum, the most prominent public figure outside the Frontier Congress, and the non-Congress Khans changed their attitude toward it. Sir Abdul Qaiyum did not publicly embrace the League while he was Chief Minister, but he covertly encouraged its development in hopes that it would help to stem the Congress' rising popularity.[142] Partly in response to his request, a small group of *ulema* and urban politicians from Hazara gathered in Abbottabad on September 3, 1937, to form a "Frontier Muslim League." They chose *Maulana* Muhammad Shuaib as their President and Qazi Abdul Hakim as General-Secretary. The organizational meeting was timed to coincide with the opening of the fall session of the Legislative Assembly, which was also meeting in Abbottabad and whose first order of business was scheduled to be a no-confidence motion against Sir Abdul Qaiyum's ministry.

The founders of the new party were self-appointed men who, with few exceptions, possessed neither political influence nor prominent social stature. As a consequence, the Khans in the United Muslim Nationalists who independently gravitated to the League after the fall of Qaiyum's ministry were unprepared to accept their leadership. To avoid the appearance of conflict with the Abbottabad "League," the Khans, in cooperation with some urban professionals and businessmen in Peshawar city, formed only a District Muslim League at a meeting on October 23, 1937. Mirza Salim Khan was elected President and Muhammad Ismail Ghaznavi General-Secretary.[143] The two Leagues reached a compromise in Nowshera on November 3, 1937. They were both disbanded, and a new provincial council was formed with *Maulana* Muhammad Shuaib as President, Mian Ziauddin and Saadullah Khan, who belonged to the Peshawar party, as the Vice-Presidents, and Muhammad Ismail Ghaznavi as the General-Secretary.[144] The compromise disguised the Peshawaris' control of the party, which was inevitable in view of their much greater social stature and political strength. Most of the Abbottabad group came to terms with them, but Shuaib refused to accept the role of a figurehead. He tried to assert his presidential authority but succeeded only in isolating himself within the provincial council, which censured him in June 1938 and then stripped him of his office six months

142. Abdul Khaliq Khaliq, *Azadi Jang. Silidili au sa Auridili* (Peshawar: Idara-i-Ishaat Sarhad, 1972), pp. 131-32.

143. *Khyber Mail*, 10/27/37 and *Sarhad*, 12/15/37. Interviews with Muhammad Ismail Ghaznavi and Nasrullah Khan.

144. *Khyber Mail*, 3/13/38.

later.[145] When Saadullah Khan was named as President in his place, the eclipse of the "Abbottabad League" was complete.

The new Provincial Muslim League quickly evolved into an umbrella organization for the non-Congress Khans who found their old, contentious brand of political individualism a liability once their rivals assumed control of the government. Their first response to the Khan Sahib ministry had been to expect the British to restore the old order in which they had acted as the government's surrogates and received its patronage.[146] Once it became apparent that the governor would not turn back the clock, the senior Khans turned to the League. Cunningham would later write:

> The Congress attitude toward the Khans was also largely the cause of the revival of the Muslim League, at the expense of Congress. . . . when some of the anti-Khan measures were taking shape, it was clear that the Muslim League was becoming popular among the Khanate, even among those old-fashioned Khans who had hitherto hardly known the name of the League. They saw in it their main bulwark against the attacks of the Congress. . . .[147]

The League's organization was created piecemeal. Khans on the provincial council persuaded other Khans to build the party in their respective regions through kin ties, factional associations, and social contacts.[148] The League's organization over much of the province consequently was a patchwork of alliances among Khans. In Peshawar *Tehsil*, for example, the League was controlled among the Mohmands by their hereditary chiefs, the Landi *Arbabs*; among the Khalils by the senior branch of the Tehkal *Arbabs*, the titular heads of the tribes; and among the Daudzais by the Babuzai Khans. These families cooperated to control the *Tehsil* League, presided over the District League, and were influential in the Provincial League.[149] A similar pattern occurred in Bannu where the party was led by two powerful families—the senior branch of the Bannuchi Maliks of Bazar Ahmad Khan, who had historically been among the most influential families in their tribe, and the chiefs of the Sperka Wazirs, who considered themselves the leaders of all Wazirs in the district.[150]

To compete with the Khudai Khidmatgars, the League tried to absorb the Khaksars who had developed a strong quasi-military organization in the

---

145. *Sarhad*, 6/22/38; *Lahore Tribune*, 10/27/38; and *Khyber Mail*, 12/11/38 and 12/18/39.

146. GR/41. No. 2, 1/24/38. Also GR/41. No. 3, 2/9/38.

147. CP/5, Part II, p. 7.

148. Interviews with Mian Ziauddin and Muhammad Ismail Ghaznavi. Saadullah Khan, the President of the Frontier Muslim League, who had connections throughout the province as a result of a long career in government service, was the primary figure behind this process.

149. Interviews with Mian Ziauddin, Muhammad Ismail Ghaznavi, and *Arbab* Nur Muhammad Khan.

150. Interviews with Malik Damsaz Khan, Habibullah Khan, and Mian Ziauddin.

Frontier. Estimates of their numbers in the NWFP ranged as high as 3,000, with most of their members belonging to the province's towns.[151] Although the two organizations shared an antipathy to the Congress, the League's hope that the Khaksars would provide a shortcut to a disciplined body of volunteers never materialized because their founder, *Alama* Inayatullah Mashriqi, was not prepared to see his movement subordinated to another organization.[152] Even the possibility that they might cooperate disappeared in 1939 when Mashriqi turned on the League with a venom which he had previously reserved for the Congress.

The Frontier League drew its strongest support from the province's non-Pakhtun regions—its towns and Hazara—where the Congress' rural, Pakhtun character was a handicap. The Frontier Congress had capitalized on the good will which existed for it after the 1937 elections to gain some support in those areas, but within a year, the alliances it had made collapsed due to the feeling that the Khan Sahib ministry was showing overt favoritism to the Pakhtun countryside. In Hazara, there was also strong disapproval of its anti-Khani policies among a Khani elite whose authority and prestige remained strong.[153] The alienation of the towns was symbolized by the shift of Pir Bakhsh and Abdur Rab Nishtar, the Peshawar city MLAs, to the opposition.[154] The Hazara Democrats, with the exception of Muhammad Abbas Khan who was unwilling to quit the ministry, also broke with the Congress; the two Congress MLAs from Hazara publicly protested against what they regarded as ministerial discrimination against their district; and the Hazara District Congress passed a no-confidence motion against the ministry.[155] This shift in non-Pakhtun political sentiment enabled the Muslim League to establish effective party units in the NWFP's towns by World War II and to acquire a base in Hazara which the Congress never challenged.

Power in the NWFP, however, belonged to whoever represented the Pakhtun countryside, and there the Muslim League could not compete with the Congress. The League attracted few Pakhtun organizers with a competence approaching that of the Congress workers. The party was disdainfully called the "Motor League" or "Calling League," even among its own adherents, because its leaders seemed to spend their time visiting one another instead of engaging in serious party work.[156]

---

151. Shad Muhammad, *Khaksar Movement in India* (Delhi: Meenakshi Prakashan, 1973), p. 16.

152. FR11/37(I), FR12/37(I), and FR6/38(II). Also, GR/42. No. 13, 7/7/38.

153. Interviews with Sardar Bahadur Khan and Ghulam Rabbani Khan.

154. The immediate cause of Nishtar's defection was Khan Sahib's failure to support his bill to repeal section of what he termed the "repressive acts." GR/42. No. 15, 8/8/38. However, the dissatisfaction of the two Peshawar city MLAs went deeper. Both objected to the ministers' favoritism of Pakhtuns and the countryside at the expense of their own constituency. Interview with Pir Bakhsh Khan.

155. *Khyber Mail*, 11/6/38; and *Lahore Tribune*, 11/1/38.

156. CD, 5/23/38. Khan Mir Hilali, *Turiyali* (Peshawar: Manzur-i-Am Press, 1967), p. 102.

The League's dependence on the senior Khans guaranteed it some Pakhtun support since each of them brought with him his core group of personal retainers and factional followers. Most, however, did not make the transition from tribal chief to political organizer. They lacked the requisite skills and experience, and usually did not have the inclination since they had not joined the League for ideological reasons but to obtain tactical backing against the Congress. They retained a parochial orientation, which focused on the affairs of their tribe and locality and placed personal and factional interests ahead of party needs. They commonly refused to abide by party directives when they felt that the power or status of other Khans in the League would be enhanced as a result. Some simply rebelled against the idea of party discipline since it ran contrary to their *Pakhto* which made political independence and equality with others a matter of honor.[157] Even within the realm of tribal politics, the senior Khans were no longer a match for their rivals in the Congress.[158] By the start of the 1930s, they had already lost their social legitimacy, and their factional strength had declined dramatically. Once the Congress assumed office, the last prop on which their influence had rested—government support—was removed, leaving them, and by extension, their new party, with only the onus of having once been the close associates of the Frontier's imperial rulers.

The leaders of the All-India Muslim League did little to aid their party in the Frontier. They made a gesture of support at the League's Calcutta session in April 1938 by passing a resolution calling on Muslims "to combat the Congress anti-Muslim activity in the Frontier Province,"[159] and they occasionally sent celebrated Muslim figures, such as *Maulana* Shaukat Ali, to the province to drum up enthusiasm for the party. Otherwise, the central leaders gave the Frontier League only general guidance, and more important, they provided it with little financial support despite repeated pleas from provincial leaders.[160] Thus, the Frontier League was forced to rely for funding on membership dues and the generosity of local donors, neither of which proved substantial. This left the party at a severe financial disadvantage to the Frontier Congress which received a large and regular subsidy from its all-India allies.[161]

Another major cause for the Frontier League's ineffectiveness was its lack of a coherent party program. Beyond resorting to communal propaganda, it had no policy other than to react opportunistically to the initiatives of the Congress government. When the ministry introduced measures beneficial to

---

157. Hilali, *op. cit.*

158. See *supra*, Ch. 3.

159. Syed Sharifuddin Pirzada (ed.), *Foundations of Pakistan* (Karachi: National Publishing House, 1970), Vol. II, p. 298.

160. GR/41. No. 7, 4/9/38.

161. Interview with Mian Ziauddin. GR/40. No. 14, 11/9/37; GR/41. No. 7, 4/9/38, and No. 8, 4/23/38.

Muslims, the League would accuse it of not being bold enough. Its legislative leaders, for instance, publicly advocated a much stronger version of the Agricultural Debtors' Relief Bill, even while they privately complained that it hurt their interests as Khans.[162] When the ministry took forceful measures to curb crime, party spokesmen denounced it for betraying its promise to protect personal liberties and for resorting to policies and police tactics which were more repressive than anything the British had ever employed. Aurangzeb Khan, the party's leader in the assembly, expressed a recurrent party refrain during an adjournment motion in March 1938:

> Repression in any form is to be condemned and more especially when a Government that has got on its programme the protection of civil liberties. If repression comes from that Government, it is all the more deplorable. We were told and we all expected that with the ushering in of this popular Government . . . a new heaven and earth would be brought about. We wished them God speed. But to my painful regret, I have to state on the floor of this House—what to talk of a new heaven and earth—even the old heaven and earth are nowhere by such repressive policy.[163]

The Peshawar District League even voted to start civil disobedience against the *Goondas* Bill in October 1939 on the grounds that the Congress was resorting to fascism in an effort to destroy its opponents.[164] (It did not have to carry through on its threat because the Congress government resigned the next month.)

To compensate for its lack of a positive program, the party placed a heavy reliance upon religious appeals. The Provincial Chief Secretary, Ambrose Dundas, noted in March 1938: "The speeches reported have contained no policy and no argument and have in about every case had no other theme but that Congress is a Hindu organisation and that no true Muslim ought to ally with it."[165] League newspapers assumed a similar approach with articles purporting to show that "the Congress . . . has plans for *Ram Raj* in their hearts" and that the members of the Frontier Congress were traitors to Islam who were furthering the Hindus' anti-Muslim designs in return for power and personal gain.[166]

The League attempted to exploit any activity or indiscretion of the Frontier Congress which could lend substance to these charges. Its members tried to use visits by Gandhi and Nehru to the NWFP to show that the party was subject to Hindu control.[167] They juxtaposed spinning, a classic Con-

162. LAD, Vol. 3, No. 12, 3/18/38, p. 754.
163. LAD, Vol. 3, No. 4, 3/4/38, pp. 188-89.
164. *Lahore Tribune*, 10/19/38.
165. FR3/38(I).
166. *Shura*, 8/1-2/38. Also see *Sarhad*, 12/30/38.
167. GR/41. No. 3, 2/9/38, and No. 4, 2/23/38.

gress symbol, with the Pakhtuns' martial values in an attempt to insinuate that the Congress wanted to emasculate the people of the Frontier and reduce them to doing women's work.[168] They extracted propaganda value from the title of "Frontier Gandhi" which Hindus had given Abdul Ghaffar Khan, suggesting that he had become so Hinduized that he took pride in being a "*naqli* [imitation] Gandhi."[169]

The League concentrated in particular on the policies of the Khan Sahib government. Its spokesmen denounced the ministers, and especially Bhanju Ram Gandhi, for showing Hindus and Sikhs undue preference in government appointments, dismissing Muslims from their jobs without cause, and tolerating injustices against Muslim civil servants by their Hindu superiors.[170] They alleged that the ministry was slighting Muslims in the distribution of government scholarships, and when it withdrew textbooks by the *Anjuman-i-Himayat-i-Islam* from government schools, the newspaper, *Sarhad*, reported that it had removed Islamic history from the curriculum and replaced the name of the Prophet with "Rama Chandra."[171] Whenever communal violence occurred, Leaguers invariably came to the defense of Muslims, blamed the tensions on Hindu prejudices, and found in the government's efforts to restore peace a bias in favor of the minorities.[172]

The League's communal rhetoric, however, was unfruitful in the late 1930s, for its basic charge against its opponents was belied by their attitudes and actions. Islam was so integral a part of the Pakhtuns' ethos that it was natural for Frontier Congressmen to use Islamic symbols and rhetoric. The very name "Khudai Khidmatgar" carried a religious meaning—Servants of God—and its objectives included service to Islam as well as the Pakhtuns. Its leaders' speeches were laced with religious allusions. Abdul Ghaffar Khan even justified the seemingly un-Islamic idea of non-violence in religious terms:

> Non-violence is not a new creed to a Muslim though Mahatma Gandhi has revived it when it was forgotten. It was followed by the Prophet all the time he was in Mecca, persecuted for his faith in one God. It has been followed by other Muslims, who had wished to throw off the yoke of Oppression.[173]

The party's policies also lent little substance to the charge that it was betraying Islam or favoring non-Muslims. Party leaders were careful to maintain their autonomy from the Indian National Congress and paid due atten-

168. *Sarhad*, 7/22/38.
169. *Ibid.*, 2/25/39. Also see *ibid.*, 6/21/38.
170. *Ibid.*, 10/15/37, 2/17/38, 7/3/38, 2/26/39, and 2/27/39.
171. *Ibid.*, 4/6/39.
172. For example, see GR/40. No. 15, 11/23/37; and LAD, Vol. 5, No. 2, 3/18/38, p. 130.
173. Quoted in C.F. Andrews, *The Challenge of the North-West Frontier* (London: George Allen and Unqin, 1937), pp. 88-89.

tion to issues with religious implications. The Khan Sahib ministry, for example, introduced Islamic texts into the school curriculum, amended the laws governing *awqaf* to improve their management, and passed a bill restricting printing and merchandizing of the Quran to Muslims. On occasion, party leaders even fought the League on its own terms by suggesting that theirs was the more Islamic party.[174]

More fundamentally, the League's propaganda rested on the inappropriate premise that people in the North-West Frontier Province identified themselves primarily by their religion rather than their ethnicity. To a large extent, the League had no choice in the matter since the Frontier Congress had defined itself as the party of Pakhtun interests, while the League drew its adherents from the province's non-Pakhtuns and senior Khans whose past connections with the British made them suspect in Pakhtun eyes. Under these circumstances, it made little sense for the League to compete for Pakhtuns' ethnic allegiance. The late 1930s, on the other hand, witnessed growing Muslim-Hindu tensions throughout India which raised the possibility that a communal appeal might overcome the Pakhtuns' ethnocentrism. Communal relations, however, had not deteriorated to the point where Pakhtuns were ready to abandon their ethnic priorities, and as long as that remained true, the League would find it difficult to compete with the Congress in the North-West Frontier.

## Communal Politics During the Khan Sahib Ministry

In July 1935, the Shahidganj mosque was demolished in Lahore to make room for a Sikh *gurdwara*. The ensuing controversy dragged on for years and adversely affected communal relations in the NWFP as well as the Punjab.[175] Closer to home, and more seriously, Musammat Ram Kaur, a minor Hindu girl in Bannu, eloped with her Muslim lover in March 1936, converted to Islam, and took the name of Islam Bibi.[176] Her parents instituted legal proceedings which led to her husband's arrest and a six-month judicial dispute which ended in their regaining custody of her. These events inaugurated a period of rising communal tensions which heightened the minorities sense of personal and political insecurity and colored party politics in the Frontier.

Shortly after the Islam Bibi case reached the courts, *Haji* Mirza Ali Khan, a religious recluse among the Tori Khel Wazirs, who was better known as the *Faqir* of Ipi, raised a *lashkar* of Daurs which momentarily threatened to in-

174. FR9/38(II).

175. FR7/35(II), FR8/35(II), FR9/35(I), FR9/35(II), and FR12/35(II).

176. *Official History of Operations on the North-West Frontier of India, 1936-37* (Delhi: Government of India Press, 1943), pp. 3-4.

vade Bannu District. When the courts returned her to her parents, he began to preach against the government again, this time among his own tribe. Two brigades of troops marched into the Khaisora Valley, the *Faqir*'s headquarters, where they were engaged in a two-day battle by his adherents in late November 1936. The *Faqir* of Ipi subsequently retreated deeper into Waziristan where he rallied elements of the Wazirs, Mahsuds, and Bhittanis in a tribal war against the government which assumed the shape of a regular military campaign in 1937. The government employed 40,000 troops to quell the tribesmen, incurred almost 1,000 casualties, spent £1,500,000, and still managed to secure only an uneasy and fragile truce in Waziristan during the rest of the decade.[177]

As had happened in all previous conflicts in Waziristan, tribal gangs also attacked settlements in Bannu, Dera Ismail Khan, and Kohat Districts. There were only thirteen attacks on the settled districts in 1936-37; but as the army pacified Waziristan, the *Faqir* of Ipi's adherents diverted their energies into raiding which minimized the risk of a direct confrontation with the military. Between October 1937 and April 1939 alone, 233 raids caused property losses estimated at Rs. 40,000,000 and led to almost one hundred kidnappings.[178] The worst single raid occurred on July 23, 1938, when a *lashkar* attacked the town of Bannu, killed twelve people, wounded twenty-five, kidnapped twenty, and looted or destroyed property estimated at four lakhs of rupees.[179]

The raids were directed principally at the religious minorities who, as the province's main traders and moneylenders, were a more enticing target than the Muslims and a safer one since Muslims were bound by their code of honor to assist their clansmen in case of attack. Traditionally, the minorities' major, though by no means infallible, source of protection had been the *naik-hamsaya* relationship.[180] A Hindu or Sikh acknowledged himself a *hamsaya* (dependent) of a powerful Pakhtun Khan, and received the protection of his *naik* (patron) in return. By the late 1930s, this relationship had broken down in the southern districts under the impact of economic changes. With their increasing wealth, many Hindus and Sikhs no longer sought protection since it carried the onus of dependency, yet Pakhtun Khans were often unwilling to defend them without it.[181] The Congress' anti-Khani policies also increased the minorities' vulnerability. As Cunningham observed:

> . . . the Khans were surly and resentful at the attitude of the Ministry towards them and at the blows which had been dealt at their pockets and prestige. They consequently saw no reason why they should take

177. Sir William Barton, *India's North-West Frontier* (London: John Murray, 1939), p. 228.
178. PJ12/23. File 99.
179. FR7/38(II).
180. CD, 12/15/38. AICC File 16, 1938. Statement by Kotu Ram, 10/25/38.
181. *Ibid.*

any particularly active part in helping to combat crime.[182]

For their part, the ordinary villagers tended to sympathize with the tribesmen. Thus, intelligence about impending raids dried up; the Frontier Constabulary and army received little assistance in tracking down the tribal gangs; and the minorities had to worry about their neighbors joining the raiders rather than helping them to defend themselves.

When a rash of raids made their sense of insecurity acute, the minorities in isolated villages sought refuge in the district towns. In 1938 alone, an estimated one-third of the minority population in Bannu was displaced in this manner.[183] The towns, however, were not the havens they were assumed to be. Communal relations there were already strained, and the migrants only made a tense situation more volatile with their suspicions and complaints. In Dera Ismail Khan, the "influx of additional, highly-strung Hindus from the outlying areas" helped, as Cunningham recounted, to turn a dispute over the slaughter of a cow on *Id* into a communal riot on February 2, 1939.[184] As was usually the case, the minorities suffered the greatest losses in the fighting and found that their position became even more insecure than before as a result of the bitterness the riot engendered.

The Muslim League sought to capitalize on the NWFP's communal troubles by giving its unswerving support to the Muslim side in every communal incident, regardless of who was at fault. Its rhetoric, as a result, tended to enflame communal animosities and, according to government reports, occasionally led directly to violence, such as the murder of two Sikhs in Mayar village in Mardan District in February 1938 and the random stabbing of minorities in Peshawar city early the following year.[185]

As much as they were alarmed by the Muslim League, the minorities felt only a little better about the Frontier Congress. Neither of the two political camps into which the province's Hindus and Sikhs were divided were pleased with Khan Sahib's ministry. Those who had opted for a party of their own found confirmation for their mistrust of the Congress in the ministry's record, while many of those who had thought that their security lay in working within the Congress were disillusioned by what they perceived as its communal bias. For example, Dr. C.C. Ghosh, a founding member of the Frontier Congress, later wrote to V.C. Savarkar that the Frontier Hindus "had placed them[selves] under Muslim majority which dominates the Red Shirt organisation here . . . Congress (Red Shirt) attitude during the Congress Ministry days towards the minorities was most tyrannous."[186]

The minorities complained that the ministry did not adequately protect them from tribal raids or take sufficiently strong punitive measures against

182. PJ8/588. Collection 117-C-3, p. 9.
183. Barton, *op. cit.*, p. 186.
184. GR/43. No. 3, 2/8/39. Also see CD, 2/8/39.
185. GR/41. No. 4, 2/23/38; and GR/43. No. 6, 3/23/39.
186. Savarkar Papers. File A18/116. Letter, 9/20/43. Ghosh to Savarkar.

their Muslim neighbors whom they believed aided the tribesmen.[187] They also thought it was squeezing them out of government employment, although the percentages on communal representation in the services did not lend credence to their suspicions,[188] and they took strong exception to two pieces of economic legislation, the Agricultural Debtors' Relief Bill and Agricultural Markets Produce Bill, which hurt their interests as moneylenders and traders. Mehr Chand Khanna expressed the general feelings of his compatriots when he call the two bills doses of poison which made a mockery of the Congress' election pledge that no one would suffer economically from its policies because of their religion.[189] A combination of governmental decisions even convinced some Hindus and Sikhs that the Frontier Congress was acting out of an Islamic bias which threatened their culture and religion.[190]

The Frontier Congress, in sum, seemed to the minorities to be committed to policies which favored Muslims at their expense, and even the Congress' predominantly Hindu all-India High Command appeared unable to act as a brake upon it. On the other hand, the strategy of relying on a separate party which would use its strength in the legislative assembly to obtain written guarantees had failed with the fall of Sir Abdul Qaiyum's government. The Congress did not need the Hindu-Sikh Nationalists' support, and the Muslim League did not want it. The only strategy left to the minorities was the weak and futile one of protest and appeal—to the ministry, the PCC, Abdul Ghaffar Khan, the AICC, and the permanent administration. Thus, at the end of Khan Sahib's tenure of office in November 1939, a solution to their political dilemma appeared as distant as at its start. It would not materialize until the advent of a Muslim League ministry in 1943 forced a reevaluation of their attitude toward the Frontier Congress.

---

187. For example, see the statements by Hindu leaders in AICC File 16(i), 1937 and Files 16 and P-16, 1938.

188. See LAD, Vol. 6, No. 1, 9/14/39, p. 30 for a breakdown of the administrative services by communal percentages.

189. LAD, Vol. 4, No. 16, 11/22/38, p. 1152.

190. For example, see statements in AICC File P-16, 1938.

# 7

# WARTIME POLITICS, 1939-1945

World War II cut short the Frontier Congress' brief regime. Dr. Khan Sahib had hoped to stay in office as late as October even if the Working Committee forced the other Congress ministries to resign, but in the end, he could not stand apart from the rest of the party on an issue of the magnitude of the war.[1] On November 7, 1939, he called a special assembly session, passed the Congress' resolution against the war, and tendered his resignation. Muhammad Ali Jinnah immediately urged Aurangzeb Khan, the Provincial League leader, to form a coalition at any cost to show that the NWFP accepted their party as the authoritative representative of India's Muslims,[2] but communal antagonism and factionalism among the non-Congress Muslims prevented him from doing so. Cunningham, therefore, assumed control of the provincial administration under Section 93 of the 1935 Government of India Act. Under renewed pressure from Jinnah, the Frontier League made a more concerted attempt to create a ministry at the beginning of 1940. Lord Linlithgow urged Cunningham to help and had Sir Henry Craik, the Governor of the Punjab, discreetly ask Sir Sikandar Hayat Khan to lend his assistance.[3] But, as Cunningham predicted, no ministry could be formed because there were "too many selfish ambitions and private feuds" among the non-Congress MLAs.[4]

During Khan Sahib's tenure, provincial politics had centered around the efforts of the Frontier Congress to alter the balance in the province's traditional polity. With the war, the party's assault on its Khani rivals abated, and its focus reverted to dismantling the British imperial system. Since their interests were no longer directly threatened, the Khans who dominated the

1. GR/44. No. 19, 10/9/39. Also, LP/24. No. 56. Telegram 27-T, 9/29/39. Parsons to the Viceroy.

2. *Lahore Tribune*, 11/12/30; and GR/44. No. 21, 11/12/39.

3. LP/175. No. 1, 6, and 7. Also, PJ8/644. No. 6206. Letter, 12/2/39. Linlithgow to Craik.

4. Cunningham explained: "Khan Bahadur Sadullah Khan would bitterly contest the premiership with Aurangzeb Khan; the Hindus would be shy of joining a party tainted with the name of Muslims; among the Hindus themselves two Rai Bahadurs [Mehr Chand Khanna and Ishar Das Sahni] are inveterate rivals, and would split the Hindu group; the two Independents (the ablest men, probably, in the Assembly) would, I think, vote with Congress in a crucial vote." GR/44. No. 1, 1/9/40.

Frontier Muslim League lacked the incentive to maintain their party activities at the same pitch as before. Many reverted to their old style of politics and sought to reestablish a privileged relationship with the government.[5] Cunningham, however, rejected every proposal which artificially enhanced the powers of the Khans since he was determined not to repeat the mistake of 1930 and create a source of popular discontent on which the Congress could capitalize.[6]

World War II underscored the parochialism of the NWFP. While the Congress' confrontation with the British threw other provinces into turmoil, the Frontier remained quiet. The issues that agitated the rest of India simply seemed less urgent or even irrelevant to the province, including most of its Congressmen. Yet the Frontier Congress was compelled by party ties to stay in step with its allies. In the process, it fell out of tune with local sentiments with the result that its popularity was temporarily eclipsed. The Frontier Congress was called on twice to join agitations devised by the all-India party: the individual *satyagraha* campaign, which was started in September 1940; and the Quit India Movement, which was launched in August 1942. Both times, it joined in late, acted indecisively, and experienced failure.

The arrest of ten Congress MLAs in the Quit India Movement allowed Aurangzeb Khan to form a Muslim League ministry in May 1943 and govern the province until March 1945. As soon as he came to power, the personal feuds and factionalism which had plagued his party from the start resurfaced. He was threatened by defections within the assembly and challenged by opponents in the provincial party organization. In order to survive, he opportunistically used his ministerial power to pacify wavering MLAs and keep his supporters happy. His manipulation of power was so blatant that within a year of assuming office he had disillusioned the general public and major segments of his party. Factional strife within the party intensified as a result, forcing the central League leadership to intervene. But its efforts to rebuild the party failed when the reorganization became one more arena into which Aurangzeb Khan's supporters and opponents extended their bitter animosities.

## The Congress Agitations of 1940 and 1942

The genesis of individual civil disobedience lay in the failure of the Congress to negotiate a suitable political trade-off with the Viceroy for its cooperation in the war. The party decided at Ramgarh in March 1940 to resort to civil disobedience and gave Gandhi sole responsibility for directing the campaign. In July, the Working Committee suspended that decision in hopes of reaching an accommodation with the government, only to reverse

5. CD, 5/3/40.
6. CD, 6/22/40.

itself again two months later when a new impasse developed. Gandhi decided on individual, rather than mass, *satyagraha* over the right to preach against the war. He ordered select individuals to court arrest by shouting anti-war slogans beginning on October 17th.

Gandhi did not choose any *satyagrahis* from the NWFP. Instead, he entrusted responsibility for the Frontier to Abdul Ghaffar Khan who prevaricated because of objections to the campaign within the PCC.[7] Slogan-shouting by twenty select leaders was finally targeted for December 14th. Notices were sent to the Deputy Commissioners specifying times and places, and meetings were held to whip up popular anticipation. But beneath the public appearances, party leaders, including many of the anointed *satyagrahis*, remained unconvinced of the efficacy of the campaign. Four days before it began, Cunningham wrote in his diary:

> It seems clear now that none of them have their hearts in it, and if left to themselves many of them will not persevere with their slogan-shouting more than a day or two. We decided, therefore, not to arrest anyone straight-away, unless a demonstration is anticipated, and to judge each case by the actual effect it is likely to have.[8]

The *satyagrahis* started on schedule, shouting the approved slogans against the war. Some made only a gesture at breaking the law. For example, the ex-Finance Minister, Bhanju Ram Gandhi, "only came out on to the steps of his house, shouted the slogan once or twice and then retreated indoors."[9] Two *satyagrahis*, including the PCC General-Secretary, Abdul Qaiyum Khan Swathi, were arrested in Hazara, but elsewhere the police simply told them to disperse or took them home.[10] The Government of India objected to Cunningham's leniency, but he resisted its demand for sterner measures on the grounds that arrests would create political martyrs who would give impetus to a campaign which had no chance of otherwise succeeding.[11] Slogan-shouting dwindled away by Christmas as the *satyagrahis* saw that they were only evoking bemusement and derision. Gandhi declared a Christmas truce which was extended in the NWFP until after *Id-uz-Zuha* in the first week of January. Subsequently, a few men half-heartedly resumed slogan-shouting until the end of the month and then stopped. Abdul Ghaffar Khan tried a new tack in March by sending Khudai Khidmatgars to shout slogans in their villages. The public's response was so negligible that the next month he gave up and called a halt to individual *satyagraha* altogether.

---

7. GR/44. No. 21, 11/8/40 and No. 23, 12/9/40.
8. CD, 12/10/40.
9. CD, 1/16/41.
10. FR12/40(I).
11. GoI File 3/22/44. Telegram 4964, 12/14/40. Home Department to Chief Secretary, NWFP; and Telegram 196-BI, 12/17/40, NWFP to Home Department.

The Frontier Congress' paltry efforts were partially obscured in 1940 by the failure of the campaign throughout India. During the Quit India Movement of 1942, it had no such cover. The Working Committee once again entrusted Abdul Ghaffar Khan with responsibility for the Frontier. In late July, he tried to stir up excitement by announcing that he would send Khudai Khidmatgars to the tribal areas to urge the people not to indulge in raiding once civil disobedience began. Cunningham saw no need to stop the emissaries because propaganda by *mullahs* and tribal *maliks* had already turned the tribesmen against the Congress.[12] The Khudai Khidmatgars met a hostile reception everywhere they went. The Mohmands and Afridis warned them not to come to their territory, while the *maliks* in Malakand forced them to turn back. Elsewhere, they received the barest reception commensurate with the Pakhtun value of *melmastia* (hospitality).

Cunningham also assumed a mild stance toward the rest of the agitation. He felt confident that the Congress "would get little sympathy here, and that Abdul Ghaffar Khan was not likely to get much support if he preached the Congress case."[13] He sought at all costs to avoid arrests which might force a confrontation and arouse hostility "not only among Abdul Ghaffar Khan's Red Shirt followers but among a considerable section of otherwise friendly opinion."[14] Moreover, he regarded the Frontier leaders as the province's best protection against the agitation turning violent. In fact, they did keep the campaign peaceful, deflecting all pressure from Congress extremists within and outside the province to redirect it into sabotage.[15]

Cunningham's policy was received with deep misgivings by the Government of India.[16] Before the agitation began, the Viceroy and Home Department urged him to adopt their hardline policy of arresting everyone capable of leading a mass movement as soon as the AICC ratified the call for civil disobedience. After August 8th, they redoubled their pressure, broadly hinting that unless he acted firmly, Cunningham would be held solely responsible for any problems which might develop in the Frontier. Events, however, proved that his confidence, and not the Government of India's apprehensions, was warranted.

No action was taken against the Frontier Congress on August 9th, leaving it the only PCC in India that was not outlawed. This caught party leaders by surprise because they had assumed that the government would take preemptive measures, thereby handing them an issue.[17] They temporized at first, holding public meetings and organizing a partial *hartal* on August 10th to keep up appearances while searching for a coherent policy. They also started

12. CP/6, No. 6. Note, 9/23/42; and PJ8/627. Collection 117-C-27Q. No. 3765, p. 1.
13. CP/6. No. 6. Confidential Note, 11/4/42.
14. *Ibid.*
15. *Ibid.* Also see CD, 9/15/42 and 6/12/45.
16. See CD, 7/29/42; and LP/77. No. 26, 9/23/42. Viceroy to Cunningham.
17. Interviews with Abdul Akbar Khan and Pir Shahinshah.

small-scale picketing of liquor stores which the authorities condoned on the theory that it "is a useful safety valve as it troubles nobody and saves the face of Congress."[18] The PCC met on August 16th but could reach no decision other than to leave the matter to Abdul Ghaffar Khan. He, in turn, decided to go on tour to gauge public feelings before starting civil disobedience in earnest.

A more definite program was charted at a second PCC meeting on August 28th.[19] Picketing of schools began on September 1st, with some property damage occurring in the towns of Mardan and Charsadda. Attempts were also made to organize student *hartals*, but these met with minimal success after the first day. Only in Bannu, where the picketers blocked access to school buildings, did the authorities respond with arrests, detaining 439 people in all. Public meetings were also intensified, with the peak coming on September 4th when a declaration of independence was read throughout the province. The Khudai Khidmatgars began to talk about occupying government offices, and Congress leaders warned on September 13th that they would shut down the courts, but neither threat materialized. In spite of all their activity and rhetoric, party workers had failed to generate a sufficient level of public interest to sustain a civil disobedience campaign. The agitation dwindled after September 13th, and *Ramzan* conveniently intervened to serve as an excuse for inactivity. Even the protests at the schools were halted by the end of the month in deference to public opinion.

Under pressure from Indian National Congress sources, Abdul Ghaffar Khan ended the lull in the agitation on October 5th.[20] Large groups of Khudai Khidmatgars from the countryside, numbering up to 750 in Peshawar and 300 in Mardan, picketed the district courts for six consecutive days before suspending their activities for *Id* on October 10th. Smaller crowds also appeared in Kohat for two days. At first, the police only detained the picketers for the day, but their activities attracted crowds which clashed with the police, most seriously in Mardan where three people were killed and thirteen wounded on October 10th. When picketing resumed on October 19th, therefore, the government modified its tactics and started selectively arresting Congress organizers. The largest number detained in any single district was only 131 in Mardan. Abdul Ghaffar Khan was arrested on October 27th. Cunningham would have preferred to have left him free since his detention gave the Khudai Khidmatgars an issue, but he had left the authorities no choice by defying a ban on his entry into Mardan District.[21] To forestall trouble, twenty-three Khudai Khidmatgar leaders from Charsadda were rounded

18. PJ8/605. Collection 117-C-27-F. No. 5941. Telegram, 8/17/42. Governor, NWFP, to Secretary of State.

19. FR8/42(II). Also see FR9/42(I) and CD, 9/13/42.

20. CP/5. Part II, pp. 22-23.

21. CP/5, Part II, pp. 22. Also see FR10/42(I), FR10/42(II), and PJ8/627. Collection 117-C-27Q. No. 3765, p. 6.

up after his arrest in the last major sweep of Frontier Congress leaders.

The government siphoned away the remaining force of the agitation by starting to jail picketers in later October rather than merely holding them for a day.[22] By then, the agitation was confined to Peshawar city and the town of Mardan. The first day's arrests ended serious picketing in Mardan. In Peshawar, the number of picketers fell to about ten a day by mid-November, and they no longer approached the courts, presenting themselves at police headquarters instead. The government arrested each new group of protestors but did not try to stop the routine altogether. Cunningham wrote in retrospect, "We let it go on because Dr. Khan Sahib and other Congress leaders here could use this as an answer to pressure from down-country to take a more active part against the Government."[23] The charade continued in a spasmodic manner until April 1943 when the Frontier Congress leaders called it off on their own accord.

General Sir Claude Auchinleck said that Sir George Cunningham's handling of the Quit India Movement was worth two Army Corps.[24] There is no doubt that his tactful policy minimized the disruptive impact of the campaign; however, he was able to use finesse rather than force only because conditions already existed which made its failure probable. During the Khan Sahib ministry, the Frontier Congress had possessed sufficient autonomy to act independent of, and even contrary to, the High Command's wishes on many questions. The war, in contrast, raised issues which were so vital to the Congress that its leaders expected the Frontier party to abide by their decisions, no matter how individualistically it implemented them. This left the Frontier Congressmen prey to the vagaries of all-India political negotiations in which they had little part. Time and again, they had to adjust to policy shifts about which they had not been forewarned and which they did not always like. Their relationship with the High Command was further confused by Abdul Ghaffar Khan, who temporarily resigned from the Working Committee twice when it adopted policies contrary to Gandhi's wishes.[25] The end-result was that the Frontier Congress often acted equivocally, contrary to the best judgment of its leaders, or not at all.

Even when the High Command issued clear orders, the party tended to act indecisively because the war was popular in the NWFP. Economically, the war brought prosperity to the Frontier after the hard time of the 1930s. Agricultural prices rose, and employment opportunities expanded as the province's contingent in the army grew almost fivefold from 8,828 to

---

22. PJ8/627. Collection 117-C-27Q. No. 3765, p. 6.

23. CP/5, p. 24.

24. Norvall Mitchell, *Sir George Cunningham* (Edinburgh: Blackwood and Sons, 1968), p. 162.

25. D.G. Tendulkar, *Abdul Ghaffar Khan* (Bombay: Popular Prakashan, 1967), pp. 326-38 and 343.

41,201.[26] Politically, the two years of self-rule under the 1935 India Act had blunted anti-British feelings so that the government no longer appeared as an obstacle in the way of local aspirations. With the heavy recruitment into the army and an intensive propaganda campaign which equated the war with the defense of Islam, the people of the Frontier adopted the British cause as their own.

Even most Congressmen did not oppose the war out of deep-seated conviction. Many made no pretense of complying with party policy, as Khan Sahib recognized when he told Cunningham in May 1940 that while he did not think any Congressmen would serve on committees set up to assist in the war mobilization, "they would be ready to perform any task allotted to them by those Committees, with a view to preserving the peace and good order of the Province."[27] Leaders like Khan Sahib and Ali Gul Khan, the PCC President, were caught in a more difficult position. They too sympathized with the British, but party policy dictated that they appear to be against the war. The contradiction between their inner feelings and public posture was so transparent that when they were called on to lead the campaigns of 1940 and 1942, people remained unconvinced of their sincerity. As Cunningham noted during the individual *satyagraha* campaign, "It is . . . commonly believed that Congress leaders, with the possible exception of A.G.K., are really in secret concord with Government."[28] There appeared to be good grounds for these suspicions. Some party leaders remained in regular contact with government officials and extended to them some cooperation even when relations were most strained. Cunningham, for instance, felt he could take a vacation in August 1942 in spite of the Quit India agitation because of private assurances from the PCC President: "Sikandar [Mirza] told me that Ali Gul Khan had said that he would see things did not boil up enough to make me curtail my trip to Kashmir."[29] Clearly, the passions which marked the unrest in 1930-1932 were absent during World War II.

The government helped foster the Frontier's positive attitude on the war by secretly enlisting on its side influential *mullahs*, *maulanas*, and *sajjada nishins* in both the settled districts and tribal area.[30] Few men of any religious consequence stood aloof. The *Faqir* of Ipi was a major exception, but some of his lieutenants took up war propaganda as did many other men who were publicly perceived as anti-British. In return for liberal subsidies, religious figures preached that Great Britain's enemies were also the enemies of

26. MIL14/234 and MIL14/236. Including the Frontier Corps and Levies which operated in the tribal area, the total in the military on January 1, 1942, was 57,599.

27. CD, 5/30/40.

28. CD, 12/24/40.

29. CD, 8/28/42. Khan Sahib was a frequent dinner and bridge guest of the governor, seeing him even while the Congress was conducting civil disobedience.

30. See CP/3 for a detailed description of how this was done.

Islam. Similar propaganda was disseminated by the province's press, which was also heavily subsidized.[31] Two parallel networks were used to recruit the religious leaders.[32] *Khan Bahadur* Quli Khan started the first in August 1939 on the request of Sir Arthur Parsons, the acting governor. His primary success was in convincing the members of the *Jamiat-ul-Ulema-i-Sarhad*, who were almost professionally anti-British, to preach that the interests of Islam and Great Britain were identical. Cunningham directed the second network himself until August 1941 when he turned it over to military intelligence. He worked primarily through the Deputy Commissioners and Political Agents who, in turn, employed influential and largely apolitical, private citizens.

A rare unanimity was created in religious circles which gave the war a powerful sanction. Religious figures initially concentrated their attacks on the "bolsheviks" who had long been held in disfavor in the Frontier for their atheism and their treatment of Central Asian Muslims. The Germans were denounced first for their association with the Russians and then for being anti-religious themselves. When the alignments in the war changed, the propaganda was suitably redirected. Italians were condemned as no longer *ahl-i-kitab* and the Japanese as *but parast* (idol worshippers). The Russians' religious attitudes were played down, and the English alliance with them was justified as expedient politics.[33]

It required little prompting to turn these polemics against the Congress. Frontier Congressmen encountered a barrage of denunciations which described them as actively in league with the anti-religious Fascists or simply labeled them as *kafirs* for opposing a war in which Islam had a stake.[34] The more actively the Congress engaged in anti-war work, the heavier the propaganda against it became. Months before the Quit India Movement opened, religious figures throughout the Frontier started to sharpen their attacks. Once the agitation began, a spate of *fatwas* were issued condemning it; the *Jamiat-ul-Ulema-i-Sarhad* disseminated tracts which Cunningham called "all good anti-Congress, anti-Japanese and [anti-]Axis stuff," and the Muslim press almost universally denounced the Congress for trying to create a Hindu *Raj* in collusion with the Axis powers.[35]

The anti-Congress propaganda was reinforced by personal attacks on its leaders. Abdul Ghaffar Khan had made no attempt to disguise his admiration for Gandhi, emulating him in ways which ran counter to Pakhtun values. He propagated *charkha* (spinning) which Pakhtuns considered women's work, and in an effort to create an awareness of cleanliness, swept village streets, an activity which was viewed as beneath the dignity of a Khan. He also established a Khudai Khidmatgar center at Sardaryab in Peshawar Dis-

31. CP/3a, p. 4.
32. CP/3b.
33. CD, 7/1/41.
34. See CP/3a for samples of the anti-Congress propaganda.
35. CP/3c and FR9/42(I).

trict which his enemies compared to Gandhi's *ashram*. *Al-Falah*, for instance, editorialized:

> The Frontier Gandhi, Abdul Ghaffar Khan, to give Hindu education and to make Pakhtuns true *kafirs*, has opened an *ashram* in the Frontier in which instruction on the Gita and Vedas will be given. Muslims will be enlightened with Hindu education. Lessons in the Hindu style of praying and the true education of Gandhi's *ashram* will be taught.[36]

More detrimental were the marriages of Abdul Ghaffar Khan's son to a Parsi and Khan Sahib's daughter to a Christian. The former excited disapproval but no major public outcry since it was assumed that women in interfaith marriages adopt the religion of their husbands. For that very reason, the marriage of Khan Sahib's daughter, Miriam, in May 1942 was blown into a major political issue. Although Miriam's mother was Christian and English, people felt Khan Sahib was allowing a Muslim woman to leave the Islamic fold. The anti-Congress press used the marriage as a springboard for a general denunciation of Khan Sahib and his brother. The *Khyber Mail* wrote in a relatively restrained manner:

> The episode of Miss Khan Sahib's engagement to a non-Muslim may well establish the Khan Brothers' claim to enlightened nationalism, but its outcome leaves no doubt regarding the fact that the Muslim public expects its leaders to live up to MUSLIM ideals. Certain circles in this country are in the habit of proclaiming loudly that a man's private life is entirely his own and has nothing to do with his public activities. The Pathans have, however, shown that so far as they are concerned this doctrine is mere trash.[37]

Other papers made much more virulent attacks.[38] Khan Sahib temporarily resigned from the party, and Abdul Ghaffar Khan disassociated himself from the marriage. Nonetheless, their personal reputations suffered, and their party lost considerable public support. As late as July 1942, Cunningham cited the marriage as a major reason why he did not expect much public enthusiasm for the Quit India Movement.[39]

External factors aside, the Frontier Congress was severely sapped during the early war years by factionalism which was a legacy from its days in power. Departure from office had produced a momentary spirit of accommodation among the feuding groups; but as time passed without a clear-cut policy and as ambivalence about opposing the war rose, infighting broke out with re-

---

36. *Al-Falah*, 7/3/42.
37. *Khyber Mail*, 5/12/42.
38. For example, see *Al-Falah*, 6/5/42 and 7/31/42.
39. PJ8/597. Collection 117-27-AA. No. 5374. Telegram 2193-S, 7/26/42. Viceroy to Secretary of State.

newed intensity throughout the party organization.[40] Ghulam Muhammad Khan renewed his feud with the PCC majority until it expelled him from the party in November 1940. Mian Jafar Shah and *Arbab* Abdul Ghafur resigned as PCC President and General-Secretary in July 1940 in a dispute over party policy. Two years later, *Arbab* Abdul Ghafur revived the Afghan Jirga as a proponent of militant Pakhtun nationalism and became a bitter foe of Abdul Ghaffar Khan and Dr. Khan Sahib, whom he denounced as apostates and servants of the Hindus.[41] When Abdul Ghaffar Khan temporarily resigned from the Congress Working Committee in July 1940, some Khudai Khidmatgars felt that they should abolish the Congress Committee hierarchy and reassert their independence from their all-India allies. The PCC fought the idea until Abdul Ghaffar Khan resolved the issue in its favor by rejoining the Working Committee in September. Just as that dispute ended, Rab Nawaz Khan resigned as the Khudai Khidmatgars' commander "on the grounds that he is merely a puppet *Salar-i-Azam* and that the non-violence clause introduced in the movement was contrary to Islamic principles and Afghan traditions."[42]

All these factors—the failure to mount a credible anti-war movement, the war's popularity, the anti-nationalist religious propaganda, the attacks on the personal behavior of the Khan brothers, and the factionalism—combined to produce a dramatic slump in the Frontier Congress' popularity which can be most readily seen from membership statistics. The number of primary Congressmen fell from 23,815 in 1939 to 10,902 by March 1941. Later figures are not available, but there is no reason to assume that the decline was reversed before 1943. While all of the districts contributed to the decrease, the southern three showing the greatest percentage decline (see Table 8). A similar drop occurred among the Khudai Khidmatgars, but its precise dimensions are unclear since accurate membership rolls were not kept.

## The Aurangzeb Khan Ministry

Immediately after the Quit India Movement began, the "obvious propaganda advantage" prompted Lord Linlithgow once more to urge Cunningham to explore the possibility of a non-Congress ministry.[43] Cunningham, however, considered the Muslim MLAs too divided by jealousies to make the enterprise worthwhile. Aurangzeb Khan, the presumptive Premier, initially concurred, calling any coalition he might put together a

40. See FR4/40(II), FR5/40(I), FR7/40(I), FR8/40(II), and FR11/40(II). Also GR/44. No. 5, 14, 15, and 16.

41. *Al-Falah*, 7/24/42 and 8/28/42; and *Civil and Military Gazette*, 9/27/42 and 11/5/42.

42. FR9/40(I).

43. LP/77. No. 21. Telegram 2402-S, 8/13/42. Viceroy to Cunningham. Also see LP/77. No. 23. Telegram 2638-S, 8/28/42. Viceroy to Cunningham.

**Table 8: Congress Membership in 1939 and 1941**[44]

| *District* | *1939* | *1941* | *% Change* |
|---|---|---|---|
| Hazara | 1,720 | 604 | – 65 % |
| Mardan | 6,008 | 4,641 | – 23 % |
| Peshawar | 9,351 | 4,004 | – 23 % |
| Kohat | 1,794 | 409 | – 77 % |
| Bannu | 3,568 | 452 | – 87 % |
| Dera Ismail Khan | 954 | 152 | – 84 % |

"bathroom majority"—one so precarious it would disappear whenever a member went to the toilet.[45] He revised his opinion in January 1943 after the assembly's membership had been reduced to thirty-four by the arrest of ten Congress MLAs and the death, resignation, or disbarment of six others. Even though he started with a block of sixteen Muslim supporters, the formation of his ministry turned into an arduous, drawn out process. The dissension among the League representatives reemerged as soon as there was a prize to fight over, while the minority MLAs refused to negotiate because their leader, Mehr Chand Khanna, was away on a trip to Canada.[46]

Cunningham had reservations about the calibre of the League leaders. He told the Viceroy in January 1943:

> . . . although Congress stock has fallen very heavily in the last year or so, this does not mean that the prestige of the Muslim League has risen. Aurangzeb Khan and his friends are looked upon generally, as an Indian friend of mine put it, as being out for the 'loaves and the fish.' Opinion does not credit them with any motives of public service.[47]

He also had strong doubts about the durability of a League government and feared that a short-lived ministry of mediocre talent might reflect badly on the government as a whole and resuscitate the Congress agitation. Due to these misgivings and the experience of having failed to promote a non-Congress ministry in 1937, Cunningham told Aurangzeb Khan that he had to have written commitments from enough MLAs to give him a majority in the assembly even if the representatives who were in jail were released before he would be allowed to form a government.[48]

Both the League and the Congress had solid blocs of supporters in the assembly, but there was a group equally as large which, if not actually up for the highest bidder, gave the impression that it was. In March, Aurangzeb

44. Compiled from AICC File G-54, 1939 and File G-1, 1941.

45. CD, 11//9/42. Also PJ8/659. Collection 177-C-68. No. 9750. Letter, 11/9/42. Cunningham to Viceroy.

46. GR/43. No. 3, 2/9/43; and PJ8/659. Collection 117-C-68. No. 4380. Letter, 3/5/42. Cunningham to Viceroy.

47. GR/43. No. 2, 1/23/43.

48. GR/43. No. 8, 4/23/43.

Khan listed three Congressmen as converts and another eight, some of them by all appearances staunch partymen, as possibilities. He also expressed hope about seven non-Congress MLAs, including three minority representatives.[49] The situation did not stabilize until May, by which time he had commitments from twenty MLAs and expected another two or three to join him once a ministry was formed. Cunningham relaxed the earlier requirements he had imposed on Aurangzeb Khan and accepted that assessment, noting in addition that two Congressmen had promised to stay neutral.[50] On May 25th, he swore in a cabinet consisting of four Muslims and a Sikh, Sardar Ajit Singh.

The formation of the League ministry finally resolved the divisions among the religious minorities over political strategy. The broad outline of their dilemma was the same as before the war, but the political environment had qualitatively changed. The minorities' maneuverability had been reduced, while their perception that they needed protection had acquired greater urgency due to the Muslim League's advocacy of Islamic separatism. The minorities had three options: to cooperate as a separate party with the Muslim League; to do the same with the Congress; or to merge wholly with the Congress. In the end, most agreed on the third alternative. Only a segment of the Sikh community continued to opt for a separate party, the Akali Dal, and to try to work with the League. A few Hindus, such as Dr. C.C. Ghosh, were so disillusioned with the Congress that they wished to retain a separate political identity, but they were in a small minority. Most were convinced that the growing communal polarization of India's politics left them with no viable alternative to joining the Frontier Congress. The key individual in this decision was Mehr Chand Khanna, who had emerged as the dominant Hindu politician in the NWFP.

Aurangzeb Khan believed at one point that he had the support of at least three minority MLAs, but in the end, only Ajit Singh joined him.[51] The rest reneged after Khanna, on his return to Peshawar in early May, refused to cooperate with the League. He declared, according to his newspaper *Sarhadi Samachar*, that the League "stands for the vivisection of Mother India" and the minorities would be committing suicide by working with it.[52] Even Ajit Singh seemed likely to back away when the Akali Dal leader, Master Tara Singh, opposed the alliance; but V.C. Savarkar, the Hindu Mahasabha President, interceded to obtain the Dal's consent.[53] Savarkar believed that

49. PJ8/659. Collection 117-C-68. No. 3473. Letter, 3/2/43. Viceroy to Cunningham.

50. PJ8/659. Collection 117-C-68. No. 4413. Telegram C.A./26, 5/13/43. Governor, NWFP, to Viceroy.

51. GR/43. No. 9, 5/4/43; and PJ8/659. Collection 117-C-68. No. 3473. Letter, 3/2/43. Viceroy to Cunningham.

52. Quoted in FR6/43(I).

53. *Dawn*, 4/20/43 and 5/21/43. For Savarkar's role in the Akali Dal decision, see Savarkar Papers. File A18/116. Letter, 9/28/43. Savarkar to Ajit Singh; and Letter, 1/14/44. Savarkar to J.P. Srivastiva.

cooperation with the League on carefully delineated terms would restrain the League, give the Mahasabha access to power, and enhance its position in the Hindu community vis-à-vis the Congress. In the face of Khanna's opposition, he could not implement his policy through his own party, so he encouraged Ajit Singh and the Akali Dal to enter into a pact with the League.

The personal slight Khanna felt as a result of Savarkar's actions reinforced the ideological impetus which was propelling him toward a rapprochement with the Congress.[54] He had started to come to terms with the Frontier Congress even before leaving for Canada in November 1942. After Aurangzeb Khan took office, he became the secretary of its Parliamentary Party. He, nonetheless, did not break completely with his past associates, for he apparently still had some doubts about the Congress' reliability.[55] He remained a member of the Mahasabha and even attended its Working Committee meeting in December 1943. Whatever doubts he may have initially felt were dispelled as he established close working relations with the Congress leaders, especially Dr. Khan Sahib. Within two years, his political conversion was complete. Ignoring requests from the Mahasabha's General-Secretary to revive the party's Frontier branch, he finally repudiated his party membership in October 1945.[56]

The Frontier Congress needed to make few adjustments to accommodate the minorities since their fears about the League left them with no choice but to trust its promises of communal impartiality. Congress leaders, therefore, did not have to make major changes in their party programs, to offer commitments on future policy, or to give anyone other than Khanna an important party post. They merely had to reiterate their pledge to promote communal harmony and to show by their actions that their intentions were genuine.

Even with the support of only one minority MLA, Aurangzeb Khan governed the province for two years. His ministry, however, rested upon an unstable assembly majority which was in constant danger of disintegrating. The League controlled the assembly only by keeping ten Congress MLAs in prison, and even then, it was so vitiated by internal feuds that Aurangzeb Khan continuously had to readjust his policies to mollify wavering supporters. His ministry survived for as long as it did only because there was no possible alternative. While the war lasted, the Frontier Congress was prevented by party policy from replacing it, and Cunningham refused to countenance a government of independents which relied upon tacit Congress support.[57]

---

54. Moonje Papers, Letter, 5/25/43. Khanna to Moonje.
55. Interviews with A.C. Bombwal and G.D. Khera.
56. HM File 113, 1945. Report of the All-India tour of Kunwar Karan Sarda, General-Secretary, All-India Hindu Mahasabha. Also see *Lahore Tribune*, 10/9/45.
57. CD, 8/16/43.

Aurangzeb Khan's first actions as Chief Minister were a harbinger of the opportunism which would bring his government into disrepute.[58] He requested that the 1943 budget authorized during governor's rule be allowed to stand. Cunningham refused because the 1935 India Act stated that a budget adopted under Section 93 automatically lapsed with a new ministry. Aurangzeb Khan then pleaded for an assembly delay until August when bye-elections were scheduled in six constituencies. This time Cunningham relented, even though that meant the province was technically being run without a valid budget.

Aurangzeb Khan needed the extra time to shore up a coalition that was already crumbling. He had enlarged his cabinet to five ministers and an equal number of Parliamentary Secretaries in order to satisfy the numerous demands for office, only to raise dissension with his choice of its personnel. Even his own appointment was not universally accepted. Saadullah Khan, who had been an aspirant for the Premiership, started to intrigue against him within weeks after the ministry was formed.[59] Dissension also cropped up over his distribution of League tickets for the assembly bye-elections. In Dera Ismail Khan, for instance, his choice for one constituency split the District League into two, temporarily alienated *Nawabzada* Muhammad Saed Khan, MLA from Tank, and gave his *tarbur*, Asadullah Jan Khan, MLA from Kulachi, an excuse to defect to the opposition.[60]

In spite of these internal problems, the ministry's public standing momentarily improved. In the bye-elections in August, two Congressmen were elected unopposed to Hindu seats, but the League won all four Muslim seats, including two in the Khudai Khidmatgars' rural stronghold of Peshawar Valley. The results produced a sense of euphoria among Leaguers and the hopeful feeling that the Congress' grip on the province had finally been broken. A writer for *Dawn* triumphally proclaimed:

> The Sage of Wardha may have tamed the stage-managed Frontier lion [Abdul Ghaffar Khan] who guzzled from the pail of the classical goat, but not the Islamic dynamism whose ever resplendent upsurge proved beyond his competency to control. The Frontier stands today as the bastion of Islam, unconquerable and inviolate, sanctified by the extinction of the treacherous fifth column.[61]

There were however, more mundane reasons for the League's success. Two of its victories were in urban, heavily non-Pakhtun constituencies where the

58. CD, 5/20/43. Also see LP/78. No. 22. Telegram C.A./30, 5/18/43. Cunningham to Viceroy; and No. 21. Telegram 1221-G, 5/20/43. Viceroy to Cunningham.

59. Aziz Javed discusses the dissension in his manuscript, *Tehrik-i-Azadi ke Namvar Mujahadin*. Also see *Dawn*, 6/13/43 and GR/43. No. 9, 5/4/43; and No. 15, 8/9/43.

60. CD, 7/19/43; *Dawn*, 8/7/43; and Collection of Aziz Javed. Letter from Mirza Abdul Wahid Khan, Vice-President of the Dera Ismail Khan Muslim League, to Liaqat Ali Khan, no date.

61. *Dawn*, 8/17/43.

Congress was not strong. The League had selected its candidates for the rural seats from the dominant families of the constituencies, while the Congress had chosen men who did not even belong to their main tribes.[62] Moreover, since its ministry was at stake, the Frontier League made an intensive effort in the bye-elections, diverting government resources into the campaign and calling upon an array of outside party figures for help. The Congress, in contrast, first refused to contest the bye-elections, and even after the PCC reversed itself, the Khudai Khidmatgars still withheld their assistance.[63]

Despite the electoral victories, party dissension, "the result of petty considerations, nearly all of them pure self-interest or pique,"[64] left the ministry's survival in doubt. Congress leaders wooed the disgruntled MLAs by hinting that they would support a ministry of independents. Cunningham, however, frustrated their designs by indicating that he would not ask defectors who did not command a majority in their own right to form a government. Since the alternative was governor's rule, the dissidents remained with the League, and the Congress boycotted the legislative session which started on August 17th.[65] Still, only twenty-three members were present when it opened, a comfortable margin out of the thirty-eight who could have attended, but a minority if the ten jailed MLAs were included.

Their failure to command a majority and party disunity preoccupied the ministers for the rest of their tenure. In the struggle to survive, they temporized, acted for short-term gain, and misused their powers on a scale that alienated former well-wishers and played into the hands of the Congress. The ministers manipulated administrative appointments, selectively distributed licenses and permits, discriminated in allocating government funds, interfered in police investigations, and tried to tamper with the judicial process.[66] The Khan Sahib government had engaged in similar actions but never so openly or on so widespread a scale. Even major segments in their own party were antagonized. The *Khyber Mail* protested:

> . . . the rule there (NWFP) seems to be: Everyone for himself and the devil take the hind-most. Corruption with a Capital C is writ large on the face of the Frontier administration and almost everybody who has anything to do with the administrative machinery there bothers about

62. In the Khalil constituency in Peshawar District, the League's candidate was *Nawabzada* Sher Ali Khan, the titular chief of the Khalil tribe, while the Congress nominee was Muhammad Ibrahim Khan of Jhagra who was not a Khalil. For the Suddam seat in Mardan, the League chose Muhammad Ayub Khan, a member of the Mir Babu Khel Khans, the dominant Mandanr Yusafzai family in the area. His opponent was *Sahibzada* Khurshid Ahmad, a descendent of a holy man who belonged to a different branch of the Mandanr Yusafzais.

63. FR5/43(II) and FR6/43(I).

64. GR/43. No. 14, 7/25/43.

65. CP/5, Part II, p. 26; and GR/43. No. 16, 8/24/43.

66. GR/44. No. 3, 2/9/44 and GR/44, No. 28, 2/23/45. Also see CP/5, Part II, p. 27.

just one thing—how best to feather his own nest.[67]

The ministers acted out of the need to please their supporters rather than for personal gain. The Frontier League depended upon Khans who had little ideological loyalty to their party. They had joined it for the tactical advantage to be gained against their rivals in the Congress and saw in the new ministry an opportunity to recoup the privileges Khan Sahib had stripped away from them. As Cunningham explained to the Viceroy: "Many of them gave their support to Aurangzeb merely for what they might be able to make out of it."[68] Unable to rely on party sentiment, Aurangzeb Khan and his colleagues had to placate them with patronage, even at the expense of their own reputations.

Much of the ministry's unpopularity derived from its handling of the primary public problems of its time—commodity scarcities and rising prices. The war had distorted normal market conditions as early as 1939, but the effects had been manageable until 1943. Almost simultaneous with the League's accession to office, the stresses that had been building up since 1939 brought about a full blown crisis which lasted for the rest of the war and beyond. Prices of food grains and other goods rose drastically, and even at the higher rates, they were often unavailable. In the first half of June, for example, rice prices increased 30 percent and in the second half of the month wheat by 75 percent.[69] The situation called for comprehensive controls: fixed prices, rationing, regulation of imports and exports from the province, compulsory requisitioning of produce, and mandatory specification of crop acreage.

Since different parts of the province were affected by the scarcities in different ways, the ministers were bound to alienate some groups no matter what steps they took. Most rural areas, which produced a surplus of food, benefited from the high prices accompanying the shortage. The major exception was Hazara, which depended on imports from Mardan and the Punjab. Urban areas, particularly Peshawar city, suffered from chronic shortages and soaring prices. The government's problem, then, was to maximize food grain production, transfer the rural surplus to deficit regions, and make up the remaining shortfall, which approached 60,000 tons annually, with imports.[70] The first two steps entailed coercing *zamindars* to act contrary to their own interests. Limits had to be placed on sugarcane acreage in 1944 because the high price of sugar encouraged farmers to expand its cultivation at the expense of food grains. Price controls were instituted to curb the soaring costs of agricultural goods, and when *zamindars* retaliated by withhold-

67. *Khyber Mail*, 4/21/44.

68. GR/44. No. 5, 3/9/44.

69. FR6/43(I) and FR6/43(II). For information on the economic situation during the war, see the Fortnightly Reports and Governor's Reports for 1943-45.

70. LAD, Vol. 10, No. 3, 3/12/45, p. 47.

ing stocks or channelling them into the black market, the government issued anti-hoarding orders, requisitioning all stocks above 150 maunds.[71]

This situation helped the Frontier Congress recover from the Quit India debacle since it pitted the interests of the predominantly non-Pakhtun towns and Hazara against the Pakhtun agricultural areas which contained the party's natural constituency. Predictably, therefore, Congressmen championed the cause of the food-producing areas. They condemned all control measures and even advised villagers not to surrender their produce when compulsory procurement began.[72] While shoring up its position among the Pakhtuns, the party's aggressive opposition to the controls curiously aroused little hostility in the non-Pakhtun, deficit areas. Resentment in the towns and Hazara were directed primarily against the League due to the manner in which it dealt with the crisis.

The ministry was not solely to blame for the inadequacies in the government's rationing system. The crisis had caught the provincial bureaucracy unprepared, and the central government was often slow to meet the NWFP's deficiency in food grains. The ministers, nonetheless, bore the brunt of public criticism because they permitted flagrant injustices to develop in the controls in their continuing effort to secure their tenuous hold on office. They used the allocation of scarce commodities to pay off supporters and turned a blind eye when their appointees as rationing administrators exploited their powers for personal and factional ends. These abuses particularly alienated members of the League itself who were concentrated in the deficit areas and tended, therefore, to suffer more from the resulting hardships than their political opponents in the Congress.

The ministry's reputation also suffered from its reluctance to release the imprisoned Congress MLAs. It freed all but 135 of the NWFP's remaining 1,400 political prisoners within two months after the assembly adjourned in August 1943.[73] The ten MLAs, however, were still in jail when the legislature reconvened in March 1944 because dissension within the League's parliamentary party had once more endangered Aurangzeb Khan's position to the point where he feared that the release of even one might tip the balance in the assembly against him.[74] To free them all would have guaranteed defeat even if none of the League's MLAs defected. Once the legislature adjourned, Cunningham told Aurangzeb Khan that the detention of the MLAs no longer served any security purpose and that he could not tolerate the League undemocratically clinging to office.[75] Aurangzeb Khan still procrastinated, searching for a means to ensure that the MLAs did not rejoin the

71. FR6/44(I).
72. For Congress propaganda see GR/44, No. 1, 8, 11, and 12.
73. FR10/43(I).
74. PJ8/659. Collection 117-C-68. No. 3755. Letter D.O. No. GH-72, 3/13/44. Cunningham to Viceroy. Also GR/44. No. 6, 3/24/44.
75. GR/44. No. 7, 4/10/44.

Congress after being freed. In May, Cunningham wrote in his diary:

> Having promised me about 10 days ago that he had actually released 4 of the Congress MLAs, he has now, I have learnt, said that he was keeping them on parole in order to get an agreement out of them and may send them back again. I told him I would refuse to agree to a further "cat and mouse" policy like this. He showed me the draft agreement he was trying to get out of them; a ridiculous agreement offering them as a "People's Party," a rather vague chance of being allowed to start some cooperative stores![76]

Four MLAs were finally freed in late July after they signed an undertaking not to vote against the ministry at the next session; one more was freed in August.

The ministry handed the Congress a new issue in October by recommending that the autumn legislative session be cancelled, ostensibly because there was no business to transact. It was widely recognized that Aurangzeb Khan's real motive was to avoid the growing likelihood of defeat.[77] The Congress Parliamentary Party sent the governor a petition in November signed by twenty MLAs which asked that the assembly be called to discuss a no-confidence motion. Cunningham refused, a decision the Congress leaders seem to have expected and desired.[78] There was no urgency to their demand, for they were not entirely confident that they had the votes to topple Aurangzeb Khan, and even if they did, they were not in a position to resume office since the Congress still opposed the war effort. Therefore, the governor's refusal allowed them to score an easy propaganda victory, to pose as the champions of democracy and to brand the League as a creature of the British, without risking defeat in the assembly.

By the time the legislature did meet again in March 1945, two more Congress MLAs had been released, and a number of Muslim League dissidents had decided to vote against their government. More important, the Frontier Congress was finally able to resume office, for the war was coming to an end. Throughout the war, Khan Sahib had made little pretense about his ambition to return to power as soon as political conditions in India permitted, and most of the other party leaders shared his desire by 1945. Gandhi bowed to their wishes and made an exception to the Congress' opposition to holding office while the war continued. He told a delegation of party leaders from the Frontier in February 1945 that they should act according to their own judgment, thereby emphasizing once again the unique position of the Frontier Congress within the party.[79]

---

76. CD, 5/27/44.
77. CP/5, Part II, p. 30.
78. GR/44. No. 21, 11/23/44.
79. *Lahore Tribune*, 3/15/45. Also GR/45. No. 2, 3/23/45.

On March 12, 1945, the Frontier Congress passed a no-confidence motion in the assembly by a vote of twenty-four to eighteen with two abstentions.[80] Two days later, Khan Sahib accepted Cunningham's invitation to resume office. The margin of difference in the no-confidence vote was provided by five Muslim League MLAs, the most influential of whom was Saadullah Khan. He had differed with the ministers on some policy issues, but the primary cause for his defection was his rivalry with Aurangzeb Khan, which had turned into a personal vendetta after the police had searched his home and violated the *purdah* of his women.[81]

The dissension in the League's Parliamentary Party was mirrored in the party at large. Aurangzeb Khan came into conflict with organizational leaders as soon as he assumed power. Many party officers were upset by his refusal to consult them on governmental decisions, while others grew uneasy with his record in office. In addition, Saadullah Khan used his influence in the party organization in pursuit of his personal feud with the Chief Minister. These dissident elements passed a no-confidence motion against the ministry at a Provincial League Council meeting on October 24, 1943.[82] Aurangzeb Khan convinced the council to rescind its resolution by promising to attend to his detractors' grievances, but instead, he sought to protect himself from future embarrassment by gaining control of the party machinery. The Provincial Council split into two camps, with Mian Ziauddin, its General-Secretary, leading the ministerial supporters and Bakht Jamal Khan, its President, their opponents. Jinnah tried to mediate between the two sides at the League's annual session in December 1943, but his efforts failed.[83] The faction-fighting continued until the organizational elections in August 1944, when Aurangzeb Khan's group elected Taj Ali Khan of Bannu as the President of the Frontier Muslim League.

Ousted from power within the party, the anti-ministerialists shifted their attention to a new front. Two months before the organizational elections, the All-India Muslim League Council, over Aurangzeb Khan's strenuous objections, had ordered its Committee of Action to conduct a full-scale investigation into the state of the Frontier League.[84] After a two-week tour of the NWFP, the committee concluded that the provincial party organization required a thorough overhauling. Liaqat Ali Khan summed up the views of the committee's members when he wrote its president that "things are in a ter-

80. Three Congress MLAs were still in jail, and a fourth had taken a job in Bhopal. One seat was vacant due to an election petition against Saran Singh (Congress).

81. *Al-Jamiat Sarhad*, 3/14/45. The others included Muhammad Afzal Khan who had been elected on a Congress ticket but joined the League in June 1943. Abdur Rashid Khan and Raja Manuchehr were both from Hazara and both Parliamentary Secretaries. For the latter, this was the fourth time he had crossed the floor. Khan Sahib appointed him a Parliamentary Secretary. The fifth dissident was Faizullah Khan of Bannu.

82. *Al-Falah*, 10/29/43. Also see Aziz Javid, *op. cit.*

83. Bakht Jamal Khan, *Meri Dastan-i-Hayat, 1900-1968* (Unpublished memoirs).

84. GR/44. No. 12, 6/24/44.

rible mess here and unless immoderate steps can be devised and taken, the Muslim League will suffer a setback from which it will be very difficult to recover."[85] The Committee of Action decided that the dissension within the provincial party made it imperative that it exercise direct control over the reorganization. It entrusted the job to one of its members, Qazi Isa, a Pakhtun from Baluchistan, who started by cancelling the membership of everyone in the Frontier League in October. He then toured the province, reenlisting members and reestablishing primary party branches. On April 15, 1945, the Committee of Action liquidated the old party structure and ordered Qazi Isa to proceed with new organizational elections. In June, he appointed a provincial board and *ad hoc* committees for each district and Peshawar city to assist in the elections and handle routine party affairs until permanent bodies were formed.

The Committee of Action's initial decision in June 1944 encouraged the anti-ministerial forces to think that Qazi Isa would be sympathetic to their point of view since it implied dissatisfaction with Aurangzeb Khan's leadership. Once they lost the party elections in August 1944, the reorganization became the only possible avenue through which they could regain control of the party machinery. At first, they individually tried to persuade Qazi Isa to push through reforms which would enhance their position vis-à-vis their rivals. Then, the anti-ministerialists in Peshawar city formed the "Progressive Muslim League" in January 1945 to act as a pressure group. In June 1945, they regrouped into the *Khudam-i-*Muslim League, allying themselves with dissidents in other districts.[86]

Aurangzeb Khan's enemies also exploited the defeat of his ministry in their effort to influence Qazi Isa. The Provincial League Council considered two motions in March 1945 condemning the ex-Ministers for corruption and a multitude of other sins. The second passed on March 26th after the anti-ministerialists, led by Saadullah Khan, physically disrupted the Council's proceedings and caused its pro-ministerial majority to walk out in protest.[87] Subsequently, no attempt was made to maintain even a superficial semblance of party harmony. The anti-ministerialists conducted an unremitting propaganda campaign against their opponents in the press, demanding that the former ministers and their supporters be expelled from the League for destroying its organization and ruining its reputation.

Qazi Isa's plans for reorganizing the party deepened the split in the party rather than healing it. To complete his assignment, he needed the assistance

85. ML/155. No. 79. Letter, 6/17/44. Liaqat Ali Khan to *Nawab* Muhammad Ismail Khan. For the Committee's decision, see ML/192. No. 18. Proceedings of the 6th Meeting of the Committee of Action at Abbottabad on June 27-28, 1944.

86. *Al-Jamiat Sarhad*, 2/14/45 and 7/11/45. Also see *Khudam-i-*Muslim League Papers. Statement on the founding of the party. No date. (Part of the collection of Aziz Javed.)

87. ML/165. No. 81. Letter, 4/26/45. Aurangzeb Khan to Liaqat Ali Khan; and *Lahore Tribune*, 4/10/46.

of provincial party workers. He chose to rely on the existing office-bearers, who were primarily members of Aurangzeb Khan's faction. As early as the start of 1945, this aroused the suspicions of the anti-ministerialists. Their mistrust hardened into open hostility with the *ad hoc* committees Qazi Isa appointed in June 1945 to run the party's new organizational elections. Out of the ten members on the Central Advisory Board besides himself, Qazi Isa had appointed only two members from their group.[88] Three others were neutrals, while the remaining five were the top leaders of their opponents' faction. The composition of the District Boards showed a similar weightage in favor of the ministerialists. The *Khudam-i*-Muslim League turned on Qazi Isa, complaining to Jinnah:

> When the League Ministry was dissolved, we endeavoured hard to organize the League in Peshawar City as well as in the rural area. In June 1945 Qazi Mohd Isa was deputed by the High Command for organizing the League. We . . . placed before him the entire position and pointed out that if we could place the situation under the right leadership of League workers, the Congress and all its tactics would be finished once for all. But to our bad luck, he did not agree with our proposals . . . he announced the names of Temporary League Committees and inserted even those men on account of whom the Public has a strong current of hatred and contempt against the League. . . . He went away placing the League command only in those hands who had no sympathy with the League, but for their own reputation and selfishness had been in League from the last few years.[89]

Nothing came of their complaint except Qazi Isa's condemnation which increased their opposition to his party reforms.

The organizational elections ordered by the Committee of Action were never held. They were indefinitely postponed in the summer of 1945 so that the party could concentrate on the forthcoming campaign for the provincial assembly. What was left of Qazi Isa's reorganization was an *ad hoc* structure which was only a cosmetic change from the old jerrybuilt, faction-ridden organization. The same people continued in the party with the same authority pursuing the same factional disputes. The only difference was the institutional setting within which they operated. Real party reforms had to await the February 1946 elections, which provided the Frontier League with a new leadership untainted by the factionalism of the war years.

---

88. *Khyber Mail*, 6/22/45. The Central Board consisted of eleven members, including Qazi Isa. The ministerialists were Aurangzeb Khan, Abdur Rab Nishtar, Taj Ali Khan, Muhammad Akbar Badshah, and Mian Ziauddin (convenor). Bakht Jamal and Karim Bakhsh represented the anti-ministerialists while *Arbab* Nur Muhammad Khan, Muhammad Ali Khan, and Pir Sayyid Shah were neutral. Interview with *Arbab* Nur Muhammad Khan.

89. *Khudam-i*-Muslim League Papers. Letter, no date. Mirza Muhammad Salim Khan to Jinnah. (Part of the collection of Aziz Javed.)

# 8

## THE RISE OF COMMUNALISM IN FRONTIER POLITICS, 1945-1946

Once the war in Europe ended, events on the all-India stage determined the direction and tempo of Frontier politics. Lord Wavell convened a conference in Simla in June 1945 to discuss a possible interim government for India. After the talks collapsed over the question of who represented India's Muslims, he scheduled new legislative elections for February 1946 to determine the relative strength of the Indian National Congress and Muslim League. While the voters divided along communal lines in the rest of India, the Congress emerged as the clear winner in the North-West Frontier due to its superior campaign organization, greater party unity, voter preference for its ideology of ethnic nationalism, and greater backing from the Pakhtuns' landed elite.

The election results turned the NWFP into an anomaly which plagued the efforts of the British Cabinet Mission to resolve India's Hindu-Muslim impasse. Frontier Congress leaders objected to the Cabinet Mission's plan for fear that the Muslim League would be able to negate their electoral victory and infringe upon the rights of the Pakhtuns by subjugating them to the wishes of the more numerous Punjabis. All-India Congress leaders, who found the plan unacceptable for other reasons, used those objections to help undermine the compromise proposed by the Cabinet Mission and thereby created a political deadlock which finally gave way to violence.

As India's communal conflict grew more embittered in 1946, the Muslim League rapidly acquired popularity in the Frontier. Integral to its new-found strength was the widespread support it received from the province's religious leaders, and especially its *sajjada nishins*. Additionally, once India exploded into violence in August 1946, the League's warning of "Islam in danger" assumed a credibility and urgency in Pakhtun eyes it had previously lacked, and its call for Pakistan acquired a powerful attraction. Together, these factors triggered a variant on the Pakhtuns' traditional response to crisis by which they temporarily set aside their mutual enmities to unite under spiritual leaders in the interest of a higher, religious cause.

## The 1946 Elections

The Frontier Muslim League had been reduced to a state of paralysis in the spring of 1945 by the failure of its ministry and rampant factionalism. The conference at Simla and the announcement of elections helped distract attention from the party's past and made its communal ideology seem more credible than before. Equally important, those events brought new organizational talent into its ranks. The most influential of the new leaders were the *Pir* of Manki, who emerged as the party's dominant personality over the next two years, and Abdul Qaiyum Khan, who became its legislative spokesman. These men were also representative of the two main sources of leadership on which the party would henceforth depend. Along with the *Pir* of Manki, the League recruited other religious leaders, including many of the Frontier's *sajjada nishins*. In addition to Abdul Qaiyum, numerous other politicians joined the League after World War II. Some of them were former Congressmen, while others were influential men who had previously been uninvolved in politics.

Amin-ul-Hasnat, the fourth *Pir* of Manki, was a model of what a *sajjada nishin* should be.[1] As the descendant of a renowned saint, he was widely believed to have a powerful aura of *baraka*. He enhanced that reputation with his piety, moral righteousness, and attentiveness to the needs of those who sought his spiritual intercession. His authority can be measured in two ways. First, as the guardian of the *ziarat* of the original *pir* in the village of Manki in Nowshera *Tehsil*, Peshawar, he was the living recipient of the devotions people made at it. The shrine attracted a steady stream of supplicants from the region around Peshawar Valley, and on the occasion of his ancestor's *urs*, drew large crowds of pilgrims from all over the northern Frontier and northwest Punjab. Second, the *Pir* of Manki had an extensive network of disciples who were bound to him through the *piri-muridi* relationship. These disciples, who were reputed to number in the tens of thousands, were concentrated mainly in Peshawar Valley and the surrounding tribal areas.[2]

The *Pir* of Manki proved to be an ideal leader for the Frontier League. His saintly reputation gave a religious validation to its ideology, while the practical skills he displayed as a *sajjada nishin*—his administrative abilities, gift for proselytizing, and tireless energy—were a welcomed addition to a party which had suffered from a lack of organizational talent. The *Pir* of Manki's emergence as the party's leader occurred gradually. He had opposed the Congress as early as the Quit India Movement, but he had abstained from

1. Even Congress leaders, who criticized his politics, considered him a religious man beyond reproach. Interviews with Mian Jafar Shah, Abdul Akbar Khan, and Sayyid Ashiq Shah.

2. Estimates of his following reach twenty *lakhs*. *Al-Falah*, 9/20/46. *Al-Jamiat Sarhad* estimated them at seven *lakhs*. *Al-Jamiat Sarhad*, 12/4/46.

public activity until the Simla Conference convinced him that Indian politics had acquired an important religious dimension.[3] Even then, he maintained a certain distance from the League, campaigning on its behalf during the elections, but independent of its provincial organization. In doing so, he acted much more as the *sajjada nishin* he was than the accomplished politician he would become. As a close associate has suggested, he was still disinterested in the mundane internal affairs of the Frontier League and wanted solely to promote its ideology, which he found far nobler than the quarrelsome and often compromising behavior of its leaders.[4]

The *Pir* of Manki's first priority was to enlist the province's religious elite behind the demand for Pakistan. He created a new organization in October 1945, the *Anjuman-us-Asfia*, which reputedly included over sixty *sajjada nishins* and other prominent clerics.[5] The organization was actually more symbolic of the growing interest among the Frontier's *sajjada nishins* in the League's goals than the vehicle through which they were mobilized. Most of the *sajjada nishins* who worked for the League did so outside of any formal organization by individually utilizing their religious authority and influence in rural society in a traditional manner. The *Anjuman-us-Asfia* also exemplified the essentially religious motivation behind their involvement in politics. At the founding meeting, the members declared that their sole objective was the realization of an Islamic state and resolved that they would assist the League in the elections only if it promised to enforce the *Shariah* as the law of Pakistan. In November, the *Pir* of Manki announced that Jinnah had accepted these conditions and that all Muslims should treat the elections as part of a *jihad* to achieve Pakistan.[6]

Independent of the *Pir* of Manki, *Maulana* Shakirullah of Nowshera and like-minded *maulanas* also tried to mobilize religious leaders behind the League. They primarily worked to bring the Frontier's *ulema* together in a single, pro-Muslim League association. Numerous bodies had claimed the title of *Jamiat-ul-Ulema-i-Sarhad* since the first one was formed in 1927. The one on-going organization with that name was affiliated with the pro-Congress *Jamiat-ul-Ulema-i-Hind* and represented the *ulema* who had maintained a working alliance with the Frontier Congress since the 1930 civil disobedience movement. *Maulana* Shakirullah united the *ulema* who were sympathetic to the League into a competing *Jamiat-ul-Ulema-i-Sarhad* in 1944 and affiliated it with *Maulana* Shabbir Ahmad Usmani's *Jamiat-ul-Ulema-i-Islam*.[7]

The new *Jamiat-ul-Ulema* played a less significant role in the growth of the League than the *Pir* of Manki and the other *sajjada nishins*. In part, its ef-

3. *Al-Jamiat Sarhad*, 6/26/45.
4. Interview with Amin Jan Khan of Landi.
5. *Al-Jamiat Sarhad*, 10/17/45.
6. *Ibid.*, 10/17/45 and 11/26/45.
7. Interview with Hasan Gilani, the Frontier correspondent for *Dawn*, 1946-47, and son of Sayyid Sultan Muhammad Shah, General-Secretary of the *Jamiat-ul-Ulema-i-Sarhad*.

fectiveness was diminished by its inability to achieve its stated goal. The League continued to face major opposition within the ranks of the Frontier *ulema* from men of Congress persuasion who shared a strong skepticism about the commitment of the League's leaders to Islam and the creation of an Islamic state. India's communal troubles, moreover, still seemed distant to the NWFP in 1945 and the Frontier Congress no less a Muslim party than the League. Thus, many of the *ulema* saw no need, as yet, to change their political allegiances.

More fundamentally, the influence of the new *Jamiat-ul-Ulema* was limited by the nature of the *ulema's* position in Frontier society.[8] While individual *maulanas* were highly respected, as a group they lacked the venerated status accorded to *sajjada nishins*. *Sajjada nishins* also had strong ties to the landed elite and filled an important structural role in tribal politics which made them effective power brokers among Pakhtuns. Most *ulema*, in contrast, were urban based and had few ties into the rural social structure. Finally, subtle but important differences existed in the messages of the *ulema* and *sajjada nishins*. Both called for the creation of Pakistan, but the *ulema* insisted that they would have to regulate the new state if it were to be truly Islamic. Some Pakhtuns regarded this as an attack on the existing social order since it would have meant transferring power from their own hands to men they considered their inferiors.[9] The *sajjada nishins*' vision of Pakistan involved a much less radical departure from the status quo. As David Gilmartin has observed for their counterparts in the Punjab:

> The thrust of their concern has always been to influence the political leaders and their followers to regulate their lives according to religious injunctions. . . . The idea of a state in the hands of such [secular] leaders was for them perfectly natural, for in the establishment of such a state based on the Shariat, they could see the projection of their local religious work into a larger political arena.[10]

Abdul Qaiyum Khan, in contrast to the *Pir* of Manki, rose to power by securing a succession of key posts in a period when the party's leadership was in flux. He had been elected to the Central Assembly on the Congress ticket to replace Dr. Khan Sahib in 1938 and had served as the party's deputy leader in the Assembly until 1945. By the end of the war, he had fallen out with the Frontier Congress leaders, partly on personal grounds and partly because he had been associated with Bhulabbhai Desai, the Congress' leader in the Assembly, who had fallen into disfavor in late 1944 for negotiating with Liaqat Ali Khan for an interim Congress-Muslim League government after the war. After prolonged secret negotiations, Qaiyum joined the

8. See *supra*, Chapter 2 for the role of *ulema* and *sajjada nishins* in Pakhtun society.

9. Interviews with Abdul Akbar Khan and Amin Jan Khan.

10. David Gilmartin, "Religious Leadership and the Pakistan Movement in the Punjab," *Modern Asian Studies*, Vol. 13, Part 3, 7/79, p. 509.

League on August 16, 1945, just days before the Viceroy ordered new elections.[11] Although he did not bring a large following with him, he possessed attributes which immediately propelled him into prominence in the Frontier Muslim League. He was the highest Frontier Congressman to date to switch parties, and while he had held little real power in the Congress, his position had given him public prominence and extensive experience in legislative politics. In addition, as a newcomer, he was not associated with any faction in the Frontier League. These factors gave him an edge over other party leaders which first became apparent when the League geared up its election campaign.

In early October, the League's Central Parliamentary Board appointed three provincial committees: the Selection Board to choose candidates, the Election Board to manage the campaign, and the Finance Board to collect funds.[12] The first was the only committee with genuine power and, in fact, the only one actually to function. The impact of its decisions extended well beyond the elections to the later evolution of the party's leadership. Most of the old leaders of the Frontier Muslim League were excluded from the board, having been discredited by their past performance in directing the party. The members of the board were either new to the party or old district workers who were untainted by the associations which disqualified their former colleagues. The *Nawab* of Mamdot, an outsider from the Punjab, was selected as its president and Abdul Qaiyum as its convenor. *Arbab* Abdul Ghafur was included as part of an agreement by which the Afghan Jirga, a party of former Congress dissidents, joined the League.[13] The other six members were chosen to ensure every district of representation: *Pir* of Zakori (Dera Ismail Khan), Habibullah Khan (Bannu), Malik-ur-Rahman Kiyani (Kohat), *Arbab* Nur Muhammad Khan (Peshawar), Sohbat Khan (Mardan), and Jalaluddin (Hazara).

The Selection Board's influence over the distribution of tickets varied from one constituency to another. In some, it deferred to a single, dominant figure or tribal *jirga*.[14] In many others, however, more than one influential man sought the League's nomination, leaving the board to make a final decision. In every case save one, Abdul Qaiyum's rivals for party leadership were denied party tickets, although in three cases the Central Parliamentary Board overturned the decision.[15] The one exception was Abdur Rab Nish-

11. *Al-Jamiat Sarhad*, 8/22/45.

12. ML/193. No. 8. Proceedings of the 13th Meeting of the Committee of Action, 9/1/45; and *Khyber Mail*, 10/12/45.

13. Interview with Sher Bahadur Khan; and *Khyber Mail*, 10/5/45.

14. For example, in the constituency of Nowshera South (Peshawar) the board confirmed the *Pir* of Manki's choice, Mir Aslam Khan, while in Abbottabad East (Hazara) it accepted *K.B.* Abdur Rahman Khan, who was proposed by a *jirga* of the leading men among the Dhonds. Interviews with *Arbab* Nur Muhammad and Jalaluddin.

15. The three were Mian Ziauddin, Sardar Bahadur Khan, and Muhammad Farid Khan. *Rehbar Mardan*, 12/21/45.

tar, whose standing in the party was too strong to be excluded from its electoral slate. Nonetheless, before obtaining a ticket, he had to defeat several challengers, including the Peshawar City League President, Fida Muhammad Khan, who had Qaiyum's covert support.[16] Although the board's decisions benefited Qaiyum, they were not due solely to his talents for intrigue, as his rivals subsequently claimed. Other factors complicated the selection procedures. Party sentiment favored denying Aurangzeb Khan a ticket; Saadullah Khan, Mian Ziauddin, and others were hurt by their past factional ties; and some prominent politicians, such as Muhammad Ramzan Khan, an ex-PCC President from Dera Ismail Khan, were passed over in favor of men with less political experience but stronger tribal credentials.

The conflict at the top of the party's slate was not unique. Disappointment over the choice of candidates led to disunity among party workers at all levels and to the alienation of party supporters whose tribal stature made their backing indispensable to the League. Many disgruntled aspirants sat out the elections, ran as independents, or threw their support to candidates opposing the League, including Congressmen. In Kohat district, for example, defections cut into the League's strength in at least three out of the four constituencies. Pir Sayyid Jalal, the Chief Parliamentary Secretary in Aurangzeb Khan's ministry, resigned from the party on being denied a ticket.[17] In the Khattak areas Sir Olaf Caroe, who became the governor of the NWFP just after the elections, later recounted:

> . . . the well-known Pir of Makhad . . . lives just on the Punjab side of the Indus but has a large number of disciples in the Kohat District of this Province. As his nominee did not get the Muslim League ticket in Kohat, he instructed his disciples to vote Congress, and it was mainly due to this that Congress got in in at least one constituency in that District.[18]

Dissension was also rampant elsewhere in the province. Unhappy ticket seekers bolted the party to stand as independents or third-party candidates in six constituencies in Hazara, while other prominent party workers in the district turned against the party because they could not reconcile themselves to the leadership of Jalaluddin, the League's strong-minded boss in Hazara.[19] In Peshawar, the Afghan Jirga's alliance with the party proved short-lived once the Selection Board gave it only one nomination rather than

16. Interviews with Fida Muhammad Khan and Mian Ziauddin.

17. *Tarjuman-i-Sarhad*, 1/5/46.

18. GR/46. Pol. 8485. Letter D.O. GH-114, 5/8/46. Caroe to Lord Wavell. Jansson states that the *Nawab* of Teri, who had sat in the Assembly as a Muslim League MLA, did not support his party's nominee in his constituency in return for a loan from the Congress government. Erland Jansson, *India, Pakistan or Pakhtunistan* (Uppsala: Studia Historica Upsalensia, No. 11, 1981), pp. 258-259.

19. For examples, see *Al-Falah*, 1/4/46 and 2/1/46; *Al-Jamiat Sarhad*, 12/26/45; and *Khyber Mail*, 2/15/46.

the three or four its leader, *Arbab* Abdul Ghafur, felt it deserved.[20] Leading Khattak Khans in Nowshera refused to support the League when their own preference was passed over to accommodate the choice of the *Pir* of Manki.[21] Peshawar city dissidents bitterly opposed Nishtar and were unhappy with Qaiyum. The League lost the support of the powerful Ghazni Khan Marwats in Bannu when Faizullah Khan, their leader, was denied a ticket, while in Dera Ismail Khan the selection of two members of the Alizai Pakhtun *Nawabs* prompted prominent leaders from numerically larger tribes in their constituencies to support their opponents.[22]

Defections cut the size of the League's vote in Hazara but hurt the party in only one constituency, Upper Pakhli, where the Congress candidate won with the help of Atai Muhammad Khan who had represented the area in the old legislative assembly as a member of the Muslim League.[23] Elsewhere, however, they provided the margins by which a number of its candidates lost. Caroe later commented on the difference:

> I am at present on tour in the Hazara District and it is interesting to see how different these people are from Pathans. . . . almost all the M.L.As. from this District are local Khans and they seem to be able to sink their family quarrels to a large extent when they come down to politics. The inability of Pathans to do this is one of the chief reasons for the success of Congress in the Pathan parts of the Province.[24]

In addition to party disunity, the League suffered in the NWFP from its ideological claim to be the sole representative of India's Muslims. The party was trapped by its pretensions into fighting all thirty-eight of the province's Muslim seats, even though the most optimistic prognoses conceded some to be hopeless. Frontier League leaders were confident that the issue of Pakistan and their opponents' ties to the Congress were all they needed to win a decisive victory in the election. Their optimism did not seem out of place in the first months of the campaign. The party attracted many Congress defectors and previously apolitical men, a process which Cunningham viewed as "symptomatic of a steadily increasing antipathy between the more highly educated Muslims and Hindus."[25] But then the growth of communal feeling slowed, and the League found that, with an organization and treasury inferior to those of its rival, it had spread its resources dangerously thin.

---

20. Interview with Sher Bahadur Khan. Also see Jansson, *op. cit.*, p. 258.
21. *Al-Jamiat Sarhad*, 2/6/46.
22. Interviews with Habibullah Khan and Muhammad Ramzan Khan. Jansson cites other examples. Most notably, Taj Ali Khan, the former president of the Provincial Muslim League, ran an uncle as an independent in a Bannu constituency when he was denied his party's ticket. Jansson, *op. cit.*, p. 261.
23. *Al-Jamiat Sarhad*, 7/17/46; Interviews with Daud Khan and Anwar Khan of Dotar and Ghulam Rabbani Khan.
24. GR/46. Pol. 8485. Letter D.O. GH-114, 5/8/46. Caroe to Lord Wavell.
25. GR/45. No. 13, 9/9/45.

The party had no real machinery with which to conduct its campaign. Its provincial organization was a facade, incapable of functioning, let alone competing with the Frontier Congress' strong party apparatus. As a result, even some of the League's backers doubted that the party would fare as well as its leaders expected. *Al-Jamiat Sarhad* acted as a frequent Cassandra, beginning in September when the electoral rolls in the province were revised:

> Since this work [enrollment of voters] needs organization and the Muslim League organization in the Frontier Province is non-existent because during its period of government its lamp [the ministry] reduced its house to dust and ashes, now Congress workers have a golden opportunity.[26]

The boards which had been specially created to direct the party's campaign fared no better.[27] Attempts by the Election Board to frame an electoral strategy never extended beyond generalities, while Mian Ziauddin, the convenor of the Finance Board, complained that it was futile to expect the party's wealthy Khani supporters to think beyond the narrow confines of their own constituencies.

In the absence of a coordinated party effort, the League had to depend upon the influence and connections of its nominees. Only Muhammad Akbar Khan Khadim received a ticket in spite of an ordinary socio-economic background, and he, in effect, was put up as a sacrificial candidate against Dr. Khan Sahib. The rest of the party's list of candidates reads like a selection from the province's wealthiest, most aristocratic families.[28] Eight were the titular heads of their tribes, and a ninth, *Arbab* Muhammad Sharif Khan, was nominated because his nephew, *Arbab* Nur Muhammad Khan, the chief of the Bara Mohmands, was too young to stand. For example, *Nawab* Sir Muhammad Akbar Khan, the Khan of Hoti, was the wealthiest man in the province. *Nawab* Qutbuddin Khan was the descendant of the pre-British rulers of Tank and one of the province's major *jagirdars*. Muhammad Farid Khan was the chief of the Palal Tanaolis in Hazara and the maternal grandson of the ruler of the state of Amb.[29] Two other candidates were the sons of hered-

26. *Al-Jamiat Sarhad*, 9/13/45. The next month, Cunningham told the Viceroy: "The Congress election campaign among the rank and file is, so far, more effective than the League's owing to better organization and more money . . . the League's chance in the Election will depend on the efforts their central command is now making to improve local organisation." GR/45. No. 15, 10/9/45.

27. Interview with Mian Ziauddin.

28. For an examination of the candidates and election by constituency, see Appendix III in Stephen Rittenberg, *The Independence Movement in India's North-West Frontier Province, 1901-1947* (New York: Ph.D. dissertation. Columbia University, 1977).

29. *Ibid.* The other five were *K.B.* Muhammad Zaman Khan, the chief of the Utmanzai tribe; Raja Haidar Zaman Khan, the head of the Gakkar tribe; *Nawabzada Arbab* Sher Ali Khan, the titular chief of the Khalil tribe; *Arbab* Attaullah Khan, the titular head of the Daudzai tribe; and *Nawabzada* Mohabbat Ali Khan, the chief of the Izzat Khel Bangash.

itary *nawabs*; another thirteen belonged to prominent families of Khans in the dominant tribes in their constituencies; four more were wealthy, high-status members of numerically smaller tribes; and two belonged to families of *sajjada nishins*.[30]

With their personal followings, *gundi* ties, wealth, and high social standing, these candidates partially compensated for the League's organizational weaknesses; but the senior Khans were no substitute for an efficient campaign organization in the face of the well-run and financially well-off Frontier Congress, especially since they had lost their once dominant position in Frontier society. Discredited by their departure from Khani norms, their standing had slipped badly since their Khani rivals and the lower classes had first openly challenged their authority in 1930. This left the League vulnerable to attack on factional grounds wholly unrelated to nationalist issues. As Cunningham observed: "... the Congress deliberately appeal to the less well-to-do, over whom the bigger Khans (most of them on the Muslim League side) are more and more losing their hold in most Districts."[31]

The Congress followed a different electoral strategy from the League, nominating candidates for only those seats where its prospects justified a campaign.[32] The party contested all twelve minority seats. The Akali Dal ran against it in the three Sikh constituencies, but its nominees were unopposed for seven Hindu seats and had only nominal opposition in an eighth. Out of the thirty-eight Muslim constituencies, the party ran candidates in only twenty-seven, most of them in Pakhtun areas.[33] It contested eighteen of twenty rural seats in Peshawar, Mardan, Kohat, and Bannu, avoiding only the Marwat constituencies in Bannu where it had the backing of neither of the *gundis* which dominated tribal politics. It nominated two men in Dera Ismail Khan, one of them in the predominantly Pakhtun *tehsil* of Tank, while three of its five nominees in Hazara ran in Mansehra *Tehsil* where the influence of Pakhtun culture was strongest.

Wherever the Congress name was a handicap, the party looked for non-Congress allies who stood a better chance of winning. Its pragmatism was most evident in the heavily non-Pakhtun areas of Dera Ismail Khan where it deferred to two sitting MLAs with great wealth and high traditional status: *Nawabzada* Allah Nawaz Khan, the son of the *Nawab* of Dera Ismail Khan; and Asadullah Jan Khan, the chief of the Gandapur tribe, who had been a member of the Muslim League until 1944.[34] Both ran under the Islamic label of the *Jamiat-ul-Ulema-i-Hind* to counteract the League's communal propaganda. In parts of Hazara and the NWFP Towns constituency where

30. *Ibid.* Abdus Shakur Bacha belonged to the family of the *Bacha* of Bamkhel, and Abdul Latif Khan was the *Pir* of Zakori.

31. GR/46. No. 4, 2/27/46.

32. Rittenberg, *op. cit.*, Appendix III.

33. *Ibid.*

34. *Ibid.*; also, *Lahore Tribune*, 10/27/45.

the electorates were predominantly non-Pakhtun, the Congress backed independents or Ahrars. Finally, in the double constituency of Peshawar city, where every voter cast two ballots, the Congress ran only one candidate and told its supporters to vote for him twice. Party leaders also encouraged two third-party candidates in the constituency, even though the more popular of them, the Khaksar nominee, was vitriolic in his criticism of the Congress.[35]

The Congress depended less heavily than the League on candidates with influential family and tribal ties, a possibility made feasible by its extensive grassroots organization. The party's selections in Peshawar Valley were indicative of the varied background of its nominees.[36] Manfatullah Khan, who ran in a Mardan constituency, came from an ordinary Khattak family, while Sayyid Yakub Shah, who stood for a seat in Peshawar, was both a non-Pakhtun and a man of modest means. More typically, the party chose its candidates from the Valley's landed elite: for example, *Arbab* Abdur Rahman belonged to a junior branch of the family which was the titular head of the Daudzai tribe; Mian Jafar Shah was a relative of one of the more influential *sajjada nishin* in the Frontier and the son of a wealthy contractor; and Muhammad Zarin Khan was a member of a leading Khani family among the Baizai Khattaks of Mardan.

The Congress nominees were chosen through a two-part procedure. First, the *Tappa* Congress Committees suggested possible candidates. In most cases, their endorsement was tantamount to nomination, although the final decision rested with a six-man subcommittee of the Provincial Working Committee. At its October 1945 meeting, the PCC ritually reaffirmed Abdul Ghaffar Khan's supreme authority by proposing that he take over complete control of the campaign. He turned down the offer, although he did influence the choice of nominees to ensure that Khudai Khidmatgar leaders were strongly represented on the Congress slate.[37] In contrast to the experience of the League, the Congress' distribution of tickets created little party dissension of any consequence. Two party members stood as independents while a few others defected to the League, but with the exception of the Bara Mohmand constituency (Peshawar), their loss did not affect the outcome of the elections.[38]

Both parties exploited local economic issues during the campaign. The League blamed the Khan Sahib government for the shortages resulting from

35. Interviews with Muhammad Yahya Jan and Abdul Akbar Khan.

36. Rittenberg, *op. cit.*, Appendix III.

37. *Lahore Tribune*, 10/2/45. The Khudai Khidmatgar's *Salar-i-Azam*, Amin Jan Khan, was given a ticket, as were three of their *Naib Salars*, or district chiefs; and one commanding general of a *tehsil*.

38. Qazi Attaullah lost the constituency by 398 votes. *Returns Showing the Results of Elections to the Central Assembly and the Provincial Legislatures in 1945-46* (Delhi: Manager, Government of India Press, 1948), Statement II. Also see *Al-Jamiat Sarhad*, 10/24/45 and 11/7/45.

the war and accused it of corruption and political favoritism in rationing essential commodities. Congress leaders retaliated with denunciations of the misdeeds of Aurangzeb Khan's government and claimed that they had reformed the grossly unjust system of rationing which they had inherited from the League. Their ministry also adjusted its policies with an eye toward winning votes. Cunningham observed:

> Congress are showing signs of nervousness about the elections. The cancellation of the increase in water rates was a bid for popularity in Peshawar and Mardan Districts. In Hazara, the Ministry has now postponed the increase in land revenue assessment proposed in the Settlement Report. In other smaller matters, they have done things with an eye to pleasing or soothing the electorate.[39]

While economic questions influenced the races in individual constituencies, they were not the central issues around which the elections revolved. The campaign revealed in the sharpest possible terms the ideological differences between the two parties. The League tied its fortunes to its vision of Pakistan, while the Frontier Congress relied upon its distinctive brand of ethnic nationalism.

The League reduced the elections to the black and white generalities of Pakistan versus *Akhand* (undivided) Hindustan, and Muslim independence versus Hindu domination. Jinnah himself toured the province in November 1945 with the message: "Every vote in favor of Muslim League candidates means Pakistan. Every vote against Muslim League candidates means Hindu Raj. That is the only choice and the only issue before us."[40] His thesis was echoed by provincial party workers. The *Pir* of Manki's *Anjuman-us-Asfia*, for example, turned voting for the League into a religious duty:

> From the standpoint of the *Shariah* there is, in reality, only one party for a Muslim. He should give his vote to the representative of the Muslim League. To give a vote to the Hindu Congress or any other party is treachery against Islam and conflicts with the unanimous opinion of the *ulema*.[41]

Every other issue in the elections was tied into this grand dichotomy. Frontier Congressmen were portrayed as Hindu agents bent on enslaving the Pakhtuns. *Al-Falah* cautioned:

> . . . you should prove your attachment to Islam by making the Muslim League candidate . . . successful. Others who demand your vote are either the bought slaves of the Hindu party or enemies of Indian Muslims appearing in Islamic garb. Work for the honor of the faith and do not accept slavery to the Hindus.[42]

39. GR/45. No. 16, 10/23/45. For example, see Jansson, *op. cit.*, pp. 258-59.
40. *Dawn*, 11/29/45.
41. *Al-Jamiat Sarhad*, 2/6/46.
42. *Al-Falah*, 12/19/45.

The Hindus, especially Mehr Chand Khanna, were pictured as the real powers in the Frontier Congress, while Abdul Ghaffar Khan and his lieutenants were presented either as having been deluded by Hindu flattery or, worse, as having sacrificed Muslim honor for personal gain.[43] League leaders also dissected the record of the Khan Sahib ministry to show that it was anti-Muslim. They pointed to numerous cases, many of them manufactured or taken out of context, in the areas of commodity controls, permits, administrative appointments, and education to prove that the ministry was systematically oppressing Muslims to satisfy Hindus.[44]

The Frontier Congress also spoke of freedom and slavery but gave those terms a different meaning. Its campaigners countered the League's religious communalism by emphasizing that their party, which they identified as the Khudai Khidmatgars rather than the Congress, was the national movement of the Pakhtuns and by presenting the real issue of the elections as Pakhtun independence from British imperialism. Abdul Ghaffar Khan told audiences:

> I have not come to beg votes because these votes and the assemblies are not worth a penny to me. I have brought a message of friendship and good will to achieve the freedom for which you fought for years. The decision to contest these elections was taken only so that this course would further the struggle for freedom. We are not fighting our brethren in the country. We are fighting British imperialism. . . . I visualize its days in this country as numbered provided you unite and stand as one Pakhtun nation. We are as good as any other nation—rather, more brave and more hospitable. Stand united as one Pakhtun race.[45]

Congress leaders gave "freedom" still another meaning by claiming to defend the Pakhtun nation against an exploitative Khani elite. When they spoke of Khans, they did not mean everyone who deserved the title, since many of them were Khans themselves. Instead, they redefined the term, as they had throughout the nationalist period, to refer only to the province's senior Khans who supported the League. At times, their rhetoric had a radical coloring, such as when they promised to expropriate the Khans' land and distribute it to the lower classes.[46] More commonly, it was phrased in an old and familiar way. They argued that the Khans, *jagirdars*, and title-holders were more interested in their own advancement than in the Pakhtuns' national cause; that in the past they had betrayed the nation to the British imperialists out of personal greed; and that they were continuing to do so by

43. See *Ibid.*, 10/2/45 and *Al-Jamiat Sarhad*, 10/15/45.
44. See *Dawn*, 1/20/46; *Al-Falah*, 12/19/45; and *Al-Jamiat Sarhad*, 10/24/45 and 12/5/45.
45. *Lahore Tribune*, 1/15/46.
46. GR/46. Pol. 8485. D.O. Letter GH-114, 5/8/46. Caroe to Lord Wavell.

contesting the elections against the Pakhtuns' nationalist party on the spurious platform of religion. Abdul Ghaffar Khan wrote in *Pakhtun* in January 1946:

> . . . we have opposed British imperialism and for this reason their friends have always disliked us. Today we are accused of being friends of the Hindus and taking bribes from them, but I will remind you about the past when we have no relations with Hindus. We came to the field of politics in 1919. We rejected the black laws of the Rowlatt Act, but these people opposed us. At the time of *Hijrat*, which was led by Muhammad Ali and Shaukat Ali, these people did not like the idea. When the Khilafat Committee, a purely Islamic party, was formed, who accepted its demand that the British should abandon Arabia? Who came forward at that time, we or these Khans and *nawabs*? . . .
>
> When Muhammad Ali announced non-cooperation, who left the service of the Government? These people with fat stomachs or us? I remember the late Mian Hamid Gul who abandoned a pension and his title, but the other Khans and *jagirdars* continued to stick to their friends, the British. . . .
>
> Again, when people, instigated by the British, rebelled against Amanullah Khan, who sympathized with him? He and Nadir Khan were given both financial and physical help by us, the poor people, while these Khans, the great lovers of Islam, remained silent. . . . If you believe we did all this out of a love of Islam, then how are we selfish? And how have these Khans, who have always served the British, become the selfless lovers of Islam?
>
> On whose sacrifices have these assemblies and councils, which have served the poor people and alleviated their burden, been formed? These Khans opposed these institutions because they promised some help to the poor and the Khans thought they would jeopardize their own position.
>
> I am surprised that some of the poor believe these Khans, *nawabs*, and *arbabs* served Islam and are the sympathizers of the poor.[47]

Since the Frontier Muslim League was closely associated with the senior Khans, Congressmen were, by extension, also attacking that party and casting doubts on the sincerity of its Islamic appeal. They often took their argument a step further and asserted that the issue of Pakistan itself was a British concoction rather than a genuine demand.[48]

While the elections did not hinge exclusively on ideology, the Frontier Congress' appeal did give it a decided advantage. Insulated from India's communal problems by distance and a population in their own region which

47. *Pakhtun*, 1/9/46.
48. *Ibid.*, 1/17/46.

was 93 percent Muslim, Pakhtuns found the League's warnings unconvincing. Cunningham calculated that its propaganda "is not really an intelligible war cry to 90 percent of . . . [its] hearers. To the average Pakhtun villagers in these parts, the suggestion that there could be such a thing as Hindu domination is only laughable."[49] The Pakhtuns' ethnic loyalties, moreover, were stronger than their communal consciousness. After the elections, Caroe reasoned: "If the Muslim League up here had had the sense to substitute Pathanistan for Pakistan, they would certainly have done a good deal better."[50] The League, however, could not have followed his advice because the Frontier Congress had preempted the issue of Pakhtun nationalism. By doing so, it had protected itself from any religiously based challenge unless and until a crisis developed that would make the differences between Pakhtuns and other Muslims less important than their common faith. It was not that Pakhtuns enthusiastically embraced the Indian National Congress' vision of a unified India with a strong central government. If anything, they expected strong constitutional safeguards, much like those the League had demanded before adopting the Pakistan resolution. Rather, most favored the Frontier Congress because they believed it faithfully reflected their ethnic interests.

Beneath the grand political issues of the campaign lay a substratum of *parajamba*. At one point, Cunningham went so far as to contend that the "elections in the Province . . . are being fought not on any kind of party programme . . . but on grounds of personal faction-feeling."[51] He was, of course, overstating the case, as he recognized himself. Nonetheless, traditional rivalries significantly influenced the contest in every constituency, and in many, their impact was decisive. In six constituencies, for example, the primary or sole contestants were cousins; *gundi* alignments influenced the choice of candidates in at least five; and tribal divisions were critical in another seven.[52] The importance of *parajamba* was even more profound than is apparent from an examination of the electoral candidates. It affected every constituency to some degree since men and factions commonly supported one party for the simple reason that their enemies backed the other. Caroe later wrote: "It is only necessary for the League to put up a Khan for a seat for the rest of the Khan's relatives to vote Congress or to abstain from voting altogether."[53] The reverse was also a common occurrence.

Factionalism produced a confusion of political alliances in some areas which is inexplicable if party labels alone are considered. The best example

49. GR/46. No. 4, 2/27/46.

50. GR/46. No. 6, 3/23/46.

51. GR/46. No. 2, 1/24/46.

52. See the description of the election by constituency in Rittenberg, *op. cit.*, Appendix III.

53. GR/46. Pol. 8485. D.O. No. GH-114, 5/8/46.

is provided by the three constituencies in Mansehra *Tehsil* in Hazara.[54] *Khan Bahadur* Ali Gohar Khan ran as a Khaksar in Mansehra North after the League ticket was given to Muhammad Abbas Khan. The two men belonged to the two leading families of Mansehra town and were bitter political foes. Also, their respective clans, the Jahangiri and Khan Khel Swathis, were at odds with each other. In Lower Pakhli, Ali Gohar Khan of Dotar, a Jahangiri Khan, was the League candidate. His family had close marriage ties to his namesake in Mansehra, so its members worked for the League in their own constituency but against it in Mansehra North. Ali Gohar Khan of Mansehra reciprocated. Atai Muhammad Khan, the leading Jahangiri Khan in Upper Pakhli, broke with the League to back the Congress in his own constituency. He, nonetheless, favored the Jahangiris standing for the other two seats—one a Leaguer and the other a Khaksar.

With the revision of the electoral rolls in 1945, over 20 percent of the province's population was registered to vote, a figure which included few women but practically every adult male.[55] Polling took place between January 26 and February 14, 1946. The Congress won eleven of the twelve minority constituencies, losing only to the Akali Dal in Peshawar. The party also captured nineteen of the twenty-seven Muslim seats it contested, while its allies in Dera Ismail Khan, the *Jamiat-ul-Ulema-i-Hind*, won two more. The Muslim League was victorious in the remaining seventeen Muslim seats.[56]

The Congress' victory among the Pakhtuns was decisive. The party did not contest two of the twenty-one rural, territorial constituencies in the Pakhtun region encompassing Peshawar, Mardan, Kohat, and Bannu Districts, and Tank *Tehsil* of Dera Ismail Khan. It won sixteen of the remaining nineteen and lost the other three by slender margins.[57] It also lost the landlord seat in Peshawar Valley. In aggregate, the party garnered 51.90 percent of the vote in the twenty-two Pakhtun constituencies and 57.71 percent in the twenty it contested. The figures for the Muslim League were 39.40 and 37.43 percent respectively.[58]

The League, on the other hand, emerged as the representative of the province's non-Pakhtun Muslims. It won eight of the nine seats in Hazara District, two of the three urban seats, and both landlord seats. Since a Hazara resident won in each of the latter two categories, that district's total con-

54. Interviews with Ghulam Rabbani Khan, Ali Asghar Khan, and Daud Khan and Anwar Khan of Dotar.

55. A.S. Dhawan, *Report on the General Elections to the Central Assembly (NWFP Constituency) and to the NWFP Legislative Assembly in 1945-46* (Peshawar: Manager, Government Stationery and Printing, 1946), p. 10.

56. For the results by constituency, see *Returns . . . op. cit.*, Statement II.

57. *Ibid.* The two Pakhtun seats the Congress did not contest were in Marwat *Tehsil*, Bannu.

58. Computed from *ibid.* See Table 9a, p. 246 *infra* for information on the election results.

tingent in the League's legislative party was ten out of seventeen.[59] The race in the double constituency in Peshawar city had the greatest bearing on the party's future. Officially, the League instructed its supporters to cast one ballot each for Nishtar and Qaiyum. Nishtar, however, lost votes due to his role in the Aurangzeb Khan government, while Qaiyum, due to the closeness of the race, urged his supporters to give him both of their votes.[60] As a result, Qaiyum placed second in the voting, edging out the Khaksar candidate, while Nishtar ran a poor fourth. This outcome left Qaiyum the logical leader of the League's assembly party, a base which he would parlay into the premiership of the province after independence.

The final alignment in the new assembly found thirty Congressmen supported by the two *Jamiat-ul-Ulema-i-Hind* MLAs. The party could also count on the vote of the Akali Dal representative in any clash with the League. The new cabinet consisted of Dr. Khan Sahib as Premier, Qazi Attaullah, Muhammad Yahya Jan, and Mehr Chand Khanna. Its composition underscored both the dominance of Abdul Ghaffar Khan's family in the party and the continuing importance of kin and marriage ties in Pakhtun politics. Caroe regarded it as "rather a queer body:"

> . . . with the exception of the Hindu Member, Mehr Chand Khanna, it is a family affair, Qazi Attaullah's daughter having been married to one of Abdul Ghaffar Khan's younger sons and Yahya Jan, the new Minister, being married to one of Abdul Ghaffar Khan's daughters. The family complexion is made even more apparent by the election of Abdul Ghani, another of Abdul Ghaffar Khan's sons, to represent the Province in the Central Assembly.[61]

The Congress held only one legislative session in 1946 which primarily served as a forum in which each side kept up the propaganda of the election campaign.[62] They argued over language, with Congressmen insisting on Pashtu while the League pressed equally hard for Urdu. They traded accusations over rationing. The League's MLAs charged the ministry with partisanship in distributing essential commodities, and Congressmen retorted that the League was only sore at losing the corrupt advantages it had enjoyed

59. *Khan Bahadur* Jalaluddin and *Khan Sahib* Sultan Hasan Ali Khan of Boi were both from Hazara.

60. Muhammad Yahya Jan, *Khan Abdul Ghaffar Khan. Un ke Khidmatgar aur Qaiyum Muslim League* (Peshawar: Imperial Press, 1970), pp. 18-19; Qaiyum's campaign manager, Fida Muhammad Khan, concedes the charge against Qaiyum. Interview.

61. GR/46, No. 5, 3/9/46.

62. For examples, see LAD. Vol. X. The third Khan Sahib ministry also passed some significant economic and social legislation, such as the Punjab Tenancy (North-West Frontier Province) Amendment Act, introduced administrative reforms, and began long-range planning for the province. Like the measures of the first Khan Sahib ministry, these tended to favor the Congress' supporters, the lower-class non-Pakhtuns and the smaller Khans, at the expense of the senior Khans in the Muslim League.

under Aurangzeb Khan. Leaguers used every opportunity, no matter how implausible, to charge the Congress with conspiring to establish a Hindu *raj*. For their part, Congress MLAs projected themselves as the champions of the Pakhtuns and the poor against the British and their henchmen in the Muslim League. None of this rhetoric was new or memorable, nor did it have a major impact on the course of provincial politics, for the assembly was overshadowed by events occurring outside its halls.

## The Cabinet Mission Plan

The British government announced on February 19, 1946 that a special delegation of three cabinet ministers would go to India to seek a solution to its constitutional problems. The trio arrived in New Delhi on March 24th and plunged into extended negotiations with India's political leaders. Their talks culminated with a conference in Simla in early May at which it became apparent that the gap between the Congress and Muslim League was too wide to be bridged by direct bargaining. On May 16th, therefore, the ministers proposed a compromise of their own which they hoped would lay the basis for a future Indian constitution and clear the way for an interim central government.

Their plan called for a decentralized, three-tiered system of government consisting of provinces, groups, and a central, or union, government.[63] The princely states would revert to an independent status and negotiate their future association with the union. The center would deal only with foreign affairs, defense, and communication, with all other powers vesting in the provinces. The authority of the union government was further restricted by requiring that any legislation with significant communal implications could be passed only if a majority of both Muslim and Hindu representatives in the central assembly supported it. The provinces would "be free to form groups with executives and legislatures, and each group could determine the provincial subjects to be taken in common."[64] The proposed groups were "A"—Madras, Bombay, Central Provinces, Orissa, United Provinces, and Bihar; "B"—Punjab, NWFP, and Sind; and "C"—Bengal and Assam.

The details of these constitutional arrangements were to be worked out by a Constituent Assembly whose composition reflected party strengths in the provincial assemblies and included representatives of the princely states. After a preliminary meeting of the whole, the representatives of British India were to divide into their respective groups to decide on provincial and group constitutions. The assembly would then reconvene to write a union

---

63. V.P. Menon, *The Transfer of Power in India* (New Delhi: Orient Longmans Ltd., 1968), p. 267.

64. *Ibid.*

constitution. Once the new constitution had been implemented, the provinces would have the right to leave their groups, should their legislatures so decide. The entire constitution was to be reconsidered at ten-year intervals.

The Cabinet Mission's plan was complex, cumbersome, and ambiguous. To make it work would have required a cooperative spirit among India's political leaders whose very absence had forced the ministers to produce their extraordinary document in the first place. The compromise proposals satisfied no one entirely but proved to be more acceptable to the Muslim League since they more nearly approximated its demands. Congress leaders were never reconciled to the decentralization of power, the communal veto, and the possibility of provincial secession contained in the plan. Ultimately, they destroyed it as a possible compromise by refusing to be bound by the very restrictions which made it tolerable to the League.

The Congress' public objections, however, focused primarily on a procedural issue, albeit one with far-reaching implications. The ministers had been vague in their May 16th statement on whether the initial grouping would be mandatory. The Congress insisted that the decision should be left to the discretion of the provincial legislatures, on the grounds that it would otherwise be "inconsistent with the freedom promised the Provinces," and its leaders adhered to this position even on being informed that its interpretation "did not express the intent of the Delegation."[65] League leaders took the opposite view that grouping had to be compulsory. To allow provinces to opt out of the groups in advance would have removed the main element of the plan that made it acceptable to their party—that it contained the "seeds" of Pakistan in Groups B and C. That, however, was precisely what the Congress envisioned, as Nehru frankly told the press on July 10th:

> The big probability is, from any approach to the question, there will be no grouping. Obviously section A will decide against grouping. Speaking in betting language, there is a four to one chance of the North-West Frontier Province deciding against grouping. Then group B collapses. It is highly likely that Bengal and Assam will decide against grouping, although I would not like to say what the initial decision may be since it is evenly balanced. But I can say with every assurance and conviction that there is going to be finally no grouping there, because Assam will not tolerate it under any circumstances whatsoever.[66]

With grouping destroyed, the possibility once more arose of creating a united India with a much stronger center than the Cabinet Mission proposed. Thus, Congress leaders raised strong objections to coercing the NWFP and Assam into any group to which their elected officials did not wish to belong.

65. PJ8/788. Collection 127-1-AA. No. 6, 6/19/46. V.P. Menon to Secretary of State. Also see PO/474. No. 27, 44, and 46; and Menon, *op. cit.*, pp. 27-28.

66. Quoted in Menon *op. cit.*, p. 284.

Unlike the Congress High Command, the Frontier Congress did not take issue with the decentralization envisioned in the Cabinet Mission's plan. Its leaders objected solely to compulsory grouping, or rather to the Frontier Province being included in Group B. They were fearful that the League, with its strength in the Punjab and Sind, would have a majority among the group's representatives and would push through a group constitution disadvantageous to their party. Grouping also potentially represented an obstacle in the way of achieving one of their most basic objectives. Officially, the Frontier Congress had never precisely defined what it foresaw for the Frontier region after independence, but its leaders were firmly wedded to the idea that the NWFP and tribal areas should enjoy the maximum possible autonomy. Thus, in his initial response to the Cabinet Mission's plan, Abdul Ghaffar Khan told the press on May 21st:

> Great stress was laid by the Muslim League on self-determination and on autonomy. The Congress has agreed to the fullest autonomy and even to a large extent of self-determination. It is curious that now the Muslim League stands for compulsion of certain provinces joining groups whether they want to or not. Surely, this is the negation of self-determination. Provinces must, of course, cooperate together, but this must be done with their own free will or goodwill.[67]

Frontier Congressmen claimed their right to autonomy on the basis of the Pakhtuns' unique identity. Modifying a statement by Jinnah to serve his own purposes, Allah Nawaz Khan, the President of the Provincial Assembly, declared:

> Pathans and Punjabis are two major nations by any definition or test of a nation, and the idea and very thought of grouping the NWFP with the Punjabis is revolting to the Pathan mind. We are a nation of three million, and what is more, we, the Frontier Pathans, are a body of people with our own distinctive culture, civilization, language, literature, art and architecture, names and nomenclature, sense of values and proportion, legal and moral codes, customs and calendar, history and traditions, and aptitudes and ambitions. In short, we have our own distinctive outlook on life and by all canons of international law a Pathan is quite separate from a Punjabi.[68]

As his statement suggests, the Frontier Congress also pandered to the chauvinistic side of the Pakhtuns' sense of ethnic pride. Pakhtuns had particularly strong biases against their immediate neighbors, the Punjabis, which party leaders blatantly manipulated by speaking about Punjabi imperialism and Punjabi contempt for Pakhtuns.[69]

---

67. *Lahore Tribune*, 5/22/46.
68. *Civil and Military Gazette*, 12/17/46.
69. For examples, see *Pakhtun*, 6/24/46 and 9/9/46.

The Frontier League responded by emphasizing the Pakhtuns' religious identity. Its members asserted that the NWFP could not stand alone and had to join some group—if not the "Islamic" Group B, than Group A with its overwhelming Hindu majority. A press statement by Abdul Qaiyum Khan in June summed up the League's position:

> Khan Abdul Ghaffar Khan has lately toured the southern districts of the N.W.F. Province where he has been chanting a hymn of hate by rousing Pathans against the domination of Punjabi Muslims. . . . He conveniently forgets that if there is danger of 16 million Punjab Muslims dominating the six million Pathans in the tribal areas, NWFP and Baluchistan, the danger of domination by the Hindu group is much more real as their population is something like 100 times the population of this province. . . . Before setting up the Government of North-West Pakistan [Group B] we will see to it that Pathan interests are adequately and satisfactorily protected and that our province has a real say in the affairs of the Pakistan Government. The bogey of Punjabi domination has no foundation and the war-cry raised by Khan Abdul Ghaffar Khan is due to the fact that his own political existence is now being increasingly threatened from all sides.[70]

Stripped of its hyperbole, one element in Qaiyum's statement was accurate. The leaders of the Frontier Congress were worried about the future and subtly shifting their political emphasis in response to the growing possibility of partition. They had always argued for Pakhtun regionalism but previously had spoken of the Frontier as part of India. In 1946, they downgraded references to India and devoted their attention more to discussing the future of the Pakhtuns. In fact, a direct correlation can made between India's political climate and the party's emphasis on Pakhtun autonomy: the greater the chance of Pakistan, the more militant the Frontier Congress' brand of regional autonomy would become.

## The Reorganization of the Frontier Muslim League

The election results showed that there was little hope of the League's Islamic ideology overcoming the Frontier Congress' ethnic appeal in the absence of a functioning party organization. That lesson was reinforced by the rapid expansion of the Frontier Congress in 1945-46. The party had 24,215 primary members by March 1946, more than three times the number enrolled during World War II. They were marshalled into a grassroots organization of formidable depth. An incomplete PCC report lists forty-four *Halqa*

70. *Civil and Military Gazette*, 6/16/46.

Congress Committees and 886 Primary (Village) Congress Committees.[71] In addition, the party, by the most conservative government estimate, had no less than 8,000 Khudai Khidmatgar volunteers at its command.[72]

After consulting with a select group of provincial leaders in Delhi, the All-India Muslim League's Committee of Action named a forty-man Organizing Committee in April 1946 to overhaul the Frontier League.[73] The new committee constituted tacit recognition that Qazi Isa's reorganization had failed, since it was instructed to repeat the tasks he had supposedly completed—to enroll new party members, establish League branches throughout the province, and conduct new party elections.

The committee's appointment completed the transformation of the provincial party's leadership. With the exception of Abdur Rab Nishtar, the men who had previously controlled it were pushed aside. Some, like Mian Ziauddin, dropped out of politics altogether; others, like Aurangzeb Khan and Bakht Jamal Khan, accepted much diminished roles. The new leaders came from three sources. Some, such as Jalaluddin, Mohabbat Ali Khan, and Malik Damsaz Khan, emerged from the ranks of the party's district organizations. Many others, such as the committee's chairman, Samin Jan Khan, were former Congressmen. They were especially numerous in Peshawar Valley where the League was weakest vis-à-vis the Congress.[74] Most of them had only joined the League after the war, but their newness was overlooked because they possessed skills the party desperately needed. Finally, the committee drew on men from a younger generation who had little prior political experience but strong tribal credentials. They were exemplified by Muhammad Ali Khan, the committee's twenty-three year old secretary, and *Arbab* Nur Muhammad, its twenty-two year old treasurer, who was the hereditary chief of the Bara Mohmands. The *Pir* of Manki did not join the Organizing Committee, even though he was acknowledged as the dominant figure in the Frontier League's leadership. He chose, instead, to act as the party's guiding spirit without holding any official title, much in the manner Abdul Ghaffar Khan presided over the Frontier Congress.

The Organizing Committee divided responsibility for rebuilding the party in each district among its members and created two three-man sub-

71. Membership figures are from AICC File G-54(I), 1946. Letter, 3/27/46. Sadiq Ali, AICC Office Secretary, to the General-Secretary of the NWFPCC. For the organizational units, see *Congress Handbook, 1946* (Allahabad: Allahabad Law Journal Press, 1946), pp. 118-21. The information for the Primary CCs is especially incomplete. Out of forty-four *Halqa* CCs listed, only twenty-five reported the number of Primary CCs they controlled.

72. FR12/46(II).

73. ML/193. No. 13. Proceedings of the Meetings of the Committee of Action in Delhi on April 11-18. The personnel of the committee are listed in *Khyber Mail*, 4/20/46.

74. Others besides Samin Jan included Mian Abdullah Shah, who had been among Abdul Ghaffar Khan's closest associates until 1931. Ghulam Muhammad Khan had served as the PCC President, as had Muhammad Ramzan Khan. *Arbab* Abdul Ghafur had been one of the Afghan Jirga's main organizers in Peshawar and later the PCC General-Secretary.

committees to aid them.[75] In addition, the *Pir* of Manki toured extensively throughout the province, often in the company of an entourage of League leaders. At a meeting in Peshawar city on May 1st, the Organizing Committee appointed Rab Nawaz Khan, the former *Salar-i-Azam* of the Khudai Khidmatgars and Abdul Ghaffar Khan's nephew, to command the party's *razakars* (volunteers). Numerous quasi-military units calling themselves "National Guards" already existed as adjuncts to local branches of the Frontier League. Rab Nawaz Khan was instructed to mold them into a single, cohesive body which would act as the party's equivalent to the Khudai Khidmatgars.[76] He was shortly replaced by Faiz Muhammad Khan, a member of the Daudzai Khans of Babuzai, who, in turn, gave way in November 1946 to Muhammad Ayub Khan of the Hoti-Mardan family, who directed the *razakars* until independence.

*Sajjada nishins* other than the *Pir* of Manki played a major role in the revitalization of the Frontier Muslim League. Their political involvement, which was already noticeable during the election campaign, intensified as India's communal impasse hardened, and especially once negotiations gave way to rioting in August 1946. By the end of the year, a high percentage of the NWFP's *sajjada nishins* were actively working for the League. The party was also helped by *sajjada nishins* from the Punjab, such as the *Pirs* of Taunsa, Makhad, and Sial, who had numerous disciples across the Indus River.[77] While some *sajjada nishins*, such as the *Pir* of Zakori, assumed high positions within the Frontier League, most continued to work outside the party. Their efforts were typified by the *Akhundzada* of Karbogha in Kohat who simply added political proselytizing to his normal religious activities.[78] He most effectively served the party by instructing his *murids* to join it and by speaking in its favor wherever he went on the frequent tours he made to keep in touch with his disciples.

Attracted into politics by what they perceived as serious religious issues, the *sajjada nishins* imparted, in turn, a religious legitimation to the League and its goal of Pakistan. Of equal importance, as Frontier politics became communally charged, they once more filled their traditional, structural role as unifiers in Pakhtun society in times of crisis. Their support for the Muslim League facilitated its evolution from merely a political party into a religiously inspired movement in which Pakhtuns could temporarily suspend

75. *Al-Jamiat Sarhad*, 5/8/46. Interviews with Muhammad Ali Khan and *Arbab* Nur Muhammad.

76. *Al-Jamiat Sarhad*, 5/8/46. Interviews with Muhammad Ayub Khan, Fida Muhammad Khan, and Muhammad Ali Khan.

77. *Al-Jamiat Sarhad*, 10/17/45. Interviews with the *Pir* of Zakori and Sher Bahadur Khan. See Gilmartin, *op. cit.* for a discussion of the Punjab's *sajjada nishins* and their participation in the Pakistan movement.

78. PS12/2300. Collection 23/60. No. 24 and 26. *Civil and Military Gazette*, 9/29/46 and 12/18/46. *Khyber Mail*, 12/13/46. Interviews with Ghulam Haidar Akhtar and Fazli Karim Asif.

their normal worldly concerns and factional disputes and unite under saintly leadership in the name of Islam.

The Organizing Committee never completed its assigned task. Before party elections could be held, the League's High Command abandoned political negotiations for direct action in August 1946 and appointed Provincial Committees of Action to assume the duties of the Provincial Leagues.[79] The Frontier Committee of Action, chaired by the *Pir* of Manki, confirmed the officers of the Organizing Committee in equivalent ranks in the provincial party and appointed officers for subordinate party branches. With these steps, the reorganization of the Frontier Muslim League ended. It did not fully achieve its objectives, for in many parts of the province the party remained little more than a patchwork of *ad hoc* bodies directed by senior Khans. Yet, despite its deficiencies, the organizational efforts of 1946 adequately met the requirements of the Frontier Muslim League. Due to the deterioration of Hindu-Muslim relations in the rest of India, the League did not need a tightly run organization to win support in the Frontier. All it required was a sufficiently sound party structure to allow it to channel the upsurge in communal feeling into coordinated activity, and this had been created by the time riots in other parts of India diverted the party away from organizational questions.

## Communal Rioting and Frontier Politics

The Muslim League had agreed to the Cabinet Mission's proposals in early June, but its leaders reconsidered when the AICC formally expressed reservations on July 7th that negated their essential clauses. In a subsequent press conference, Nehru effectively repudiated the entire scheme by stating that the Congress was committed to going to the Constituent Assembly and nothing more.[80] The All-India Muslim League Council reacted by withdrawing its approval of the plan at a special meeting on July 27th-29th and passing a resolution which declared in part:

> . . . whereas recent events have shown that power politics and not justice and fair play are the deciding factors in Indian affairs . . . the Council of the All-India Muslim League is convinced now that the time has come for the Muslim nation to resort to Direct Action to achieve Pakistan, to assert their just rights, to vindicate their honour and to get rid of the present British slavery and the contemplated future Caste-Hindu domination.[81]

---

79. ML/193. No. 18. Proceedings of the Committee of Action, pp. 39-40.

80. Menon, *op. cit.*, p. 283.

81. Syed Sharifuddin Pirzada (ed.), *Foundations of Pakistan* (Karachi: National Publishing House, 1970), Vol. II, pp. 557-58.

Jinnah then dramatically told the Council: "This day we bid goodbye to constitutional methods. . . . Today we have also forged a pistol and are in a position to use it."[82]

In spite of the bellicose rhetoric, nothing drastic was immediately intended. The League merely planned to hold meetings throughout India on August 16th and have its members renounce whatever titles the government had conferred upon them. But Calcutta exploded into three days of communal rioting which left thousands dead or injured. The Great Calcutta Killing set off a succession of bloody disorders in Bombay in September, Noakhali in October, and Bihar and the eastern part of the United Provinces in November. At the all-India level, this sequence of unprecedented communal violence destroyed the last faint hopes for a political settlement that stopped short of partition. In the North-West Frontier Province, it accomplished in a few short months what the League had failed to achieve through years of work—a massive swing in public opinion away from the Frontier Congress and its ethnic nationalism in favor of Pakistan.

The Frontier Congress' strength had started to erode even before the rioting began. Every week, a few more of its members transferred their allegiances to the Muslim League. Some, no doubt, switched out of political opportunism or after losing out in factional struggles within the Congress, while others were alienated by the Khan Sahib government, and particularly its rationing policies.[83] Many, however, were swept up by the growing communal polarization of India, and all, regardless of their motives, represented their conversion as stemming from religious convictions. Yet, as long as India's communal conflict was confined to words, the Frontier Congress was protected by the Pakhtuns' strong ethnocentrism and by the widely held perception that it was an autonomous Pakhtun party committed to advancing their ethnic interests. The Pakhtuns' provincialism was finally shattered when the deadlock at the bargaining table gave way to bloodshed in the streets. As the rioting reached a level unparalleled in India's troubled communal history, the contradiction between the Pakhtuns' religious and political loyalties became acute. Their sense of ethnic uniqueness did not disappear, but it was superseded temporarily by a religious awareness which led them to give their primary allegiance to their Muslim identity for the duration of the crisis.

League leaders ensured that the disorders received the maximum publicity in the Frontier in order to sustain the sense of crisis at the highest possible pitch. They flooded the province with stories of Hindu atrocities, sent investigative teams to the disturbed areas, and brought Muslim eyewitnesses and victims from the riot areas to the NWFP. Their propaganda

---

82. Quoted in Menon, *op. cit.*, p. 287.

83. GR/46, No. 7, 4/10/46 and Pol. 9836 and 11332.

stressed that the riots proved that the Hindus were bent on destroying Islamic culture in India and physically exterminating Muslims. In the face of this danger, they argued, Pakhtuns had to give up their unnatural alliance with the Indian National Congress and join the struggle for Pakistan. The riots in Bombay and Bihar were exploited with an especially telling effect, the first because many of the victims were Pakhtuns and the second because of the sheer magnitude of the death and destruction that was involved.

The trouble in Bombay consisted of random stabbings rather than large-scale mob violence. Nonetheless, it received particular attention in the Frontier because Bombay contained a large number of Pakhtuns, most of them transient laborers who regularly traveled back and forth between the city and the Frontier.[84] Once the stabbings began, they sent back descriptions of their situation to the Muslim League's newspapers in the NWFP which were designed to arouse the Pakhtuns' sense of ethnic honor. Part of one account in *Al-Jamiat Sarhad*, for example, read:

> Though the Pakhtuns did not take any part in the opening of the Hindu-Muslim riots in Bombay on September 1st, a great number of them were killed later on. The police also helped in killing them in factories, nearby villages, and on the main streets. The situation went to the extent that while burying them we could not distinguish among their limbs, and some bodies were buried with a lesser or greater number of arms and legs.[85]

In late September, a delegation returned to Peshawar to plead their case in person. In response, the Frontier League sent a committee under Bakht Jamal Khan to Bombay to investigate the conditions of the Pakhtuns residing there. The committee's report described the Pakhtuns' suffering in graphic detail and accused the Bombay Congress government of aiding the Hindu assailants.[86] Provincial party workers, in turn, used its conclusions to support the contention that the Hindus of Bombay had embarked on a campaign of genocide against the Pakhtuns in the city.[87]

In Bihar, rioting began on October 25th after a *hartal* called in sympathy for the Hindus of Noakhali. It rapidly escalated into disturbances which the Government of India declared: "For ferocity, barbarity and size, seem to have surpassed all communal or political outbursts in recent Indian history."[88] After only one month, official estimates put the number of dead at 5,000 and the number of Muslim refugees at over 120,000.[89] League esti-

84. PJ8/574. "Summary of Events on the Bombay Riots."
85. *Al-Jamiat Sarhad*, 11/13/46.
86. Bakht Jamal Khan, *Meri Dastan-i-Hayat, 1900-1968* (Unpublished memoirs. Collection of Aziz Javed).
87. *Al-Falah*, 9/24/46.
88. PJ8/788. Collection 127-1-AA. No. 11, 11/20/46.
89. PO/474. No. 68, 11/22/46.

mates were much higher. The leaders of the Frontier League focused on the plight of the Biharis almost to the exclusion of other events in India for the rest of the year, due to a genuine sense of compassion for fellow Muslims and an awareness of the political capital they could earn among the Pakhtuns from the defenselessness and suffering of the Biharis. They sent three medical missions consisting of doctors and party volunteers to fan out through the affected region to aid Muslims. Besides offering help and comfort, the members of these missions wrote articles for the NWFP press in which they painted gruesome pictures of murder, torture, rape, arson, and the desecration of everything Muslims held sacred.[90] Many returned to describe what they had seen at public meetings, displaying objects picked up in Bihar to dramatize the destruction—blood-stained clothing, torn pages of the Quran, and in one case, a skull of an alleged Muslim victim.[91] Their accounts were corroborated by Bihari Muslims who were brought to the province especially for propaganda purposes.

In the midst of the communal riots, Nehru decided to visit the Frontier in October. A Congress-dominated interim central government had been formed the previous month in which Nehru, as the member for foreign affairs, was responsible for the tribal areas. Ostensibly, his trip was undertaken in his official capacity, but party motives lay behind his decision. As Caroe has suggested, he also wished to enhance the Congress' standing by showing that it controlled the strategic and sensitive subject of border security.[92] Additionally, Abul Kalam Azad has written:

> . . . Jawaharlal was receiving official reports that a large section of the people in the Frontier were against Congress and the Khan brothers. Local officers repeatedly said that the Congress had largely lost local support and that the people had transferred their loyalty from the Congress to the League. Jawaharlal was of the view that these reports were not correct and were fabricated by British officers who were against Congress. Lord Wavell did not agree with Jawaharlal, though he did not either accept the official reports, in toto. His view was that the Frontier was almost equally divided between the Khan brothers and the Muslim League. The impressions in Congress circles was that the overwhelming majority of the people were with the Khan brothers. Jawaharlal said that he would tour the Frontier and assess the situation for himself.[93]

The trip was made against the advice of Gandhi, Azad, and other high Congress leaders who felt it might provoke a reaction in the Frontier which

90. For examples, see *Al-Jamiat Sarhad*, 11/3/45; and *Al-Falah*, 11/8/46 and 11/29/46. Also see Muhammad Yusaf, "Mazlumin Bihar ki Ankhon Dekhi Kihani, Un ki Zabani," *Khatun*, 8/14/73, pp. 5-6.

91. *Pakhtun*, 3/9/47 and *Lahore Tribune*, 1/10/47.

92. Interview with Sir Olaf Caroe.

93. Abul Kalam Azad, *India Wins Freedom* (New Delhi: Orient Longmans, 1959), pp. 151-52.

would hurt their party locally and throughout the rest of India as well.[94] The Viceroy and Frontier administration were also against the idea. Caroe flew to Delhi to try to dissuade Nehru:

> I told him that he would undermine the influence of my ministers and heighten communalism. I said that if he wanted the Frontier to join a united India peacefully, he should bide his time and that if he still insisted on going, he should do so on a nonpartisan basis by taking with him Muslim League members.[95]

For the leaders of the Frontier Congress, the visit was a gamble. A successful trip would have dispelled any doubts the High Command might have had about their popularity and would have strengthened their position locally by demonstrating their influence with the party in charge of Frontier affairs in the central government. They also sought access through Nehru to the tribal territories from which they had hitherto been barred. On the other hand, the risks involved in the trip were considerable. A hostile reaction to Nehru would undermine the party's standing locally, in the central councils of the Congress, and in the estimation of the British. Recognizing this, the Frontier League set out to whip up public opinion in both the settled districts and tribal areas in the weeks preceding Nehru's visit. The *Pir* of Manki was particularly active, touring the tribal region around Peshawar Valley with the message that the tribesmen had to unite against the Hindu Congress and preserve their freedom by joining the *jihad* for Pakistan.[96]

Nehru's visit turned out to be a fiasco for the Frontier Congress.[97] He was greeted in Peshawar on October 16th by a mammoth, hostile demonstration mounted by the Muslim League. The next day, he embarked on a series of disastrous trips to the tribal agencies. The Wazirs shot at his plane and confronted him in an angry *jirga*. The Afridis refused to see him and stoned his party. He by-passed the Mohmands due to intelligence of possible trouble and went to Malakand instead where his party was attacked again; Abdul Ghaffar Khan was hit by stones; shots were fired; and Khan Sahib had to draw a pistol to disperse a menacing crowd.

Caroe reported that the demonstrations in the Khyber and Malakand were organized by the League.[98] The advantages to the party were obvious and sufficiently compelling to cause its provincial leaders to make a concerted effort to arouse the tribesmen. They would not, however, have been as suc-

---

94. *Ibid.*, p. 152. Also, PO/474. No. 59, 10/22/46.

95. Interview with Sir Olaf Caroe.

96. GR/46. Pol. 11878. D.O. No. GH-196, 10/23/46. Caroe to Lord Wavell.

97. The trip is described in a number of sources. See H.V. Hodson, *The Great Divide* (Karachi: Oxford University Press, 1969), pp. 279-81 for the official version; and D.G. Tendulkar, *Abdul Ghaffar Khan* (Bombay: Popular Prakashan, 1967), pp. 384-94 for the nationalists' version.

98. GR/46. Pol. 11878. D.O. No. GH-196, 10/23/46. Caroe to Lord Wavell.

cessful as they were if the tribesmen had not already been upset by India's communal problems and uneasy about their own future. The rioting in India had created strong tribal animosities toward Hindus and the Congress. The sentiments expressed by a *jirga* of Wazirs and Daurs during Nehru's visit typified the common feeling. They told him that they sympathized with those "who repeat the word *Bismillah*" and threatened to retaliate against those who were persecuting their Muslim brethren in India.[99] While their religion led them to sympathize with the Muslim League, most tribesmen, as the same *jirga* informed Nehru, wished to remain independent. They did not want to be ruled by anyone—the British, League, Pakhtuns from the settled districts, and, above all, the Congress which stood for Hindu domination in their minds. Nehru's visit suggested to the tribesmen that the British might well be replaced by the Hindus with independence, an outcome which had hitherto seemed remote and implausible. As Caroe put it, it seemed like the coming of a second Birbal.[100]

Nehru's visit aside, India's troubles upset the communal peace in the Frontier. This too was to the League's advantage, since any violence within the province reinforced local feelings of solidarity with the rest of India's Muslims. Even before August 1946, the party had added to the growing communal tensions in the region with its persistent charge that Hindus were using the Congress' control of the NWFP government to exploit Muslims. Once the rioting began, they added the allegation that the minorities were stockpiling arms with the ministers' connivance.[101] More seriously, the League's dissemination of accounts of Hindu atrocities encouraged the desire to extract revenge for the wrongs suffered by Muslims elsewhere on the Frontier's minorities. Some party spokesmen even urged their followers to answer violence with violence. *Al-Jamiat Sarhad* editorialized: "The only way to stop these anti-Muslim riots is for all Muslims to unite and organize and prove to the Hindus that the blood of every Muslim will be definitely avenged."[102]

Communal tensions in the Frontier became so serious by the autumn of 1946 that the minorities started to seek refuge in flight.[103] In late September, many Hindus and Sikhs left the rural areas of Peshawar for the safety of the district's towns. Similar migrations occurred from villages in Mardan, Hazara, and the tribal state of Swat in November. In the south, some Hindus quit Tank for Dera Ismail Khan city in December, while many others left the Frontier altogether.

99. PS12/2300. Collection 23/60. No. 42, 10/19/46.

100. Sir Olaf Caroe, *The Pathans* (London: MacMillan and Co., 1965), p. 435. Birbal, a Mughal general, was killed in 1586 while trying to subdue the Pakhtuns.

101. *Al-Jamiat Sarhad*, 9/11/46 and 11/20/46.

102. *Ibid.*, 11/13/46. Also see *ibid.*, 12/8/46 and *Dawn*, 11/3/46.

103. *Civil and Military Gazette*, 10/5/46 and 12/28/46; *Khyber Mail*, 11/29/46; and *Lahore Tribune*, 11/21/46 and 12/8/46.

In spite of these scares, the province managed to escape the pattern of violence experienced elsewhere in India until December 8th when Black Mountain tribesmen raided two border villages in Hazara, burnt their bazars, and killed or abducted their Hindus and Sikhs.[104] The province's Chief Secretary reported: "The raids were well organized and instigated by *Mullahs* working on fanatical tribes in retaliation for events in Bihar."[105] Additionally, the tribesmen believed that Hindu and Sikh merchants in the border villages were holding back badly needed supplies of cloth and other scarce goods for sale on the black market. For the rest of the month, the tribal raiders roamed at will throughout the border areas of Mansehra *Tehsil*, receiving help from some of the local Muslims.

In January 1947, the trouble spread to the mountainous regions of Abbottabad *Tehsil*, producing similar scenes of violence. The government deployed police, Frontier Constabulary, and a full army division to deal with the crisis, arming them with sweeping authority by promulgating an emergency ordinance. Bad weather and the inaccessibility of the mountain regions of the district impaired the government's effort to end the violence and protect the minorities until late January. By then, more than 10,000 Hindus and Sikhs had been driven from their homes; fifty-five people had been killed; and another 108 were missing and presumed dead.[106] True communal peace, moreover, was never restored in Hazara. Before the emotions aroused by the violence could subside, the Muslim League started civil disobedience against the Khan Sahib ministry which threw Hazara, along with the rest of the province, into communal turmoil until independence.

---

104. *Lahore Tribune*, 12/13/46.

105. FR12/46(I). Also see PJ8/788. Collection 127-1-AA. No. 1 and 2. Information on the violence was released daily in government statements and reprinted in the *Lahore Tribune*.

106. For statistics on deaths and injuries, see *Civil and Military Gazette*, 1/30/47. Estimates of the number of refugees varied greatly. Mehr Chand Khanna put the figure at 10,000. Master Tara Singh claimed there were over 15,000 outside the province alone, while Sardar Patel put the total at more than 20,000. *Ibid.* and Pyarelal, *Mahatma Gandhi, The Last Phase* (Ahmedabad: Navajivan Publishing House, 1956), p. 13.

# 9

# THE TRIUMPH OF THE MUSLIM LEAGUE, 1947

By 1947, the election results of the previous year were no longer an accurate gauge of public opinion. Political sympathies had shifted, but there was no institutional way for the change to be reflected in the provincial assembly. The Muslim League could call for Dr. Khan Sahib's resignation, but with its solid majority in the assembly, the Frontier Congress could not be expected to surrender willingly its control of the provincial government. Since the Muslim League had no legal recourse, it resorted to extraconstitutional means to displace the Frontier Congress. It launched an agitation which brought the normal operations of government to a halt, touched off a wave of communal violence, and encouraged tribal raiding into the southern districts.

With its ministry paralyzed by the agitation and its leaders convinced of British enmity, the Frontier Congress embarked upon a new tack to win back public support. It adopted more aggressive political tactics and a more militant ethnic rhetoric focusing on the demand for Pakhtunistan. These steps failed, however, to arrest the decline in its popularity, for in the crisis atmosphere of the day, most people in the province gave their loyalties to their religious identity. Equally important, the League's agitation convinced the British and the Indian National Congress that there would be no peace in the Frontier and, hence, no transfer of power in India without a further test of public opinion in the NWFP. Lord Mountbatten conducted a series of delicate negotiations in which Congress leaders gradually abandoned their Frontier allies. To the satisfaction of everyone but the Frontier Congress, a compromise was eventually reached with the June 3rd partition plan which included a referendum on whether the NWFP should join India or Pakistan. The referendum produced a strong verdict in favor of Pakistan, resolving the immediate question of the disposition of the Frontier. It left, however, an inheritance of political divisions and ill will to the new state.

## The Direct Action Campaign

The leaders of the Frontier Muslim League had seriously discussed the idea of civil disobedience as early as autumn 1946, both among themselves and with the all-India High Command which indicated that it wanted to see the Khan Sahib government toppled.[1] With the new year and particularly the start of the League's movement against the government of Khizr Hayat Khan in the Punjab on January 24th, provincial leaders actively began to look for an excuse for a confrontation. At the start of February, the party's executive council decided to challenge the ministry over Hazara. It appointed a "war committee" with the *Pir* of Manki at its head and ordered "all the [League] committees of the province to keep an army of *mujahidin* [warriors for the faith] ready to undertake civil disobedience against the Hazara Safety Ordinance."[2] The start of the campaign was temporarily postponed in order to contest a bye-election in Mardan in mid-February. The League won the seat but by a narrow margin which demonstrated that, among Pakhtuns at least, the Frontier Congress retained significant support.[3] Once the polling was over, the final restraint on the League was lifted. Seven days later it started direct action on the first available pretext.

A pregnant Sikh woman had been abducted in January from her village in Hazara and her family murdered. She was then forcibly converted to Islam and married to a Muslim. The police rescued her in early February, and Khan Sahib brought her to Peshawar where he kept her in his own home. Although she told a magistrate in the presence of her new husband on February 18th that she wanted to go back to her own people, the rumor quickly spread that Khan Sahib had coerced her into reverting to the Sikh religion. The next day, according to the *Pakistan Times*, Khan Sahib satisfied a delegation of League leaders, including Abdul Qaiyum, that "no kind of compulsion or coercion had been used."[4] Nonetheless, the party distorted the incident into a justification for a confrontation. Its version of the case was summarized by *Al-Jamiat Sarhad*:

> Recently, a non-Muslim woman openly declared in the main mosque of Abbottabad that she had changed her religion and heartily accepted Islam. She spent a month with her Muslim husband when she was taken away by the government. She made a clear statement before the Deputy Commissioner that she was a Muslim and the person concerned was her lawful husband. This statement, however, was not recorded. Then she was kept in the Haripur jail, and even there she made the same statement.

---

1. Interviews with Muhammad Ali Khan, Abdul Qaiyum Khan, *Arbab* Nur Muhammad, and Mian Abdullah Shah.

2. *Al-Jamiat Sarhad*, 2/22/47

3. The League won by 588 votes out of 17,294, only a slight improvement over 1946 when it captured the seat by 169 votes out of 16,539. *Khyber Mail*, 2/21/47. *Returns Showing the Results of Elections to the Central Legislative Assembly and the Provincial Legislatures in 1945-46* (Delhi: Manager, Government of India Press, 1948), Statement II.

4. The paper went on to say: "The tension has considerably lessened after the meeting between the Premier and the Muslim League leaders." *Pakistan Times*, 2/20/47.

> Eventually, Dr. Khan Sahib called her to his home where she repeated the same story. He was obviously not satisfied with her plea and sent her to the house of his driver for a week. During this period no Muslim was permitted to see her, while Hindus and Sikhs visited her frequently. They threatened that if she did not reconvert, her husband would be killed and she would be accused of his murder. At last, she was so tortured and terrified that she said she was converted to Islam by force and was no longer a Muslim. And then she was handed over to the Sikhs.[5]

While the Sikh woman served as the immediate pretext for civil disobedience, she was quickly replaced as the League's "cause celebre" by the broader issue of civil and religious liberties. On February 20th, a procession was taken out in Mardan in defiance of Section 144 of the Criminal Procedure Code to protest the "reconversion." The protesters were dispersed, and Abdul Qaiyum was arrested along with two prominent party workers from Mardan. Whether by coincidence or design, the procession gave the Provincial League Council, which was scheduled that evening to discuss plans for a campaign to restore civil liberties, something concrete to seize upon. Added urgency was provided the same day when Clement Attlee, the British Prime Minister, announced to Parliament that India would be given independence by June 1948 and that his government would relinquish power as it saw fit if Indians could not agree upon a constitution.

The Council issued a sweeping indictment of the Congress ministry:

> . . . the Congress Government have deliberately embarked on a policy of crushing the Muslim League organisation and its legitimate constitutional activities; . . . in pursuance of that policy the Congress Government have been deliberately suppressing civil liberties in every possible manner as evidenced by the unnecessary and uncalled for promulgation in Hazara of the medieval and black laws; and . . . the Government have intentionally been encroaching on the Muslim religious rights as has been evidenced by the recent high-handed and unjustified action of the Ministry in enforcing apostasy on a Muslim convert under duress. . . .[6]

It went on to demand that the government immediately halt its "unjustified" policies and appointed a Provincial War Council to go underground to "carry on the struggle which has been forced upon them by the Government in a strictly non-communal manner."[7]

Mian Abdullah Shah, the Peshawar District League President, who had served as one of the Afghan Jirga's underground leaders in 1930, was chosen as the War Council's president. Two other members, Sher Bahadur Khan and

---

5. *Al-Jamiat Sarhad*, 2/30/47.
6. *Pakistan Times*, 2/22/47.
7. *Ibid.*

Mian Muhammad Shah, both with experience in the 1930 agitation, managed to avoid arrest throughout the campaign.[8] These three were aided during the first month by the Pir of Manki whom the Congress government did not detain until March 28th on Caroe's advice for fear of arousing his *murids*, especially those in the tribal area. While he was free, the *Pir* of Manki toured the province and tribal areas, rallying public support for the agitation and advising local Leaguers on its conduct. Also advising the War Council was the shadowy figure of Major Khurshid Anwar, the *Naib Salar-i-Ala* of the All-India Muslim League National Guard, who came to the NWFP from the Punjab on February 28th and remained until April 24th. For the most part, though, he operated separately from the War Council, most notably organizing cells to plant bombs and commit other acts of sabotage.[9]

The leaders of the All-India Muslim League maintained only sporadic correspondence with their Frontier workers during the campaign. Direct consultations were even more infrequent, consisting of occasional trips by provincial leaders to Delhi and periodic missions by central leaders, most importantly Abdur Rab Nishtar, to the Frontier. Thus, the High Command realistically could play only an advisory role, leaving the provincial party with almost complete freedom in the daily conduct of the agitation.[10]

The Provincial War Council was no more able to control district workers than the High Command was able to regulate its own activities. The Council directed the agitation in Peshawar city where it was based but left the campaign outside the city to district leaders and confined its supervision to periodically sending one of its members or a surrogate on tour to advise them. At its February 20th meeting, the Provincial League Council appointed some of its members as "dictators" for the campaign in their respective districts.[11] The War Council also directed some individuals to act as underground organizers, as did the different District Muslim Leagues. Many other men went underground on their own, often to form autonomous cells whose activities could only be minimally controlled from above. Additionally, the *Zenana* (Women's) Muslim League in each district functioned autonomously from the male side of the party.[12]

With this confusion of leadership, direct action was necessarily decentralized. Greater coordination, however, was not needed. The campaign's

8. The identities of the rest of the War Council are unclear since party records have been destroyed or lost. Most of the party leaders agree that Bakht Jamal Khan was one member, a point substantiated by his memoirs. Bakht Jamal Khan, *Meri Dastan-i-Hayat, 1900-1968* (Unpublished memoirs. Collection of Aziz Javed). Sher Bahadur Khan suggested in an interview that Ghulam Muhammad Khan and Ibrahim Khan of Jhagra were two others.

9. PJ8/660. Collection 117-C-68-A. Pol. 8145. Telegram 186/CB-5/29/47. Governor to Secretary of State.

10. Interviews with Mian Abdullah Shah, Sher Bahadur Khan, and Muhammad Ali Khan.

11. Interviews with Malik-ur-Rahman Kiyani, Habibullah Khan, Muhammad Ali Khan, and Jalaluddin.

12. See *infra*, pp. 222-225.

immediate objective was to throw the province into turmoil, and this was readily achieved through a loosely structured agitation conducted by local party units with a minimum of centralized direction. The League thoroughly disrupted normality and order, and before it finished, packed the jails with over 6,000 political prisoners.[13] By mid-April, the province's Chief Secretary, A.N. Mitchell, wrote:

> . . . things cannot go on as they are. The strain on the administration is too great, and in many respects it has already begun to cease to function, such as if the province were the scene of a war. . . .[14]

Following the initial demonstration in Mardan, civil disobedience spread to Peshawar city where a large crowd, estimated at over 5,000, forced its way through the cantonment's barbed-wire gates on February 21st, broke two police cordons, fought off tear gas, and reached and ransacked Khan Sahib's garden. Direct action in the rest of the province began by the end of the month. The early phase of the campaign was characterized by noisy but mostly peaceful demonstrations in the form of processions, picketing, and the blocking of railway tracks. A few Hindu and Sikh shops were looted in Peshawar city, but otherwise, violence was limited to isolated, minor damage to railway lines and telegraph wires.[15] The authorities broke up the demonstrations with *lathi* charges as well as tear gas and made sweeping arrests which rounded up most of the well-known figures in the Frontier Muslim League within three weeks.

The agitation was confined to the province's urban centers where it received enthusiastic support from the largely non-Pakhtun population. The rural areas remained quiet, in part because of the continuing strength of the Frontier Congress. Additionally, since direct action was a calculated effort to influence the British to include the Frontier in Pakistan, the League intentionally focused its campaign on the towns where the government's administrative machinery and its British personnel were concentrated. By doing so, it managed to create a heightened but somewhat misleading impression of popular opposition to the Frontier Congress, as Mitchell acknowledged.[16] While the countryside was not the scene of protest, it was involved in the campaign. League organizers, most notably the *Pir* of Manki, toured the villages to mobilize public opinion behind their campaign and funnelled a steady stream of volunteers into the towns every day to protest and court arrest.

Within two weeks, the League had unsettled the NWFP to the point that British officials questioned the viability of the Congress ministry.[17] Those

13. GR/47. Pol. 7918. D.O. GH-53, 5/8/47.
14. MP. Letter to Mrs. M.A. Mitchell, 4/13/47.
15. For the early phase of the campaign, see FR2/47(II) and FR3/47(I).
16. FR5/47(II).
17. GR/47. Pol. 6744. D.O. GH-21, 2/22/47.

doubts increased after March 10th when the nature of direct action qualitatively changed. Demonstrations intensified and took on destructive dimensions. Women not only joined the agitation but assumed a major role in its conduct due to the ministry's reluctance to act against them. The League embarked upon a campaign of sabotage against government facilities, roads, and communication lines. Finally, the NWFP exploded into a fury of communal violence under the influence of events in the Punjab, the passions generated by direct action, and deliberate planning by the Frontier Muslim League. Together, these factors turned the League's campaign into a crippling upheaval with which the authorities could not contend.

In contrast to the first phase of direct action, during which they had kept the crowds within relatively peaceful bounds, party leaders encouraged their supporters to adopt much more militant and destructive tactics after March 10th.[18] Demonstrators invaded and vandalized government offices, attempted to break into jails and police stations, occupied railroad stations where they destroyed records and issued free train tickets, closed schools with sit-ins, and damaged court buildings. Party workers did not cease their protests on being arrested. They turned the overcrowded jails into additional fronts by resisting regulations and conducting demonstrations. In the most serious incident, an attempt to free condemned criminals in Peshawar Central Jail on May 19th touched off two days of prison rioting and forced the authorities to call in the military to restore order.[19] The League also extended its protests to the countryside for the first time in May.[20] Crowds in Mardan District broke into rural government offices, burnt land revenue and irrigation records, and destroyed furniture in P.W.D. (Public Works Department) Rest Houses. In Peshawar District, demonstrations were even conducted in the Khudai Khidmatgar strongholds of Charsadda and Utmanzai, an indication that the Muslim League had acquired sufficient strength to challenge its political opponents on their home territory, the province's Pakhtun villages.

Much of the League's campaign after March 10th was conducted by women, a new and unusual feature in Frontier politics. Frontier Muslims, and especially Pakhtuns, had a highly conservative attitude about the place of women, as illustrated by the Pashtu proverb, "For the woman, either the house or the grave."[21] While economic necessity forced many women to work, the ideal was for them to maintain strict *purdah* within the confines of their homes in seclusion from all men but their closest relatives. A woman

18. Interviews with Mian Abdullah Shah and Sher Bahadur Khan. For a daily account of the agitation, see the government's communiques in the *Lahore Tribune*.

19. FR5/47(II) and GR/47. Pol. 8154. D.O. GH-58, 5/22/47.

20. FR5/47(II). Also see *Lahore Tribune*, 5/18/47, 5/20/47, 5/21/47, 5/24/47, 5/25/47, and 5/26/47.

21. Akbar S. Ahmed, *Mataloona* (Peshawar: Pakistan Academy for Rural Development, 1973), p. 44.

could wield great influence within her family, but even there her position was circumscribed to ensure male dominance. Due to these social strictures, women had virtually no freedom in normal times to engage in politics. But 1947 was hardly an ordinary year. Direct action produced an upheaval which temporarily liberated them from the restraints which customarily governed their lives.

The first major procession of women was organized in Abbottabad in early March by Begum Kamaluddin. She led a second march in Peshawar city on March 10th and three days later chaired a meeting which resuscitated a moribund Frontier *Zenana* (Women's) Muslim League and committed it to working actively in the direct action campaign.[22] The new party inflated its importance by calling itself a provincial body. Its officers and twenty-three woman Working Committee were all residents of Peshawar city and with a few exceptions, most notably Begum Qazi Mir Ahmad, its new president, non-Pakhtuns.[23] The "provincial" council exercised little, if any, authority over the other districts where local women organized and ran separate *Zenana* Leagues. Those bodies were also composed almost entirely of urban women, few of whom were Pakhtun. None were able to penetrate into the countryside where the conservative influence of custom prevailed.

The *Zenana* Leagues loosely coordinated their efforts with the male side of the party. On occasion, the women marched in processions with the men, but more often, they operated on their own in deference to the customary separation of the sexes. Direct contact between the female and male party leaders was also minimal, due to the constraints of *purdah*. Usually, instructions and information passed back and forth through the male relatives of the women leaders.[24] The regular party officials would broadly indicate what they wanted the women to do, but except when joint demonstrations were organized, they left the *Zenana* League free to carry out their own plans. The women kept the male leaders informed of their intentions and abided by the general guidelines they received, but they resisted any effort to regulate their activities more closely.[25]

Paradoxically, women enjoyed greater freedom during the agitation than men as a result of the social conservatism that had curtailed their previous involvement in politics. To protect one's women, both in the sense of guarding their physical well-being and reputations, is central to a Pakhtun's *Pakhto*, or code of honor. By extension, his honor is affected by the way he acts towards women outside his family. If he brings a woman into disrepute,

---

22. Register *Ruadad*. Muslim League Subcommittee *Khavatin*. Part II, pp. 3-5. Part I, pp. 1-2 contains a list of its officers. For further information, see the chapters on the Frontier women in Aziz Javed, *Pakistan ki Namvar Khavatin* (Peshawar: Diba Publications, n.d.).

23. Interviews with Zari Sarfaraz and Sherin Wahab.

24. Interviews with Zari Sarfaraz, Sherin Wahab, Mian Abdullah Shah, and Sher Bahadur Khan.

25. Register *Ruadad*. Part I, p. 10.

he will not only incur the enmity of her male relatives but also public odium. The Khan Sahib ministry, therefore, was caught in a cultural trap by the women demonstrators. To respond with force risked offending Pakhtun cultural sensibilities, while handling them gently was likely to make the agitation more difficult to contain.

The ministers opted for dealing leniently with the women, despite the inherent drawbacks to that decision. When they marched in procession with men, women were liable to be dispersed with *lathis* or tear gas; otherwise, the ministers' policy was to avoid arresting them and to use coercion only as a last resort.[26] Police linked arms to block the women's processions, and when their lines were broken, they retreated and reformed their passive barriers. If the women reached government offices, officials tried to persuade them to leave or ignored them; and if all else failed, the offices were closed up for the day. Only when all other means had been exhausted and the women threatened vital government installations, such as the jails or police stations, were the police ordered to use their *lathis*.[27]

The advantage of this approach in the eyes of the ministers was that it did not antagonize their party's supporters by infringing on customary taboos. There was even a partially redeeming feature to allowing the women to engage in activities which were not tolerated from men. Their conduct so completely flaunted traditional Pakhtun mores that the Congress used it for propaganda purposes, deriding the Muslim League for letting their women act in a shameful, unwomanly manner. Abdul Hanan Bijli, a Congress supporter, satirized the League in a poem which reflected the sentiment of many Pakhtuns:

> You have clung to the excuse of Pakistan;
> You have brought out your ladies;
> You must be ashamed, my dear Khans;
> You have abased the honor of your Pakhtun nation.[28]

On balance, however, the freedom the women enjoyed worked to the disadvantage of the Frontier Congress since they sustained direct action at a high level of intensity once arrests, *lathi* charges, tear gas, and increasing government surveillance took their toll on the male members of the party.[29] Recognizing the government's dilemma, the League shifted increasing responsibility for its campaign to its female workers. In Peshawar city, for example, women in *burqas* took out almost daily demonstrations, stormed into the Secretariat, forced their way through the outer gates of the central jail, beset police stations, and invaded government schools. They broke into rail-

26. Interviews with Yahya Jan Khan and Abdur Rashid Khan who was the Senior Superintendent of Police in Peshawar in 1947. Also see *Lahore Tribune*, 4/11/47.

27. Interviews with Yahya Jan Khan and Abdur Rashid Khan.

28. *Pakhtun*, 7/17/47.

29. FR5/47(I).

road offices where they distributed free "Pakistan tickets" and delayed trains by blocking the tracks. It was in the course of attempting to impede a train on April 15th that the only serious injuries of women occurred. Five had to be hospitalized, while another forty suffered minor injuries after they sat down on the tracks too abruptly for the engine driver to stop.

Only a small portion of the violence in the direct action campaign was committed by crowds of demonstrators. From the beginning of the agitation, important segments within the Frontier Muslim League had argued for sabotage against government facilities and attacks upon the minorities. One of the earliest and strongest proponents was Major Khurshid Anwar who brought a supply of explosives to the province and instructed party workers on how to manufacture homemade bombs.[30] He found a receptive audience among many of the party's rank-and-file, such that its leaders would have had difficulty preventing violence had they so desired. As it was, they were readily convinced by March 10th of the political efficacy of violence.[31] Direct action had already taxed the police and administration to their limit. Party leaders hoped that communal disorders and sabotage would destroy what little effectiveness they retained, cause a general breakdown in law-and-order, and thereby convince the British to remove the Khan Sahib ministry from office. Moreover, the risks of such a campaign seemed minimal, since the government's resources were stretched too thin to retaliate effectively against more violent forms of protest. Thus, while the Provincial War Council and other high-ranking League officials continued after March 10th to issue appeals to their followers to remain peaceful, they were only engaging in public posturing.[32] They acquiesced to and helped organize a clandestine campaign of sabotage and bombing. More seriously, they encouraged and, in some instances, actually instigated a wave of communal disorders which caused deaths, injuries, widespread property damage, and the exodus of a majority of the province's Hindus and Sikhs.

The League's sabotage and bombings were amateurish by the standards of terrorist movements in the twentieth century. They were directed at property rather than people and intended more to create an impression of unrest than to do real harm. There were no attacks on government personnel *per se*. The Hindus and Sikhs in the administration faced danger, but only because of their religion and not their jobs. Muslim and British officers were safe throughout the campaign since the League did not want to antagonize either. Muslims in the Frontier Congress were also safe, for the potential costs, both political and personal, were too great and the likely returns too small to warrant an assault on them. Had any been injured, the Pakhtuns'

30. PJ8/660. Collection 117-C-86-A. Pol. 8145. Telegram 186/CB (9357), 5/29/47. Governor to Secretary of State.

31. Interviews with Mian Abdullah Shah, Sher Bahadur Khan, Fida Muhammad Khan, Muhammad Ali Khan, Muhammad Ayub Khan, and Muhammad Ramzan Khan.

32. Interviews with Sher Bahadur Khan and Mian Abdullah Shah.

social code would have required their relatives to seek revenge, thereby creating blood enmities which would have continued long after the Frontier's political future had been decided. Any such attacks, moreover, would have solidified the Frontier Congress' hold on the loyalties of its supporters and roused it to a more aggressive, even violent, opposition to the League. As it was, Frontier Congressmen were already openly carrying arms as if to dare their opponents to a test of strength.[33] The League's saboteurs, therefore, were careful not to hurt anyone who might retaliate and precipitate bloodshed between the two parties.

The primary targets of the League's saboteurs were the province's communication and transportation systems.[34] Bombs were planted on roads and railroad bridges, along tracks, and in railroad quarters. Usually, they were discovered and defused, and even those that did explode caused only minor damage. Telegraph and telephone wires were cut, poles uprooted, and office equipment smashed. On occasion, the damage to the communication lines was sufficient to cut towns off temporarily from the outside. As the agitation progressed, directed sabotage was augmented by the random explosion of bombs, especially in Peshawar city, which were meant to contribute to the general atmosphere of unrest prevailing in the province rather than damage any government installation or injure anyone in specific.[35]

As a form of violence, sabotage of this type was overshadowed by the communal disorders the League's campaign touched off. Relations between the Frontier's religious communities had been peaceful, though strained, during the first three weeks of direct action, even in Hazara which had not yet recovered from the violence of the previous two months. Beneath this calm, however, tensions were building toward an explosion. The initial spark was supplied by the Punjab, where heavy rioting broke out after the resignation of Khizr Hayat Khan on March 5th. Law-and-order quickly collapsed in Haripur *Tehsil* of Hazara, which was culturally as well as geographically an extension of the Punjab plain. Before the month was over, the rest of the district followed Haripur into the communal maelstrom. The Punjab riots also enflamed communal antagonisms elsewhere in the NWFP, but the incident that precipitated violence was local in origin. The Frontier Muslim League mobilized a large procession in Peshawar city on March 10th in an effort to disrupt the start of the provincial assembly. The demonstrators clashed with police and army troops at a bridge between the city and cantonment, leaving two dead and fifteen injured. They then retreated to the city where they broke up into angry, roving gangs which sought out Hindus

33. GR/47. Pol. 7918 and 8154.

34. See the daily government communiques in *Lahore Tribune* and PJ8/660. Collection 117-C-68-A for samples of the specific incidents.

35. FR4/47(II) and FR5/47(II). Also see *Lahore Tribune*, 3/17/47, 4/9/47, 4/12/47, 4/19/47, 4/23/47, 5/1/47, 5/3/47, 5/7/47, 5/15/47, and 5/24/47, for a sample of the incidents that occurred.

and Sikhs. Mitchell explained:

> . . . they turned their anger against Hindus and Sikhs, partly because of the very bad communal rioting in the Punjab, which had roused feelings here; partly because they regarded the firing as an attack by the Congress party, which is represented as a Hindu party, on the Muslims. Then and on subsequent days about twenty-five Hindus and Sikhs had been stabbed or shot in the city and cantonment.[36]

Henceforth, attacks on Hindus and Sikhs became an integral part of direct action. League leaders continued to issue appeals to keep the agitation nonviolent, but their actual behavior contradicted their public statements. Party officials from the War Council down to the local level not only tolerated the disturbances but actually helped plan many of them.[37]

Communal violence was confined in March primarily to Hazara and Peshawar Districts. Animosity toward the minorities was universally felt, but the rest of the province was quiet except for a few stabbings in Bannu, Mardan, and Kohat.[38] In Peshawar Valley, only Peshawar *Tehsil* was seriously affected, and in its rural areas, the trouble was minimized by the partial evacuation of Hindus and Sikhs, frequent military patrolling, and the Frontier Congress' moderating influence. Peshawar city witnessed a week of random stabbings, bombings, and scattered incendiarism before the police and military restored a semblance of order. Even then, tensions remained so high that the city's normal commercial and administrative activities could not resume. The ministry responded by importing over 10,000 Khudai Khidmatgars from the countryside on March 19th in hopes both of quieting the city and impressing the British with their party's capacity to counter the League's campaign. Far from helping, the move added to the strained atmosphere in the city, since its largely non-Pakhtun Muslim inhabitants bitterly opposed the Congress. Muslim shops suspended business under the League's directions, and minority merchants were intimidated into also remaining closed.[39] After a momentary lull, violence also picked up again, forcing the ministry to withdraw the Khudai Khidmatgars and impose a twenty-four hour curfew on the city on April 6th.

Hazara experienced much more serious trouble because of its close affinities with the northern Punjab where devastating riots were taking place. Additionally, the Frontier Congress could not help dampen animosities because

---

36. MP. Letter to Mrs. M.A. Mitchell, 3/16/47. For an account of the clash between the police and crowd, see FR3/47(I) and *Civil and Military Gazette*, 3/14/47.

37. Interviews with Mian Abdullah Shah, Sher Bahadur Khan, and Muhammad Ramzan Khan.

38. MP. Letter to Mrs. M.A. Mitchell, 3/16/47. For the disorders in Peshawar Valley, see the government communiques in *Lahore Tribune* between 3/14/47 and 4/6/47.

39. PJ8/660. Collection 117-C-68-A. Pol. 7069. Telegram CA/26 (4913), 3/19/47. Governor to Viceroy. Also see FR4/47(I).

it had very little influence among Hazara's non-Pakhtun population. The disorders were not localized to any one part of Hazara, and the total number of casualties was much higher than in Peshawar.[40] The initial incident occurred in Haripur *Tehsil* when a party of minority evacuees was ambushed on March 12th. The next day, Muslims killed forty-seven Hindus and Sikhs in village Chajian and set fire to the bazar in village Kotnajibullah. Violence spread to the rest of the district within days and reached a peak on March 21st when Muslims looted and burnt the main bazar in the town of Mansehra. A complete breakdown of order was averted only because army troops were already in place due to the disorders of December and January. The authorities maintained "the most rigid control in all the towns,"[41] set up road blocks to prevent the free flow of rioters, evacuated large numbers of Hindus and Sikhs from the district, and fired on crowds when they appeared out of hand.

The center of communal disorder moved south in April. Violence continued in Hazara but at an endemic level until rioting ravaged the town of Nawanshehr on June 3rd. Similarly, while disturbances occurred throughout Peshawar Valley during the rest of the spring, they moderated in intensity, primarily because of the Congress' counterefforts in the area. In Kohat city, in contrast, tensions had become acute by the end of March. The Khudai Khidmatgars tried to undertake a peace effort similar to the one in Peshawar city on March 27th, only to be routed by a hostile Muslim League crowd.[42] An outbreak of looting, arson, and murder followed which drove a large part of the city's minorities from their homes.

Communal violence climaxed with ten days of rioting in Dera Ismail Khan in April. Like Hazara, that district was oriented more toward the Punjab, of which it was a geographic and cultural extension, than the rest of the NWFP. Its inhabitants, therefore, were adversely influenced by severe rioting in nearby Multan, just as the people of Hazara had been affected by the violence in neighboring Rawalpindi. In addition, the Frontier Congress was weak in the district and unable to moderate communal relations. On the evening of April 14th, local League leaders aroused a large public meeting gathered in Dera Ismail Khan city with a call for violence against its minorities. Muhammad Ramzan Khan, the District "Dictator," went so far as to urge his listeners to sack the Hindu-controlled business section of town.[43] The next morning random attacks began on Hindu homes and stores and quickly escalated into rioting and arson which raged out of control for two days. The

---

40. For information on the Hazara disorders, see the communiques published daily in *Lahore Tribune* in March. Also see GR/47. Pol. 7269. D.O. GH-34, 3/22/47.

41. FR4/47(I).

42. *Lahore Tribune*, 3/29/47, 4/3/47, 4/4/47, and 4/5/47.

43. Interview with Muhammad Ramzan Khan. Also, FR4/47(II) and *Lahore Tribune*, 5/17/47.

trouble spread to Tank on April 17th where "fires . . . burnt out practically the whole town owing to strong winds" and to Kulachi on April 22nd.[44] Numerous smaller outbursts occurred in the villages, and Mahsuds and Bhitanis from the tribal territory added to the strife and unrest by sending raiding parties which roamed virtually at will throughout the district for ten days.[45]

By April 25th, when the military finally restored a semblance of order, 121 people had been killed, and almost all of the 16,000 minorities living in rural Dera Ismail Khan, plus thousands more from its towns, had fled the province or collected in refugee camps in Dera Ismail Khan city.[46] The economic toll was also extremely heavy. Mitchell reported:

> The damage in Dera Ismail Khan City is estimated to be of the value of nearly rupees one crore; while the town of Tank has very largely ceased to exist . . . it is no exaggeration to say that the effects on commerce also imply economic calamity to the district and the adjacent Tribal Areas not only through the destruction of property and goods but also through the emigration of many thousands of those upon whom commerce depended.[47]

The effects of the riots extended into Bannu as well. According to Mitchell,

> The neighbouring District of Bannu, being forewarned, has so far escaped similar tragedies. But the City has remained in a constant state of anxiety behind locked gates with commercial and Government business almost at a standstill. Tribal gangs had constantly menaced the City and the smaller towns of the district and worse might have occurred but for a prompt action of the political authorities in North Waziristan in arresting on April 24th 400 Mahsuds who were on their way to the plains for mischief.[48]

Throughout the rest of the province, the riots heightened communal tensions and contributed to an ever-increasing exodus of Hindus and Sikhs from their homes. An estimated 60 percent of the minorities in Peshawar, Mardan, Kohat, and Bannu Districts had left the NWFP by mid-May, and the percentages for Hazara and Dera Ismail Khan were even higher.[49]

---

44. GR/47. Pol. 7674. D.O. GH-46, 4/21/47.

45. FR4/47(II). The tribesmen remained unchecked until the police and the Frontier Constabulary inflicted severe casualties on a raiding party of Mahsuds which was on its way home after attacking the town of Kulachi. Thereafter the tribesmen were more cautious, but they continued to raid isolated villages when the chances of evading the police seemed good.

46. *Civil and Military Gazette*, 5/23/47.

47. FR5/47(I).

48. FR4/47(II).

49. *Lahore Tribune*, 5/17/47.

Communal violence continued during May but at a much reduced level, as though the convulsions in Dera Ismail Khan had temporarily sated passions. One crucial reason for the relative improvement was that the League's attitude changed when it became apparent at the end of April that Lord Mountbatten, the new Viceroy, would insist on new elections or a referendum before deciding the NWFP's future.[50] With that concession, the party no longer needed to push the agitation to extremes. Jinnah, who had issued an appeal for peace with Gandhi on April 15th, sent orders to the Provincial War Council that the violence should end, and he repeated those instructions to a delegation of provincial leaders which conferred with him in Delhi at the start of May.[51] The provincial leaders henceforth tried to discourage communal violence, but it was a mark both of the involvement of non-partymen and of the agitation's decentralized nature that while violence tailed off, it did not end, nor did the participation of members of the Muslim League in it.

## The Frontier Congress' Response to Direct Action

The Frontier Congress government was neither systematic nor severe in dealing with direct action. It did not resort to preemptive detention and even delayed arresting some men despite clear evidence of their political activities. League leaders enjoyed considerable freedom of movement throughout the campaign. Surveillance and the risk of arrest were greatest in the towns, the focal points of the agitation, but even there, party leaders did not need to take strict precautions.[52] In the countryside, they moved about, held meetings, recruited volunteers, and planned demonstrations with only a modicum of care. Thus, the League retained the initiative during the campaign, while the government confined itself to reacting on an *ad hoc* basis to each new demonstration and outburst of communal violence. Mitchell complained: "The ministry does not seem to have a long term policy for dealing with the situation other than hanging on grimly from day to day and hoping to tire the other side out."[53]

The leniency of the ministry can be explained in part by the political dilemma it faced.[54] Party leaders were fearful that a harsher, more repressive policy would alienate the public, and especially the core of supporters they still retained. If that were to happen, the restoration of order would be of

50. FR5/47(I). For Lord Mountbatten's plans, see *infra*, pp. 236-239.

51. Interviews with Mian Abdullah Shah, Sher Bahadur Khan, and *Arbab* Nur Muhammad Khan.

52. *Pakistan Times*, 3/30/47 and 4/24/47; and *Al-Jamiat Sarhad*, 5/18/47. Interviews with Muhammad Ramzan Khan, Sher Bahadur Khan, and Qazi Shafiuddin.

53. MP. Letter to Mrs. M.A. Mitchell, 4/6/47.

54. Interviews with Yahya Jan Khan, Abdul Akbar Khan, and Mian Jaffar Shah.

little value since their bargaining position in the negotiations over the Frontier's future would be undermined, as would their popularity after independence.

Beyond these political calculations, the British, for their own reasons, imposed restraints on the ministry. As long as direct action continued, Caroe and Lord Mountbatten agreed that the government had no choice but to enforce the law. However, the level of repression they were prepared to sanction was limited since they did not want to complicate India's overall political deadlock by antagonizing All-India Muslim League leaders over the Frontier. In fact, with a view toward easing the all-India problem, both urged the Frontier Congress to adopt a more conciliatory policy and to end the confrontation through compromise.[55] Far from accepting this advice, party leaders took it as proof of British hostility to their government. Hence, as the agitation progressed, relations between the ministry and permanent administration deteriorated into recriminations and suspicions which demoralized both sides. Eventually, Khan Sahib and his colleagues openly accused British officers, and especially Caroe, of aiding the League. At their behest, Indian National Congress leaders began in mid-March to demand that Caroe be replaced.[56]

The Congress ministers were equally convinced, and with good reason, that they could not count on many Muslim officers in the provincial administration. In the very first demonstration in Peshawar on February 21st, the police disobeyed orders to fire on the crowd. In Caroe's estimation, this incident was not only "proof of police demoralization" but evidence that already "all Mohammadan Government servants, except a few at the very top, are disloyal in their hearts to a regime which represents in their eyes Hindu domination."[57] During the campaign that followed, some officials went beyond passively resisting ministerial orders. They passed on intelligence to the League, helped to hide its leaders and facilitate their movements, served as conduits for party communications, and even covertly participated in its campaign of sabotage and communal violence.[58]

Since its ministry could not end the agitation, the Frontier Congress had to adjust its own tactics and find new means with which to recoup its political strength. This became particularly imperative once negotiations in New Delhi pointed to the likelihood of a further electoral contest in the province. Party leaders responded with greater militancy. One of the movement's curiosities in the minds of contemporary observers had always been the Pakhtuns' support for Gandhian ideas. Abdul Ghaffar Khan was a close personal

---

55. GR/47. Pol. 7072. D.O. GH-27, 3/8/47; and PO/433. No. 4, 4/24/47.

56. PJ8/660. Collection 117-C-68-A. Letter, 3/19/47. Lord Wavell to Secretary of State. PO/433. No. 5 and 6.

57. GR/47. Pol. 6774. D.O. GH-21, 2/22/47.

58. Interviews with Sher Bahadur Khan, Mian Abdullah Shah, and Amin Jan Khan of Landi.

disciple of Gandhi, and the Khudai Khidmatgars had included a pledge of non-violence in their by-laws. As direct action gained momentum, however, party members reverted to a more traditional Pakhtun posture. In increasing numbers, they showed up at meetings or paraded through the province's villages with arms. They also began to discharge their weapons randomly in the air. At first, party leaders only tacitly encouraged this trend, but in time, they too spoke in vague but menacing terms about using force. To back up their threat, they formed the *Zalmai Pakhtun* which repudiated non-violence in favor of "armed defence against violence and terrorism."[59]

The idea of the *Zalmai Pakhtun* had been raised as early as the start of March, but its actual formation was put off until it became clear that the British intended to hold a referendum in the NWFP. At the start of May, Amir Muhammad Khan, the FPCC President, announced its creation under the leadership of Abdul Ghani Khan, Abdul Ghaffar Khan's son and the Frontier's representative in the Central Assembly. The *Zalmai Pakhtun* did not attract many members, despite Ghani Khan's claims to the contrary, but those who did join were highly visible with their guns and military paraphernalia. One indication of their prominence was that the League felt compelled to form a rival armed body, the *Ghazi Pakhtun*.[60]

While the Frontier Congress adopted a more martial posture, its members, like those in the Muslim League, were extremely cautious about provoking an armed conflict. They hoped to win public support by appearing to be more aggressive, to intimidate their opponents, and to pressure the British; but they shied away from an actual fight. Thus, confrontations with the League were reduced to ritualistic but harmless expressions of hostility whose value for both parties lay in their symbolism. The annual celebration of the 1930 Takar "massacre" in Mardan District serves as a good example. Caroe recounted:

> This year the League decided to participate in the show as well and crowds of about 3000 or 4000 (nearly half of these were armed) collected on either side. The district authorities played the game in persuading the Congress to hold their meeting in the morning and the League to hold theirs in the afternoon, thus bearing out the point that these people are more interested in posturing than in setting at one another.[61]

The appearance of armed Khudai Khidmatgars was part of a more general increase in the level of Congress activity. Initially, the party had left the task of dealing with the direct action campaign to its ministry. Abdul Ghaffar Khan even went to Bihar to work for communal peace for three months and did not return to the province until the middle of April. Once the ministry's

59. *Lahore Tribune*, 5/9/47. GR/47. Pol. 7918. D.O. GH-53, 5/8/47.
60. FR5/47(II).
61. GR/47. Pol. 8423. D.O. GH-78, 6/8/47.

ineffectiveness became apparent, party leaders actively organized public meetings, and the Khudai Khidmatgars started to tour the province's villages.

In their attempt to win back popular support, Congress leaders denounced the League for conducting a campaign of lawlessness against a democratically elected government, for stirring up religious fanaticism, and for committing communal atrocities which were a stain on the honor of the Frontier Province.[62] Additionally, they resorted to the time-honored party practice of representing themselves as the defenders of the masses against a reactionary feudal elite which was intent on exploiting India's political crisis for its own selfish ends. For example, Qazi Attaullah, the Revenue Minister, told one meeting:

> The Muslim League movement in the Frontier is nothing but an organised attempt on the part of big landlords and nawabs, parasitic pirs and mullahs, who have hoarded enormous wealth and accumulated large estates to deprive the poorer classes of their legitimate rights and seize power on the day the Britishers quit India.[63]

This line of attack was not confined to rhetoric alone. The party fitfully tried to organize a "no rent" campaign against the large Khans in parts of Mardan, Kohat, and Hazara, claiming that there was no need to pay since its ministry planned to enact legislation fundamentally altering landlord-tenant relations.[64] Previous anti-landlord campaigns had almost invariably elicited interest. This one, however, failed because of the public preoccupation with India's political crisis and because the League's identification with the senior Khans had been blurred in the preceding two years by an influx of new members from other segments of Frontier society.

The centerpiece of the Frontier Congress' new strategy was to retreat into greater ethnic militancy, to slough off its damaging alliance with the Congress and face the League purely as the champions of Pakhtun interests. This too was a technique the party had used in the past time and again to shore up its popularity. Symbolic of the move, its leaders ceased to call their party the Congress, using "Khudai Khidmatgar" instead.

Party rhetoric sought to exploit the anti-Punjabi biases which went hand in hand with the Pakhtuns' ethnic pride. A recurrent theme in the speeches of party leaders was that Pakistan was merely another name for Punjabi exploitation. Qazi Attaullah, for instance, told the press:

> We had a connection with the Punjab . . . but unfortunately our last memories are not happy, and it appears to me as if the Punjab element

62. For instance, see the FPCC resolution in *Lahore Tribune*, 3/10/47. Also see *ibid.*, 3/2/47 and 3/25/47.

63. *Ibid.*, 4/12/47. Also see *ibid.*, 4/2/47 and 4/30/47.

64. GR/47. Pol. 8154. D.O. GH-58, 5/22/47; and FR5/47(II).

again wants to dominate over us secretly by appealing to the masses in the name of religion.[65]

More positively, party leaders embraced the vague but attractive concept of Pakhtunistan as their new political goal. Initially, the demand for Pakhtunistan was not a call for separatism. The party used it as no more than a shorthand for the right to join India or Pakistan while retaining complete internal autonomy.[66] Thus, in terms of its actual content, the idea barely differed from the party's previous goals. The change was tactical, with the demand for autonomy being repackaged under a new, more appealing label. By mid-April, party leaders stopped talking about mere autonomy, substituting in its place a demand for sovereignty. But even at this point, they were not advocating a totally independent state. As Khan Sahib explained to the press: ". . . a small state like NWFP cannot but associate itself with others for defense and other purposes."[67] Even hardliners like Qazi Attaullah concurred:

> First of all we want to have an independent sovereign state of Pathans and then we will visualise a joint jirgah (council) of [the] whole Pathan nation which will ultimately negotiate on equal footing either with Hindustan or Pakistan, whichever offers us better terms.[68]

The party did not abandon this position for complete separatism until Lord Mountbatten's partition plan forced them to do so.

## Mountbatten's Partition Plan and the North-West Frontier Province

Lord Louis Mountbatten arrived in New Delhi as the new Viceroy on March 22nd and immediately initiated a period of intensive political discussions which culminated on June 3rd with the announcement of a plan to partition India and advance the date of independence from June 1948 to August 15, 1947. The North-West Frontier Province formed an important topic in those negotiations, one which complicated his attempts to reach a settlement to India's political crisis. At one point, in fact, he wrote that the Province "is the greatest danger spot in India and the bone of contention between Congress and Muslim League."[69] Mountbatten had to deal with three parties on the Frontier. While the All-India Muslim League and its provincial branch were united in wanting to see the region included in Pakistan, the interests of the Indian National Congress and Frontier Congress, despite

65. *Lahore Tribune*, 5/15/47.

66. *Ibid.*, 5/17/47. For Abdul Ghaffar Khan's first public reference to Pakhtunistan carried by the press, see *Civil and Military Gazette*, 5/3/47.

67. *Lahore Tribune*, 5/17/47.

68. *Ibid.*, 5/15/47.

69. PO/433. No. 5, 5/1/47.

their common name, diverged as the negotiations progressed. In the early stages, Nehru and his colleagues vigorously backed their Frontier allies, but once they accepted partition, support for Pakhtun nationalism conflicted with their desire to see power transferred as quickly as possible to a unified state in the territories inherited by India. Thus, the Indian National Congress agreed in the end to a compromise which was acceptable to the British and Muslim League but not to their Pakhtun allies.

As far back as Nehru's visit to the Frontier in October 1946, Sir Olaf Caroe had accepted the League's position that it, and not the Congress, represented local political feelings and that there would be no peace until the Frontier's government reflected that fact. At the start of direct action, he wrote to Lord Wavell:

> I am afraid we shall never be able to achieve any sort of stability with the present unnatural Government, and this is sad, for the personalities of my Ministers are much above the run of anyone which could be produced by other parties.[70]

With few exceptions, his subordinates shared his views. Mitchell, on taking over as Chief Secretary, was more cautious in assessing the relative strength of the two parties:

> Facts conceded by members of the Congress party . . . are that all large towns and Hazara district are now Muslim League sympathisers, active or otherwise. . . . One opinion, from a person whose opinion is entitled to respect was to the effect that D.I. Khan and Bannu would show a Muslim League majority, the rural areas of Peshawar and Mardan a Congress majority, with Kohat doubtful but inclined to the Muslim League.[71]

Nonetheless, he too concluded that decisive measures were required to end the existing, unsatisfactory situation.

The conviction that something had to be done was based on the belief that conditions would only get worse as long as the Congress clung to office, for it lacked the public support needed to bring direct action to a halt on its own terms. Mitchell also warned that the police and administrative personnel were too exhausted to cope with the situation much longer.[72] Compounding the sense of crisis, British officers feared that the disorders would spill across the administrative border into the tribal areas where sentiment overwhelmingly favored the Muslim League. While tribal elders tried to keep their people out of the conflict, many influential individuals actively spoke out for the party, and *jirgas* all along the border threatened to intervene on its be-

70. GR/47. Pol. 6774. D.O. GH-21, 2/22/47.

71. "Appreciation of Muslim League Movement Situation on 5-4/47," in Durga Das, ed., *Sardar Patel's Correspondence, 1945-50* (Ahmedabad: Navajivan Publishing House, 1973), p. 258.

72. *Ibid.*, pp. 257-58.

half.[73] Although tribal involvement assumed serious proportions only in Dera Ismail Khan, Mitchell nevertheless expressed the general consensus among his colleagues when he wrote:

> I see the possibility of tribal inroads on a large scale culminating in general war. It happened in 1897 and to a less extent 1916 and 1919, and there is nothing inherently improbable in the same thing happening again.[74]

Caroe and his subordinates believed that new elections would restore order by bringing the provincial government in line with public opinion. The Frontier Congress flatly rejected that proposal when Caroe made it to the provincial cabinet in early March.[75] Caroe, nonetheless, forcefully argued for elections to Lord Ismay, whom Mountbatten sent to the Frontier Province within a week after taking over as Viceroy, and in subsequent correspondence with the Viceroy himself. He also told both that "the best way to do this would probably be to dismiss the Ministry, dissolve the House, and for the Governor to take powers under Section 93."[76] At a Governors' Conference in Delhi on April 15-16, he made a personal appeal to Mountbatten for an announcement "straight away, rather than at a later stage," on the grounds that the province "was liable to 'drop to bits' at any moment" and he "would rather risk any disturbances the elections themselves might bring."[77]

Lord Mountbatten did not rely exclusively on the Governor for information, seeking out opposing views from Congress leaders and other sources. Nonetheless, within his first three weeks in India, he too had concluded that Section 93 and new elections were desirable. He also accepted Caroe's assessment that the Muslim League had greater popular support in the Frontier than the Congress.[78] He did not act immediately, however, due to the wider ramifications such a step might have had. By mid-April, he had a sense of how to resolve the Indian deadlock:

> In the first place, I am convinced that we have to make up our minds some way or the other in the very near future if we are to avert civil war and the risk of a complete breakdown of the administration. . . . Secondly, I have very slender hopes of getting acceptance of the Cabinet Mission plan, and I am very much afraid that partition may prove to be the only possible alternative.[79]

---

73. For information on the tribal reaction to direct action, see PS12/3201. Collection 23/60. Intelligence Summaries for 1947.

74. Das, *op. cit.*, p. 259.

75. GR/47. Pol. 7072. D.O. GH-27, 3/8/47.

76. PO/433. No. 2, 4/9/47.

77. PO/433. Minutes of Governors' Conference. Caroe also added that if elections were held, "he had very little doubt that the Northwest Frontier Province would, in fact, come in on the Pakistan side."

78. PO/433. No. 4 and 14.

79. PO/433. No. 3, 4/17/47.

With this decided, his problem was one of formulating a partition plan and coaxing both the League and Congress into quickly accepting it. He, therefore, could not afford to jeopardize his relations with either party by taking unilateral action on the Frontier, and as he noted on first hearing of Caroe's proposal, it was "clearly a big and difficult move which might infuriate Congress."[80]

Mountbatten raised the idea of new elections at a meeting after the Governors' Conference which included Nehru, Liaqat Ali Khan, and Caroe. As expected, Nehru objected, both because "he thought it would appear that the Provincial Government's hand had been forced by the agitation" and because the Frontier Congress had not had a chance to present its case.[81] Khan Sahib, therefore, was summoned to Delhi to confer with the Viceroy, Caroe, and Nehru on April 18th. Nehru conceded in principal at that meeting that a further test of the public will would have to be made in the NWFP, and Khan Sahib agreed to release those political prisoners not charged with violence as a first step toward a compromise to end direct action. For his part, Mountbatten agreed, as he later told Jinnah, that "I could not be party to surrendering to any form of violence" even though it was his unspoken conviction that "fresh elections will be necessary in due course."[82]

Mountbatten was still thinking in terms of Governor's Rule and a general election when he went to Peshawar on April 28th to assess the situation for himself. Instead of relaxing over "a nice quiet lunch" after his arrival, he found himself, in the words of his Press Secretary, Alan Campbell-Johnson, "confronting a situation of crisis bordering on panic."[83] The Muslim League had assembled a large crowd, estimated at between 50,000 and 100,000 strong, which threatened to storm into the cantonment to see the Viceroy. To avert a clash with security forces, Mountbatten and his wife went to the crowd instead. Campbell-Johnson recalled:

> We climbed up the railway embankment close to the historic Bala Hissar Fort and looked down upon a vast concourse gathered at Cunningham Park and stretching into distant fields. There was much gesticulation and the waving of innumerable but illegal green flags with the white crescent of Pakistan, accompanied by a steady chant of Pakistan "Zindabad." . . . For nearly half an hour Mountbatten, in his khaki bush shirt, and Lady Mountbatten, also in a bush shirt, stood waving to a crowd. . . . Any sort of speech was out of the question.[84]

---

80. PO/433. No. 2, 4/9/47.
81. PO/433. No. 4, 4/24/47.
82. *Ibid.*
83. Alan Campbell-Johnson, *Mission with Mountbatten* (Bombay: Jaico Publishing House, 1951), p. 61.
84. *Ibid.*, pp. 61-2.

This episode made a strong impression on Mountbatten and helped confirm, as he later recounted, his view that the NWFP would join Pakistan.[85]

Afterwards, Mountbatten returned to Government House where he met with the provincial cabinet. He later wrote to London:

> The Ministry, of course, was violently opposed to my ordering fresh elections, but I warned them that I should require to know whether they had a mandate from their people before I could possibly decide who was to inherit the Province. . . . I also warned them I should probably go into Section 93 for at least two months beforehand to ensure that the elections were fair.[86]

Next, he met a deputation of leaders from the Frontier Muslim League (including six on parole from jail) which demanded that he impose Governor's Rule immediately and order fresh elections. Although he had spoken to the ministers of precisely these steps, he replied: ". . . I could not possible yield to duress and . . . so long as they were trying to overthrow the present Provincial Government by violence, that Government must have my support."[87] The Frontier League, however, knew from all-India party sources that the Viceroy was inclined to accept its demands. To push him into acting, its Provincial Council, which was reunited in Peshawar jail, adopted an intransigent resolution on May 1st, scorning an offer of amnesty by Khan Sahib and vowing to continue direct action until he was ousted and fresh elections were ordered.[88] Their decision received Jinnah's public support on May 7th.

On May 2nd, in fact, Mountbatten sent a draft of a partition plan to London that included general elections in the North-West Frontier Province under a Section 93 Government.[89] Within two days, however, he was forced by the Congress' reaction to change his mind. In a series of public and private messages, Congress leaders conveyed their intense objection to the proposal, warned of possible trouble in the Frontier, and most ominously, hinted that they might upset the entire negotiations on India's future over the issue. The *Hindustan Times*, for instance, reported on the basis of authoritative sources:

> The Congress Working Committee has made the Frontier question a test case. It has been made clear to the Viceroy that any proposal to dis-

---

85. PO/433. No. 14, 7/25/47. For his impressions of the trip, also see PJ8/660. I.B. (47)61. 5/8/47; Letter, 4/30/47. Mountbatten to Nehru.

86. PO/433. No. 5, 5/1/47.

87. *Ibid.*

88. *Pakistan Times*, 5/2/47. For Jinnah's statement, see *Civil and Military Gazette*, 5/8/47.

89. PO/428. Part I. Telegram 955-S, 5/2/47. Viceroy to Secretary of State.

> miss the Frontier Ministry and hold fresh elections will make the Congress change its entire attitude toward the British Government.[90]

Taking these warnings seriously, Mountbatten abandoned the idea of elections for a simple referendum on which successor state the NWFP should join. The referendum would be run by permanent officials rather than the provincial government to ensure its fairness, but the Khan Sahib ministry would be left in office.[91]

The League accepted this alternative, despite initial suspicions raised by the omission of Governor's Rule, since it guaranteed a further test of the public will under an impartial authority. A referendum, in fact, had certain attractions for the party. It eliminated the weightage the minorities enjoyed in the provincial assembly and assured that the decision would not be clouded by factional and tribal considerations, as would have happened in an election of representatives to the legislature.[92] The Frontier Congress, in contrast, found the new proposal as objectionable as the old. Party leaders saw little chance of winning either an election or referendum. They wanted to postpone any polling until after the Indian and Pakistani Constituent Assemblies had drafted their constitutions.[93] This would permit them to fight the League on concrete proposals about the Frontier's future, grounds which were much more conducive to their ethnic appeal than the emotionally charged atmosphere of the spring of 1947. Moreover, it would take time to frame the two constitutions. In the interim, the Frontier Congress would remain in power, have time to recoup its political strength, and possibly even find a way to circumvent the referendum altogether.

The referendum offered a face-saving compromise for the Indian National Congress. Having resigned themselves to partition, Congress leaders no longer regarded the Frontier as a vital interest, especially since some, Sardar Patel and Abul Kalam Azad for example, doubted that the Frontier Congress was still a match for the League.[94] They, therefore, were looking for a way to remove the Frontier as an impediment to the speedy transfer of power without seeming to surrender to the League. The attraction of Mountbatten's new plan was that it appeared to give in to neither of the League's key demands—the ouster of the Khan Sahib ministry and new elections. At the same time, since they had already agreed that some sort of further vote was necessary, Congress leaders could publicly, at least, insist that they were not bowing to pressure from the League by agreeing to a referendum. Once Mountbatten made the substitution, therefore, the Congress continued to

90. *Hindustan Times*, 5/3/47. Also see R/3/151. Telegram 968-S and Telegram 975-S; PO/433. No. 5, 5/1/47; and PJ8/660. Telegram B365. Information Department Bulletin.

91. PO/433. No. 6, 5/8/47.

92. Interviews with Muhammad Ali Khan, Abdul Qaiyum Khan, and Habibullah Khan.

93. R/3/1/151. Telegram 26-SC, 5/8/47. Viceroy to Secretary of State.

94. D.G. Tendulkar, *Abdul Ghaffar Khan* (Bombay: Popular Prakashan, 1967), p. 429, and Abdul Kalam Azad, *India Wins Freedom* (New Delhi: Orient Longmans, 1959), p. 174.

support the Frontier Congress but in a more restrained manner, no longer making an overall settlement contingent on further concessions on the Frontier. Nehru presented the Frontier Congress' case against a referendum to the Viceroy on at least two occasions, but in a manner which indicated that the Congress was much more receptive to the idea than its allies. Significantly, even while he urged that the referendum be delayed, he reaffirmed his commitment to it in principle:

> As I have told you, I am in agreement with the idea that the will of the people in the Frontier Province should be consulted before final decisions in regard to the position of the Province are taken. But it is very important when this is done and in what context.[95]

With the decision on a referendum made, the only question left was its terms. If the choice were limited to Pakistan and India, Frontier Congress leaders saw their defeat as inevitable; if independence were an option, they saw some chance of winning.[96] Thus, they pushed Pakhtunistan during May with one eye on convincing the Viceroy that only the more broadly defined referendum would accurately indicate the political wishes of the province and the other on regaining the popular support necessary to win it. Mountbatten favored the more narrow terms on the grounds that an independent Frontier was not economically viable and that Afghan irredentism might be aroused.[97] Nonetheless, the very nature of his first plan introduced the possibility of independence. Part of the partition announcement being drafted in London stated:

> His Majesty's Government are satisfied that the most practical procedure in the time available is to enable different parts of India to decide, though representatives chosen for the purpose, whether their constitutions shall be framed:
> a) in collaboration with the existing [Indian] Constituent Assembly;
> b) jointly with other parts of India; or
> c) separately.[98]

To be consistent, the Secretary of State at one point prepared the paragraph on the NWFP to read that if a referendum on Pakistan and India showed that "a majority of those voting favor the partition of British India, a general election will be held and representatives will be appointed by the new Legislative Council to choose between options (b) and (c)."[99] Because Mountbatten objected, the wording on the Frontier Province was narrowed by

95. R/3/1/151. Letter, 5/10/47. Nehru to Mountbatten.

96. Interviews with Abdul Akbar Khan, Mian Jafar Shah, and Mian Shakirullah.

97. PO/428. I.B. (47)56; and R/3/1/151. Telegram 36-SC, 5/10/47. Viceroy to Secretary of State.

98. PO/428. I.B. (47)56.

99. *Ibid.*

eliminating the third option. The general operative paragraph, however, remained unchanged, leaving an ambiguity which the Frontier Congress might have tried to exploit. Even that opportunity was lost, however, as a result of the Congress' reaction to the central principle of the plan.

On a "hunch," Mountbatten showed Nehru his plan on May 10th and received in return a scathing denunciation. He had assumed that all the provinces would join one state or the other, but his plan did not compel them to do so. Recent events, such as demands for a separate Sikhistan and negotiations among some Bengali Congress and Muslim League leaders for a united, independent state, were enough to make the idea of sovereignty devolving to the provinces intolerable to Nehru. Even before consulting his colleagues, he gave Mountbatten his reaction to the proposals:

> Not only do they menace India but also they endanger the future relation between Britain and India. Instead of producing any sense of certainty, security and stability, they would encourage disruptive tendencies everywhere and chaos and weakness. . . . The proposals start with the rejection of an Indian Union as the successor to power and invite the claims of large numbers of the succession States who are permitted to unite if they so wish in two or more States. . . . His Majesty's Government should be left in no doubt as to the total unacceptability of and opposition to both these proposals and the approach made in them, and also to the consequences which are bound to follow if His Majesty's Government were to persist in them. . . . It appears to me that the inevitable and obvious consequences of the proposals and the approach in them are (a) to invite the Balkanisation of India, (b) to provoke certain civil conflict and to add to violence and disorder, (c) to a further breakdown of the central authority which alone can prevent the chaos that is growing, (d) to demoralise the army, the police and the Central Services.[100]

V.P. Menon, the Reforms Commissioner, hastily drafted a new plan which eliminated Nehru's fears by removing the option of independence for the provinces and transferring authority to two successor states only. In doing so, he removed the Frontier Congress' last hope of retaining control of the NWFP

When the Congress Working Committee accepted the redrafted plan on June 2nd, it tried to reintroduce the option of independence into the referendum in the NWFP. The request was intended less as a serious proposition than as a last gesture to show that the High Command had exhausted every avenue of recourse on behalf of the Frontier Congress. Its members were reconciled to partition. They considered Mountbatten's proposals the best

100. PO/429. Note by Nehru, 5/11/47. For a full description of Mountbatten's initial partition plan and its revision, see V.P. Menon, *The Transfer of Power in India* (New Delhi: Orient Longmans, 1968), p. 368.

available under the circumstances and were not prepared to press the question of the Frontier to the point of jeopardizing the entire plan. Thus, when Mountbatten objected that the Congress could not reasonably revive for one province a principle it had previously rejected for all, the party withdrew its suggestion.[101]

Frontier Congressmen reacted to the referendum with bitterness, even though they had known it was coming. Abdul Ghaffar Khan told the Working Committee: "We Pathans stood by you and had undergone great sacrifice for attaining freedom, but you have now deserted us and thrown us to the wolves."[102] Their immediate inclination was to reject the plan out of hand, as Abdul Ghaffar Khan explained:

> We shall not agree to hold [the] referendum because we had decisively won the elections on the issue of Hindustan versus Pakistan and proclaimed the Pakhtun view on it to the world. Now as India has disowned us, why should we have a referendum on Hindustan and Pakistan? Let it be on Pakhtunistan or Pakistan.[103]

A PCC-Khudai Khidmatgar meeting in Peshawar on June 11th-12th, however, split over whether to try to have the terms of the referendum changed or to boycott it, concede Pakistan, and fight for the party's objectives within the new state. The meeting ended by authorizing Abdul Ghaffar Khan to act as he thought best.[104]

Abdul Ghaffar Khan spent the next week in Delhi in fruitless consultations with Congress and League leaders. He received little help from the High Command, other than Gandhi who expressed his personal sympathies but was as unwilling as the other Congress leaders to jeopardize the partition agreement. The Working Committee favored contesting the referendum as it existed; Nehru even believed it could be won. When Abdul Ghaffar Khan refused to consider that suggestion at its June 16th meeting, the Committee absolved itself of further responsibility for the Frontier, leaving the provincial party to decide upon its own policy.[105] While refusing to agree to a broadening of the terms of the referendum, the League was ready to explore the possibility of a settlement that would reconcile the Frontier Congress to Pakistan. Abdul Ghaffar Khan, however, asked for concessions which Jinnah found unacceptable: assurances that the NWFP would be given internal autonomy within Pakistan, including exclusive control of all tribal matters, and that the province and tribal areas could opt out of the new state if its consti-

101. PO/433. No. 8, 6/5/47.

102. Quoted in Tendulkar, *op. cit.*, p. 424.

103. Quoted in *ibid.* Also see R/3/1/151. Telegram 1519-S, 5/4/47. Governor to Viceroy.

104. Minutes of the June 11th-12th Joint PCC, Congress Parliamentary Party and Khudai Khidmatgar Meeting. Personal Papers of Abdul Akbar Khan.

105. Tendulkar, *op. cit.*, pp. 411-12.

tution was unacceptable to their people.[106] Since these conditions would have unnecessarily undermined the new state, there was never any chance of their being accepted, as some PCC leaders themselves recognized.[107] Their only effect was to leave the League all the more determined to have the referendum held on the terms announced by Mountbatten.

Abdul Ghaffar Khan reported his failure to the PCC and Khudai Khidmatgar leaders in Bannu on June 21st-22nd. They decided in response to boycott the referendum and officially adopted complete independence as their party's objective for the first time. They resolved "that a free Pathan state of all the Pakhtuns be established. The constitution of the state will be framed on the basis of Islamic conceptions of democracy, equality and social justice."[108] The party's leaders, however, were not irrevocably committing themselves to a free Pakhtun state with this resolution. Within six months after independence, they would reinterpret the idea of Pakhtunistan to mean that the NWFP should be an autonomous unit within Pakistan.[109] Essentially, they were making yet another tactical shift. By refusing to contest the referendum, they conceded the inevitability of Pakistan. By recasting their aims in the language of extreme ethnic nationalism, they were trying to lay the foundations for their revival within the new state.

Although the boycott reduced the referendum to a formality, the voting was still preceded by a lively campaign. Frontier Congress leaders encouraged people to stay away from the polls in the hopes of a low turnout which would strengthen their own position and minimize the legitimacy of Pakistan. The League conducted an even more energetic campaign. Its workers represented the referendum as an event with great religious import, telling the public it had the chance to create a truly Islamic society. At its most extreme, their propaganda equated a vote for India with heresy.[110] The League dismissed Pakhtunistan as the effort of an un-Islamic clique to cling to power and the boycott as a last Hindu attempt to harm Muslims. At the same time, they felt compelled to address the substance of the Frontier Congress' demand by trying to convince Pakhtuns that the NWFP was too small to survive on its own and by assuring them of autonomy, in some unspecified form, within Pakistan.[111]

Direction of the referendum was entrusted to British army officers, who were invested with police and administrative powers under a special ordinance and supported by 17,000 soldiers.[112] Civilians were included only in

106. *Ibid.*, pp. 436-47. For Abdul Ghaffar Khan's version of the negotiations, see *Pakhtun*, 7/1/47 and 7/9/47.

107. Interviews with Abdul Akbar Khan and Mian Jafar Shah.

108. *Lahore Tribune*, 6/23/47.

109. Tendulkar, *op. cit.*, p. 451.

110. *Lahore Tribune*, 6/27/47; *Al-Jamiat Sarhad*, 7/2/47.

111. For example, see Jinnah's statement in *Khyber Mail*, 7/14/47.

112. *Gazette of India Extraordinary*, 7/2/47. See *Lahore Tribune*, 7/3/47, 7/4/47, 7/5/47, and 7/8/47 regarding the referendum machinery.

the lower echelons of the referendum machinery and only under the close supervision of army personnel. The ministry was excluded entirely to ensure that no interested party unfairly influenced the outcome of the polling. Sir Olaf Caroe went on leave due to the Congress' allegations against him, even though Mountbatten regarded them as unfounded, and Lieutenant-General Sir Rob Lockhart replaced him as governor.

The results of the referendum were made public on July 20th. Only 50.99 percent of the 572,798 eligible voters cast ballots. Pakistan received 289,244 votes, or 50.49 percent of the electorate, while 2,874 voted for India.[113] At first glance, these figures suggest that the Frontier Congress' boycott evoked a widespread response. A closer examination of the results in comparison with those for the 1946 elections argues for the opposite conclusion, that the boycott was ineffectual and the NWFP overwhelmingly favored Pakistan. At the same time, however, they showed that the Frontier Congress still retained strong support in Peshawar Valley.

The 1946 electoral rolls had been adopted without amendment for the referendum, even though they were out of date and included some people who had died or moved out of their constituency. Additionally, some voters undoubtedly stayed home on polling day simply because the Congress had conceded the outcome and they saw no need to vote. Nonetheless, the percentage of those voting was off only 11.20 percent from 1946, and Hindus and Sikhs accounted for over one-third of that decline.[114] The minorities, who formed 13.9 percent of the electorate, could have been expected to boycott the referendum under any circumstances. As it was, a majority of them had fled the province during the turmoil of the preceding eight months and were in no position to vote. Thus, the real issue concerns the response of the Muslim electorate and, more specifically, the eligible Pakhtun voters. Dr. Khan Sahib, a seasoned observer of the Frontier political scene, had summed up the situation before the results were known:

> In the last election about 63% of the total votes were cast. . . . Therefore, if the League polls in this referendum more than 50 percent of the votes cast on the basis of 63 percent of total electorate voting, I will be morally bound to resign.[115]

By his definition, as Tables 9a and 9b show, the Muslim League scored a spectacular victory in the referendum.

The turnout in the Muslim constituencies fell by only 8.03 percent from 1946.[116] The 288,350 votes for Pakistan represented 87.17 percent of the Muslim electorate voting in 1946. That figure was 109.87 percent higher

113. *Lahore Tribune*, 7/22/47.

114. The minorities accounted for 3.8 percent of the decline and the Muslims 7.4 percent. Computed from Tables 9a and 9b.

115. *Civil and Military Gazette*, 7/9/47.

116. Computed from figures in Tables 9a and 9b.

than the 146,235 total votes the Muslim League received in 1946 and 111.46 percent higher than the 145,139 votes for the Congress and its *Jamiat-ul-Ulema-i-Hind* allies. In the twenty-one territorial constituencies dominated by Pakhtuns, turnout dropped by 22.31 percent, suggesting some continued strength on the part of the Frontier Congress. Nonetheless, Pakhtuns sided with the other Muslim voters in the province. The 86,003 votes for Pakistan represented 68.18 percent of those voting in the same constituencies in 1946, exceeded total Muslim League votes in that election by 72.84 percent, and was 31.57 percent greater than the votes for the Congress and *Jamiat-ul-Ulema-i-Hind*. Constituency results show how widespread the shift in party strength actually was. The non-Pakhtun turnout was significantly up in Hazara, Dera Ismail Khan, and the urban areas. While there was some decline in the numbers voting in Bannu and Kohat, the two districts swung heavily in favor of Pakistan. In Bannu, the votes for Pakistan equalled 86.54 percent of those voting in 1946 and in Kohat 94.24 percent. The Frontier Congress could muster support for its boycott only in rural Peshawar and Mardan where the turnout fell in all twelve constituencies and in seven by amounts ranging from 32.1 to 57.2 percent. Nonetheless, votes for Pakistan exceeded the 1946 Congress vote in half of the Valley's constituencies, and the aggregate figures for the two districts suggest that the two parties were almost evenly balanced in what had been the heartland of the Frontier Congress.[117]

Viewing the events of 1947 from the vantage point of the province he had once governed, Sir Olaf Caroe later wrote that Mountbatten's entire partition plan hung in the balance until the referendum.[118] While he may have exaggerated the region's importance, it certainly was true that the League would have settled for nothing less than its inclusion in Pakistan. To ensure that end, it had abandoned constitutional methods, thrown the province into turmoil, and condoned communal violence. Yet the party had no other choice, for the British might not have acceded to its wishes without the pressure of its extralegal tactics. The NWFP did not have a comparable importance for the Indian National Congress once the party accepted partition. In fact, its leaders shared the League's interest in seeing the referendum held. With demands for separatism cropping up in other parts of India, the option of independence in the Frontier would have set a dangerous precedent for the new state of India. The referendum's real losers were the Pakhtun nationalists who had cast their lot with the Congress. Following the vote, they faced an uncertain future in a state in which their enemies held power and they labored under the suspicion of disloyalty.

117. See Table 10

118. Olaf Caroe, "The End of British India," *Round Table*, no. 237, 1/70, p. 62.

**Table 9a: Results of the 1946 Elections**[119]

| *Constituency* | *Electorate* | *Total Votes Cast* | *Percent Voting* | *Muslim League Votes* | *Percent of Electorate* | *Congress & JUH† Votes* | *Percent of Electorate* |
|---|---|---|---|---|---|---|---|
| Muslim | | | | | | | |
| Urban | 80,556 | 50,567 | 62.77 | 23,055 | 28.62 | 11,241 | 13.95 |
| Rural | | | | | | | |
| Hazara | 109,762 | 61,508 | 54.03 | 29,378 | 26.77 | 7,686 | 7.00 |
| Peshawar | 97,088 | 70,726 | 72.85 | 25,853 | 26.63 | 43,316 | 44.62 |
| Mardan | 86,777 | 63,601 | 73.33 | 23,162 | 26.69 | 35,443 | 40.84 |
| Kohat | 52,020 | 34,176 | 65.70 | 13,922 | 26.76 | 19,860 | 38.18 |
| Bannu | 51,080 | 38,289 | 75.00 | 17,592 | 34.44 | 9,405 | 18.41 |
| Dera Ismail Khan | 45,642 | 31,896 | 69.88 | 12,466 | 27.31 | 17,741 | 38.87 |
| Total | 442,369 | 300,196 | 67.86 | 122,373 | 27.66 | 133,451 | 30.17 |
| Total territorial seats | 522,925 | 350,763 | 67.07 | 145,428 | 27.81 | 144,692 | 27.67 |
| Landlord | 1,836 | 1,359 | 73.75 | 807 | 43.95 | 447 | 24.34 |
| Total Muslim | 524,761 | 352,117 | 67.10 | 146,235 | 27.87 | 145,139 | 27.66 |
| Hindu | | | | | | | |
| Urban | 21,117 | 9,748 | 46.16 | — | — | 7,512 | 35.57 |
| Rural | 35,521 | — | — | — | — | — | — |
| Total | 56,638 | 9,748 | 17.21 | — | — | 7,512 | 13.26 |
| Sikh | 23,164 | 14,124 | 60.97 | — | — | 7,598 | 32.80 |
| Total Minority | 79,802 | 23,872 | 29.91 | — | — | 15,110 | 18.93 |
| TOTAL | 604,563 | 375,989 | 62.19 | 146,235 | 24.19 | 160,249 | 26.51 |
| PAKHTUN* | 301,527 | 218,023 | 72.31 | 86,003 | 28.52 | 112,982 | 37.47 |

* 21 rural constituencies, including all those in Peshawar, Mardan, Kohat, and Bannu plus Tank *Tehsil* in Dera Ismail Khan

† *Jamiat-ul-Ulema-i-Hind*

119. Tables 9a and 9b are derived from the figures in *Returns Showing the Results of Elections to the Central Legislative Assembly and the Provincial Legislatures in 1945-46* (Delhi: Manager, Government of India Press, 1948) and R/3/1/151.

**Table 9b: Results of the 1947 Referendum**

| *Constituency* | *Electorate* | *Total Votes Cast* | *Percent Voting* | *Votes for Pakistan* | *Percent of Electorate* | *Percent of Total Votes in 1946†* | *Percent of Muslim League Votes in 1946†* | *Percent of Congress & JUH‡ Votes in 1946†* | *Votes for India* |
|---|---|---|---|---|---|---|---|---|---|
| Muslim | | | | | | | | | |
| Urban | *50,627 | 35,942 | 70.99 | 35,680 | 70.48 | 112.28 | 246.26 | 505.23 | 262 |
| Rural | | | | | | | | | |
| Hazara | 109,762 | 83,656 | 76.22 | 83,269 | 75.86 | 135.38 | 283.44 | 1083.39 | 387 |
| Peshawar | 97,088 | 40,470 | 41.68 | 39,902 | 41.10 | 56.42 | 154.34 | 92.12 | 568 |
| Mardan | 86,777 | 36,062 | 41.56 | 34,852 | 40.16 | 54.80 | 150.48 | 98.33 | 1,210 |
| Kohat | 52,020 | 32,323 | 62.14 | 32,207 | 61.91 | 94.24 | 231.34 | 162.17 | 116 |
| Bannu | 51,080 | 33,282 | 65.16 | 33,137 | 64.87 | 86.54 | 188.36 | 352.33 | 145 |
| Dera Ismail Khan | 45,642 | 29,461 | 64.55 | 29,303 | 64.20 | 91.87 | 235.06 | 165.17 | 158 |
| Total | 442,369 | 255,254 | 57.70 | 252,670 | 57.12 | 84.17 | 206.48 | 189.34 | 2,584 |
| Total Muslim | *492,996 | 291,196 | 59.07 | 288,350 | 58.49 | 87.17 | 209.87 | 211.46 | 2,846 |
| Total Minority | 79,802 | 922 | 1.16 | 894 | 1.12 | 3.75 | — | 5.92 | 28 |
| TOTAL | 572,798 | 292,118 | 50.99 | 289,244 | 50.50 | 81.20 | 208.76 | 190.49 | 2,874 |
| PAKHTUN** | 301,527 | 150,731 | 50.00 | 148,649 | 49.30 | 68.18 | 172.84 | 131.57 | 2,082 |

* The difference between the 1946 and referendum electorates arose due to two changes in the voting.
1) In 1946, each voter in Peshawar city could cast two votes; in 1947, they cast only one.
2) In 1946, a small number of rural Muslims voted twice: in their regular constituency and in special landlord constituencies. In 1947, there was no voting in the latter.

** These figures are for the same 21 rural constituencies used in Table 9a.

† Due to the differences in the electorates, the votes in 1946 and the referendum are not directly comparable. These percentages, therefore, have been computed by comparing the percentage of the electorate voting for Pakistan in 1947 with the percentage in 1946 of the electorate voting, of the electorate voting for the Muslim League, and of the electorate voting for the Congress and *Jamiat-ul-Ulema-i-Hind*.

‡ *Jamial-ul-Ulema-i-Hind*

**Table 10: Voting in the 1946 Elections and 1947 Referendum in Peshawar Valley**[120]

| Constituency | 1946 | | Referendum | | Decrease | |
|---|---|---|---|---|---|---|
| | *Votes Cast* | *Percent Voting* | *Votes Cast* | *Percent Voting* | *In Votes* | *In Percent Voting* |
| Peshawar District | | | | | | |
| Bara Mohmands | 9,364 | 70.4 | 7,401 | 55.7 | 1,963 | 14.7 |
| Khalil | 7,335 | 78.7 | 4,362 | 46.6 | 2,993 | 32.1 |
| Hashtnagar North | 7,703 | 82.3 | 3,499 | 37.5 | 4,204 | 44.8 |
| Hashtnagar South | 9,591 | 72.0 | 2,769 | 20.6 | 6,822 | 51.4 |
| Doaba-Daudzai | 11,484 | 82.0 | 3,469 | 24.8 | 8,015 | 57.2 |
| Nowshera South | 13,881 | 66.0 | 10,778 | 51.1 | 3,103 | 14.9 |
| Nowshera North | 11,348 | 67.6 | 8,192 | 48.9 | 3,156 | 18.7 |
| Total | 70,726 | 72.9 | 40,470 | 41.7 | 30,256 | 31.2 |
| Mardan District | | | | | | |
| Baizai | 14,418 | 69.0 | 9,502 | 50.2 | 4,916 | 18.8 |
| Kamalzai | 16,539 | 65.9 | 12,082 | 48.2 | 4,457 | 17.7 |
| Utmannama | 9,718 | 73.8 | 4,917 | 37.5 | 4,801 | 36.3 |
| Razzar | 9,977 | 76.6 | 3,546 | 27.3 | 6,431 | 49.3 |
| Amazai | 12,949 | 78.0 | 6,015 | 36.3 | 6,934 | 41.7 |
| Total | 63,601 | 73.3 | 36,062 | 41.6 | 27,539 | 31.7 |
| Total for the Valley | 134,327 | 73.1 | 76,532 | 41.6 | 57,795 | 31.5 |

120. *Ibid.*

# 10

## CONCLUSION

In the decade before independence, the Muslim League faced strong opposition in the North-West Frontier Province from powerful ethnic forces whose particularistic interests stood in the way of the party's goal of communal solidarity. It was not that Pakhtuns devalued their religion; rather, Islam was subsumed within a much narrower ethnic definition which set them off from other peoples, regardless of religion. A belief in a common descent, myths which connected them with both the Prophet Muhammad and ancient Biblical kings, their segmentary tribal organization, language, code of values, and pool of distinctive cultural attributes had for centuries given them a sense of being different and special. In combination with a history as the dominant group in the Frontier, these attributes fostered an ethnic pride and self-confidence which often gave way to chauvinism. One need only look at their proverbs to see the premium they placed on their unique identity and the demanding code of personal conduct to which they insisted one had to conform in order to retain his honor as a Pakhtun.

Predictably, therefore, Frontier politics in the twentieth century were dominated by ethnic issues in contradiction to what appeared to be the communal norm elsewhere in India. What is not straightforward are the political alignments which resulted: the Indian National Congress became the party of Pakhtun interests, while the Muslim League urged them to transcend their ethnic loyalties in the interest of Islamic unity. Religious loyalties and ethnicity were not intrinsically in conflict in the NWFP. In fact, to the extent that Pakhtuns had any political associations with other Indians before the late 1920s, they were affiliated with Muslims, primarily in the Khilafat movement. Ideology alone, therefore, cannot account for the intense competition between the proponents of Pakhtun and Muslim nationalism which, under one guise or another, has been at the center of Frontier politics since the 1930s. That was the product of the way in which party politics evolved in interaction with the Pakhtuns' traditional tribal life.

By their own accounts, Pakhtuns first moved into the region of the NWFP in the fifteenth century. They quickly acquired a monopoly over the land and created a society in which they exercised almost exclusive control over public affairs. Non-Pakhtuns were relegated to the status of landless dependents, and to the extent that they took part in politics at all, they did so as clients of their Pakhtun patrons. The Pakhtuns were organized into a hierarchy of patrilineal descent groups which determined residence, defined landholding patterns, and structured social and political relationships. While other types of disputes occurred, the greatest likelihood of conflict within this system existed among close relatives and particularly patrilineal first cousins, the archetypal Pakhtun rivals. These conflicts were formalized into a series of local factions which were central to traditional political life. Leadership was provided by Khans who combined control of significant amounts of land with powerful personalities and the skills necessary to attract and retain political followers.

The Pakhtuns' dominance of public life carried over into the independence movement. The Frontier Congress was run by members of the landed Pakhtun elite, while the rural lower classes were relegated, for the most part, to the party's rank-and-file. The Frontier Muslim League conformed less closely to this pattern since it drew significant support from the non-Pakhtun towns and Hazara. In the rural areas of the central districts, however, its organization was controlled just as strongly by prominent Pakhtun Khans. The Pakhtuns' factional alignments also strongly influenced nationalist affiliations and party structures. As a rule, rival groupings joined opposing parties. Factions and local party branches were virtually indistinguishable in many areas, and the Khans who dominated the former also directed the latter. At higher levels of provincial political life as well, Congress and League leaders were commonly from rival families and in more than a few instances, were close patrilineal cousins.

The alignment of party and faction did not occur in a random manner. The changes British rule produced in the eighty years before 1930 ensured that the Frontier Congress became the party of the junior Pakhtun Khans and the Frontier League the organization of their senior Khani rivals. The British displayed a perceptive understanding of the fluid nature of Pakhtun politics in their ethnographies and histories of the Frontier. As administrators, however, they followed policies which froze Pakhtun society into an artificial mold in the twentieth century. With limited resources of their own, the British were forced to use members of the landed elite to maintain control over the countryside. In exchange for patronage and privileges, their surrogates policed the province's villages, helped collect the land revenue, and in general, served as a prop for colonial rule. The men to whom the British turned were, most commonly, senior Khans—the wealthier and in the early years of colonial rule, the more influential individuals in their localities.

The system of Khani alliances worked quite well until World War I, not because the Khans were the natural leaders of society, as some British came to believe, but because they exhibited the qualities of leadership expected by the rest of Pakhtun society. By the 1920s, however, social and economic changes had started to undermine their authority. An array of public works projects and the intrusion of the market economy had produced a marked rise in the overall prosperity of the NWFP, but the new wealth was not shared equally by all its inhabitants. Landownership, and with it, the benefits which accrued from the commercialization of agriculture, were concentrated in the hands of a small elite, and especially the Khans on whom the government depended. These economic changes had far-reaching social consequences. Most significantly, wealth and governmental backing replaced personal dynamism as the basis for the senior Khans' power in Frontier society.

The senior Khans antagonized the rest of Pakhtun society by departing from the traditional model of leadership. Membership in their factions declined, and their authority came under attack from their rivals, the junior Pakhtun Khans. Their growing isolation and inability to act effectively as the government's surrogates first became apparent after World War I with the ferment created by the Third Afghan War, and the Hijrat and Khilafat movements. Recognizing that the old methods of governing had lost their utility, the Chief Commissioner, Sir Hamilton Grant, urgently pressed for the extension of the Montagu-Chelmsford reforms to the NWFP. Before they could be implemented, however, he retired, and his successor, Sir John Maffey, took a drastically different approach to the Frontier's problems. Maffey assumed that the senior Khans still enjoyed widespread legitimacy as the leaders of Frontier society. He, therefore, set out to rebuild their authority, instead of broadening the government's base of support by granting reforms or seeking new allies from among the junior Khans.

Maffey's policy succeeded in buying another decade of political quiet, but at the cost of driving most of the province's junior Khans, smallholding Pakhtun majority, and lower class non-Pakhtuns into the Congress-Khudai Khidmatgar agitation in 1930-31. The Frontier had a long list of grievances by then, such as the lack of reforms, the civil war in Afghanistan in which the British were suspected of having had a hand, and the hardships caused by the depression; but Pakhtuns were primarily antagonized by the British reliance upon an outmoded system of social control which artificially propped up the senior Khans at the expense of everyone else.

Maffey's policy also ensured that once civil disobedience began, it would be difficult to suppress. Having lost their legitimacy, the senior Khans were incapable of controlling the countryside in the face of serious unrest without the active assistance of the police and military. In the spring of 1930, however, the government was temporarily unable to give them the help they needed, thereby rendering them useless as instruments of control in precisely the sort of situation for which the British had maintained them at such a price.

The agitation of 1930 was concentrated in Peshawar and Bannu Districts. The outer districts of Hazara and Dera Ismail Khan, with their large non-Pakhtun populations, were barely disturbed, while Kohat was the only

Pakhtun district to be pacified without difficulty. The campaign attracted strong non-Pakhtun support in both Peshawar and Bannu from urban activists who vigorously participated for reasons of their own. The bitter anti-British feelings aroused by the agitation, and especially by the Peshawar riots of April 23rd, which was the single most dramatic event in the Frontier's nationalist history, drove them into a common front with the rural movement, temporarily obscuring the very real differences and animosities which existed between town and countryside in the NWFP. In rural Peshawar and Bannu, the repudiation of British rule was even more intense and sustained. The ordinary operations of government came to a standstill for three months and more as the authorities lost control over wide stretches of territory. Along the border, moreover, tribesmen were induced by sympathy for the nationalists to take up arms against the government. In Waziristan, hostilities were confined to the tribal areas, but the tribesmen around Peshawar actually invaded the district. Most seriously, the Afridis twice reached the outskirts of Peshawar city, forcing the Viceroy to declare martial law in the district in August 1930.

The severity of civil disobedience caught the government by surprise. Having misjudged both the depth of popular discontent and the strength of their allies, the authorities had failed to make adequate contingency plans to deal with the campaign. As a consequence, the province was not brought under full control before August, and even then, a strong undercurrent of popular hostility remained. The British drew two lessons from this experience. Realizing that they could no longer rely exclusively upon the senior Khans, they pressed for political reforms in the hopes of redirecting popular aspirations into constitutional channels. Additionally, they concluded that in future confrontations only preemptive action against the nationalists could prevent serious political unrest. Thus, after political controls were lifted in March 1931 with the Gandhi-Irwin Pact, the provincial authorities carefully prepared for what they regarded as the inevitable resumption of political hostilities.

This two-pronged strategy proved effective when civil disobedience resumed at the end of 1931, despite the strong support the nationalists had recruited during the intervening year and the powerful organization they had developed. After months of intelligence gathering and planning, the government cracked down decisively before the agitation could gain momentum and quickly reestablished its authority throughout the province. While civil disobedience officially continued until March 1934, it was reduced to little more than an ineffectual, symbolic protest within its first six weeks. The prospect of reforms also contributed to the ease with which the nationalists were suppressed by providing an alternative outlet for political energies. Most notably, it ensured that members of the province's urban intelligentsia, who had been estranged from the rural movement in 1931 by personal and ethnic differences, remained neutral in the conflict and turned their attention to legislative politics instead.

While the ferment of 1930-32 was fueled by local issues and organized by indigenous forces, it was part of a larger, all-India movement. Due to the compatibility of their political goals, the Pakhtun nationalists entered into an informal cooperation with the Indian National Congress even before the first civil disobedience campaign began. In August 1931, their relationship was formalized with the transformation of the Afghan Jirga into the Frontier Congress. This alliance endured for the next sixteen years due to the mutual benefits the two sides derived from it. For the Congress, the support of the Pakhtuns strengthened its position vis-à-vis the British and improved its standing in India's communal politics. The Khudai Khidmatgars, in turn, received the backing of India's strongest political organization on terms which did not compromise their ethnic aspirations. Congress leaders always allowed their Frontier allies much greater latitude than other Provincial Congress Committees and tolerated their regional brand of nationalism.

The local orientation, as well as the autonomy of the Frontier Congress was clearly evident after it formed a ministry in September 1937. The party deferred to the Congress' High Command on all-India matters, as though they were of little moment. In contrast, it zealously pursued its own policies on provincial issues, and in those matters, carefully maintained its autonomy from its Congress allies. The Khan Sahib government systematically used its powers to promote the interests of its constituents, favoring Pakhtuns over non-Pakhtuns and the junior Khans over their senior rivals. Simultaneously, the Frontier Congress' revitalized party organization attacked the position of its opponents at the village level. By the time Khan Sahib resigned in November 1939, the combination of these forces had materially altered the social balance in Pakhtun society and the complexion of Frontier politics. The remnants of the informal alliance system the British had used to administer the province were dismantled to the detriment of the senior Khans, rectifying at last the grievances which had driven the junior Khans and their supporters into the Congress-Khudai Khidmatgar movement.

The parochialism of Frontier politics was also underscored by the failure of the Quit India Movement in the province. Unlike the agitations of the early 1930s, the campaign of 1942 did not seriously affect the NWFP because it focused on issues with little appeal to the Pakhtuns. The reforms of the Khan Sahib ministry had satisfied their most pressing demands against the British, while the war itself was popular in the Frontier. The Congress' campaign, therefore, was viewed with disapproval in the province, even among the bulk of its party members. Thus, when the Frontier Congress leaders were forced by their alliance to join the agitation, they did so equivocally, knowing full well that they would elicit little public support.

The Frontier Congress preempted the single most potent political cause in the NWFP by espousing Pakhtun interests; by gaining the allegiance of the junior Khans, it absorbed the most dynamic elements in the province into its ranks. Thus, when the Muslim League started to organize in the North-West Frontier, it was at a severe disadvantage. In fact, the party was effectively excluded from the province until September 1937 by the Frontier Congress' popularity. It did not take root until the policies of the Khan Sahib government alienated non-Pakhtun Muslims and forced the senior Khans to unite behind the League. While responsible for its overall political preeminence in the province, the Frontier Congress' ethnic nationalism geographically limited its appeal to the rural areas of the central districts. The party never firmly established itself among the non-Pakhtuns of Dera Ismail Khan, Hazara, and the Frontier's towns. Aroused by the party's obvious favoritism toward Pakhtuns, those people turned to the Muslim League during the years of the first Khan Sahib ministry. For their part, the senior Khans joined the League out of the realization that they no longer could afford to pursue their individualistic style of politics in the face of the government's concerted attack on their interests. They needed a defender, and whatever its shortcomings, the League was the best available. At its inception, therefore, the Frontier League assumed a character which, much to its detriment, it would retain until the final, tumultuous year before independence. It was a coalition of non-Pakhtun Muslims and senior Pakhtun Khans who had banded together principally to defend personal interests. Its leadership was weak, its organization inadequate, and its membership divided by debilitating factionalism. In addition, the senior Khans on whom it depended carried the onus in the popular mind of having once been the favorites of the British.

Inseparable from the Frontier League's organizational weakness was its choice of ideology. Since the Congress monopolized the ethnic appeal, it made little sense for the party to compete for the Pakhtuns' ethnic loyalties. Instead, it challenged them with a communal rhetoric which demanded of Pakhtuns that they subordinate their ethnic concerns to the needs of the Indo-Muslim community as a whole. Before the crisis of 1946-47, however, the call for Muslim solidarity made little headway in the face of the Pakhtuns' ethnocentrism, in no small part because they were largely unaffected by the fears other Muslims in India held about their future. As long as external events did not upset that sense of security, the Frontier Congress had a greater attraction for them. It championed their ethnic interests, while the League seemed to reject their claim to a unique identity by insisting that they were part of a larger, homogeneous community defined by Islam.

For nine years, then, the Frontier League remained weak, disorganized, and wedded to an ineffective rhetoric. The nadir came with the elections of February 1946, by which time politics elsewhere in India had polarized to the point that the League captured over 92 percent of all Muslim seats.[1] In

1. Computed from *Returns Showing the Results of Elections to the Central Legislative Assembly and the Provincial Legislatures in 1945-46* (Delhi: Manager, Government of India Press, 1948).

the North-West Frontier, in contrast, it managed to win only seventeen out of thirty-eight seats, and only six of those were in Pakhtun constituencies. Eighteen months later, however, the people of the Frontier overwhelmingly favored the League and the creation of Pakistan. So rapid and decisive a shift in the political climate cannot be explained in ordinary political terms. In fact, as long as it was politics as usual, the League could not compete with the more vigorous Frontier Congress. The key to its triumph lay elsewhere, in a time-honored mechanism within Pakhtun society which the communal crisis of 1946-47 triggered once more.

One of the serious problems traditionally facing Pakhtuns was how, in the face of their deep-seated factional divisions, to unite when their collective clan or tribal interests were threatened. Lineage solidarity was one answer, but it was not entirely dependable given the intensity of their mutual enmities. Throughout their history, therefore, Pakhtuns had turned to their religion and its interpreters in times when they needed to combine for their common good. Islam provided an inspiration for Pakhtuns, a way of conducting their lives which was nobler than their tribal customs. Whenever, therefore, a conflict could plausibly be portrayed as involving a religious issue, the normal rules of their political lives could be set aside, their factional divisions transcended, and even their sense of ethnic separateness temporarily muted. Such situations invariably thrust charismatic men, believed to possess special spiritual powers, into positions of leadership. With a reputation for holiness and a seeming indifference to Pakhtuns' worldly concerns, those individuals were able, in an emotionally charged atmosphere, to unite Pakhtuns much more effectively than tribal leaders who were forever open to the suspicion of exploiting the crisis for personal ends.

A variant of this pattern recurred in 1946-47. As communal relations elsewhere in India degenerated into rioting and bloodshed, Pakhtuns temporarily subordinated their ethnic loyalties to their Muslim identity and transferred their political allegiance to the Muslim League. Aided by the wholesale support of the province's *ulema* and *sajjada nishins*, the party was transformed from an ordinary political organization into a vehicle for a religiously sanctioned political crusade with strong millenial overtones.

While the inspiration behind the League's success transcended normal political concerns, the practicalities of bringing the NWFP into Pakistan remained: the 1946 elections had solidly entrenched the Frontier Congress in power. With no legal means to achieve its objectives, the League had to launch a direct action campaign in February 1947 to break the hold of its rival and convince the imperial authorities that the people of the province favored Pakistan. The agitation threw the NWFP into political turmoil and touched off widespread communal violence which persuaded Lord Mountbatten of the necessity of holding a referendum to determine the wishes of the people of the province. That step was strongly opposed by the Frontier Congress, but its objections were swept aside, for the League would not end its campaign or any other terms, and the Indian National Congress, having accepted partition, was no longer willing to hold up the transfer of power on behalf of its allies.

The July referendum resolved the immediate problem of the North-West Frontier Province's disposition after independence, but it did not eliminate the underlying political issues of the preceding two decades. Independence was not greeted on August 15th with a new spirit of unity. The conflicts of the nationalist period were simply reformulated to fit the new context of Pakistan. Until the Pakistan government suppressed the Khudai Khidmatgar movement in July 1948, the political contest between the former Congressmen and Muslim League continued unabated, with each side appealing to the province's inhabitants in much the same manner as before. Even the drastic step of outlawing the Khudai Khidmatgars and arresting their leaders did not fundamentally alter the nature of Frontier politics. Every time political restrictions were eased in succeeding decades, issues, alignments, and personalities remarkably similar to those in the independence movement reemerged.[2] This is not surprising, for the Pakhtuns' ethnic loyalties and their social organization have continued to endure and, in turn, have given provincial politics a stability which has survived the periodic upheavals in Pakistani politics since independence.

---

2. See Stephen Rittenberg, "Continuities in Borderland Politics," in Ainslie Embree, ed., *Pakistan's Western Borderlands. The Transformation of a Political Order* (Durham: Carolina Academic Press, 1977), pp. 67-84.

# GLOSSARY

This is a selected list of those important terms which appear more than once or twice in the text. Other Pashtu and Urdu words are defined in parentheses within the text.

| | |
|---|---|
| *anjuman* | association, society |
| *alim* | man learned in Islamic religious sciences |
| *astanadar* | individual with inherited spiritual status |
| *azad* | free, independent |
| *baiat* | vow of spiritual allegiance given by a *murid* to his *pir* |
| *baraka* | spiritual power of a holy man |
| *fatwa* | decree by a learned religious figure |
| *gundi* | Pakhtun faction |
| *hamsaya* | (lit.: one who shares shade); client, dependent |
| *hartal* | strike |
| *hijrat* | religiously motivated exodus |
| *hujra* | men's house |
| *inam* | cash grant bestowed by the government |
| *jagir* | land grant bestowed by the government |
| *jagirdar* | one who holds a *jagir* |
| *jihad* | struggle for the faith; war against non-Muslims |
| *jirga* | Pakhtun tribal council; party |
| *kafir* | heretic, non-believer |
| *kamin* | landless menial laborer |
| *kandi* | village ward |
| *khel* | lineage; clan or smaller subdivision of a tribe |
| *kisan* | peasant |
| *lambardar* | village revenue official |
| *lashkar* | tribal army |
| *mujahid* | warrior for the faith |
| *murid* | religious disciple |
| *nang* | honor |
| *nawab* | (lit.: deputy, governor); honorific title bestowed by the government; may be held for life or hereditarily |
| *Pakhto* | shortened form of *Pakhtunwali* |
| *Pakhtunwali* | Pakhtun's system of values |
| *parajamba* | factionalism |

| | |
|---|---|
| *pir* | *astanadar* from a Pakhtun background; also applied generically to any hereditary spiritual leader |
| *razakar* | volunteer |
| *sajjada nishin* | (lit.: one who sits on a prayer carpet); hereditary religious leader; successor to leadership of a *ziarat* and order of sufi devotees |
| *salar* | general, commander |
| *Salar-i-Azam* | Commander in Chief |
| *satyagraha* | Gandhian non-violent civil disobedience movement |
| *shariat* | Islamic law |
| *tarbur* | (lit.: first cousin); enemy anong one's close patrilineal cousins |
| *tarburwali* | rivalry between patrilineal cousins |
| *tappa* | traditionally, the area inhabited by a major Pakhtun clan; under the British, an administrative division of a *tehsil* |
| *tehsil* | largest administrative subdivision within a district |
| *ulema* | plural of *alim* |
| *urs* | (lit.: marriage with God); death anniversary of a holy man |
| *wesh* | periodic redistribution of land |
| *zenana* | women's quarters; used to refer to something associated with women |
| *ziarat* | tomb of a holy man |

# BIBLIOGRAPHY

## UNPUBLISHED SOURCES

### I. Private Papers

F.L. Brayne Papers. India Office Library. London, Great Britain. Mss Eur F152.

Lord Chelmsford Papers. India Office Library. London, Great Britain. Mss Eur E204.

Sir George Cunningham Papers. India Office Library. London, Great Britain. Mss Eur D670. Diary of Sir George Cunningham lent by Sir John Dring. Now part of the Cunningham Papers.

Sir Hamilton Grant Papers. India Office Library. London, Great Britain. Mss Eur D660.

Sir Fazli Husain Diaries. India Office Library. London, Great Britain. Mss Eur E352.

Lord Halifax Papers. India Office Library. London, Great Britain. Mss Eur C125.

Abdul Akbar Khan Papers. Peshawar, Pakistan.

Lord Linlithgow Papers. India Office Library. London, Great Britain. Mss Eur F125.

A.N. Mitchell Papers. Twyholm, Kirkcudbright, Scotland.

Jawaharlal Nehru Papers. Nehru Museum. New Delhi, India.

Sir Arthur Parsons Papers. India Office Library. London, Great Britain. Mss Eur D696.

Lord Reading Papers. India Office Library. London, Great Britain. Mss Eur E238.

Sir George Roos-Keppel Papers. India Office Library. London, Great Britain. Mss Eur D613.

### II. Government Records

India Office Library. London, Great Britain. Records of the Political and Secret Department, 1914-1917; L/P&S/10; L/P&S/12; and L/P&S/20.

Records of the Public and Judicial Department, 1918-1947; L/P&J/5; L/P&J/6; L/P&J/7; L/P&J/8; L/P&J/9; L/PO; and R/3/1.

Records of the Military Department, 1940-1942; L/MIL/14.
Indian National Archives. New Delhi, India. Records of the Home Department (Political) of the Government of India, 1927-1945.
North-West Frontier Province Archives. Peshawar, Pakistan. Records of the Peshawar Deputy Commissioner's Office, 1897-1930.

## III. Political Party Records

All-India Congress Committee Files. Nehru Museum. New Delhi, India. 1928-1947.
All-India Hindu Mahasabha Files. Nehru Museum. New Delhi, India. 1932-1947.
All-India Muslim League Files. Karachi University. Karachi, Pakistan. 1936-1947.
*Khudam-i-*Muslim League Papers. Personal Collection of Aziz Javed. Peshawar, Pakistan.
*Sarhadi* Muslim League. Subcommittee *Khavatin*. Register *Ruadad*. Personal Collection of Aziz Javed. Peshawar, Pakistan.

## IV. Interviews (the number is in parentheses.)

Abdul Akbar Khan (4)
Abdul Aziz Chishti (2)
Abdul Ghani Avezi (1)
Abdul Ghani Khan (2)
Abdul Khaliq Khaliq (1)
Abdul Qaiyum Khan (1)
Abdur Rahman Awan (1)
Abdur Rashid Khan (1)
Ali Asghar Khan (1)
Amir Chand Bombwal (4)
Amirzada Khan (2)
Amin Jan Khan of Kochian (2)
Amin Jan Khan of Landi (1)
Anwar Khan [Son of Ali Gohar Khan of Dotar] (1)
*Arbab* Muhammad Ashraf Khan [Son of *Arbab* Abdur Rahman Khan](1)
*Arbab* Nur Muhammad Khan (1)
*Arbab* Saif-ur-Rahman [Brother of *Arbab* Abdul Ghafur] (1)
*Arbab* Usman Khan [Son of *Arbab* Abdur Rahman Khan] (1)
Caroe, Sir Olaf (1)
Curtis, Gerald (1)
Daud Khan [Nephew of Ali Gohar Khan of Dotar] (1)
Dost Muhammad Khan Kamil (1)
Dring, Sir John (1)

Emerson, Gerald (1)
Fazl-i Haq Shaida (1)
Fazl-i Karim Asif (1)
Fida Muhammad Khan (2)
Ghazanfar Ali Shah Bukhari (1)
Ghirdhari Lal Puri (1)
Gopal Das Khera (4)
Ghulam Haidar Akhtar (2)
Ghulam Muhammad Gama (1)
Ghulam Rabbani Khan (1)
Habibullah Khan (1)
Hasan Gilani [Son of Sayyid Sultan Muhammad Shah] (1)
Hasan Gul Khan (1)
Inzar Gul Khan (1)
Jalaluddin (1)
Khadim Husain (1)
Khair Muhammad Jalali (2)
Kotu Ram (1)
Low, A.P. (2)
Mahbub Alam Awam [Son of Malik Amir Alam Awan] (1)
Malik Damsaz Khan (1)
Malik-ur-Rahman Kiyani (1)
Mehr Dil Khan (1)
Mian Abdullah Shah (2)
Mian Muhammad Shah [Son of Mian Ahmad Shah] (1)
Mian Shakirullah (1)
Mian Ziauddin (3)
Mian Jafar Shah (4)
Mir Abdus Samad Khan (1)
Mitchell, A.N. (2)
Muhammad Ali Khan (1)
Muhammad Aslam Khan [Son of Zain Muhammad Khan] (1)
Muhammad Ayub Khan (1)
Muhammad Ismail Ghaznavi (1)
Muhammad Ramzan Khan (1)
Muhammad Yahya Jan Khan (1)
Muhammad Zarin Khan (1)
Nasrullah Khan (1)
Pir Bakhsh Khan (2)
Pir Jamal Piri (1)
Pir Masum Shah (1)
Pir Sayyid Zaigham Birjees [Son of Mazhar Gilani] (1)
Pir Shahinshah (1)
*Pir* of Zakori (1)

Qalandar Mohmand (1)
Qazi Shafiuddin (1)
Qazi Surajuddin (1)
Rahim Bakhsh Ghaznavi (2)
Saadullah Khan (1)
Sardar Bahadur Khan (1)
Sayyid Ashiq Shah (1)
Sher Bahadur Khan (4)
Sher Dil Khan (1)
Sherin Wahab (1)
Yusaf Khan Khattak (1)
Zari Sarfaraz (1)

### V. Manuscripts and Theses

Dani, Ahmad Hasan. *Islam in South Asia: Politics and Society. The Pathan Society: A Case Study*. Unpublished paper.

Harrison, Thomas. *Origins of the Pakhtunistan Dispute*. M.A. Thesis. Columbia University, 1953.

Javed Aziz. *Tehrik-i-Azadi ke Namvar Mujahidin*. Manuscript of an unpublished book.

Khan, Bakht Jamal. *Meri Dastan-i-Hayat, 1900-1968*. Unpublished memoirs. Personal collection of Aziz Javed. Peshawar, Pakistan.

Khan, Ghulam Rabbani. Memoirs.

Rittenberg, Stephen. "Agrarian Change and the Rise of Nationalism in Peshawar Valley." Unpublished Paper.

———. *The Independence Movement in India's North-West Frontier Province, 1901-1947*. Ph.D. Dissertation. Columbia University, 1977.

Shakirullah. *Aghaz da Subah-i-Sarhad da Nave Daur*. Unpublished memoirs. Personal collection of Aziz Javed. Peshawar, Pakistan.

## PUBLISHED SOURCES

### I. Newspapers

*Al-Falah*, 1940-1947.
*Al-Jamiat Sarhad*, 1942-1947.
*Azad Pakhtun*, 1933-1934.
*Civil and Military Gazette*, 1928-1947.
*Dawn*, 1942-1947.
*Frontier Advocate*, selective issues from 1928-1929, 1932-1935 and 1937-1941.
*Frontier Mail*, selective issues from 1960-1961, 1967 and 1970.
*Islah-i-Sarhad*, selective issues from 1928 and 1935.

*Khyber Mail*, 1932-1947.
*Lahore Tribune*, 1929-1947.
*Pakhtun*, 1928-1947.
*Pakistan Times*, 1947.
*Rehbar-i-Sarhad*, selective issues from 1936-37.
*Rehbar Mardan*, selective issues from 1946.
*Sarhad*, selective issues from 1928-1929 and 1935-1941.
*Shura*, selective issues from 1936-1937.
*Tarjuman-i-Sarhad*, 1945-1947.
*Young India*, 1930-1931.

## II. Government Publications

*Administration Report of the North-West Frontier Province*. Peshawar: Government Stationery and Printing. (annual) 1918-1939.

Barron, C.A., *Settlement Report of the Kohat District, 1900-1905*. Lahore: Civil and Military Gazette Press, 1907.

Bolton, H.N. *Settlement Report of the Dera Ismail Khan District*. Lahore: Civil and Military Gazette Press, 1907.

*Census of India, 1891*. Vol. XIX. "The Punjab and Its Feudatories." E.D. Maclagen. Calcutta: Office of the Superintendent of Government Printing, 1892. Part I.

*Census of India, 1901*. Vol. XVII. "Punjab and North-West Frontier Province." H.A. Rose. Simla: Government Central Printing Office, 1902. Part I.

*Census of India, 1911*. Vol. XIII. "North-West Frontier Province." C. Latimer. Peshawar: Commercial Press, 1912. Parts I and II.

*Census of India, 1921*. Vol. XIV. "North-West Frontier Province." Lehna Singh. Peshawar: North-West Frontier Government Press, 1922. Parts I and II.

*Census of India, 1931*. Vol. XV. "North-West Frontier Province." G.L. Mallam and A.D.F. Dundas. Peshawar: Government Stationery and Printing, 1933. Parts I and II.

*Census of India, 1941*. Vol. X. "North-West Frontier Province." I.D. Scotts (ed.). Delhi: Government of India Press, 1942.

*Constituency Assembly of Pakistan Debates*. 1948.

Dane, Louis. *Final Report of the Settlement of Peshawar District, 1898*. Lahore: Civil and Military Gazette Press, 1898.

Dhawan, A.S. *Report on the General Elections to the Central Legislative Assembly (NWFP Constituency) and to the North-West Frontier Province Legislative Assembly in 1945-46*. Peshawar: Manager, Government Stationery and Printing, 1946.

*Despatches from Provincial Governments in India Containing Proposals for Constitutional Reforms*. Parliamentary Papers. 1930-31. Cmd 3712.

*Gazetteer of the Bannu District, 1883-84*. Calcutta: Central Press Co., n.d.

*Gazetteer of the Dera Ismail Khan District*. Lahore: Arya Press, 1884.

*Gazetteer of the Hazara District, 1907*. London: Chatto and Windus, 1908.

*Gazetteer of the Peshawar District, 1883-84*. Compiled and published under the authority of the Punjab Government, 1884.

*Gazetteer of the Peshawar District, 1897-98*. Compiled and published under the authority of the Punjab Government, 1898.

General Staff, India. *Military Report and Gazetteer on the Peshawar District, 1939*. Calcutta: Manager, Government of India Press, 1940. (2nd edition).

———. *Official History of Operations on the North-West Frontier of India, 1920-1935*. Delhi: Government of India Press, 1945.

———. *Official History of Operations on the North-West Frontier of India, 1936-1937*. Delhi: Government of India Press, 1943.

———. *Who's Who. North-West Frontier Tribes*. Simla: Government Monotype Press, 1916.

Glancy, R.I.R. *Final Report of the Second Regular Settlement of the Bannu District*. Peshawar: Commercial Press, 1908.

*Government of India Despatch on Proposals for Constitutional Reforms, dated 20th September 1930*. Parliamentary Papers. 1930-31. Cmd 3700.

*Guide to the North-West Frontier Provincial Assembly*. Lahore: Pakistan Printing Works, 1952.

Hastings, E.G. *Report of the Regular Settlement of the Peshawar District*. Lahore: Central Jail Press, 1878.

*Imperial Gazetteer of India*. Provincial Series. "North-West Frontier Province." Calcutta: Superintendent of Government Printing, 1908.

*India in 1929-30. A Statement Exhibiting the Moral and Material Progress and Condition of India During 1929-30*. Calcutta: Government of India Central Publication Branch, 1931.

*India in 1930-31. A Statement Exhibiting the Moral and Material Progress and Condition of India During 1930-31*. Calcutta: Government of India Central Publication Branch, 1932.

*India in 1931-32. A Statement Exhibiting the Moral and Material Progress and Condition of India During 1931-32*. Calcutta: Government of India Central Publication Branch, 1933.

*India in 1934-35. A Statement Exhibiting the Moral and Material Progress and Condition of India During 1934-35*. Calcutta: Government of India Central Publication Branch, 1936.

*Indian Legislative Assembly Debates*. 1921, 1926-1927, 1929-1931, and 1934-1935.

*Indian Round Table Conference. Statement by the Prime Minister to the Conference at the Conclusion of its Second Session on 1st December 1931*. Parliamentary Papers. 1931-32. Cmd 3972.

*Indian Round Table Conference. 12th November 1930-19th January 1931. Proceedings*. Parliamentary Papers. 1930-31. Cmd 3778.

*Indian Round Table Conference. 12th November 1930-19th January 1931. Proceedings of the Subcommittees*. London: His Majesty's Stationery Office, 1931. Part II.

Indian Statutory Commission. *Report of the Indian Statutory Commission*. 2 Vols. Parliamentary Papers. 1929-30. Cmd 3568 and 3569.

James, Hugh. *Report on the Settlement of the Peshawar District*. Lahore: Published by the authority of the Punjab Government, 1865.

Khan, Mir Abdus Samad. *Shimal Maghribi Subah-i-Sarhad ki Aini Tarikh*. Peshawar: Mahakma-i-Itilaat, Shimal Maghribi Subah-i-Sarhad, 1972.

*North-West Frontier Province Government Gazette*. 1931-1935.

*North-West Frontier Province Gazetteer. Bannu District, 1907*. Peshawar: Commercial Press, 1908.

*North-West Frontier Province Gazetteer. Peshawar District, 1913*. Peshawar: Commercial Press, 1913.

*North-West Frontier Province Gazetteer. Peshawar District, 1931*. Lahore: Civil and Military Gazette Press, 1934.

*North-West Frontier Province Legislative Assembly Debates*. 1937-1939 and 1943-1947.

*North-West Frontier Province Legislative Council Debates*. 1932-1936.

*Population Census of Pakistan, 1961*. District Census Reports on Bannu, Dera Ismail Khan, Hazara, Kohat, Mardan, and Peshawar.

*Report of the Indian Delimitation Committee*. Delhi: Manager of Publications, n.d. 2 Vols.

*Report of the North-West Frontier Enquiry Committee and Minutes of Dissent by Mr. T. Rangachariar and Mr. N.M. Somarth*. Delhi: Government Central Press, 1924.

*Report of the North-West Frontier Province Subjects Committee*. Calcutta: Government of India Central Publication Branch, 1931.

*Report on Police Administration in the North-West Frontier Province*. (annual) 1926-1933.

*Report on Public Instruction in the North-West Frontier Province*. (annual) 1919-1932.

*Report on the Administration of the Border of the North-West Frontier Province*. (annual) 1918-1938.

*Report on the Administration of Land Revenue, Land Records and Agriculture Estates under the Court of Wards and the Alienation of Land Act in the North-West Frontier Province*. (annual) 1919-1932.

*Report on the Administration of Criminal Justice in the North-West Frontier Province*. (annual) 1927-1935.

*Report on the Legislative Council Elections in the North-West Frontier Province for the Year 1932*. Peshawar: Manager, Government Stationery and Printing, 1933.

Report on the Season and Crops of the North-West Frontier Province. (annual) 1923-1932.
*Report on the Working of District Boards in the North-West Frontier Province.* (annual) 1934-1938.
*Returns Showing the Results of Elections in India, 1937.* Parliamentary Papers. 1937-38. Cmd 5589.
*Returns Showing the Results of Elections to the Central Legislative Assembly and the Provincial Legislatures in 1945-46.* Delhi: Manager, Government of India Press, 1948.
*The North-West Frontier Provincial Election Manual.* Peshawar: Government Stationery and Printing Office, 1940.
Watson, H.D. *Final Report of the Second Regular Settlement of the Hazara District, 1900-1907.* Peshawar: Commercial Press, 1907.
*Who's Who in the Bannu District.* Peshawar: NWFP Government Printing and Stationery, 1931.
*Who's Who in the Dera Ismail Khan District.* Peshawar: NWFP Government Printing and Stationery, 1931.
*Who's Who in the Hazara District.* Peshawar: NWFP Government Printing and Stationery, 1931.
*Who's Who in the Kohat District.* Peshawar: NWFP Government Printing and Stationery, 1931.
*Who's Who in the Peshawar District.* Peshawar: NWFP Government Printing and Stationery, 1931.
Wylie, F.V. *Assessment Report of the Charsadda Tahsil of the Peshawar District.* Calcutta: Government of India Central Publications Branch, 1926.
———. *Assessment Report of the Mardan Tahsil of the Peshawar District.* Calcutta: Government of India Central Publications Branch, 1926.
———. *Assessment Report of the Nowshera Tahsil of the Peshawar District.* Calcutta: Government of India Central Publications Branch, 1928.
———. *Assessment Report of the Peshawar Tahsil of the Peshawar District.* Peshawar: NWFP Government Printing and Stationery, 1929.
———. *Assessment Report of the Swabi Tahsil of the Peshawar District.* Calcutta: Government of India Central Publications Branch, 1928.

## III. Secondary Works: Books and Articles

Afghani, Abdul Majid. *Sir Sahibzada Abdul Qaiyum Khan.* Peshawar: Imperial Electric Press, 1938.
Ahmad, Jamil-ud-din. *The Final Phase of the Struggle for Pakistan.* Lahore: Publishers United, 1968.
———. *Middle Phase of the Muslim Political Movement.* Lahore: Publishers United, 1969.
Ahmad, Mushtaq. *Government and Politics of Pakistan.* Karachi: Space Publishers, 1970.

Ahmed, Akbar S. *Economic and Social Change in the Tribal Territories*. Karachi: Oxford University Press, 1977.

———. *Mataloona*. Peshawar: Pakistan Academy for Rural Development, 1973.

———. *Millenium and Charisma among Pathans*. London: Routledge and Kegan Paul, 1976

———. *Pukhtun Economy and Society*. London: Routledge and Kegan Paul, 1980.

Ahmed, Makhdum Tasadduq. *Social Organization of Yusafzai Swat*. Lahore: Punjab University Press, 1962.

Akhtar, Shahnaz. "Tehrik-i-Pakistan ke Sarhadi Shahido. Tum peh Lakhon Salam." *Khatun*. Vol. 2, No. 22 (August 14, 1973), pp. 7-9.

Andrews, C.F. *The Challenge of the North-West Frontier*. London: George Allen & Unwin, 1937.

Ashraf, Khalid. *Tribal People of West Pakistan*. Peshawar: Board of Economic Enquiry, 1962.

Auqab, Muhammad Sarfaraz Khan Khattak. *Tarikh-i-Khattak*. Peshawar: Hamidiya Press, 1964.

Azad, Abul Kalam. *India Wins Freedom*. New York: Orient Longmans, 1960.

Baden-Powell, B.H. *The Indian Village Community*. London: Longmans, Green and Company, 1896.

Badrashi, Akbar Shah. *Da Azadi Talash*. Peshawar: Manzur-i-Am Press, n.d.

Baha, Lal. *N.-W.F.P. Administration Under British Rule, 1901-1919*. Islamabad: National Commission on Historical and Cultural Research, 1978.

Bailey, F.G. *Strategms and Spoils*. Oxford: Basil Blackwell, 1970.

Barth, Fredrik. "Ecological Relationship of Ethnic Groups in Swat, North Pakistan." *American Anthropologist*. Vol. 58, No. 6 (December 1956), pp. 1079-80.

———. *Indus and Swat Kohistan*. Oslo: Forenede Trykkerier, 1956.

———. "Pathan Identity and Its Maintenance." *Ethnic Groups and Boundaries*. Edited by Fredrik Barth. Boston: Little, Brown and Co., 1969. Pp. 117-34.

———. *Political Leadership Among the Swat Pathans*. London School of Economics Monographs on Social Anthropology, No. 19. London: Athlone Press, 1965.

———. "Segmentary Opposition and the Theory of Games: A Study of Pathan Organization." *Journal of the Royal Anthropological Institute of Great Britain and Ireland*. Vol. 89, Parts I and II (January-December 1959), pp. 5-21.

———. "The System of Social Stratification in Swat, North Pakistan." *Aspects of Caste in South India, Ceylon and North-West Pakistan*. Edited by E.R. Leach. Cambridge Papers in Social Anthropology, No. 2 Cambridge: Cambridge University Press, 1959. Pp. 113-46.

Barton, William. "Hindu and Afghan on the Indian Frontier." *Contemporary Review*. Vol. 171 (February 1947), pp. 77-80.

———. *India's North-West Frontier*. London: John Murray, 1939.

———. "The North-West Frontier." *Fortnightly*. Vol. 172 (August 1949), pp. 105-11.

———. "The Problems of Law and Order Under a Responsible Government in the North-West Frontier Province." *Journal of the Royal Central Asian Society*. Vol. 19, No. 1 (January 1932), pp. 5-21.

Bellew, H.W. *A General Report on the Yusafzai*. Lahore: Sang-e-Meel Publications, 1977.

Berry, Willard. *Aspects of the Frontier Crimes Regulations in Pakistan*. Duke University Program in Comparative Studies on Southern Asia. Monographs and Occasional Papers Series, No. 3.

Bhattacharya, Shanti Ranjan. *Pakhtunistan ka Mutalaba*. Calcutta: New Commercial Art Press, 1967.

Biddulph, C.E. (trans.). *Afghan Poetry of the Seventeenth Century, Being Selections from the Poems of Khush Hal Khan Khattak*. London: Kegan, Paul, Trench, Trubner and Company, 1890.

Bondurant, Joan. *Conquest of Violence*. Berkeley: University of California Press, 1965.

Brass, Paul. "Ethnicity and Nationality Formation." *Ethnicity*. Vol. 3, No. 3 (September 1976), pp. 225-40.

———. *Language, Religion and Politics in North India*. New York: Cambridge University Press, 1974.

Bright, Jagat. *Frontier and Its Gandhi*. Lahore: Allied Indian Publishers, 1944.

Bruce, C.E. *Waziristan, 1936-37*. Aldershot: Gale and Polden, 1938.

Bukhari, Farigh. *Bacha Khan. Khan Abdul Ghaffar Khan ke Savanah Hayat*. Peshawar: Niya Maktuba, 1957.

Byrt, A.H. "The Indian North-West Frontier Under Modern Political Conditions." *Journal of the Royal Central Asian Society*. Vol. 28, Part III (July 1941), pp. 279-94.

Campbell-Johnson, Alan. *Mission with Mountbatten*. Bombay: Jaico Publishing House, 1951.

Caroe, Olaf. "The End of British India." *Round Table*. Vol. 70, No. 237 (January 1970), pp. 59-66.

———. "The North-West Frontier, Old and New." *Journal of the Royal Central Asian Society*. Vol. 48, Parts III and IV (July-October 1961), pp. 289-98.

———. *The Pathans*. London: MacMillan & Co., 1965.

Coatman, J. "The North-West Frontier Province and Trans-Border Country Under the New Constitution." *Journal of the Royal Central Asian Society*. Vol. 18, Part III (July 1931), pp. 335-48.

Coen, Terence Creagh. *The Indian Political Service*. London: Chatto and Windus, 1971.

*Congress Handbook, 1946*. Allahabad: Allahabad Law Journal Press, 1946.

Coupland, Reginald. *Report on the Constitutional Problem in India*. London: Oxford University Press, 1943-44. 2 Vols.

Crane, Robert (ed.). *Regions and Regionalism in South Asian Studies: An Exploratory Study*. Duke University Program in Comparative Studies on Southern Asia. Monograph and Occasional Papers Series, No. 5.

Cunningham, George. "Reforms in the North-West Frontier Province of India." *Journal of the Royal Central Asian Society*. Vol. 24, Part I (January 1937), pp. 90-101.

Curtis, Gerald. "The North-West Frontier of Pakistan." *Army Quarterly*. Vol. 56, No. 2 (July 1948), pp. 176-86.

*Da Sarhadi Islamia Jirga. Dastur-ul-Amal au Qavaid*. Peshawar: Yusafi Printing Press, n.d.

Dani, Ahmad Hasan. *Peshawar: Historic City of the Frontier*. Peshawar: Khyber Mail Press, 1969.

Das, Durga (ed.). *Sardar Patel's Correspondence. 1945-50*. Ahmedabad: Navajivan Publishing House, 1972.

Davey, Cyril J. *A Handbook to the North-West Frontier*. Madras: Diocesan Press, 1942.

Davies, C. Colin. "British Relations with the Afridis of the Khyber and Tirah." *Army Quarterly*. Vol. 23, No. 2 (January 1932), pp. 251-67.

———. *The Problems of the North-West Frontier, 1890-1908*. Cambridge: Cambridge University Press, 1932.

Desai, Mahadev. *Two Servants of God*. Delhi: Hindustan Times Press, 1935.

deVos, George and Romanucci-Ross, Lola (eds.). *Ethnic Identity: Cultural Continuities and Change*. Palo Alto: Mayfield Publishing Company, 1975.

Dichter, David. *The North-West Frontier of West Pakistan*. Oxford: Clarendon Press, 1967.

Diwarkar, R.R. *Satyagraha: Its Technique and History*. Bombay: Hind Kitabs, 1946.

Douie, J. *The Punjab, North-West Frontier Province and Kashmir*. London: Cambridge University Press, 1932.

Dupree, Louis. *Afghanistan*. Princeton: Princeton University Press, 1973.

Edwardes, Herbert. *A Year on the Punjab Frontier in 1848-49*. Lahore: Printed under the authority of the Government of West Pakistan, 1963. 2 Vols.

Edwardes, Michael. *The Last Years of British India*. London: NEL Mentor, 1967.

Elphinstone, Mountstuart. *An Acount of the Kingdom of Caubul*. Karachi: Oxford University Press, 1972. 2 Vols.

Enevoldsen, Jan. *Sound the Bells, O Moon, Arise and Shine*. Peshawar: University Book Agency, 1969.

Enloe, Cynthia. *Ethnic Conflict and Political Development*. Boston: Little, Brown and Company, 1973.

Enriquez, S.M. *The Pathan Borderland*. Calcutta: Thacker, Spink and Company, 1910.

Evans-Pritchard, E.E. *The Nuer*. Oxford: Oxford University Press, 1970.

Ewart, J.M. and Howell, E.B. *Story of the North-West Frontier Province*. Peshawar: Government Printing and Stationery Office, 1930.

Fortes, Meyer. "The Structure of Unilineal Descent Groups." *American Anthropologist*. Vol. 55, No. 1 (January-March 1953), pp. 17-41.

Fortes, M. and Evans-Pritchard, E.E. (eds.). *African Political Systems*. Oxford: Oxford University Press, 1970.

Gankovsky, Yu. V. *The Peoples of Pakistan*. Moscow: Nanka Publishing House, 1971.

———. & Gordon-Polonskaya, L.R. *A History of Pakistan*. Lahore: People's Publishing House, 1964.

Gilmartin, David. "Religious Leadership and the Pakistan Movement in the Punjab." *Modern Asian Studies*. Vol. 13, Part 3 (July 1979), pp. 485-517.

Goodwin, Buster. *Life Among the Pathans (Khattaks)*. London: Privately published, 1969.

Gopal, S. *The Viceroyalty of Lord Irwin, 1926-1931*. Oxford: Clarendon Press, 1957.

Govindan, E.R. *The Khan Brothers*. Madras: Sunday Times Office, n.d.

Gupta, Amit Kumar. *North-West Frontier Province Legislature and Freedom Struggle, 1932-47*. New Delhi: Indian Council of Historical Research, 1976.

H.R.S. "Unrest in the Peshawar District, 1930-32." *Journal of the Royal Central Asian Society*. Vol. 19, Part IV (October 1932), pp. 624-42.

Halide. Ebib. *Inside India*. London: George Allen and Unwin, 1937.

Hilali, Khan Mir. *Pakhtana Nangiyali*. Peshawar: Maktabah-i-Jamhuriyat, 1377 A.H.

———. *Turi Yali*. Peshawar: Manzur-i-Am Press, 1967.

Hodson, H.V. *The Great Divide*. London: Hutchinson and Company, 1969.

Howell, Sir Evelyn. *Mizh*. London: MacMillan and Company, 1958.

———. "Some Problems of the Indian Frontier." *Journal of the Royal Central Asian Society*. Vol. 2., Part II (April 1934), pp. 181-98.

———. and Caroe, Olaf (trans.). *The Poems of Khushhal Khan Khatak*. Peshawar: Pashto Academy, University of Peshawar, 1963.

Husain, Azim. *Fazl-i-Husain*. Bombay: Longmans, Green and Company, 1946.

Ikram, S.M. *Modern Muslim India and the Birth of Pakistan*. Lahore: Sh. Muhammad Ashraf, 1970.

Inayatullah and Shafi, G.M. *Dynamics of Development in a Pakistani Village*. Peshawar: Pakistan Academy for Rural Development, 1963.

"India: Conference or Intransigence." *Round Table*. Vol. 21, No. 81 (December 1930), pp. 59-69.

"India: The Struggle with Congress." *Round Table*. Vol. 22, No. 86 (March 1932), pp. 322-42.

*Indian Year Book*. Bombay: Bennett, Coleman and Company. 1935-36 to 1947.

Ismay, Hastings L. *Memoirs*. New York: Viking Press, 1960.

Jaffar, S.M. *Peshawar, Past and Present*. Peshawar: S. Md. Sadiq Khan, 1946.

Jan, Muhammad Yahya. *Khan Abdul Ghaffar Khan. Un ke Khudai Khidmatgar aur Qaiyum Muslim League*. Peshawar: Imperial Press, 1970.

———. *Haqiqat Kya Hai*? Peshawar: Imperial Press, 1967.

Jansson, Erland. *India, Pakistan or Pakhtunistan*. Uppsala: Studia Historica Upsaliensia, No. 119. 1981.

Javed, Aziz. *Pakistan ke Namvar Khavatin*. Peshawar: Diba Publications, n.d.

———. "Tehrik-i-Pakistan me Sarhadi Khavatin ka Hissa." *Khatun*. Vol. 2, No. 22 (August 14, 1973), pp. 13-14.

———. "1930 aur Sarhad. Hissa 2." *Khatun*. Vol. 2, No. 3 (January 28, 1973), pp. 5-6.

———. "1930 aur Sarhad. Hissa 3." *Khatun*. Vol. 2, No. 9 (March 21, 1973), p. 9.

———. "1930 aur Sarhad. Hissa 5." *Khatun*. Vol. 2, No. 15 (July 21, 1973), pp. 7-8.

Javed, Irshad. "Sarhad me Tehrik-i-Azadi ke Qafila Salar." *Khatun*. Vol. 2, No. 22 (August 14, 1973), pp. 2 and 14.

Kabuli, Khan Ghazi. *Tehrik-i-Pakhtunistan*. Delhi: Punjab National Press, 1950.

Kalim, Muhammad Musa Khan. "Malik Khuda Bakhsh Marhum." *Jahan Nama*. (August 30, 1967), pp. 13-18.

Kamil, Dost Muhammad Khan. *Khushhal Khan Khattak*. Peshawar: Idara-i-Ishaat Sarhad, 1961.

———. *On A Foreign Approach to Khushhal*. Peshawar: Maktabah-i-Shaheen, 1963.

Kerkvliet, Benedict and Scott, James. "How Traditional Rural Patrons Lose Legitimacy: A Theory with Special Reference to Southeast Asia." *Friends, Followers and Factions: A Reader in Political Clientelism*. Edited by Steffen Schmidt, James Scott, Carl Lande and Laura Guasti. Berkeley: University of California Press, 1977.

Khadim, Muhammad Akbar Khan. *Pakistan*. Peshawar: Manzur-i-Am Press, 1938.

Khaliq. Abdul Khaliq. *Dazadi Jang. Silidili au sa Auridili*. Peshawar: Idara-i-Ishaat Sarhad, 1972.

———. *Za au Zama Zamana*. Peshawar: Idara-i-Ishaat Sarhad, 1968.

Khaliquzzaman, Choudry. *Pathway to Pakistan*. Lahore: Longmans, Green and Co., 1961.

Khan, Abdul Akbar. *Da Mazlum Duniya*. n.p., n.d.

———. *Karavan-i-Azadi. Manzil Aval. Safarnama-i-Russi Turkestan, 1920-21*. Peshawar: n.p., n.d. Translated from Pashtu by Purdil Khan Khattak.

Khan, Abdul Ghaffar. *My Life and Struggle*. Delhi: Orient Paperbacks, 1969. Translated from Urdu by Helen H. Bouman.

Khan, Abdul Ghani. *The Pathans, a Sketch*. Peshawar: University Book Agency, 1958.

Khan, Munawar Ali. "The Beginning of Political Consciousness in the N.W.F.P." *The Journal of History and Political Science*. Vol. 1, No. 2 (1971-72), pp. 37-47.

Khan, Sher Bahadur. *Tarikh-i-Hazara*. Abbottabad: Dar-us-Shifa, 1969.

Khan, Umar Faroq. *Maulana Abdur Rahman Popalzai*. Lahore: Sindh Sagar Akademy, 1970.

Khosla, Jagannath. "Provincial Autonomy in the NWFP." *Indian Journal of Political Science*. Vol. 1, No. 3 (January-March 1940), pp. 324-42.

Kiani, A.B., Ansari, M.A.S., Haider, S.M. and Khan, Imdad Ali. *Emerging Patterns of Rural Leadership in West Pakistan*. Peshawar: Pakistan Academy for Rural Development, 1971.

Lindholm, Charles. "Contemporary Politics in a Tribal Society: Swat District, NWFP, Pakistan." *Asian Survey*. Vol. 19, No. 5 (May 1979), pp. 485-505.

———. *Generosity and Jealousy. The Swat Pukhtun of Northern Pakistan*. New York: Columbia University Press, 1982.

———. "Images of the Pathan: The Usefulness of Colonial Ethnography." *Archives Europeennes de Sociologie*. Vol. 21, No. 2 (1980), pp. 350-61.

———. "Models of Segmentary Political Action: The Examples of Swat and Dir, NWFP, Pakistan." *Anthropology in Pakistan: Recent Socio-Cultural and Archaeological Perspectives*. Edited by Stephen Pastner and Louis Flam. Ithaca: Cornell University South Asia Program. South Asia Occasional Papers and Theses, No. 8. 1982.

Low, Donald A. "'Civil Martial Law': The Government of India and the Civil Disobedience Movement, 1930-34." *Congress and the Raj*. Edited by Donald A. Low. Columbia: South Asian Books, 1977.

———. "The Climatic Years, 1917-1947." *Congress and the Raj*. Edited by Donald A. Low. Columbia: South Asian Books, 1977.

Mackenzie, D.N. (trans.). *Poems from the Divan of Khushal Khan Khattak*. London: George Allen and Unwin, 1965.

Majumdar, R.C. and Majumdar, A.K. (eds.). *Struggle for Freedom*. Vol. XI of *The History and Culture of the Indian People*. Edited by K.M. Munshi: Bombay: Bharatiya Vidya Bhavan, 1969.

Mansergh, Nicholas (ed.). *The Transfer of Power, 1942-47*. London: Her Majesty's Stationery Office, 1970-74. 5 Vols.

Masson, Charles. *Narrative of Various Journeys in Balochistan, Afghanistan, the Panjab and Kalat, during a Residence in Those Countries*. London: Richard

Bentley, 1844. 4 Vol.
Mayne, Peter. *The Narrow Smile*. London: John Murray, 1955.
Mazdki, Anwar (ed.). *Bacha Khan aur Pakhtunistan*. Lahore: Navai Vaqt Printers, 1972.
Menon, V.P. *The Transfer of Power in India*. London: Longmans, Green and Company, 1957.
Middleton, John and Tait, David. *Tribes Without Rulers*. London: Routledge and Kegan Paul, 1967.
Miller, Charles. *Khyber: British India's North-West Frontier*. New York: Macmillan Publishing Company, 1977.
Mitchell, Norval. *Sir George Cunningham*. London: William Blackwood, 1968.
Mitra, N.N. (ed.). *The Indian Annual Register*. Calcutta: The Annual Register Office. (annual) 1930-1939.
Moregenstierne, Georg. "Khushhal Khan." *Journal of the Royal Central Asian Society*. Vol. 47, Part I (January 1960), pp. 49-57. Translated from Norwegian by Athelstan Caroe.
Mosley, Leonard. *The Last Days of the British Raj*. London: Widenfeld and Nicholson, 1961.
Muhammad, Shad. *Khaksar Movement in India*. Delhi: Meenakshi Prakashan, 1973.
Nagina, Ram Saran. *Attock par ki Yaden*. Delhi: Maktuba Jamal Printing Press, n.d.
———. *Manzil ki Taraf. Political Conference ki Mufassil Karavai*. Peshawar: Imperial Electric Press, 1945.
Nasr, Nasrullah Khan. *Sir Sahibzada Nawab Abdul Qaiyum*. Peshawar: Azim Publishing House, 1949.
Newman, R.E. *Pathan Tribal Patterns*. Ridgewood, N.J.: Foreign Studies Institute, 1965.
North, Roger E. (ed.). *The Literature of the North-West Frontier of India: A Selected Bibliography*. Peshawar: n.p., 1946.
Nowshervi, Nur Muhammad. *Mujahid Sarhad. Jangnama Haji Bahadur Sahib Turangzai*. Peshawar: Sadiq Brothers, n.d.
Obhrai, Diwan Chand. *The Evolution of North-West Frontier Province*. Peshawar: The London Book Co., 1938.
Office of the All-India Congress Committee. *Congress Bulletin*. Allahabad: Allahabad Law Journal Press. 1929-31 and 1935-38.
*Pakhtunistan. The Khyber Pass as the Focus of the New State of Pakhtunistan*. Hove: Key Press, n.d.
"Pakistan and the Tribes: The Legacy of the North-West Frontier." *Round Table*. Vol. 39, No. 156 (September 1949), pp. 329-36.
Pal, Dharm. *North-West Frontier, 1843-1947*. Bombay: The National Information and Publications, 1947.

Patel, Gordhanbhai. *Vithalbhai Patel*. Bombay: Shree Laxmi Narayan Press, n.d. Vol. II.

Pirzada, Syed Sharifuddin (ed.). *Foundations of Pakistan*. Karachi: National Publishing House, 1970. 2 Vol.

Popalzai, Abdur Rahim (ed.). *Rodad Vafd Ulema-i-Subah-i-Sarhad*. Peshawar: Barqi Press, n.d.

Pyarelal. *A Pilgrimage for Peace*. Ahmedabad: Navajivan Publishing House, 1950.

———. *Mahatma Gandhi. The Last Phase*. Ahmedabad: Navajivan Publishing House, 1956. 2 Vols.

———. *Thrown to the Wolves*. Calcutta: Loyal Art Press, 1966.

Qadri, Muhammad Amir Shah. *Tazkira Ulema-o-Mushaikh Sarhad*. Peshawar: Azim Publishing House, 1964. 2 Vols.

Qaiyum, Abdul. *Gold and Guns on the Pathan Frontier*. Bombay: Hind Kitab, 1945.

———. "Reflections on Some of the Causes of the Partition of the Indo-Pakistan Sub-Continent." *The Partition of India*. Edited by C.H. Philips and Mary D. Wainwright. London: George Allen and Unwin, 1970.

Qaiyum, Mian Abdul. *Doctor Khan Sahib. Niya Roshan Sitara*. Peshawar: Ilmi Publishing Press, n.d.

*Qavaid-o-Hidayat Intikhabat Muslim League Subah-i-Sarhad*. Peshawar: Manzur-i-Am Press, n.d.

*Qavaid-o-Zawabit Barai Intikhab Muslim League Subah-i-Sarhad, 1947-48*. Peshawar: Manzur-i-Am Press, 1948.

Qayyamuddin. *Pakhtunwali*. Kabul: n.p., 1331 A.H.

Qureshi, Ishtiaq Husain. *Ulema in Politics*. Karachi: Ma'aref Ltd., 1972.

Raverty, H.G. (trans.). *Selections from the Poetry of the Afghans from the Sixteenth to the Nineteenth Century*. London: Williams and Norgate, 1867.

Razi, M.S. *Surkh Phul*. Peshawar: Pakhtun Kutab Khana, 1972.

Rittenberg, Stephen. "Continuities in the Borderland Politics of Pakistan." *Pakistan's Western Borderlands: The Transformation of a Political Order*. Edited by Ainslie Embree. Durham: Carolina Academic Press, 1977.

Sahir, Faqir Husain. *Pashtu Zaban-o-Adab per ek Nazr*. Peshawar: Shahin Printing Press, 1965.

Sahlins, Marshall. "The Segmentary Lineage: An Organization of Predatory Expansion." *American Anthropologist*. Vol. 63, No. 2 (April 1961), pp. 322-45.

Saifi, Gul Ayub Khan. *Bannu aur Waziristan Tarikh*. Peshawar: Shahin Printing Press, 1969.

Sayeed, Khalid B. "Pathan Regionalism." *The South Atlantic Quarterly*. Vol. 63, No. 4 (Autumn 1964), pp. 478-506.

———. *Pakistan. The Formative Phase. 1857-1948*. Karachi: Oxford University Press, 1968.

Schermerhorn, R.A. *Comparative Ethnic Relations*. New York: Random House, 1970.
Scott, George B. *Afghan and Pathan*. London: Mitre Press, 1929.
Scott, James. *The Moral Economy of the Peasant*. New Haven: Yale University Press, 1976.
Seal, Anil. "Imperialism and Nationalism in India" *Locality, Province and Nation: Essays on Indian Politics, 1870-1940*. Edited by John Gallagher, Gordon Johnson and Anil Seal. Cambridge: Cambridge University Press, 1973.
Seth, Hira Lal. *Abdul Ghaffar Khan. Frontier Gandhi*. Lahore: Indian Printing Works, 1942.
Shah, Mian Abdullah and Shah, Mian Jafar. *A Statement of Facts About the Present Situation in the North-West Frontier Province (India) II*. Lahore: Ripon Printing Press, 1930.
———. *The Forbidden Land*. Lahore: Ripon Printing Press, n.d.
Shahab, Qudratullah. *Pathans*. Karachi: The People of Pakistan Series, 1964.
Shridharani, Krishnalal. *War Without Violence*. Bombay: Harcourt, Brace and Co., 1962.
Sitaramayya, Pattabhai. *The History of the Indian National Congress*. Bombay: Padma Publications, 1947, 2 Vols.
Smith, Wilfred C. *Modern Islam in India*. Lahore: Ripon Printing Press, 1947.
Spain, James. "Pakistan's North-West Frontier." *The Middle East Journal*. Vol. 8, No. 1 (Winter 1954), pp. 27-40.
———. *The Pathan Borderland*. The Hague: Mouton and Company, 1963.
———. *The People of the Khyber*. New York: Frederick Praeger, 1963.
Spate, O.K.K. and Learmouth, A.T.A. *India and Pakistan. A General and Regional Geography*. London: Methuen and Company, 1967.
Swinson, Arthur. *The North-West Frontier*. New York: Frederick Praeger, 1963.
Talwar, Bhagat Ram. *The Talwars of Pathan Land and Subhas Chandra's Great Escape*. New Delhi: People's Publishing House, 1976.
Takar, Sohbat Khan. *Pakistan aur Khan Abdul Ghaffar Khan, al-Maruf Badshah Khan*. Peshawar: Shahin Printing Press, 1970.
Tendulkar, D.G. *Abdul Ghaffar Khan*. Bombay: Popular Prakashan, 1967.
"The First Elections in the North-West Frontier Province." *Journal of the Royal Central Asian Society*. Vol. 19, Part I (January 1932), pp. 65-69.
"The Unrest on the Indian Frontier." *Round Table*. Vol. 21, No. 82 (March 1931), pp. 351-70.
Tinker, Hugh. *Experiment with Freedom*. London: Oxford University Press, 1967.
Trimingham, J. Spenser. *The Sufi Orders in Islam*. London: Oxford University Press, 1967.
Waheed-uz-Zaman. *Towards Pakistan*. Lahore: Publishers United, 1964.

Warburton, Robert. *Eighteen Years in the Khyber, 1879-1898*. Karachi: Oxford University Press, 1970.

Wavell, Lord Archibald. *The Viceroy's Journal*. Delhi: Oxford University Press, 1977.

Wingate, Ronald. *Lord Ismay*. London: Hutchinson and Company, 1970.

Wylly, H.C. *From the Black Mountains to Waziristan*. London: MacMillan and Company, 1912.

Woodruff, Philip. *The Men Who Ruled India*. New York: Schocken Books, 1954. Vol. II.

Yunus, Muhammad. *Frontier Speaks*. Bombay: Hind Kitab, 1947.

———. *Qaidi ke Khat*. New Delhi: Idara-i-Shama, 1969.

Yusaf, Muhammad. "Mazlumin Bihar ki Ankhon Dekhi Kahani, Un ki Zabani." *Khatun*. Vol. 2, No. 22 (August 14, 1973), pp. 5-6.

Yusafi, Allah Bakhsh. *Afghan ya Pathan*. Karachi: Muhammad Ali Educational Society, 1960.

———. *Sarhad aur Jad-o-Jihad-i-Azadi*. Lahore: Markazi Urdu Board, 1968.

———. *Sarhadi Gandhi se Mulaqat*. Peshawar: Manzur-i-Am Barqi Press, 1939.

———. *Siyasiyat Sarhad ke Irtiqai Manazil*. Karachi: Muhammad Ali Educational Society, 1972

Zafar, Sayyid Bahadur Shah. *Pakhtana da Tarikh pa Renake*. Peshawar: University Book Agency, 1965.

Zaidi, Z.H. "Aspects of the Development of Muslim League Policy." *The Partition of India*. Edited by C.H. Philips and Mary D. Wainwright. London: George Allen and Unwin, 1970.

Zia-ud-din, Mian. *Memoirs of a Pakistani Diplomat*. Peshawar: University Book Agency, 1976.

Zutshi, G.L. *Frontier Gandhi*. Delhi: National Publishing House, 1970.

# INDEX